ANIMAL LAND

By Makoto Raiku

Translated and adapted by Stephen Paul

Lettered by North Market Street Graphics

KC
KODANSHA
COMICS

Animal Land volume 1 is a work of fiction. Names, characters, places, and incidents are the products of the author's imagination or are used fictitiously. Any resemblance to actual events, locales, or persons, living or dead, is entirely coincidental.

A Kodansha Comics Trade Paperback Original

Animal Land volume 1 copyright © 2010 Makoto Raiku
English translation copyright © 2011 Makoto Raiku

Published in the United States by Kodansha Comics, an imprint of Kodansha USA Publishing, LLC, New York.

Publication rights for this English edition arranged through Kodansha Ltd., Tokyo.

First published in Japan in 2010 by Kodansha Ltd., Tokyo, as *Doubutsu no Kuni*, volume 1.

ISBN 978-1-935-42913-5

Printed in the United States of America.

www.kodanshacomics.com

9 8 7 6 5 4 3 2 1

Translator/Adapter: Stephen Paul
Lettering: North Market Street Graphics

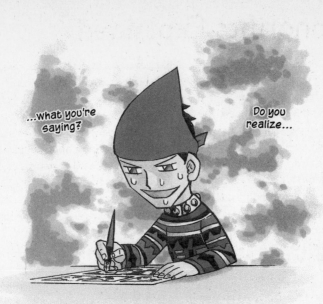

Do you realize...
...what you're saying?

I was hoping to use this story to describe the process of raising an adorable little baby. But in the chapter that I'm drawing at the moment I write this (April 2010), this sweet little baby is making one hell of a momentous decision. I wish he would have some consideration for the guy who draws him.

Makoto Raiku

Honorifics Explained

Throughout the Kodansha Comics books, you will find Japanese honorifics left intact in the translations. For those not familiar with how the Japanese use honorifics and, more important, how they differ from American honorifics, we present this brief overview.

Politeness has always been a critical facet of Japanese culture. Ever since the feudal era, when Japan was a highly stratified society, use of honorifics—which can be defined as polite speech that indicates relationship or status—has played an essential role in the Japanese language. When addressing someone in Japanese, an honorific usually takes the form of a suffix attached to one's name (example: "Asuna-san"), is used as a title at the end of one's name, or appears in place of the name itself (example: "Negi-sensei," or simply "Sensei!").

Honorifics can be expressions of respect or endearment. In the context of manga and anime, honorifics give insight into the nature of the relationship between characters. Many English translations leave out these important honorifics and therefore distort the feel of the original Japanese. Because Japanese honorifics contain nuances that English honorifics lack, it is our policy at Kodansha Comics not to translate them. Here, instead, is a guide to some of the honorifics you may encounter in Kodansha Comics.

-san: This is the most common honorific and is equivalent to Mr., Miss, Ms., or Mrs. It is the all-purpose honorific and can be used in any situation where politeness is required.

-sama: This is one level higher than "-san" and is used to confer great respect.

-dono: This comes from the word "tono," which means "lord." It is an even higher level than "-sama" and confers utmost respect.

-kun: This suffix is used at the end of boys' names to express familiarity or endearment. It is also sometimes used by men among friends, or when addressing someone younger or of a lower station.

-chan: This is used to express endearment, mostly toward girls. It is also used for little boys, pets, and even among lovers. It gives a sense of childish cuteness.

Bozu: This is an informal way to refer to a boy, similar to the English terms "kid" and "squirt."

Sempai/
Senpai: This title suggests that the addressee is one's senior in a group or organization. It is most often used in a school setting, where underclassmen refer to their upperclassmen as "sempai." It can also be used in the workplace, such as when a newer employee addresses an employee who has seniority in the company.

Kohai: This is the opposite of "sempai" and is used toward underclassmen in school or newcomers in the workplace. It connotes that the addressee is of a lower station.

Sensei: Literally meaning "one who has come before," this title is used for teachers, doctors, or masters of any profession or art.

-[blank]: This is usually forgotten in these lists, but it is perhaps the most significant difference between Japanese and English. The lack of honorific means that the speaker has permission to address the person in a very intimate way. Usually, only family, spouses, or very close friends have this kind of permission. Known as *yobisute*, it can be gratifying when someone who has earned the intimacy starts to call one by one's name without an honorific. But when that intimacy hasn't been earned, it can be very insulting.

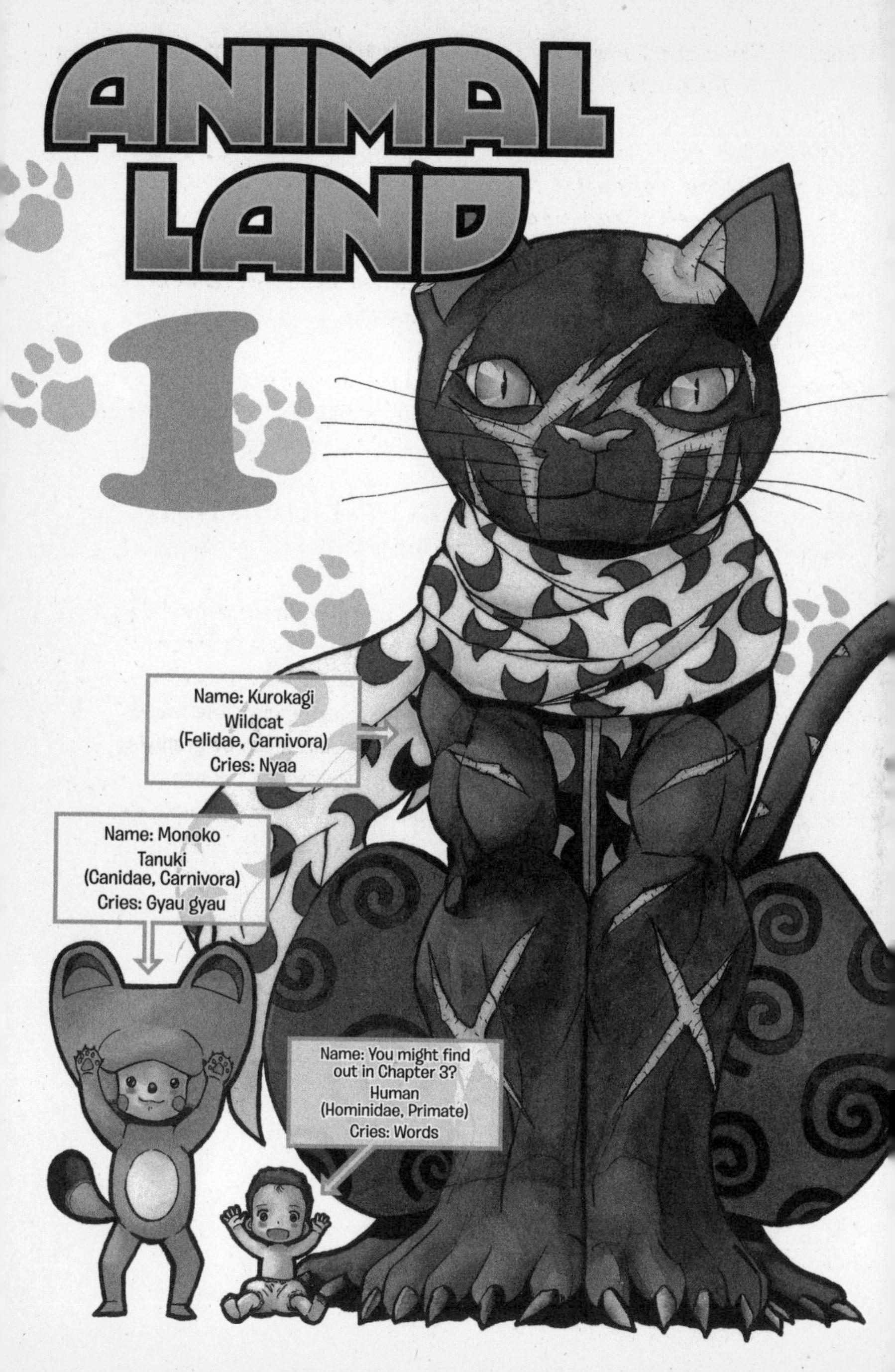
ANIMAL LAND
1
Name: Kurokagi
Wildcat
(Felidae, Carnivora)
Cries: Nyaa
Name: Monoko
Tanuki
(Canidae, Carnivora)
Cries: Gyau gyau
Name: You might find out in Chapter 3?
Human
(Hominidae, Primate)
Cries: Words

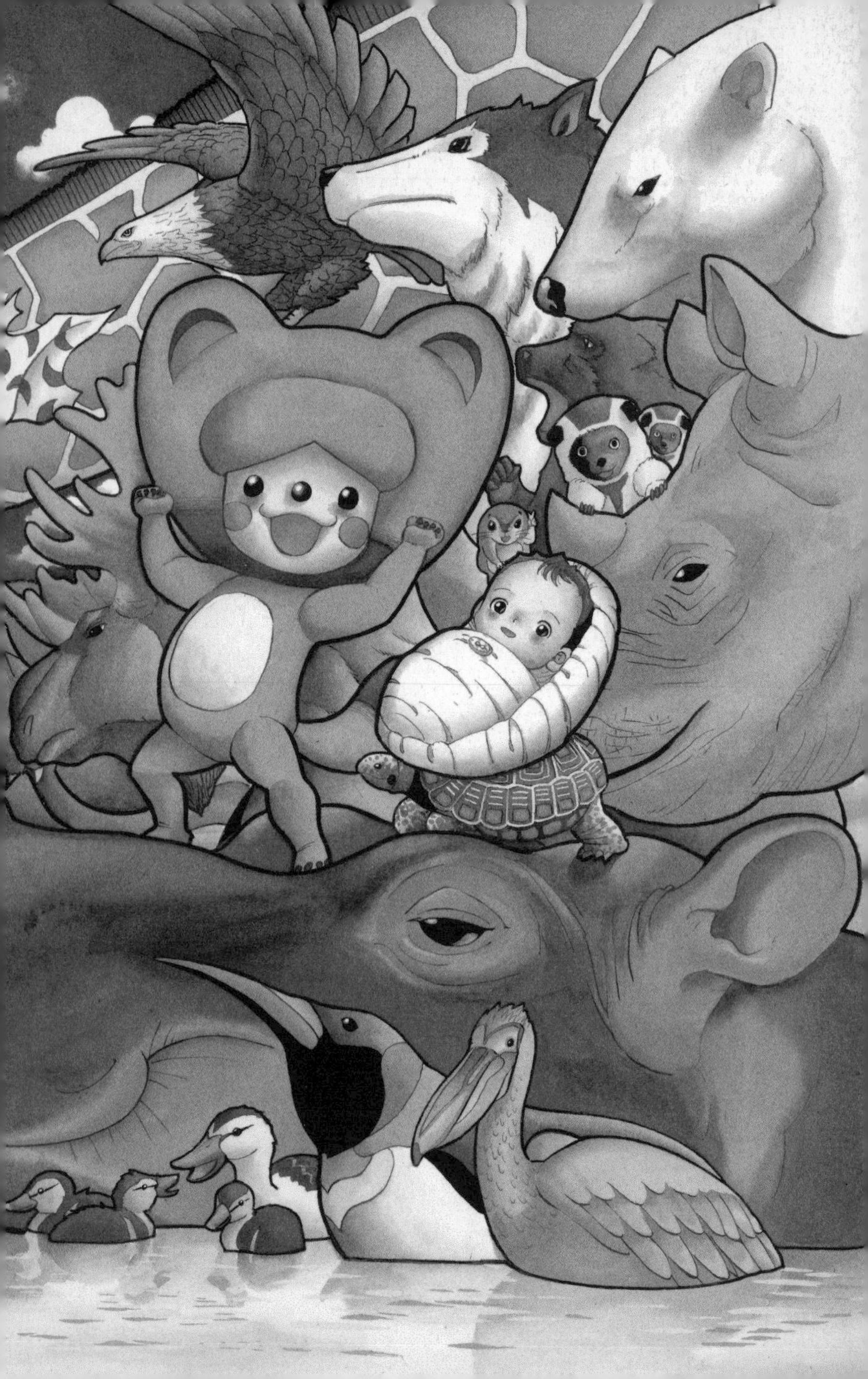

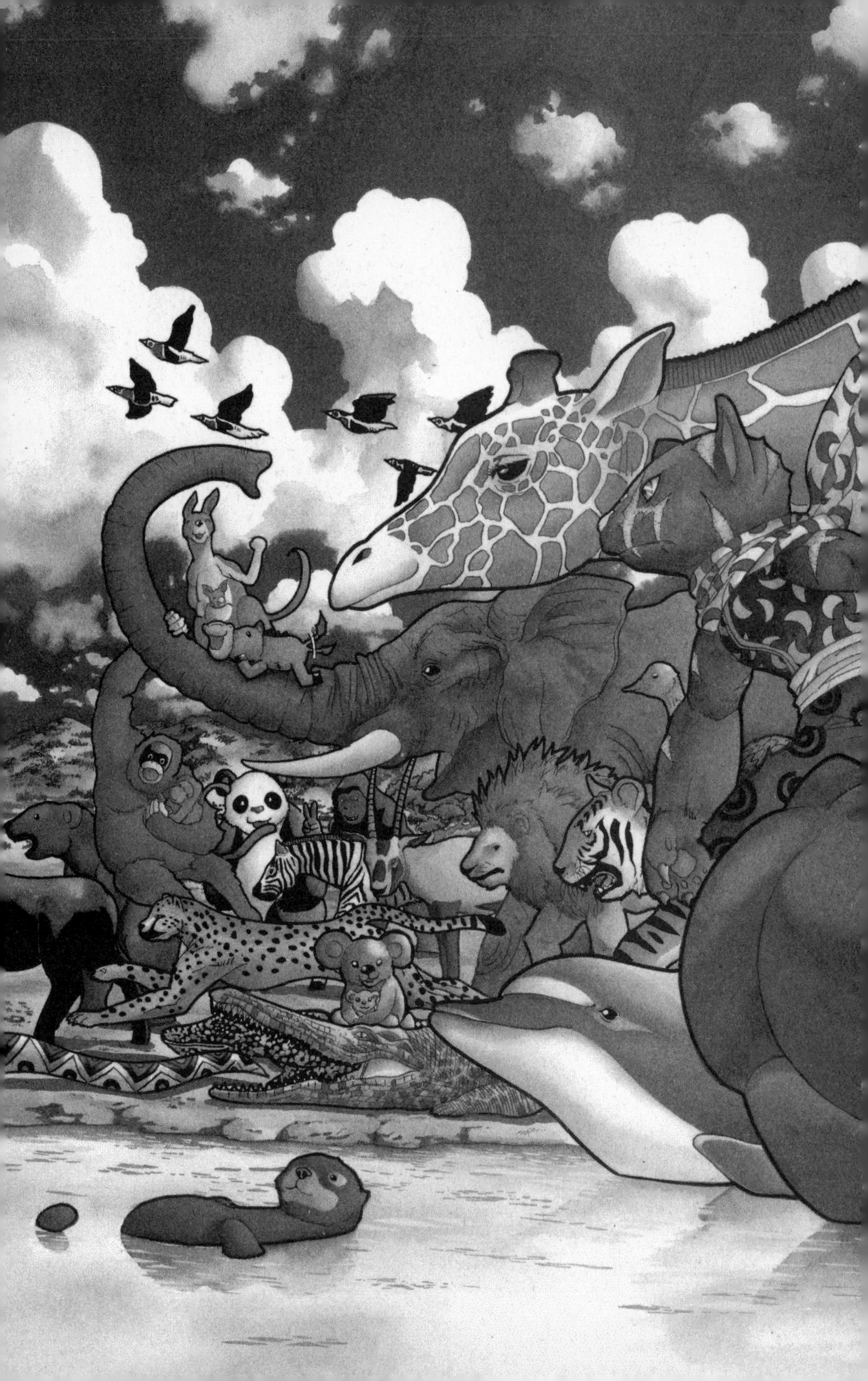

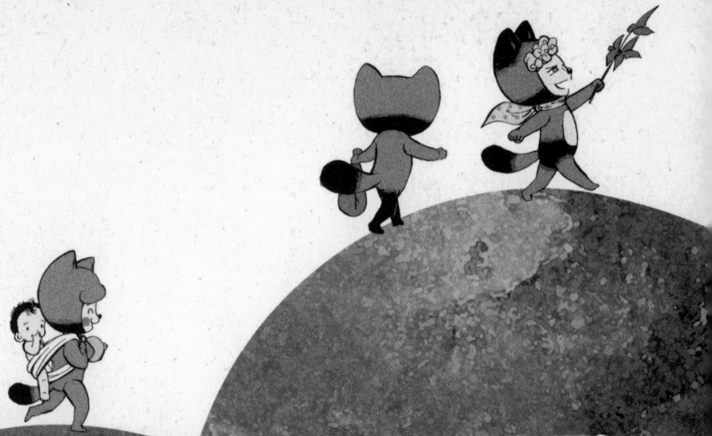

CONTENTS

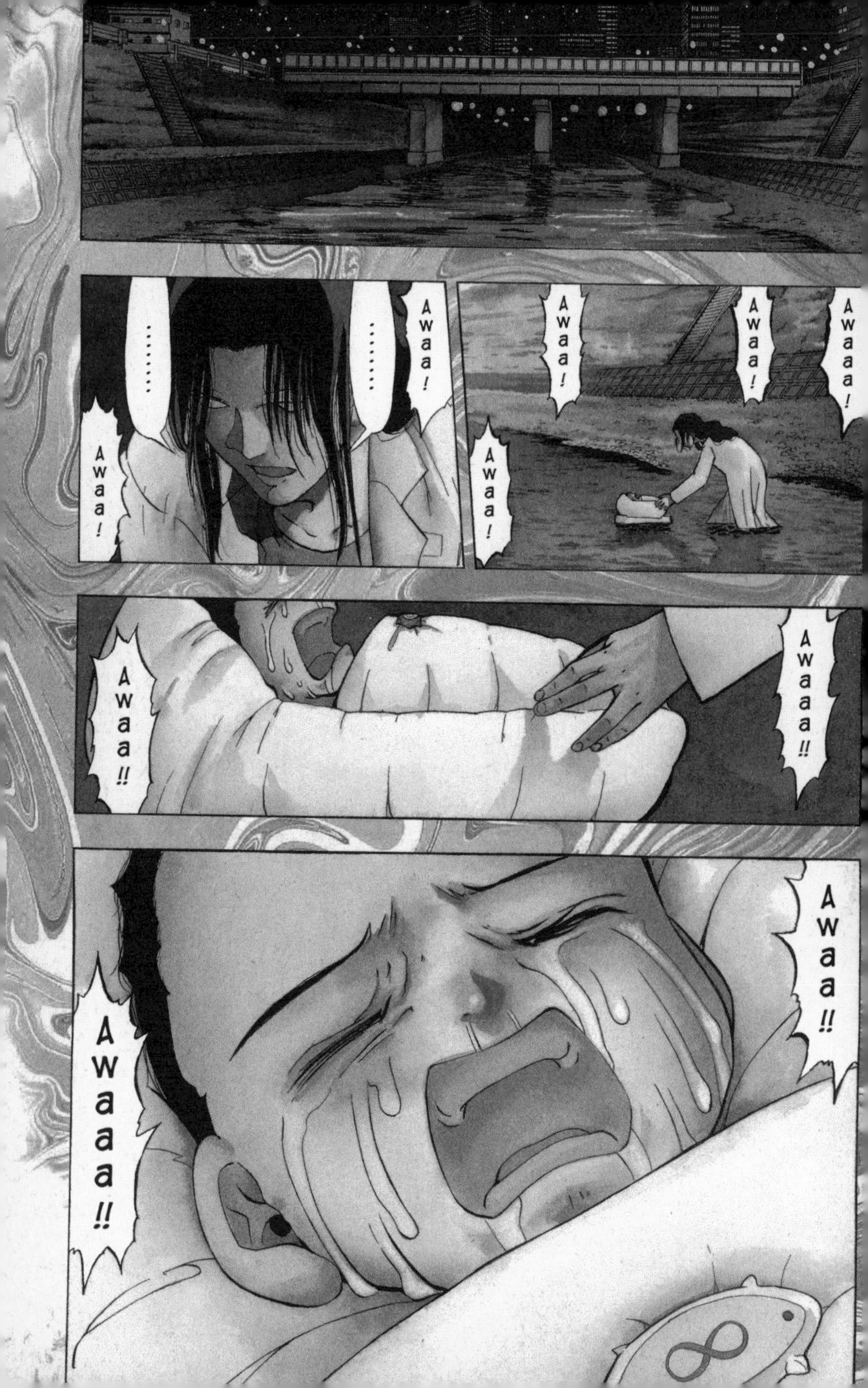
Awaaa!
Awaa!
Awaa!
Awaa!
Awaa!
....
....
Awaa!
Awaaa!!
Awaa!!
Awaa!!
Awaaa!!

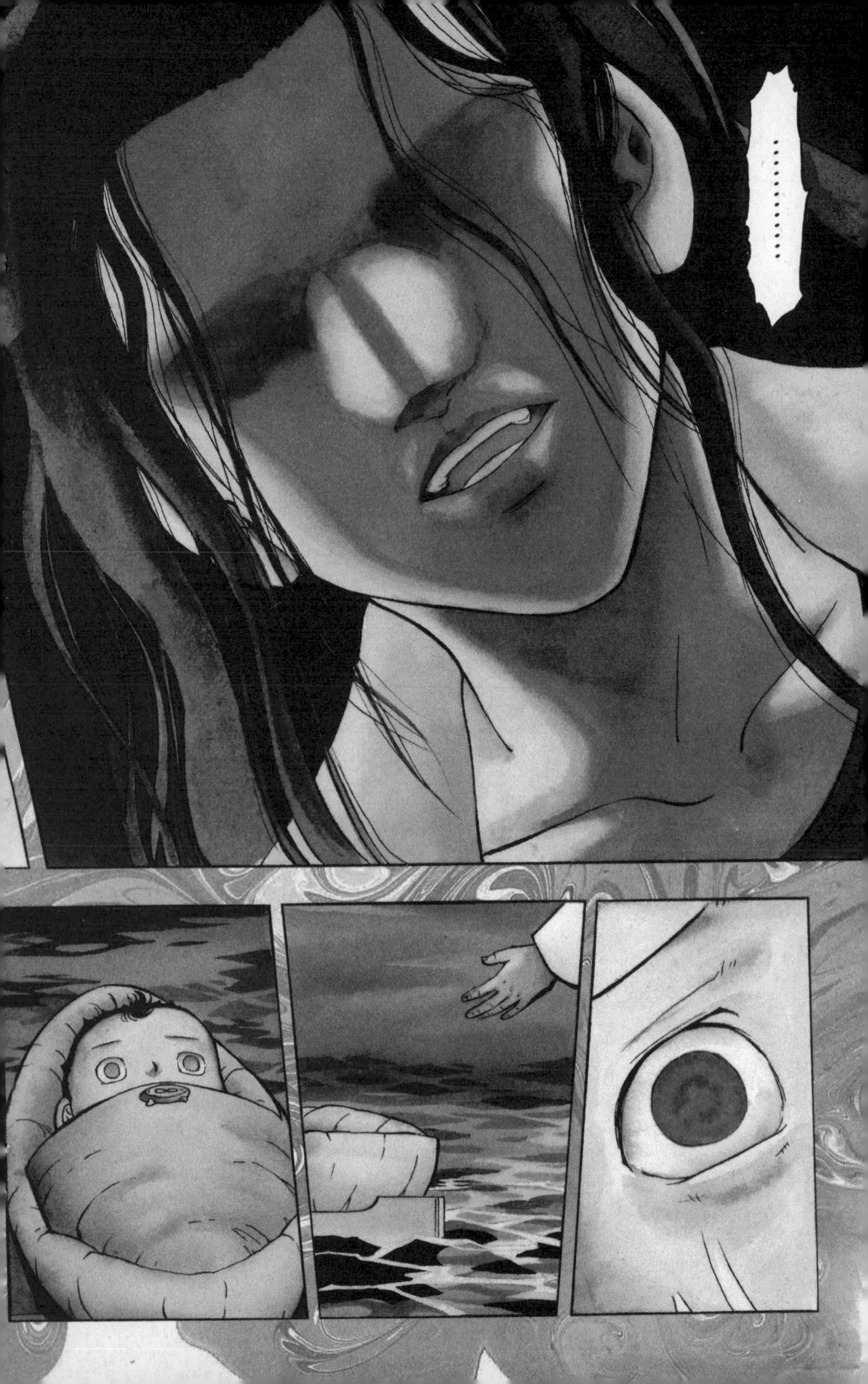
……

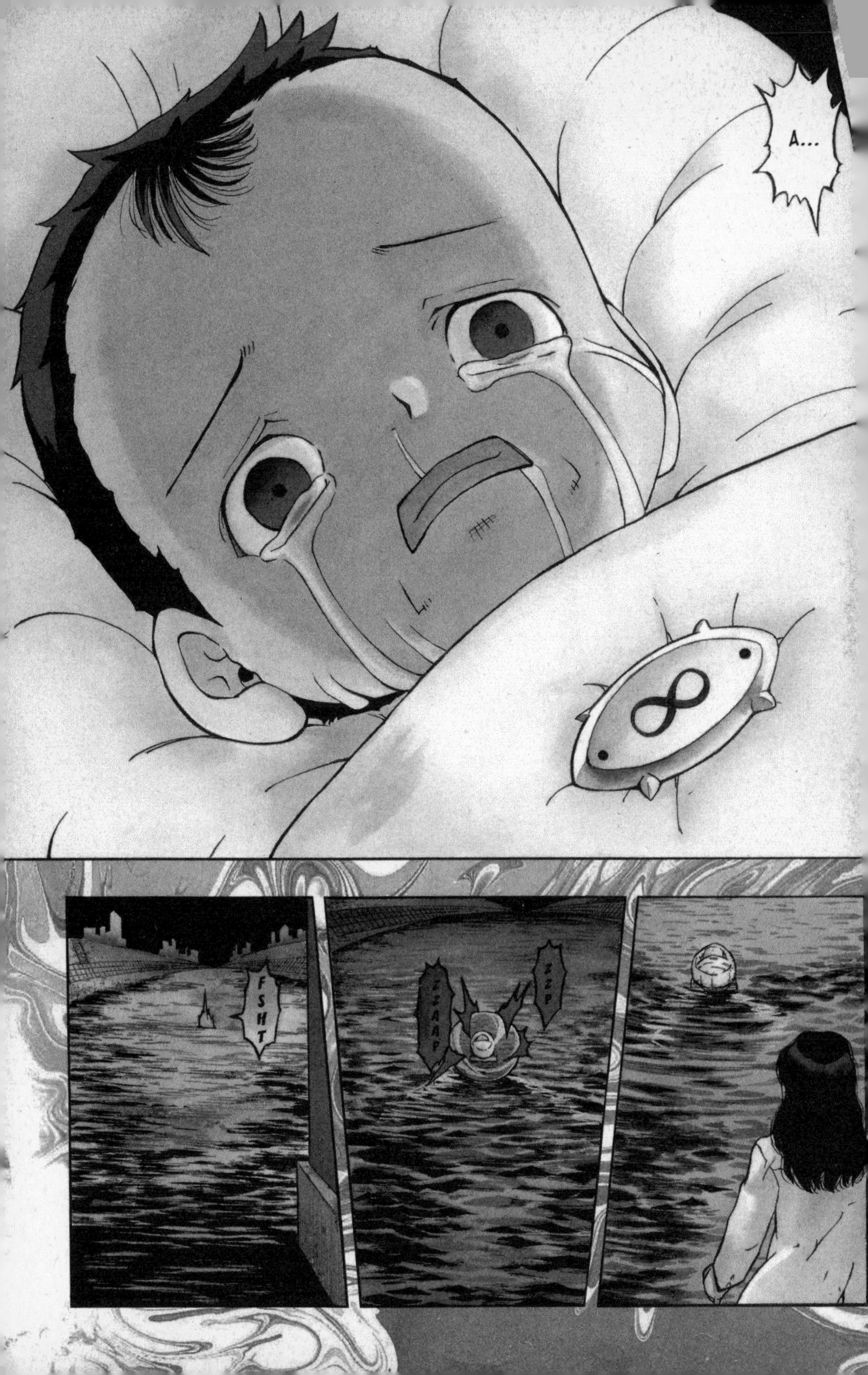
A...
ZZP
ZZAAP
FSHT

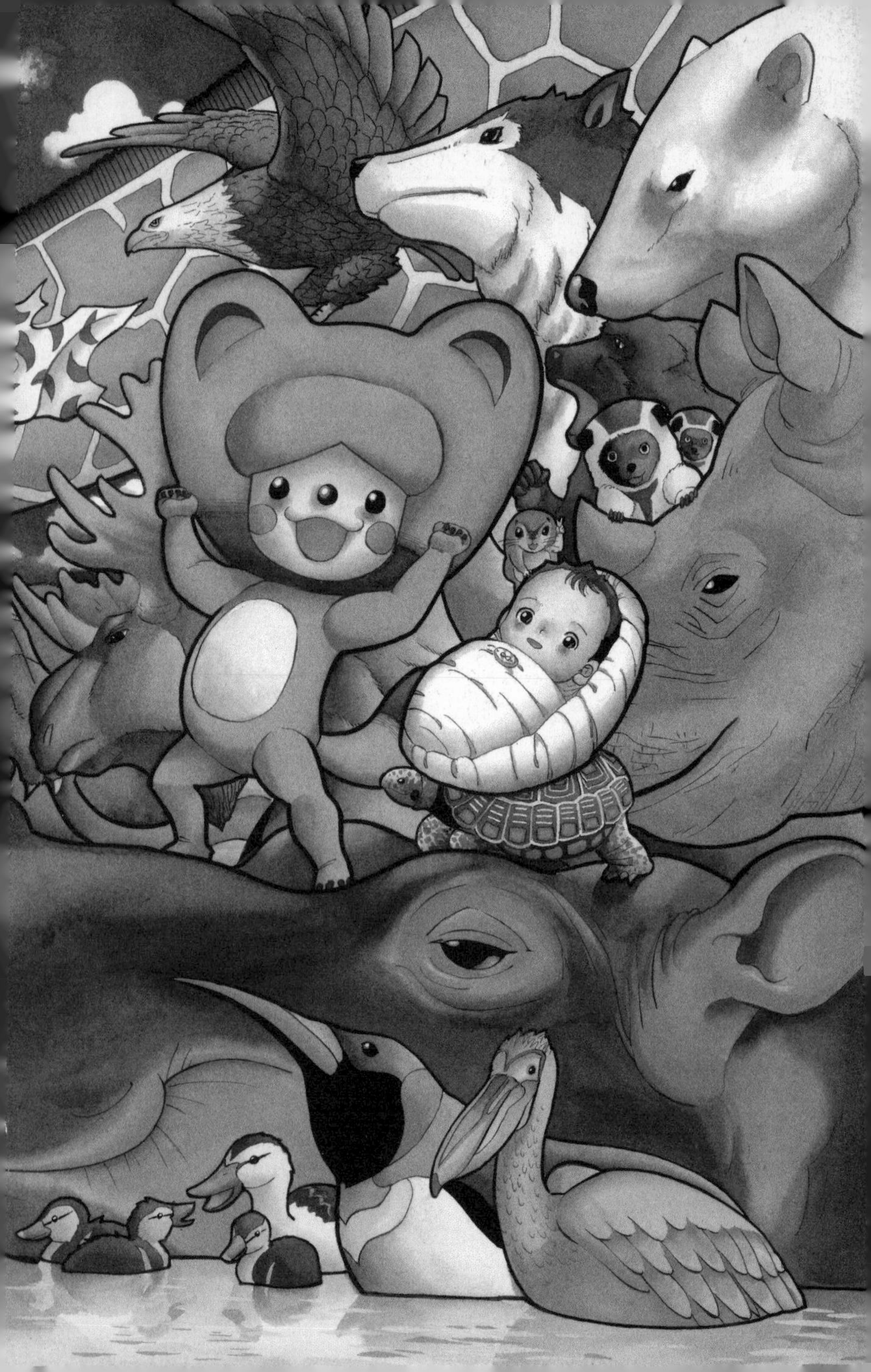

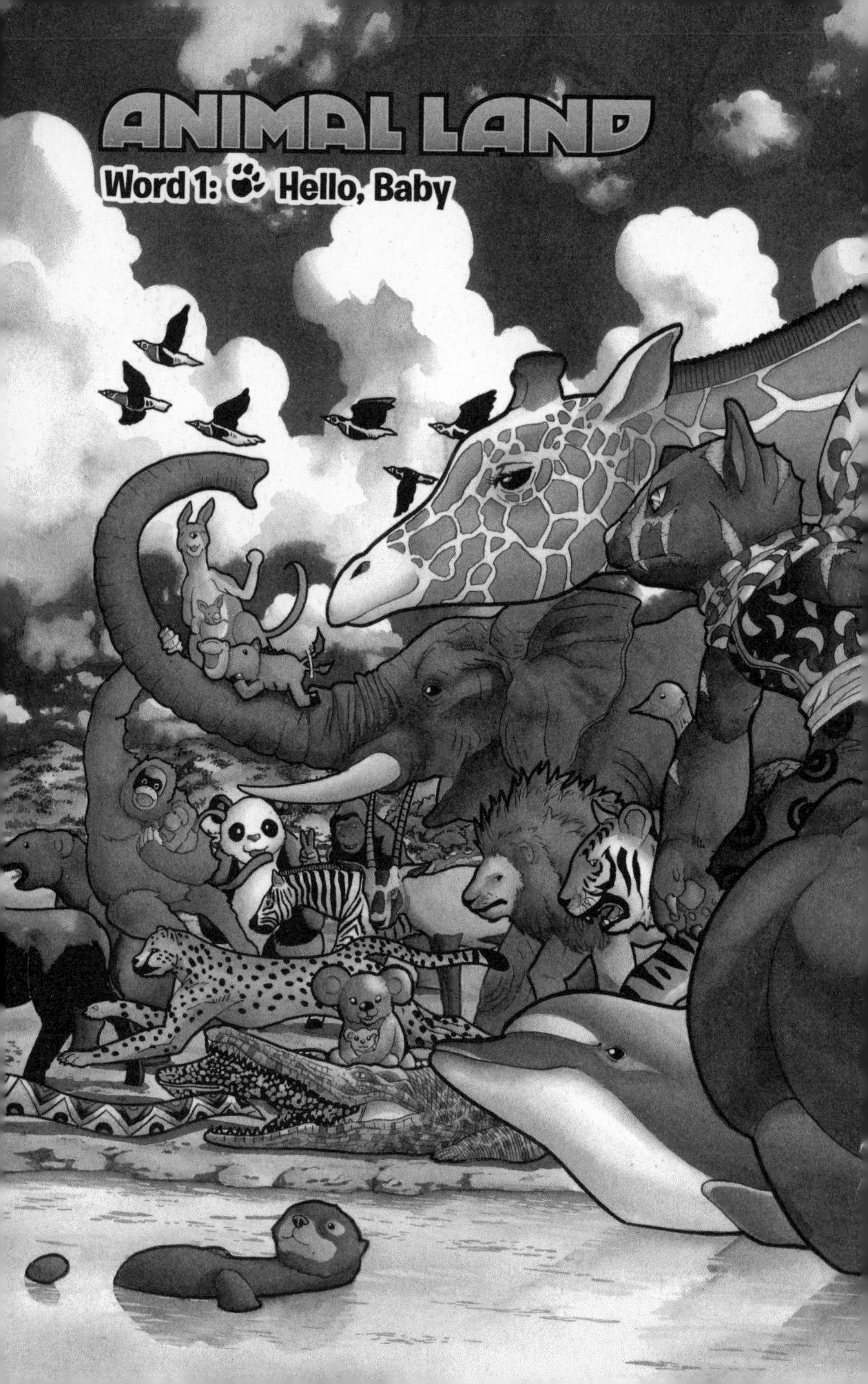
ANIMAL LAND
Word 1: Hello, Baby

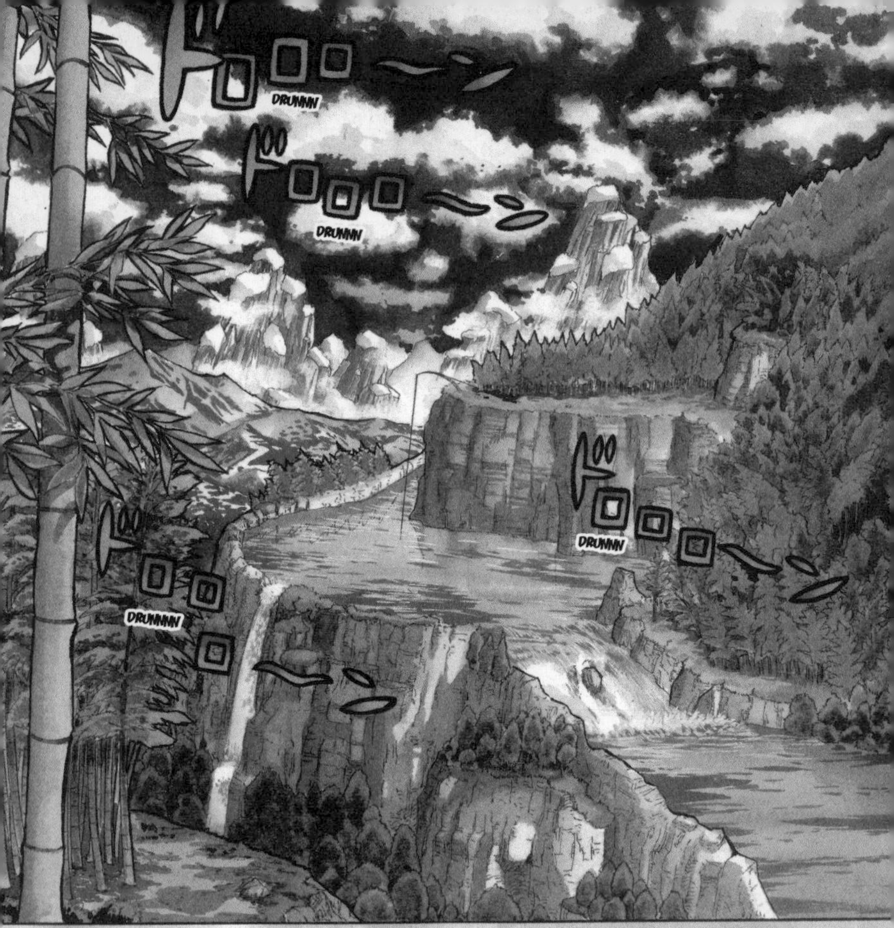
DRUNNN
DRUNNN
DRUNNN
DRUNNNN
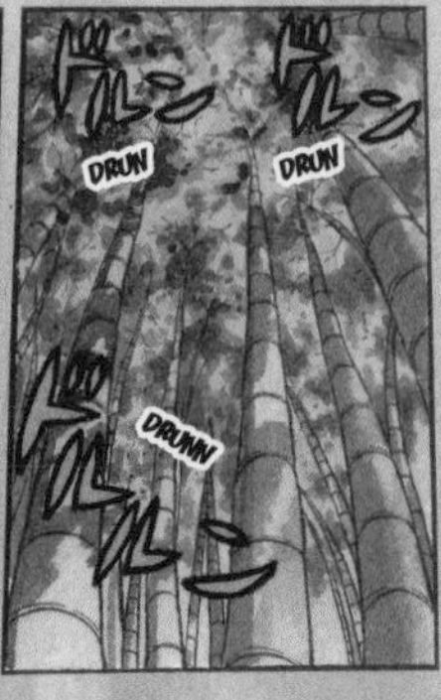
DRUN
DRUN
DRUNN
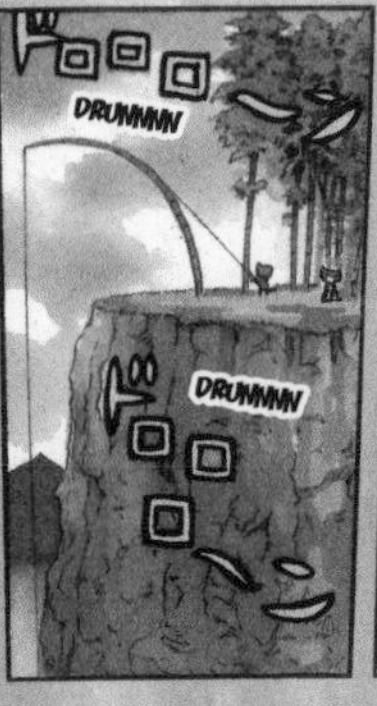
DRUNNNN
DRUNNNN
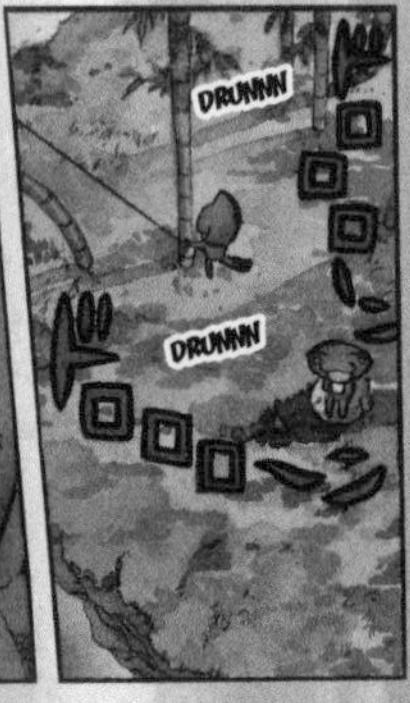
DRUNNN
DRUNNN
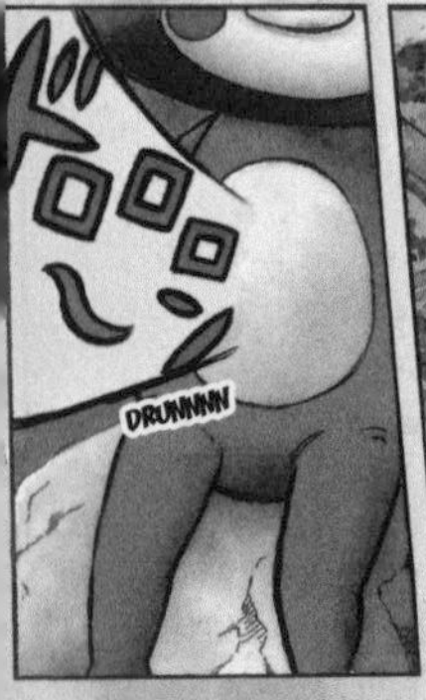
DRUNNNN

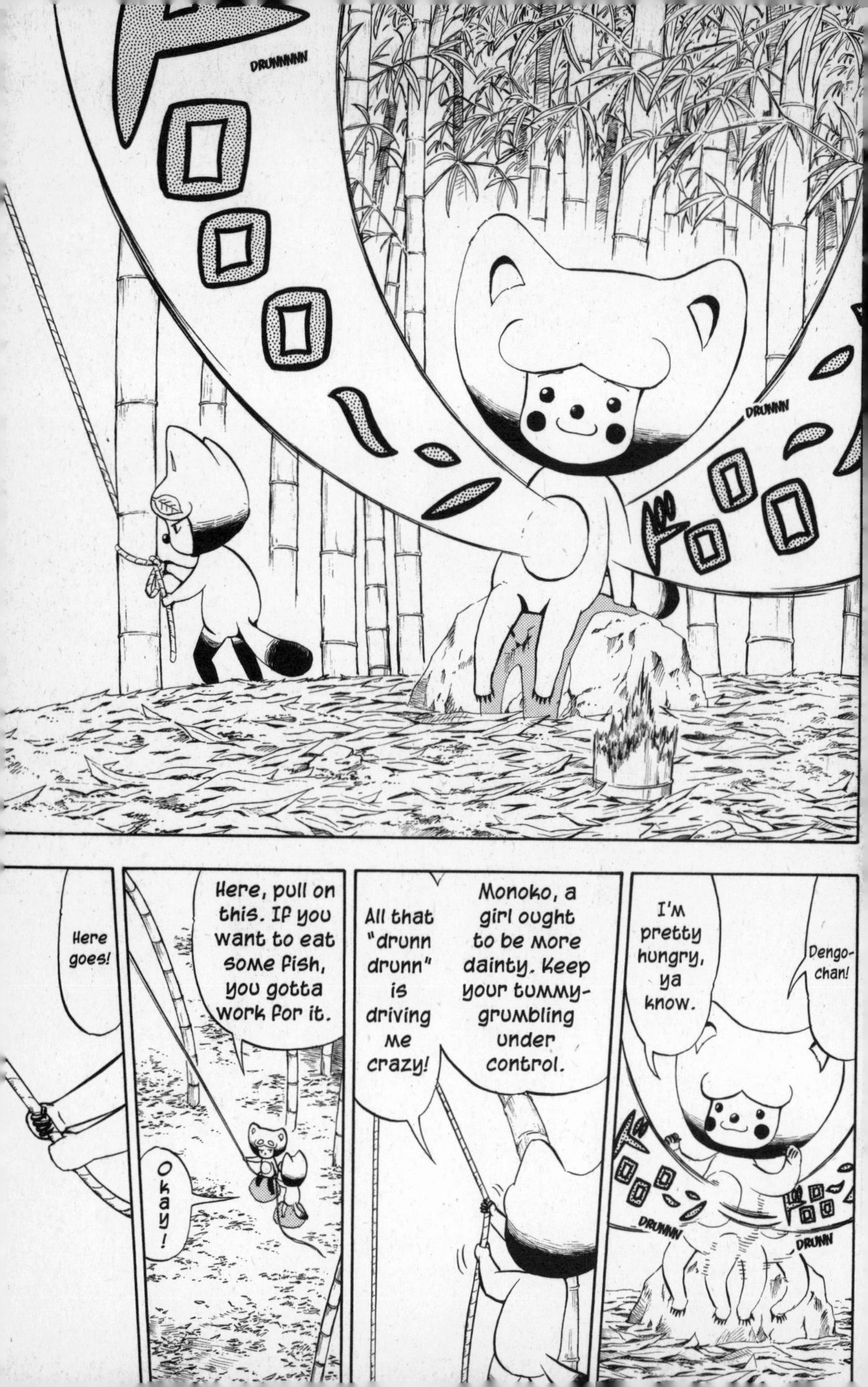
DRUNNNNN
DRUNNN
Dengo-chan!
I'm pretty hungry, ya know.
DRUNN
DRUNN
Monoko, a girl ought to be more dainty. Keep your tummy-grumbling under control.
All that "drunn drunn" is driving me crazy!
Here, pull on this. If you want to eat some fish, you gotta work for it.
Okay!
Here goes!

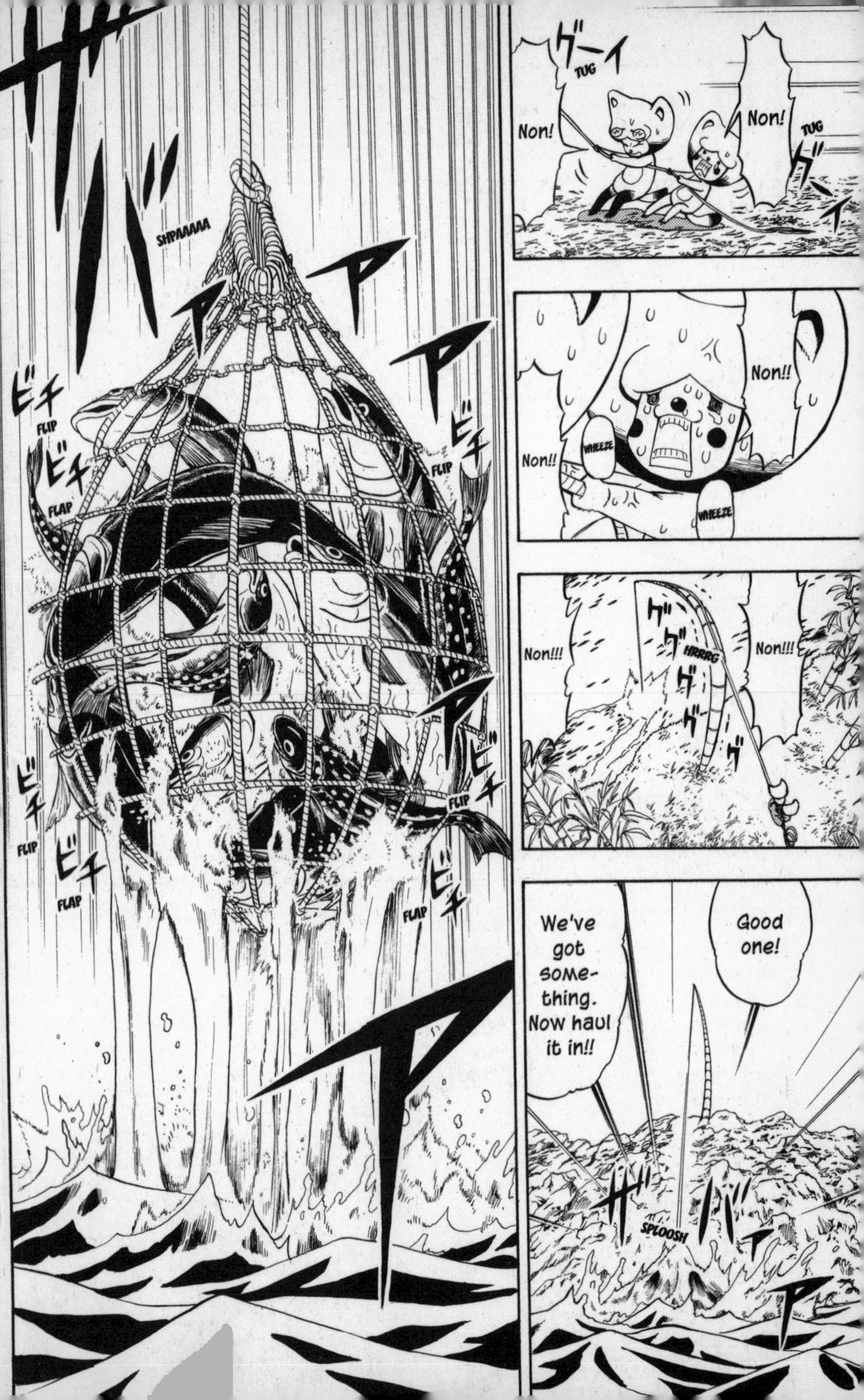
TUG
Non!
Non!
TUG
Non!!
WHEEZE
Non!!
WHEEZE
Non!!!
HRRRG
Non!!!
Good one!
We've got some-thing. Now haul it in!!
SPLOOSH
SHPAAAAA
FLIP
FLIP
FLAP
FLIP
FLAP
FLIP
FLAP
FLAP

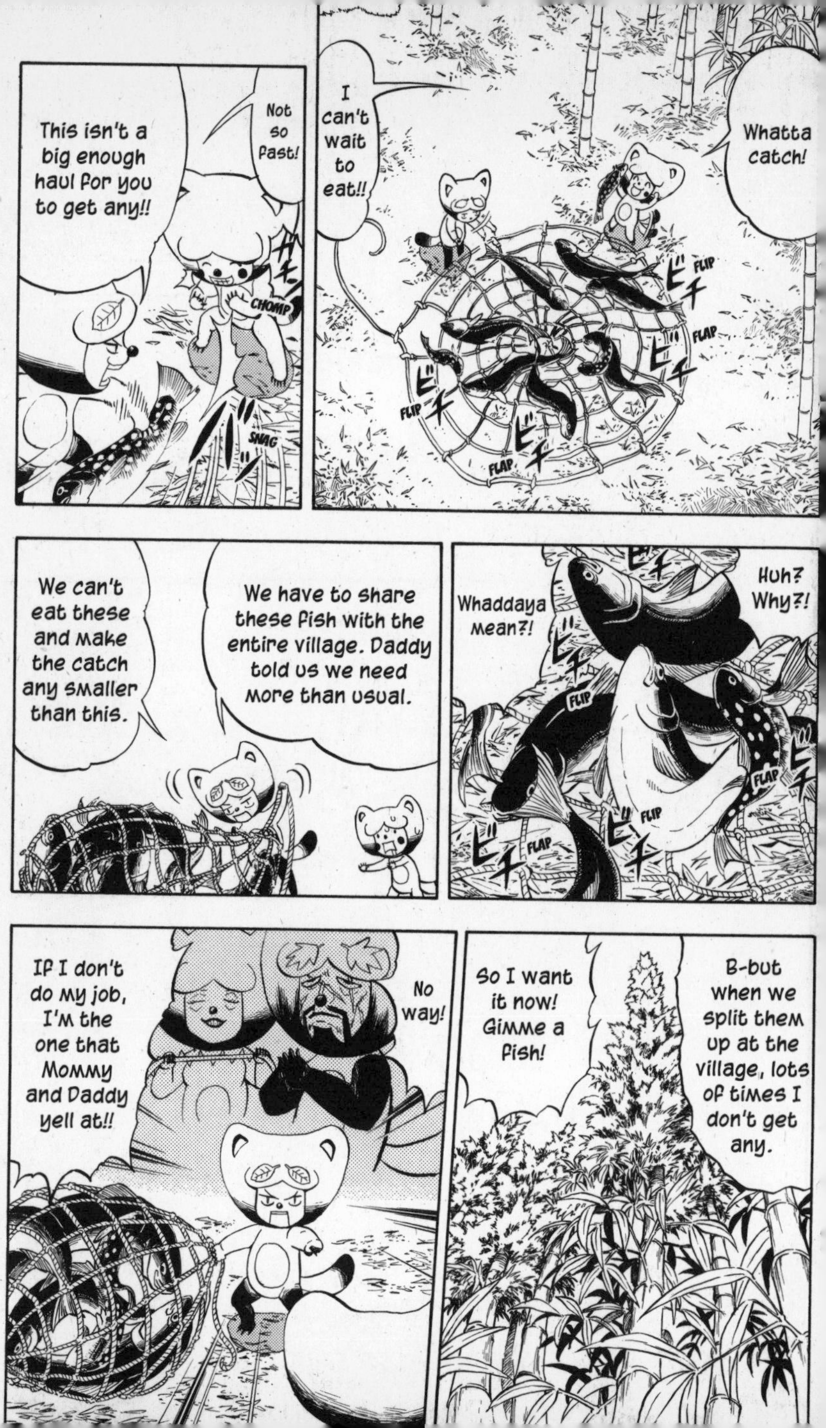
Whatta catch!
I can't wait to eat!!
FLIP
FLAP
FLIP
FLAP
Not so fast!
This isn't a big enough haul for you to get any!!
CHOMP
SNAG
Huh? Why?!
Whaddaya mean?!
FLIP
FLAP
FLIP
FLAP
We have to share these fish with the entire village. Daddy told us we need more than usual.
We can't eat these and make the catch any smaller than this.
B-but when we split them up at the village, lots of times I don't get any.
So I want it now! Gimme a fish!
No way!
If I don't do my job, I'm the one that Mommy and Daddy yell at!!

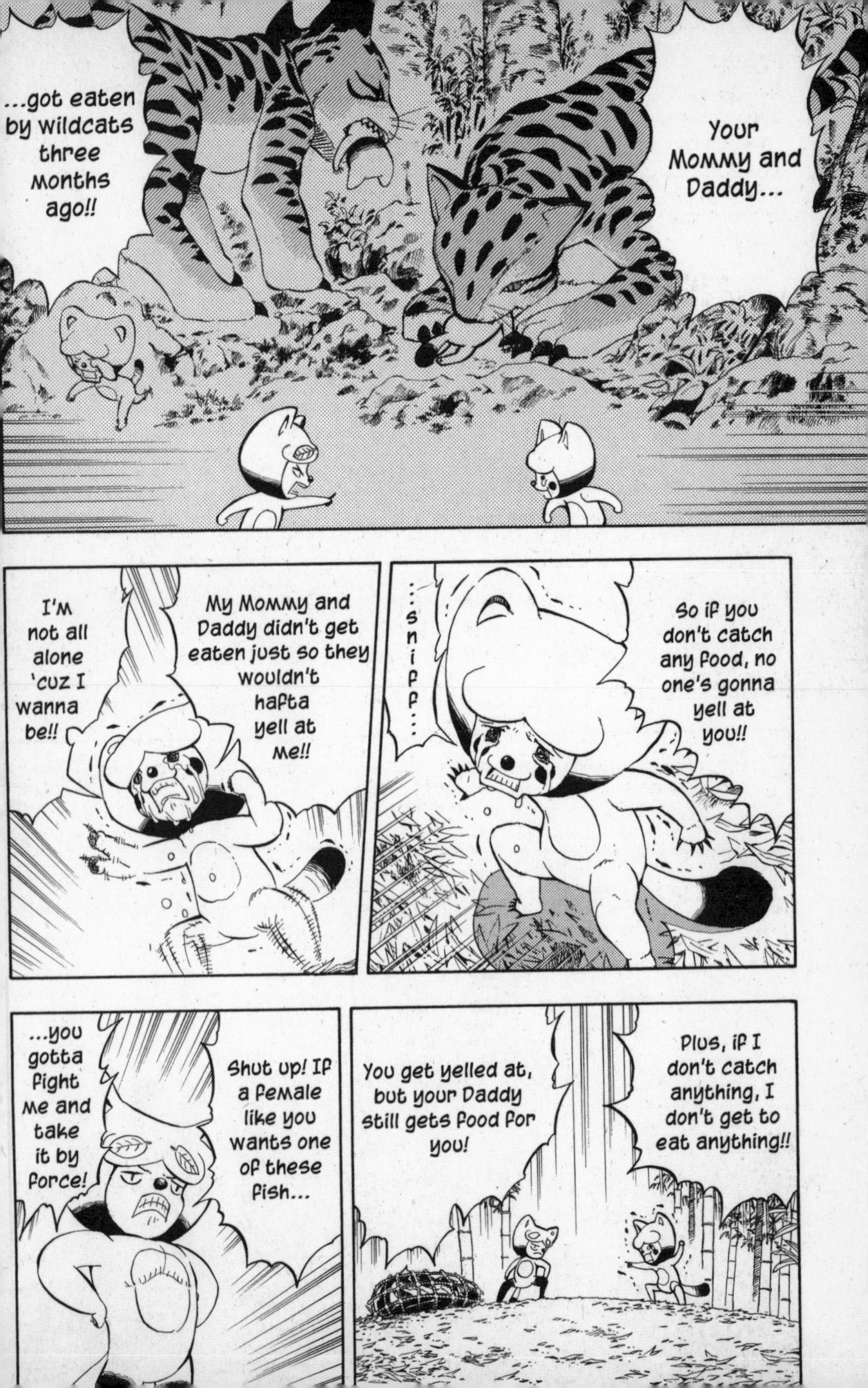
Your Mommy and Daddy...
...got eaten by wildcats three months ago!!
So if you don't catch any food, no one's gonna yell at you!!
...sniff...
My Mommy and Daddy didn't get eaten just so they wouldn't hafta yell at me!!
I'm not all alone 'cuz I wanna be!!
Plus, if I don't catch anything, I don't get to eat anything!!
You get yelled at, but your Daddy still gets food for you!
Shut up! If a female like you wants one of these fish...
...you gotta fight me and take it by force!

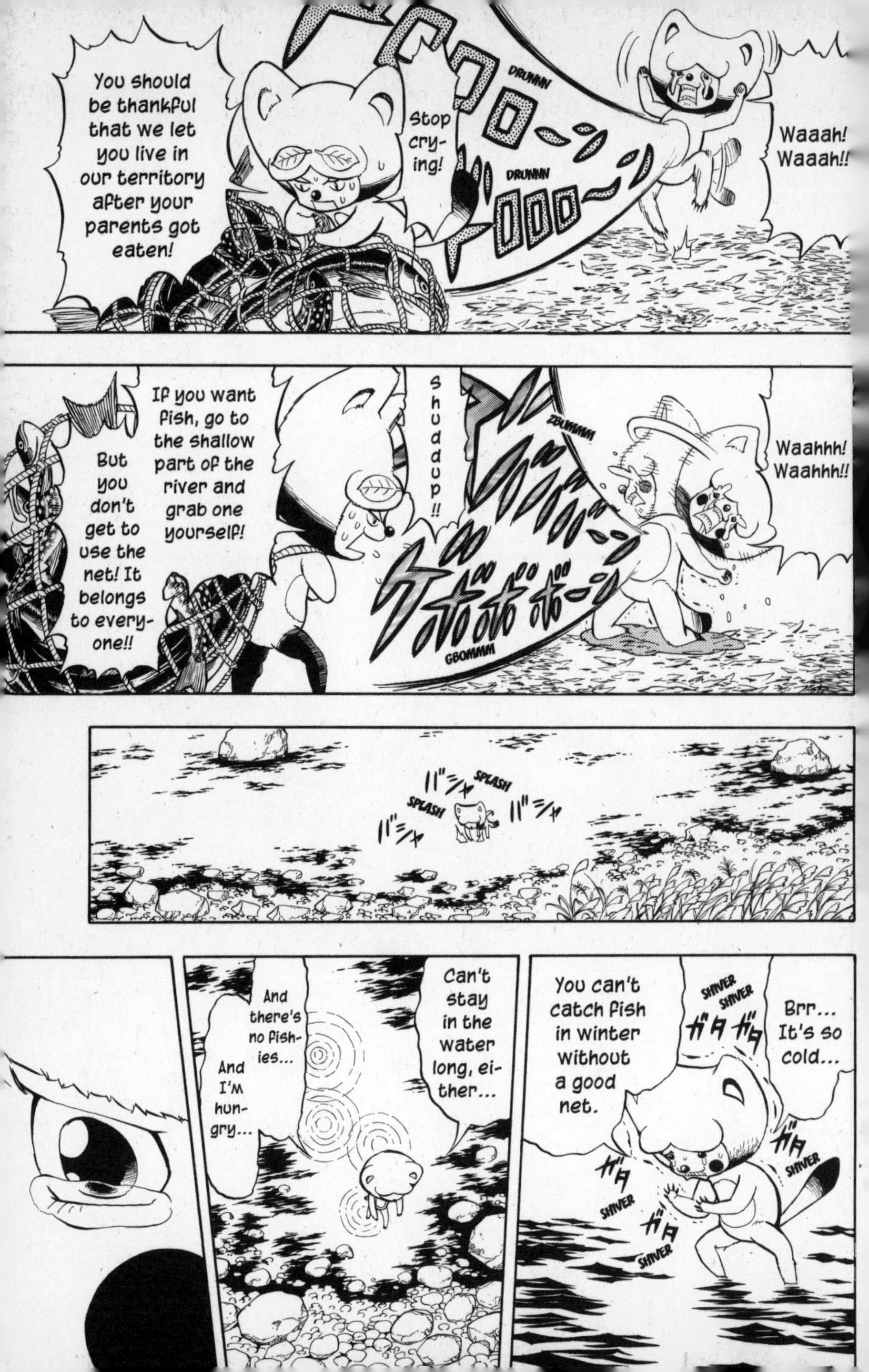
Waaah! Waaah!!
DRUNNN
DRUNNN
Stop crying!
You should be thankful that we let you live in our territory after your parents got eaten!
Waahhh! Waahhh!!
ZBUMMM
GBOMMM
Shuddup!!
If you want fish, go to the shallow part of the river and grab one yourself!
But you don't get to use the net! It belongs to everyone!!
SPLASH
SPLASH
Brr... It's so cold...
SHIVER
SHIVER
SHIVER
SHIVER
SHIVER
You can't catch fish in winter without a good net.
Can't stay in the water long, either...
And there's no fishies...
And I'm hungry...

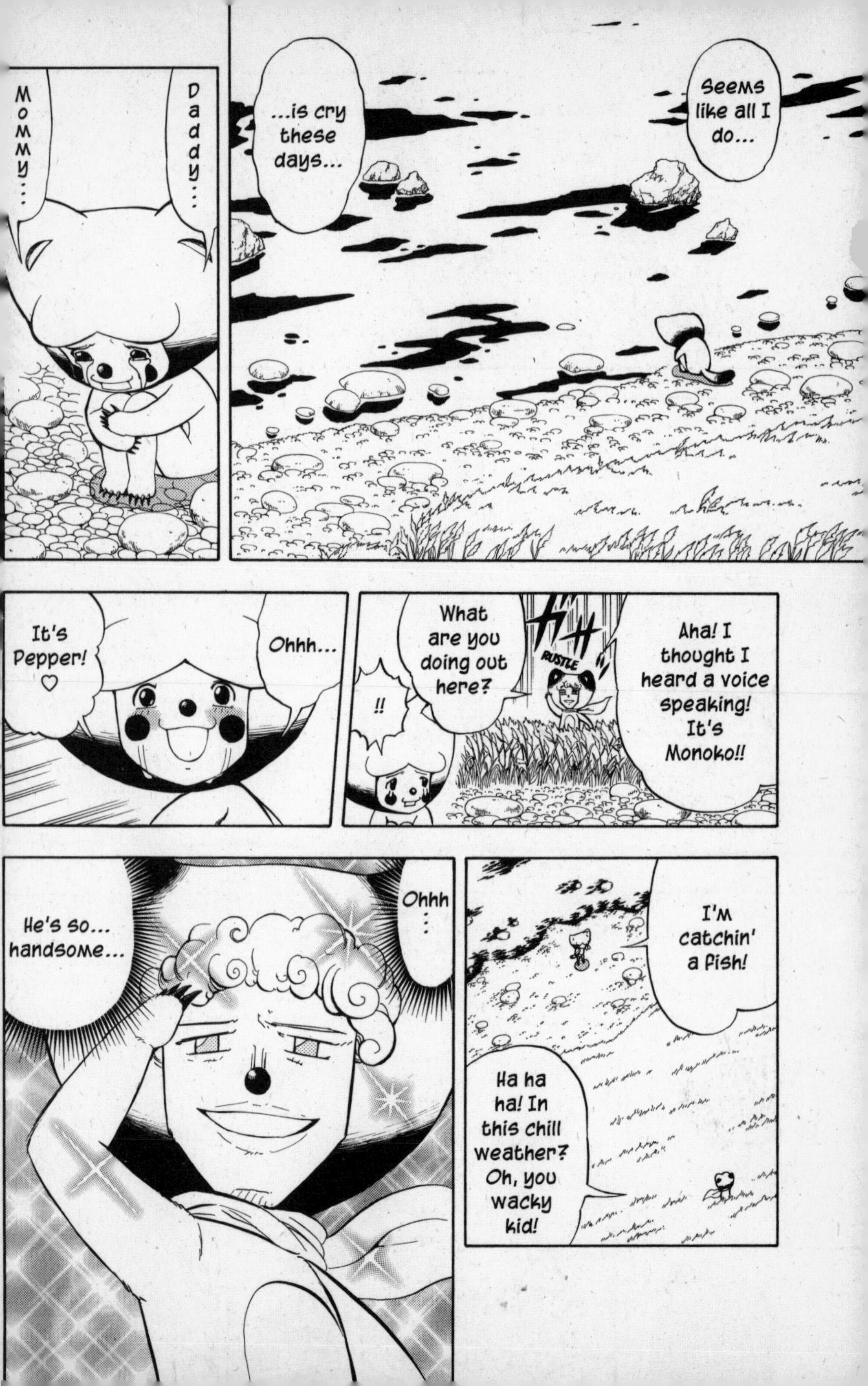
Seems like all I do...
...is cry these days...
Daddy...
Mommy...
Aha! I thought I heard a voice speaking! It's Monoko!!
RUSTLE
What are you doing out here?
!!
Ohhh...
It's Pepper! ♡
I'M catchin' a fish!
Ha ha ha! In this chill weather? Oh, you wacky kid!
Ohhh...
He's so... handsome...

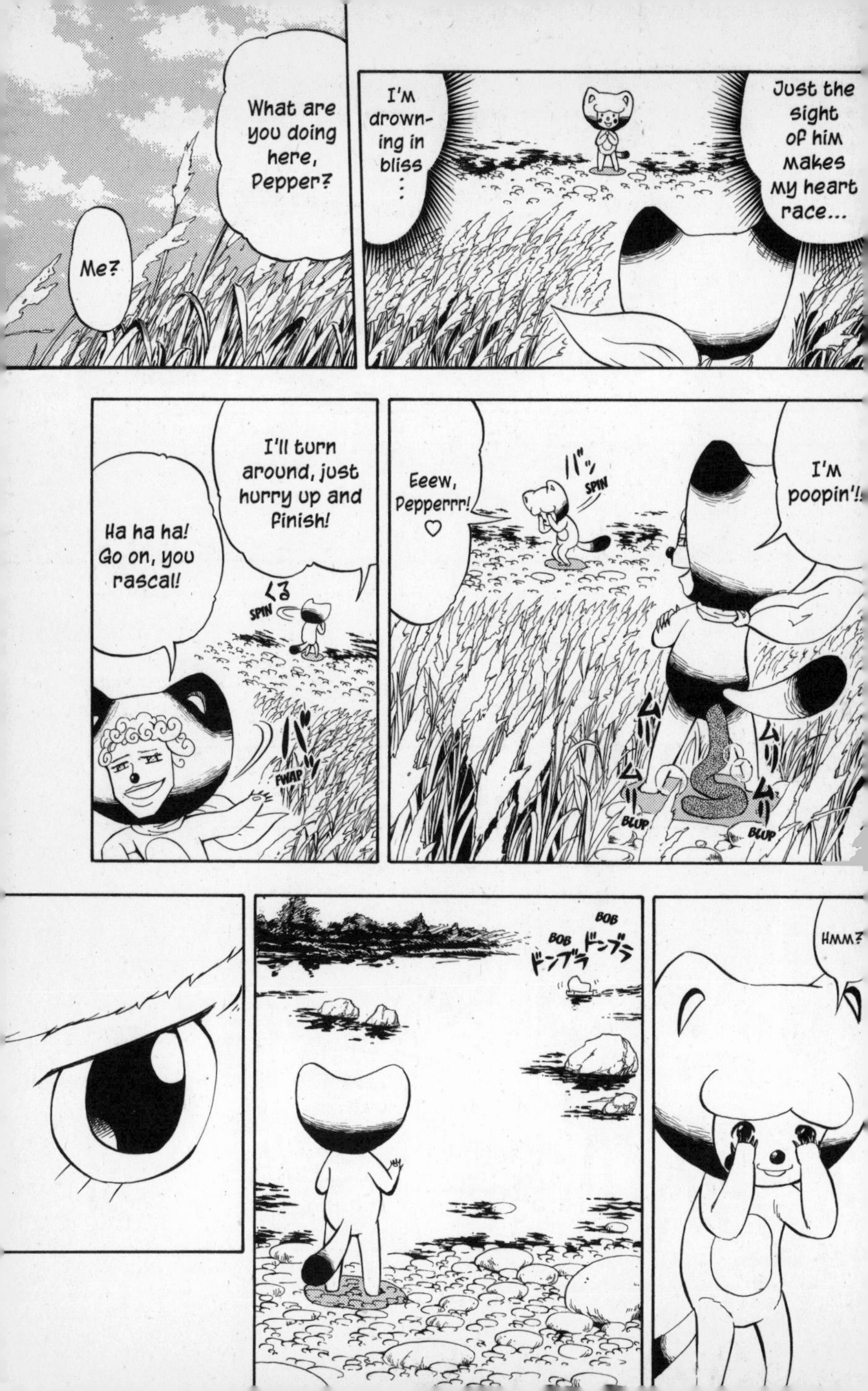

Just the sight of him makes my heart race...
I'm drowning in bliss...
What are you doing here, Pepper?
Me?
I'm poopin'!!
バッ
SPIN
Eeew, Pepperrr! ♡
BLUP
BLUP
I'll turn around, just hurry up and finish!
Ha ha ha! Go on, you rascal!
くる
SPIN
FWAP
HMM?
ドンブラ
BOB
ドンブラ
BOB

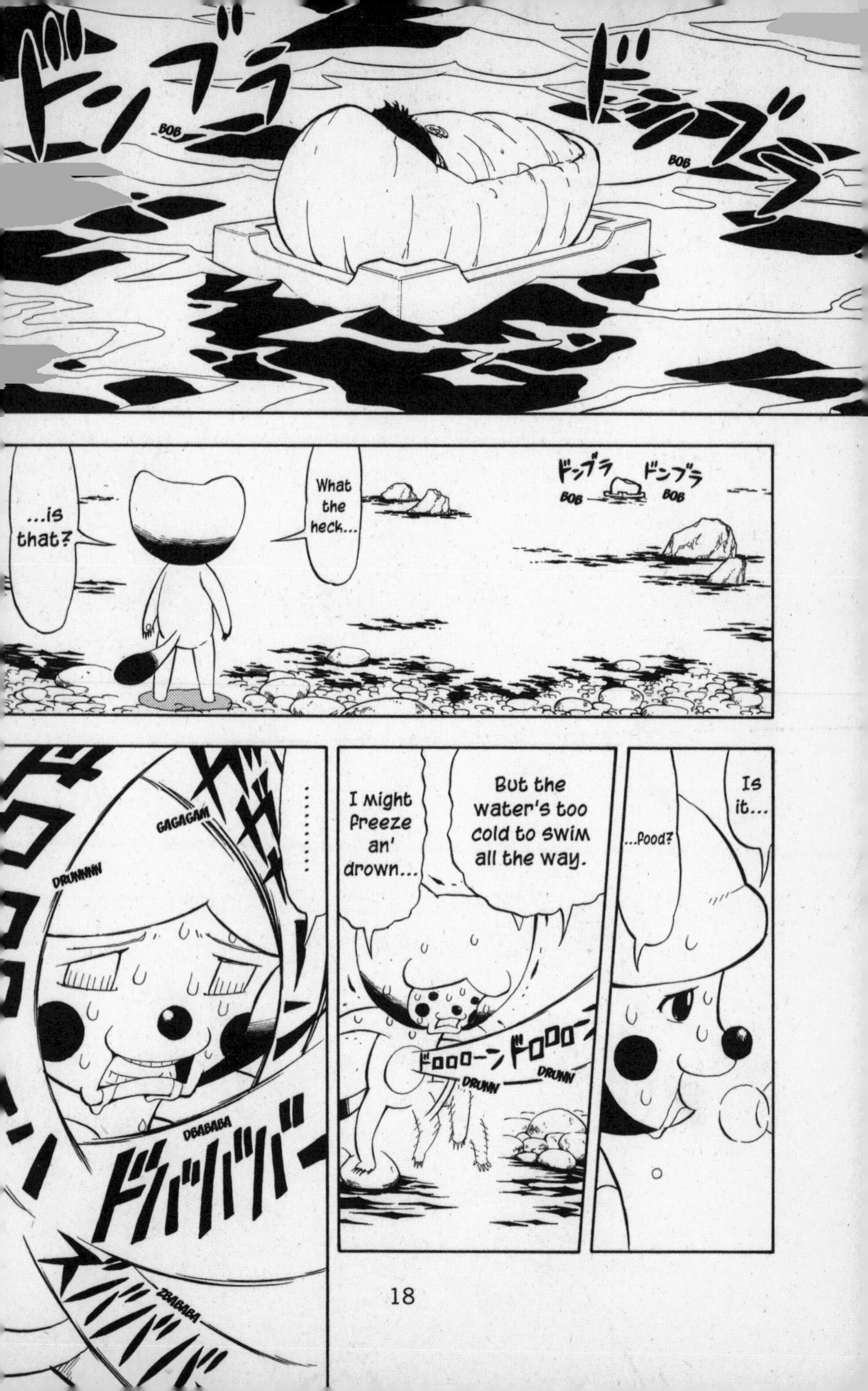
ドンブラ
BOB
ドンブラ
BOB
ドンブラ
BOB
ドンブラ
BOB
What the heck...
...is that?
Is it...
...food?
But the water's too cold to swim all the way.
I might freeze an' drown...
ドロローン
DRUNN
ドロロー
DRUNN
......
GAGAGAM
DRUNNNN
DBABABA
ZBABABA

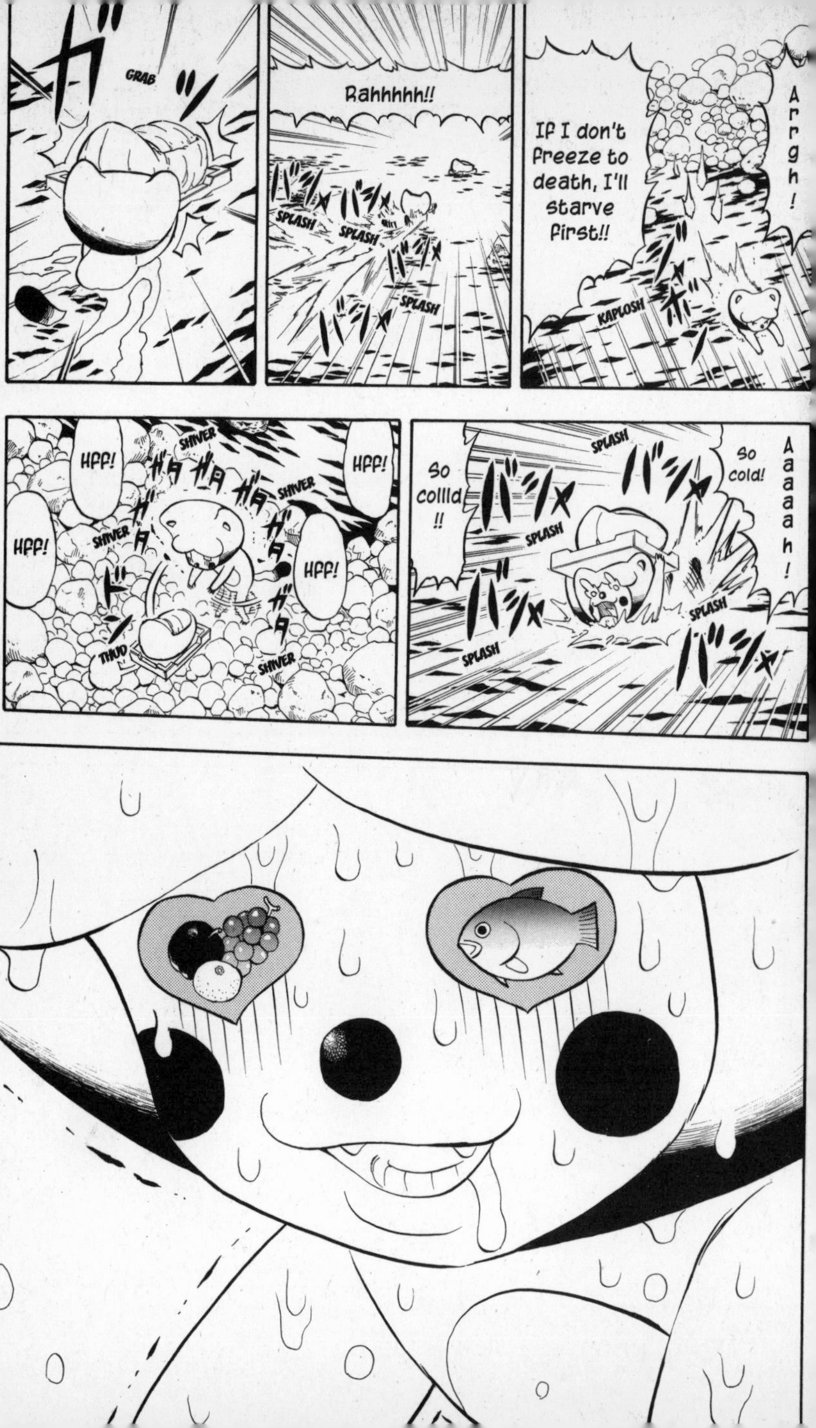
Arrgh!
If I don't freeze to death, I'll starve first!!
KAPLOSH
Rahhhhh!!
SPLASH
SPLASH
SPLASH
GRAB
Aaaaah!
So cold!
SPLASH
So collld!!
SPLASH
SPLASH
SPLASH
HFF!
SHIVER
SHIVER
HFF!
SHIVER
HFF!
HFF!
SHIVER
THUD

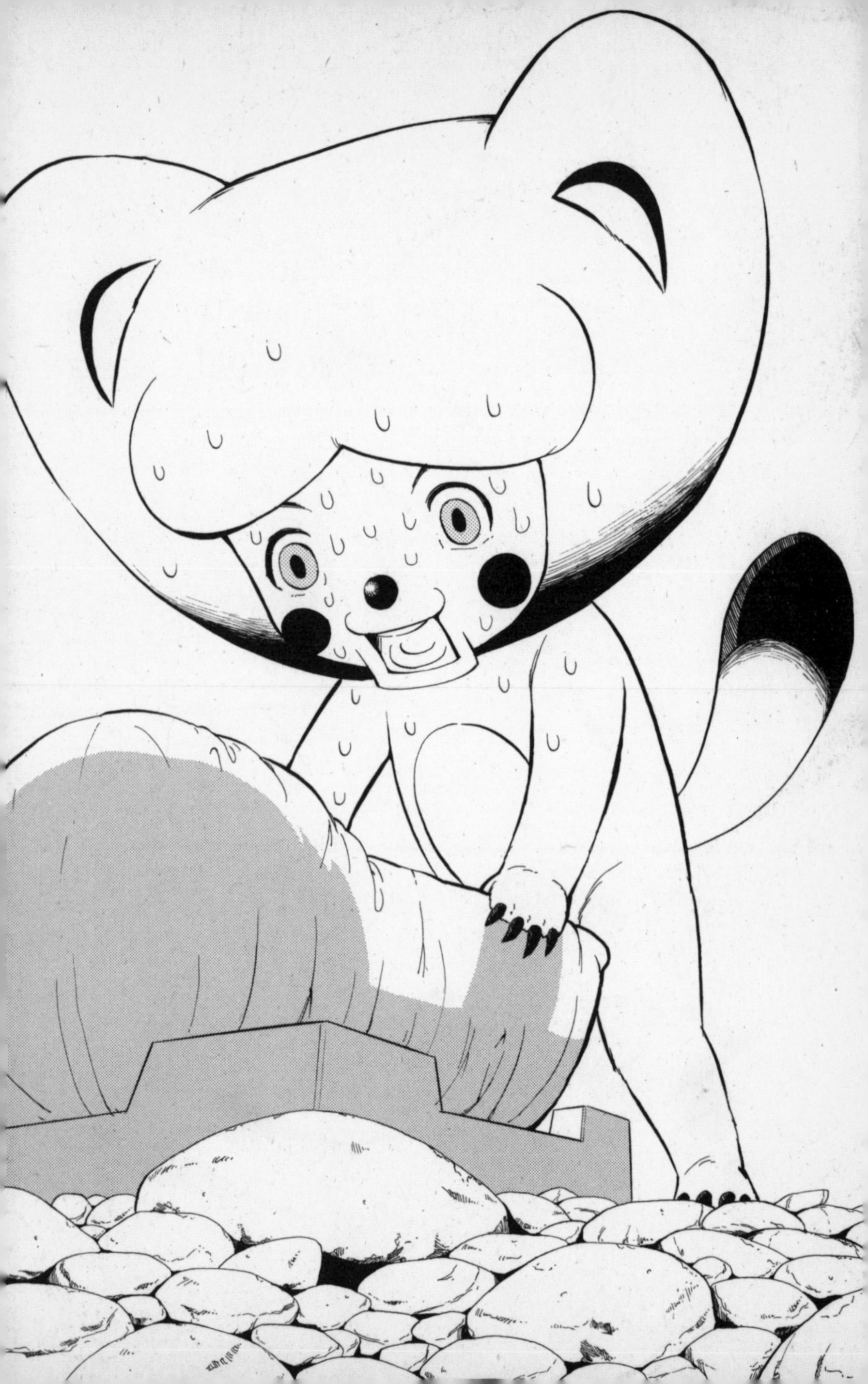

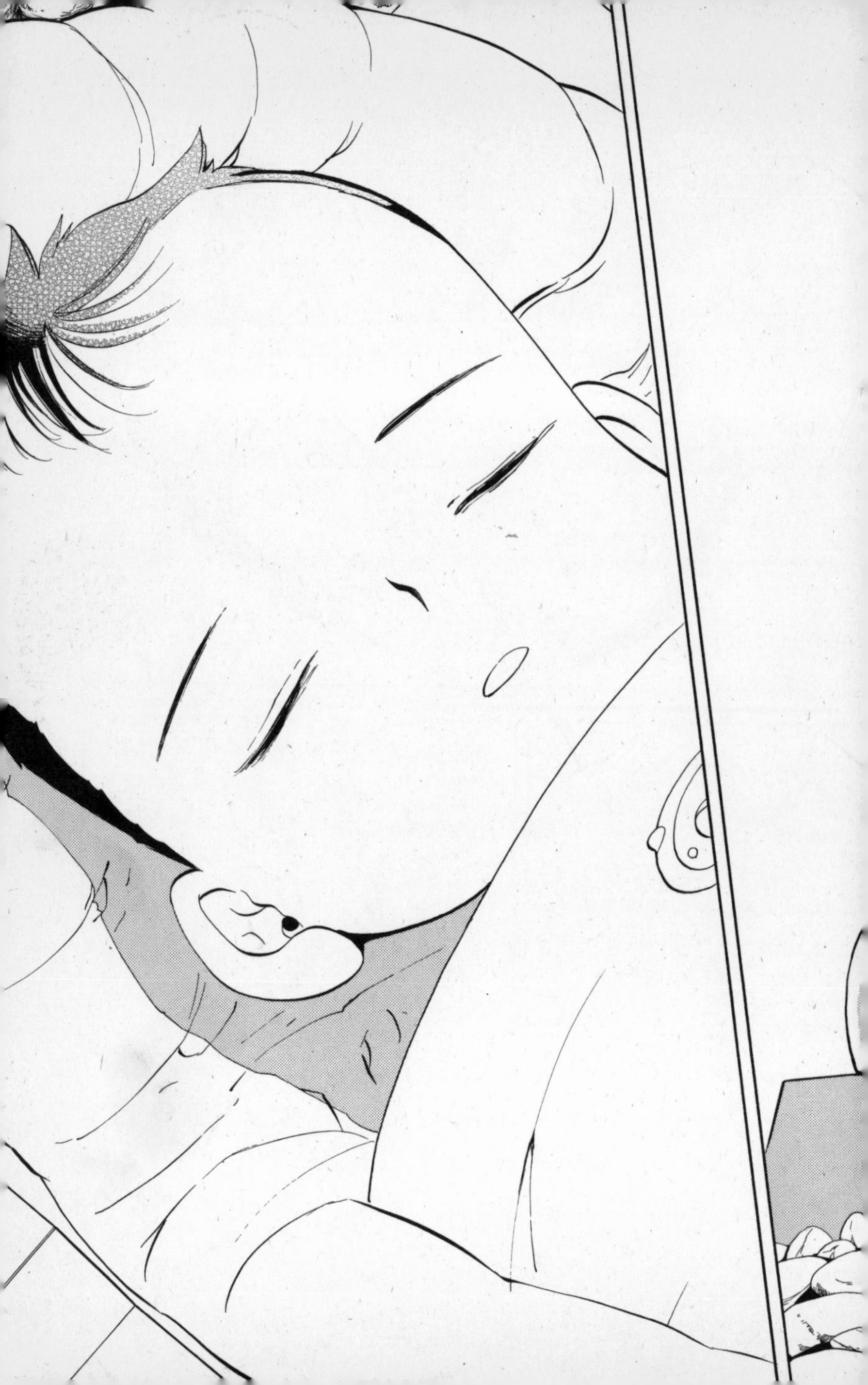

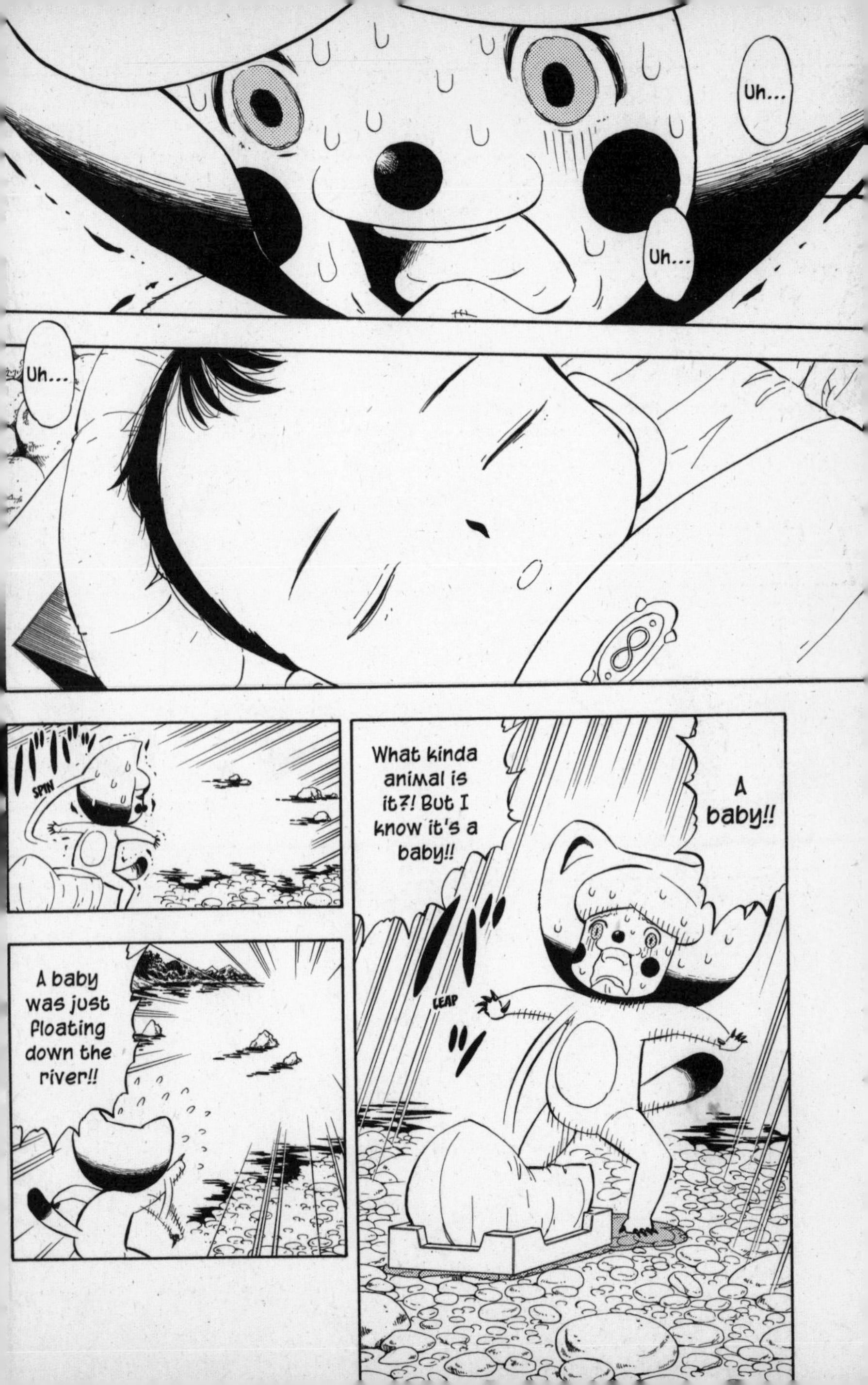
Uh...
Uh...
Uh...
A baby!!
What kinda animal is it?! But I know it's a baby!!
LEAP
SPIN
A baby was just floating down the river!!

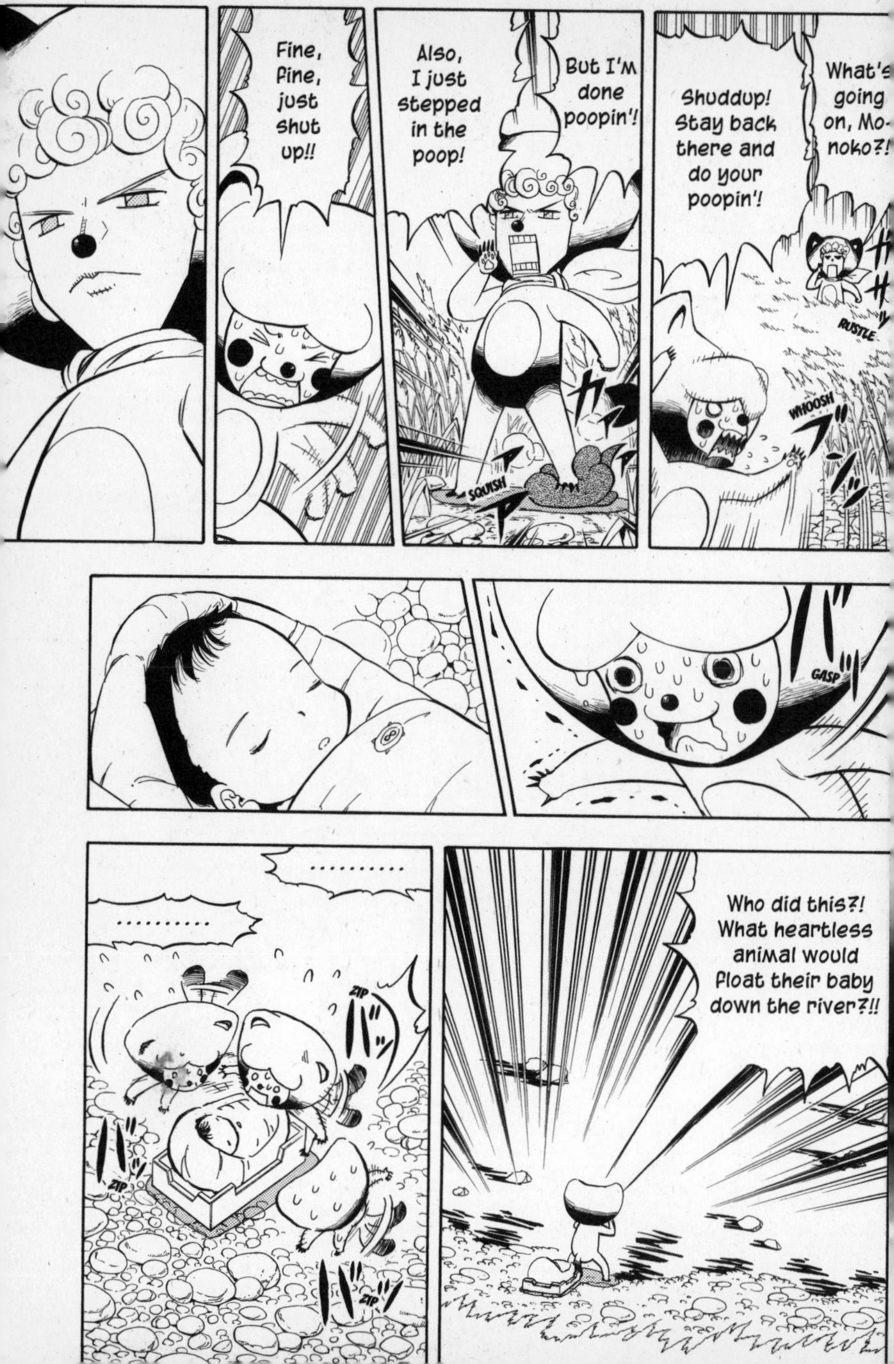
What's going on, Mo-noko?!
Shuddup! Stay back there and do your poopin'!
RUSTLE
WHOOSH
But I'M done poopin'!
Also, I just stepped in the poop!
SQUISH
Fine, fine, just shut up!!
GASP
Who did this?! What heartless animal would float their baby down the river?!!
....
....
ZIP
ZIP
ZIP

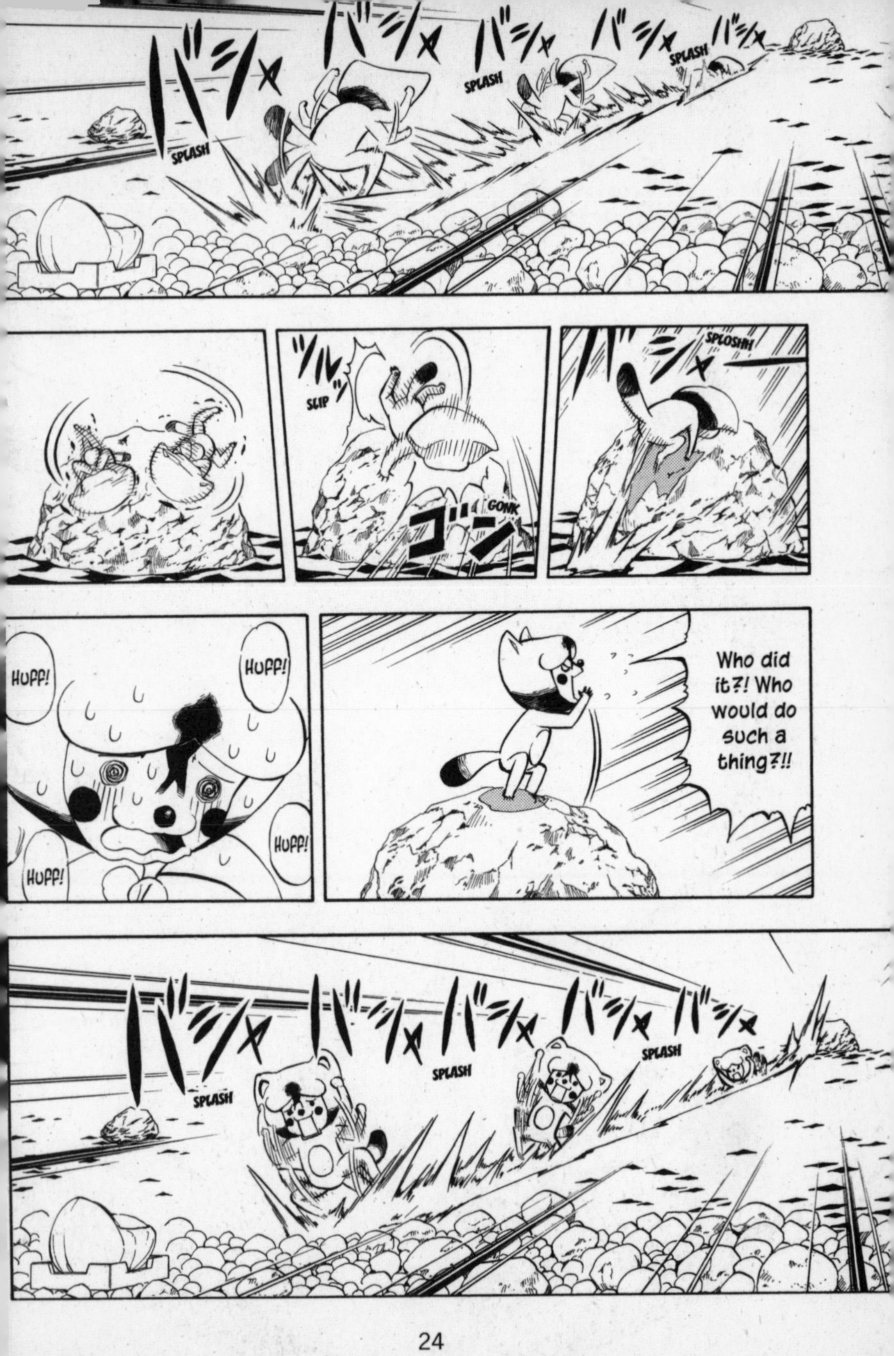

バシャ
SPLASH
バシャ
SPLASH
バシャ
SPLASH
バシャ
SPLOSHH
バシャ
ツル
SLIP
ゴン
GONK
Who did it?! Who would do such a thing?!!
HUFF!
HUFF!
HUFF!
HUFF!
バシャ
バシャ
SPLASH
バシャ
SPLASH
バシャ
SPLASH
バシャ

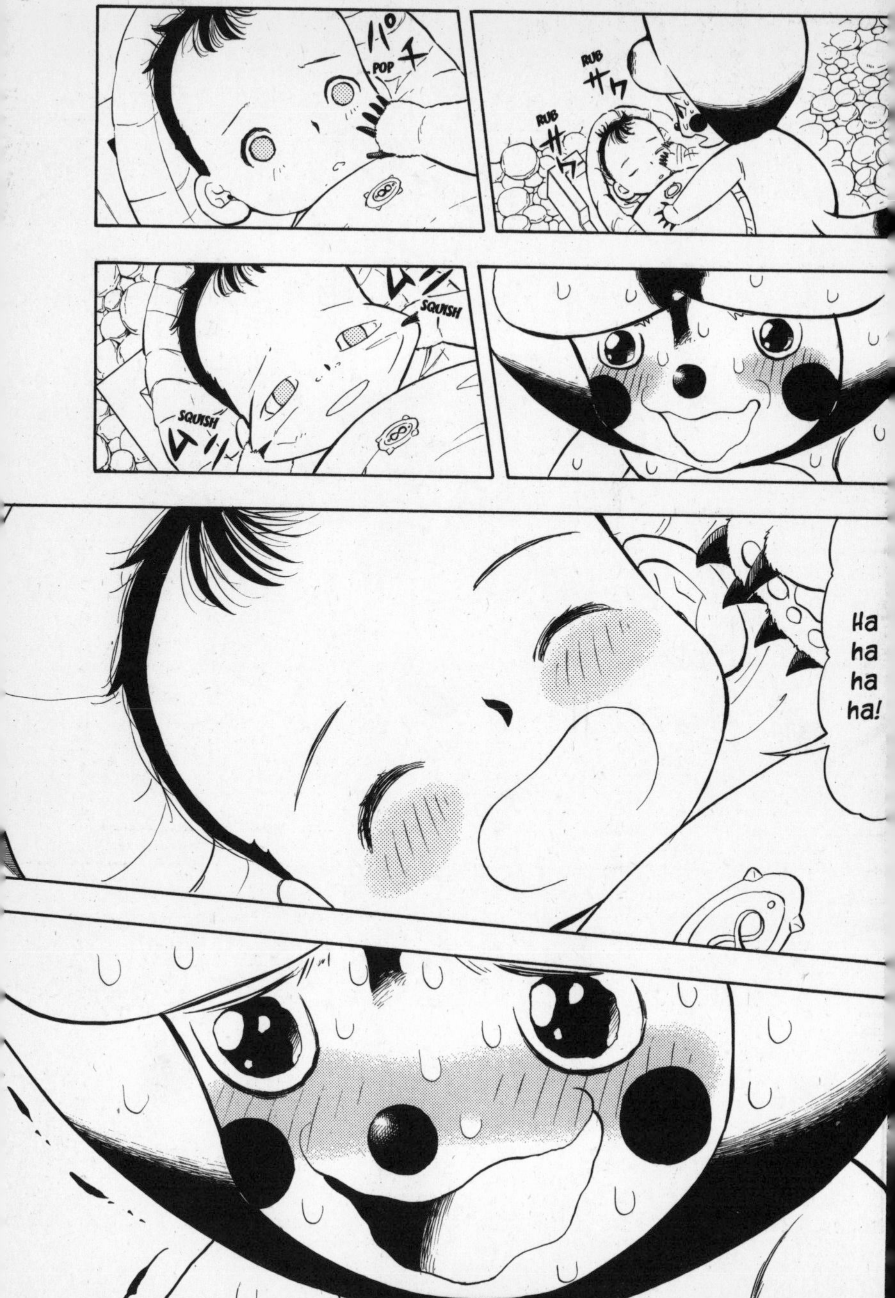

RUB
RUB
POP
SQUISH
SQUISH
Ha ha ha ha!

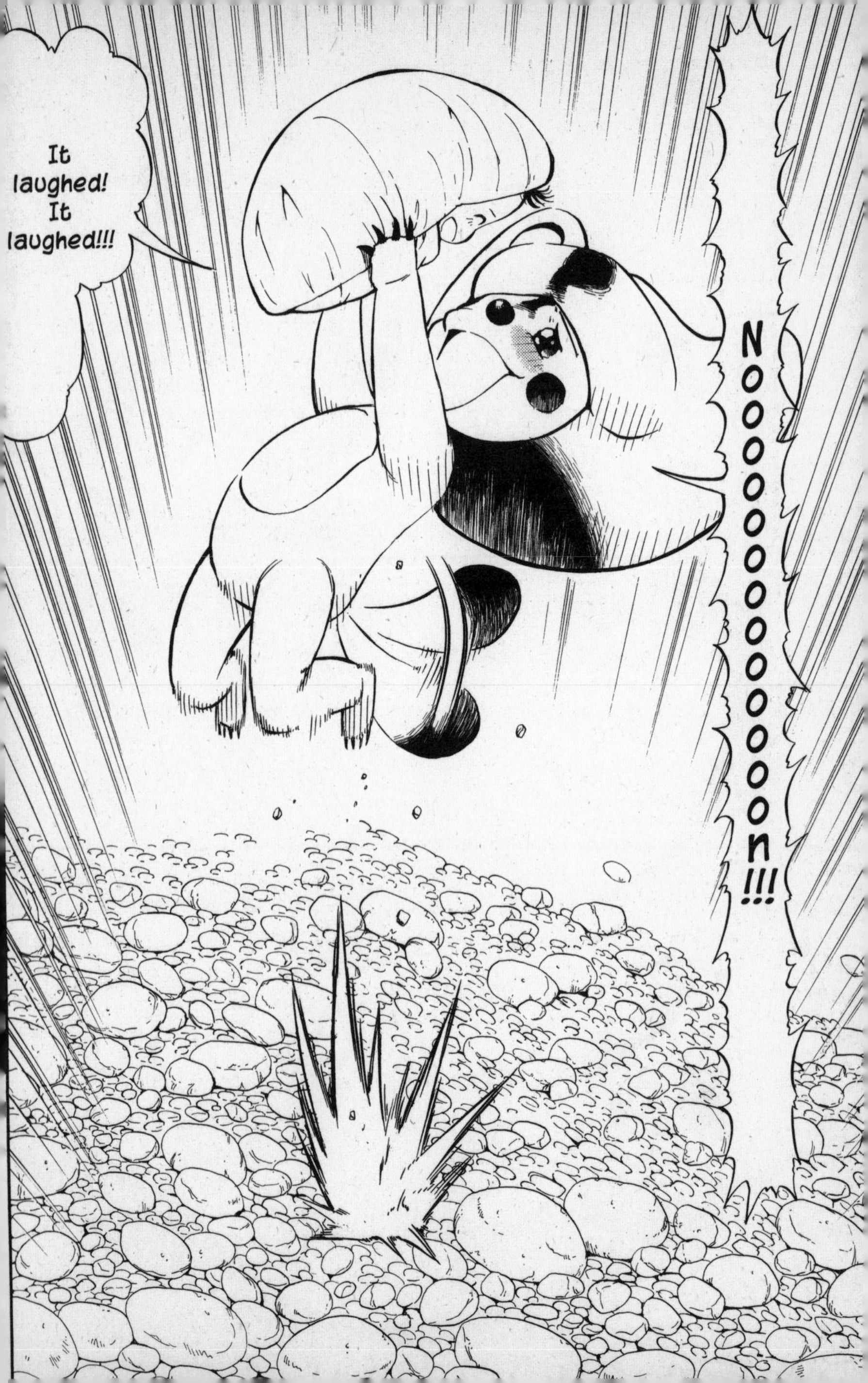
NOOOOOOOOOOOOOOn!!!
It laughed! It laughed!!!

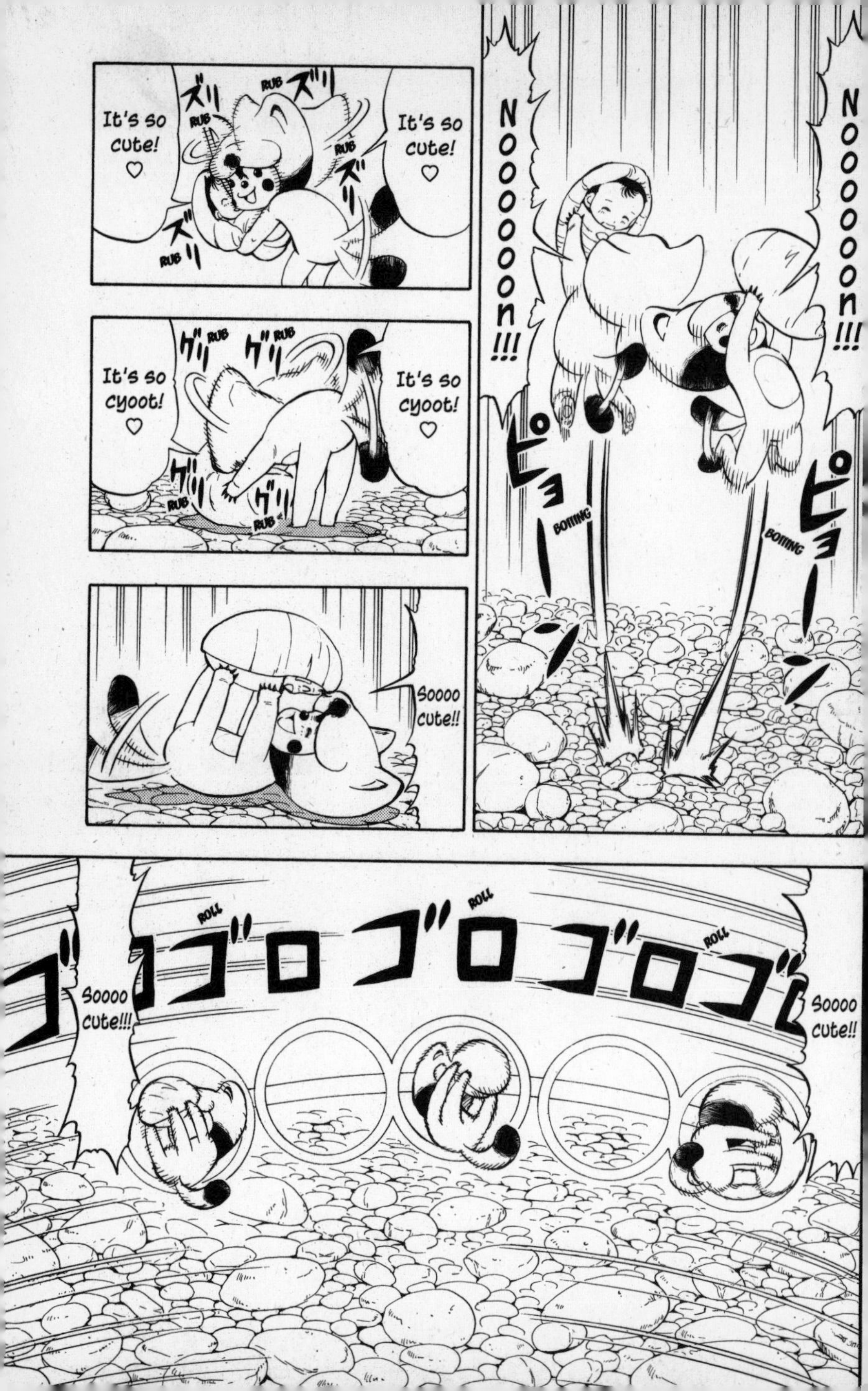
NOOOOOOn!!!
NOOOOOOn!!!
ピョーン
BOING
ピョーン
BOING
ズリ RUB
ズリ RUB
It's so cute! ♡
It's so cute! ♡
ズリ RUB
ズリ RUB
グリ RUB
グリ RUB
It's so cyoot! ♡
It's so cyoot! ♡
グリ RUB
グリ RUB
Soooo cute!!
ゴロゴロゴロゴロ
ROLL ROLL ROLL
Soooo cute!!
Soooo cute!!!

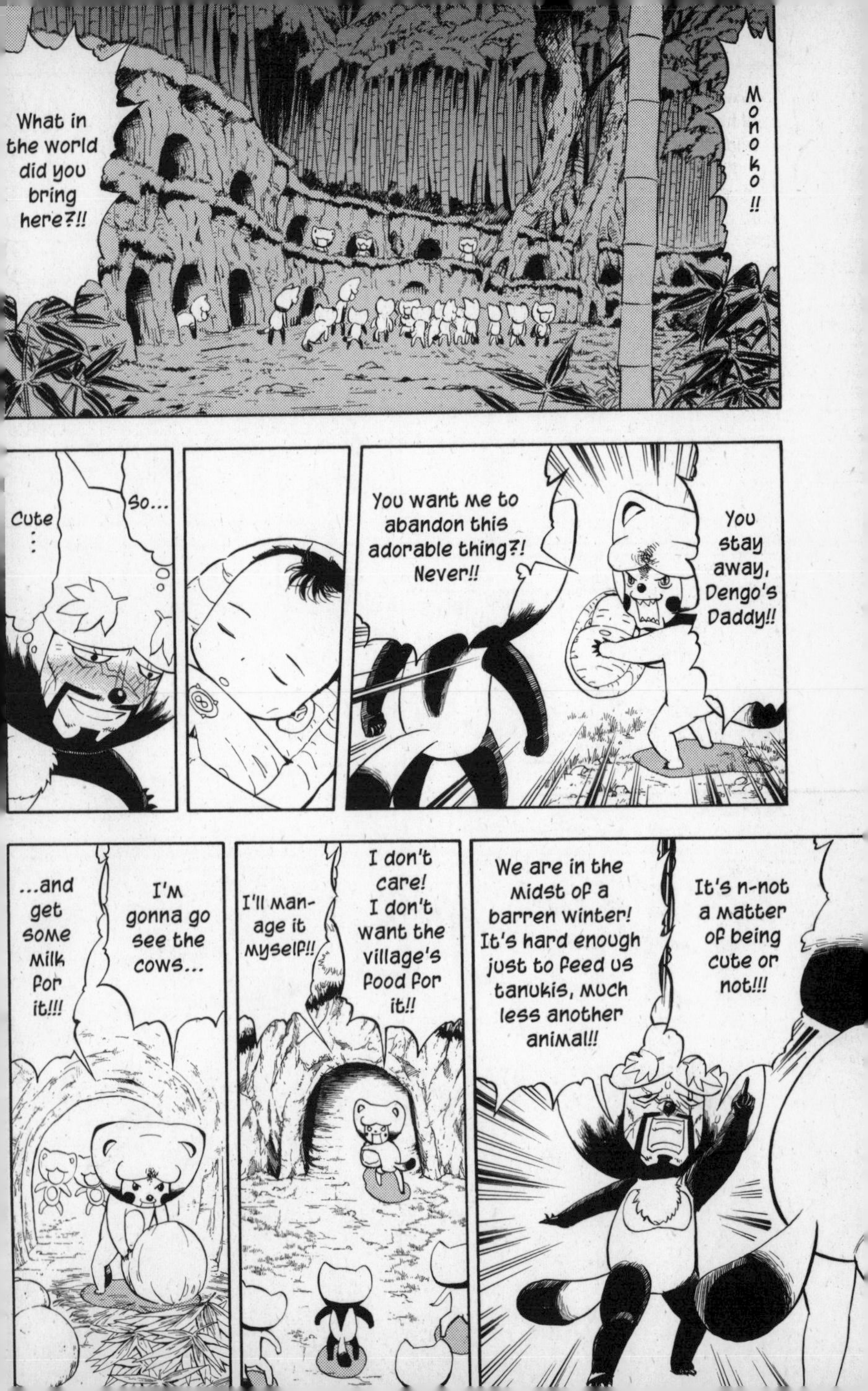
Monoko!!
What in the world did you bring here?!!
You stay away, Dengo's Daddy!!
You want me to abandon this adorable thing?! Never!!
So...
Cute...
It's n-not a matter of being cute or not!!!
We are in the midst of a barren winter! It's hard enough just to feed us tanukis, much less another animal!!
I don't care! I don't want the village's food for it!!
I'll manage it myself!!
I'm gonna go see the cows...
...and get some milk for it!!!

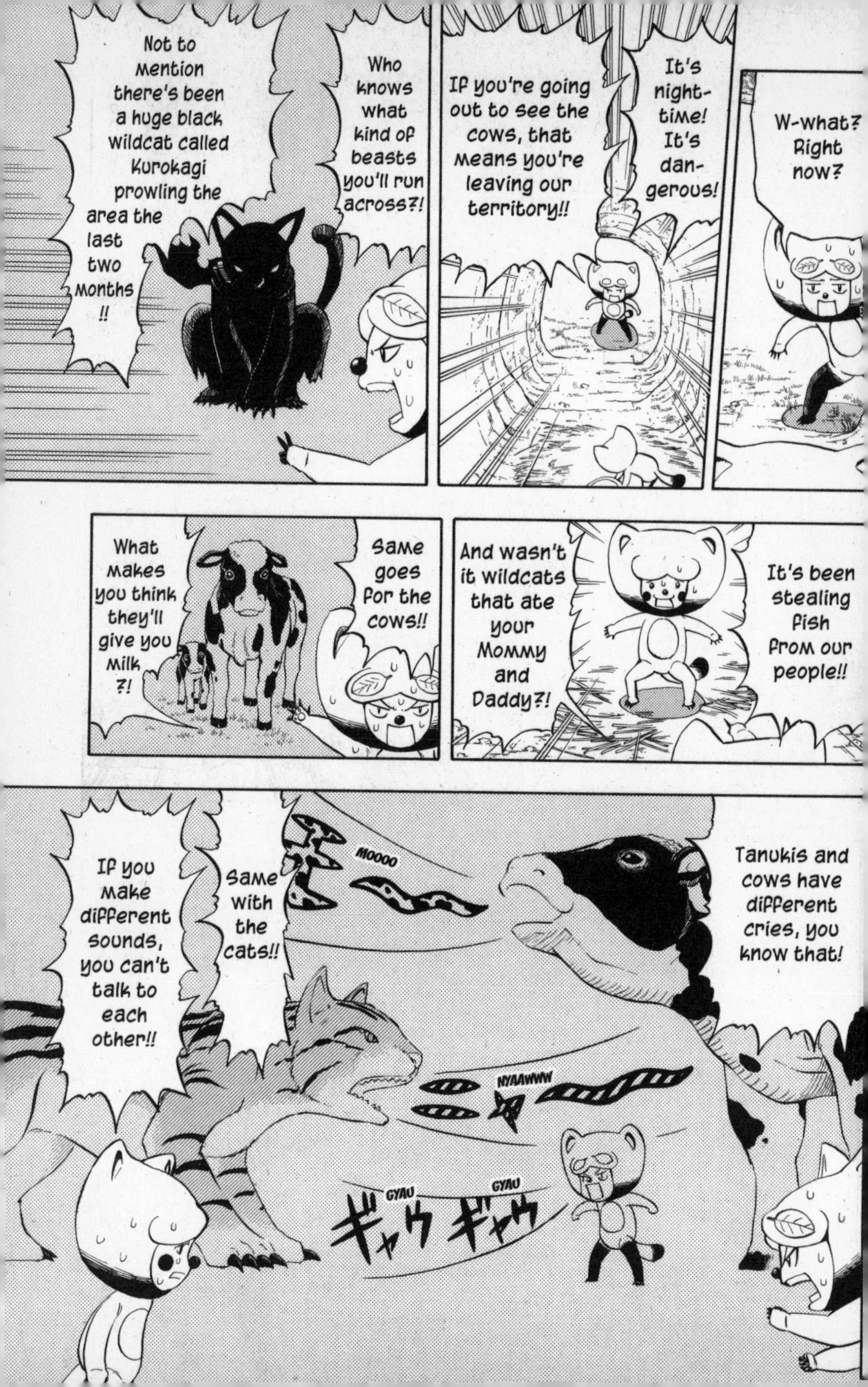
W-what? Right now?
It's night-time! It's dangerous!
If you're going out to see the cows, that means you're leaving our territory!!
Who knows what kind of beasts you'll run across?!
Not to mention there's been a huge black wildcat called Kurokagi prowling the area the last two months!!
It's been stealing fish from our people!!
And wasn't it wildcats that ate your Mommy and Daddy?!
Same goes for the cows!!
What makes you think they'll give you milk?!
Tanukis and cows have different cries, you know that!
MOOOO
Same with the cats!!
If you make different sounds, you can't talk to each other!!
NYAAWWW
ギャウ GYAU
ギャウ GYAU

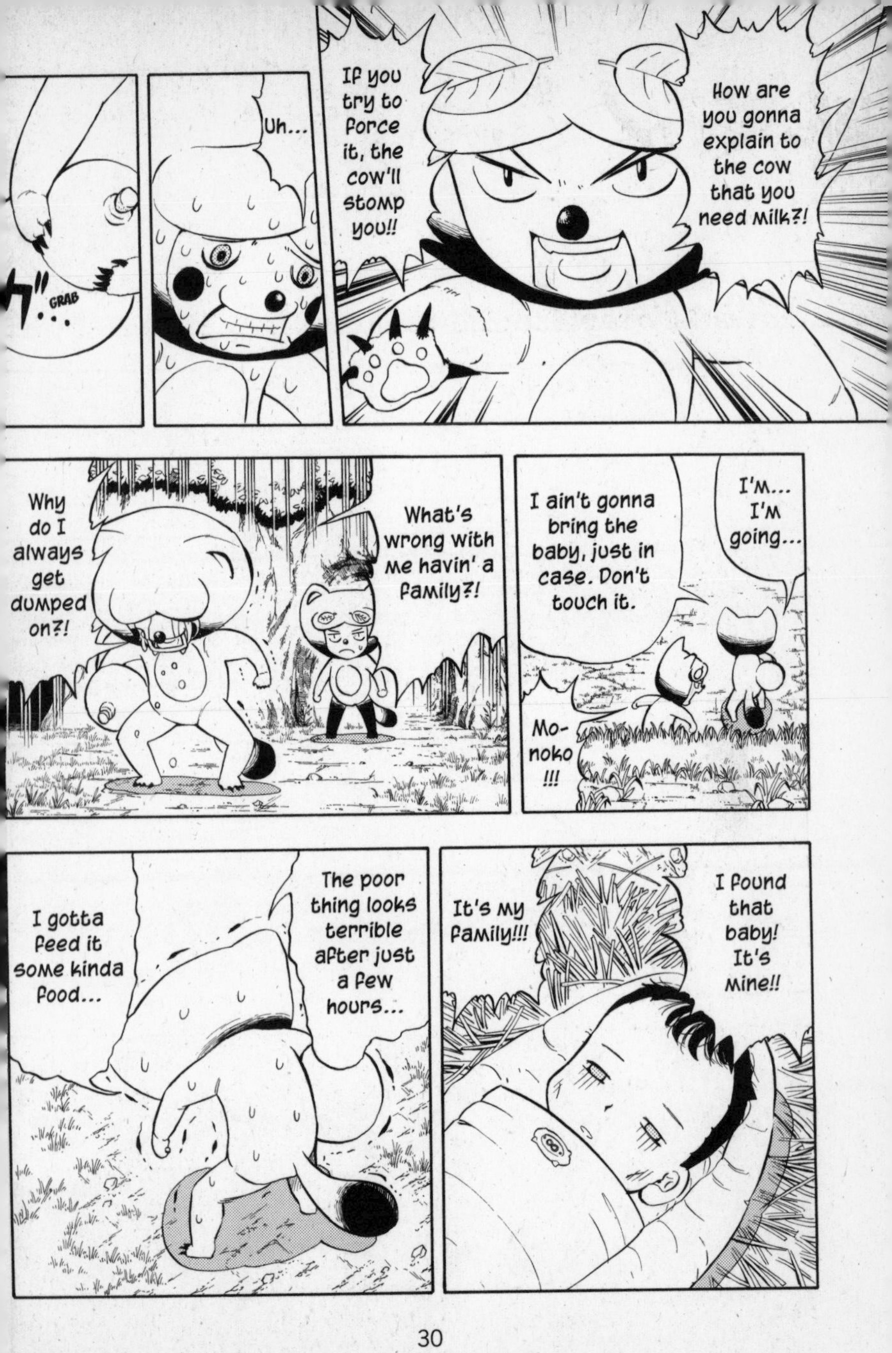
How are you gonna explain to the cow that you need milk?!
If you try to force it, the cow'll stomp you!!
Uh...
GRAB
I'm... I'm going...
I ain't gonna bring the baby, just in case. Don't touch it.
Mo-noko!!!
What's wrong with me havin' a family?!
Why do I always get dumped on?!
I found that baby! It's mine!!
It's my family!!!
The poor thing looks terrible after just a few hours...
I gotta feed it some kinda food...

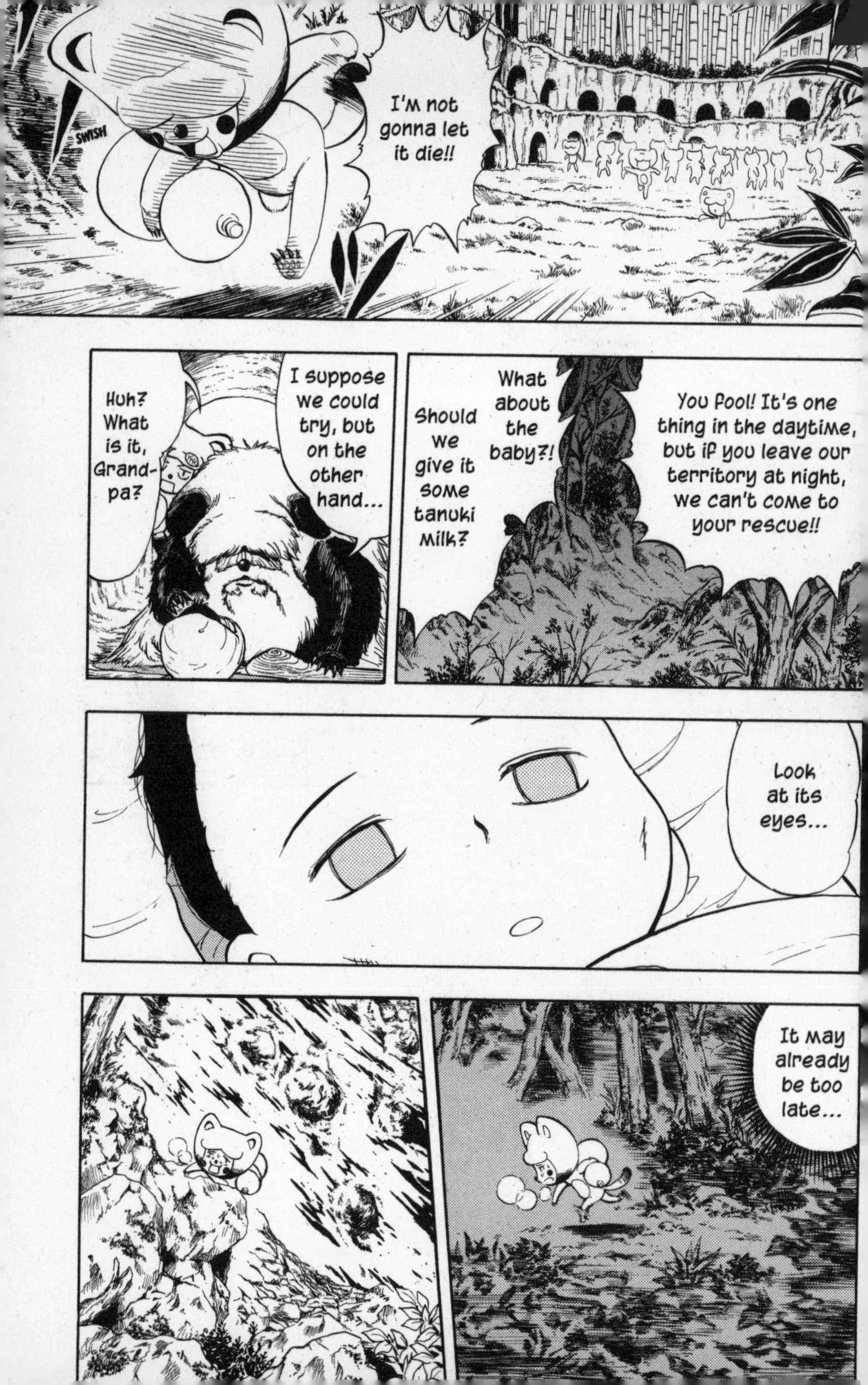
I'm not gonna let it die!!
SWISH
You fool! It's one thing in the daytime, but if you leave our territory at night, we can't come to your rescue!!
What about the baby?!
Should we give it some tanuki milk?
I suppose we could try, but on the other hand...
Huh? What is it, Grand-pa?
Look at its eyes...
It may already be too late...

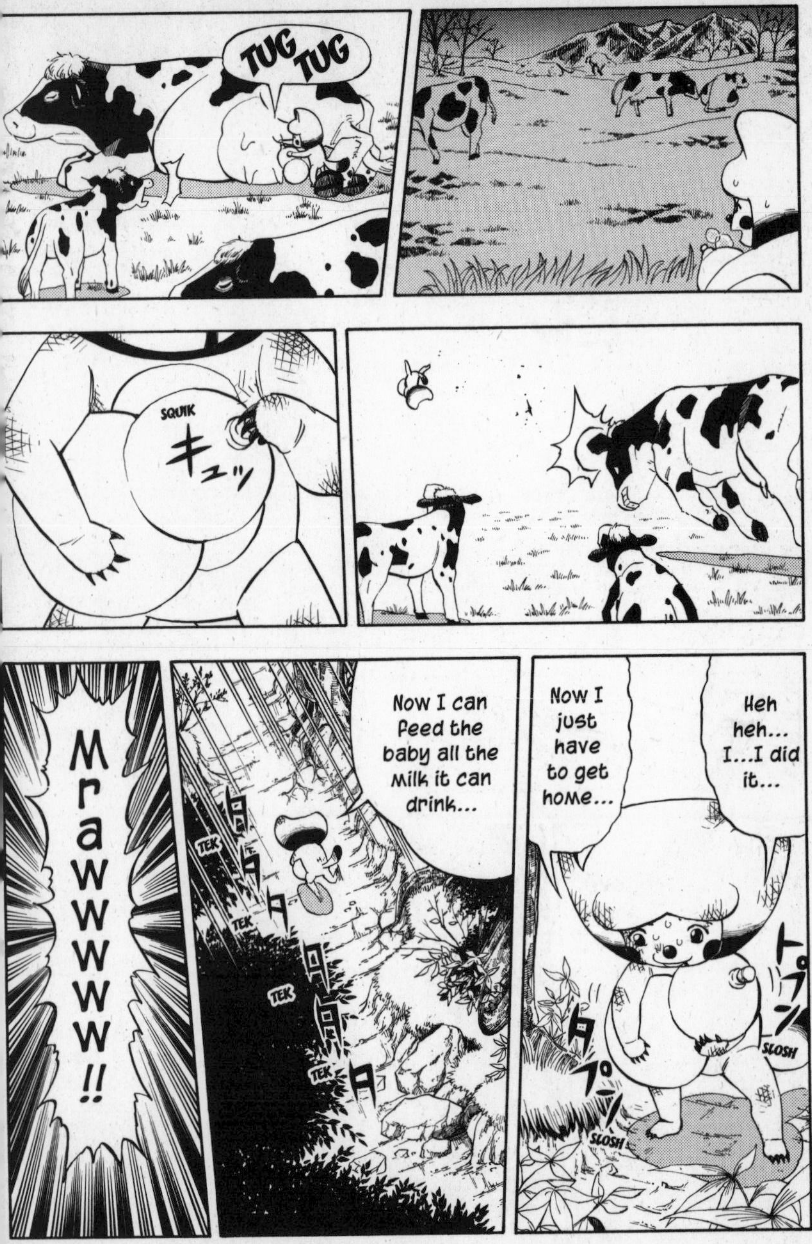

TUG TUG
SQUIK
キュッ
Heh heh... I...I did it...
Now I just have to get home...
SLOSH
SLOSH
Now I can feed the baby all the milk it can drink...
TEK
TEK
TEK
TEK
Mrawwwwww!!

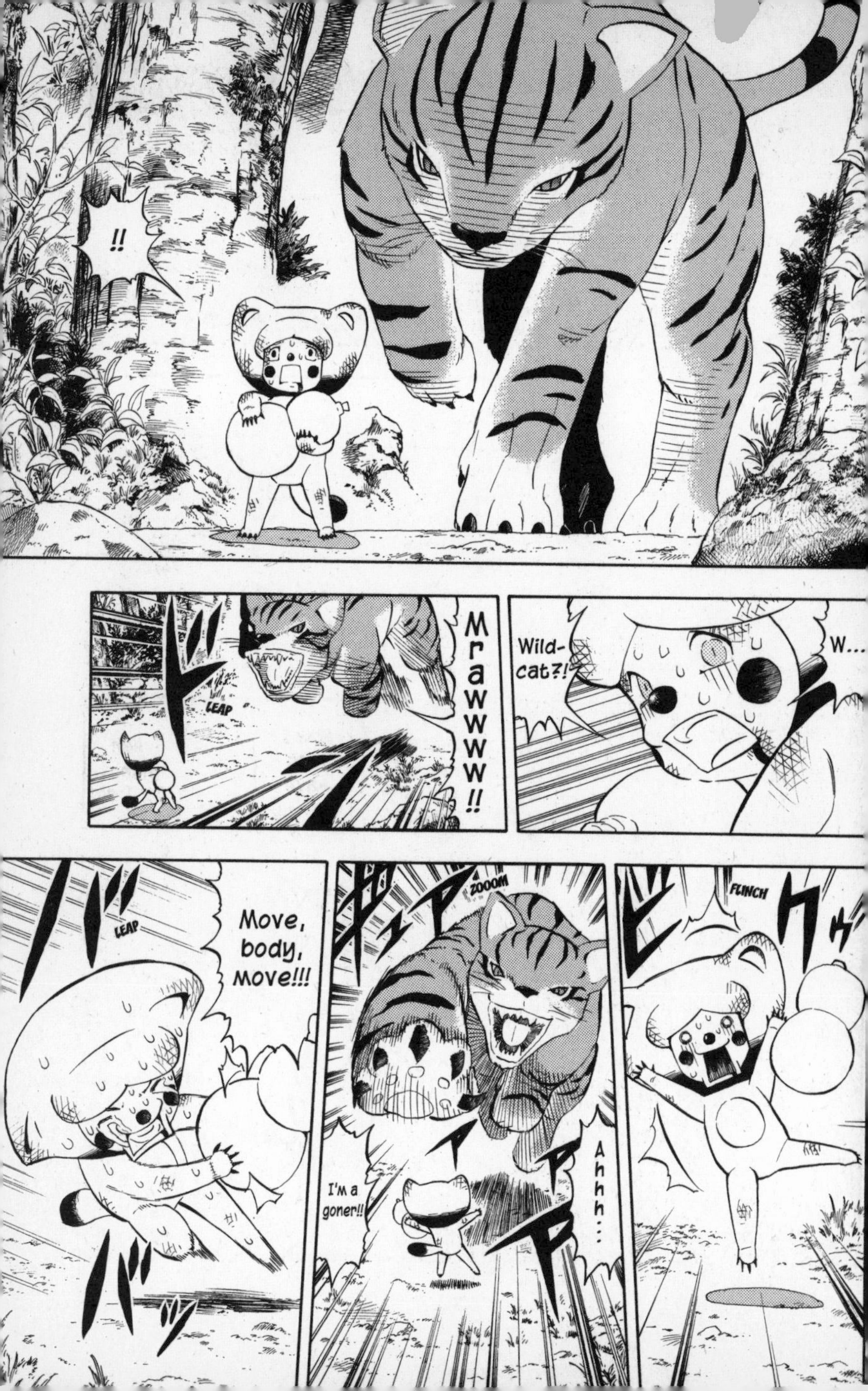
!!
W...
Wild-cat?!
Mrawwwww!!
LEAP
FLINCH
ZOOOM
Ahhh...
I'm a goner!!
Move, body, move!!!
LEAP

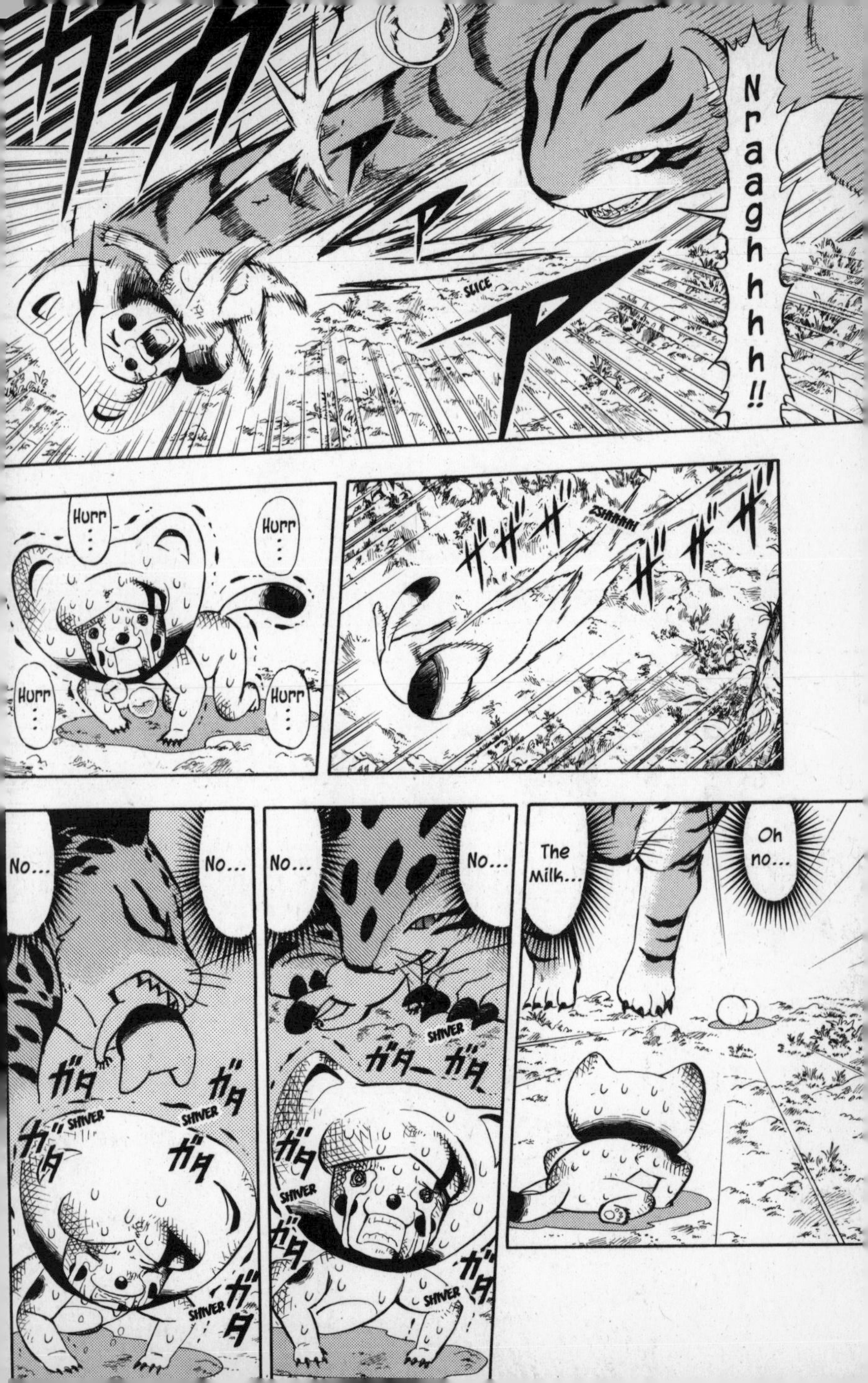
Nraghhhh!!
SLICE
ZSHHHH
ザザザ
ザザザ
Hurr...
Hurr...
Hurr...
Hurr...
Oh no...
The milk...
No...
No...
SHIVER
ガタ ガタ
SHIVER
SHIVER
No...
No...
SHIVER
SHIVER
ガタ
ガタ
SHIVER

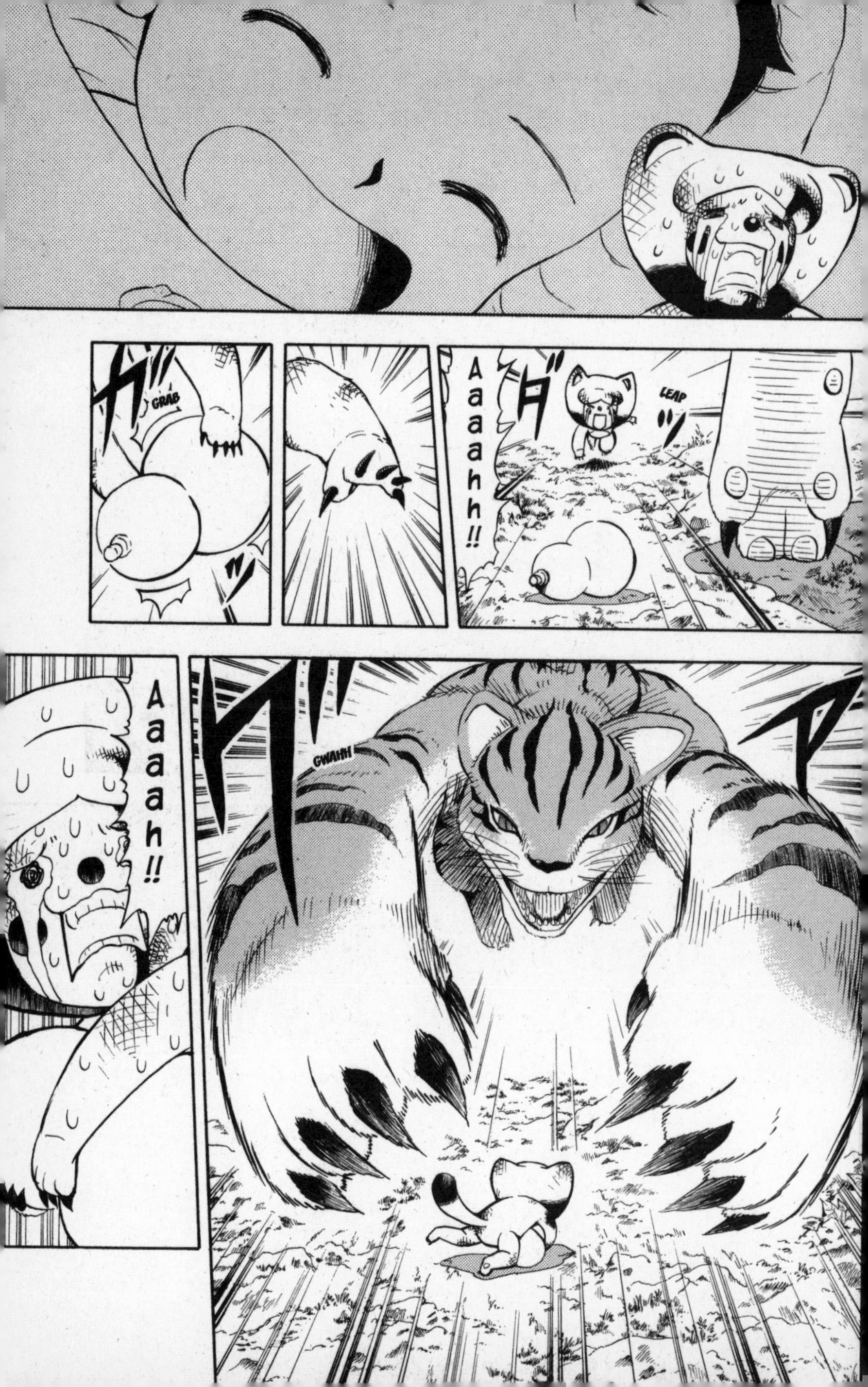

LEAP
Aaaaahh!!
GRAB
GWAHH
Aaaaah!!

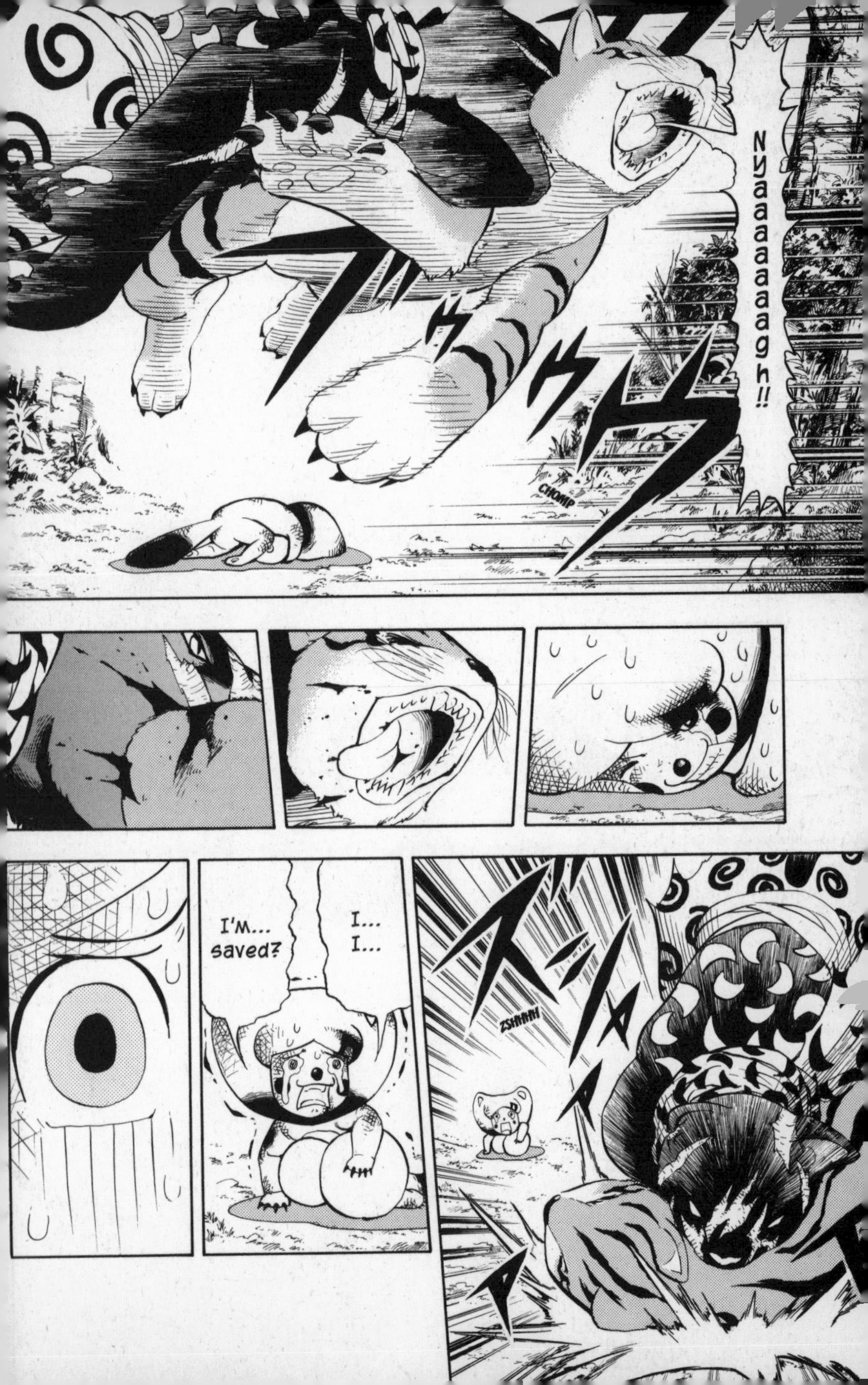
Nyaaaaaagh!!
CHOMP
ZSHHHH
I... I...
I'M... saved?

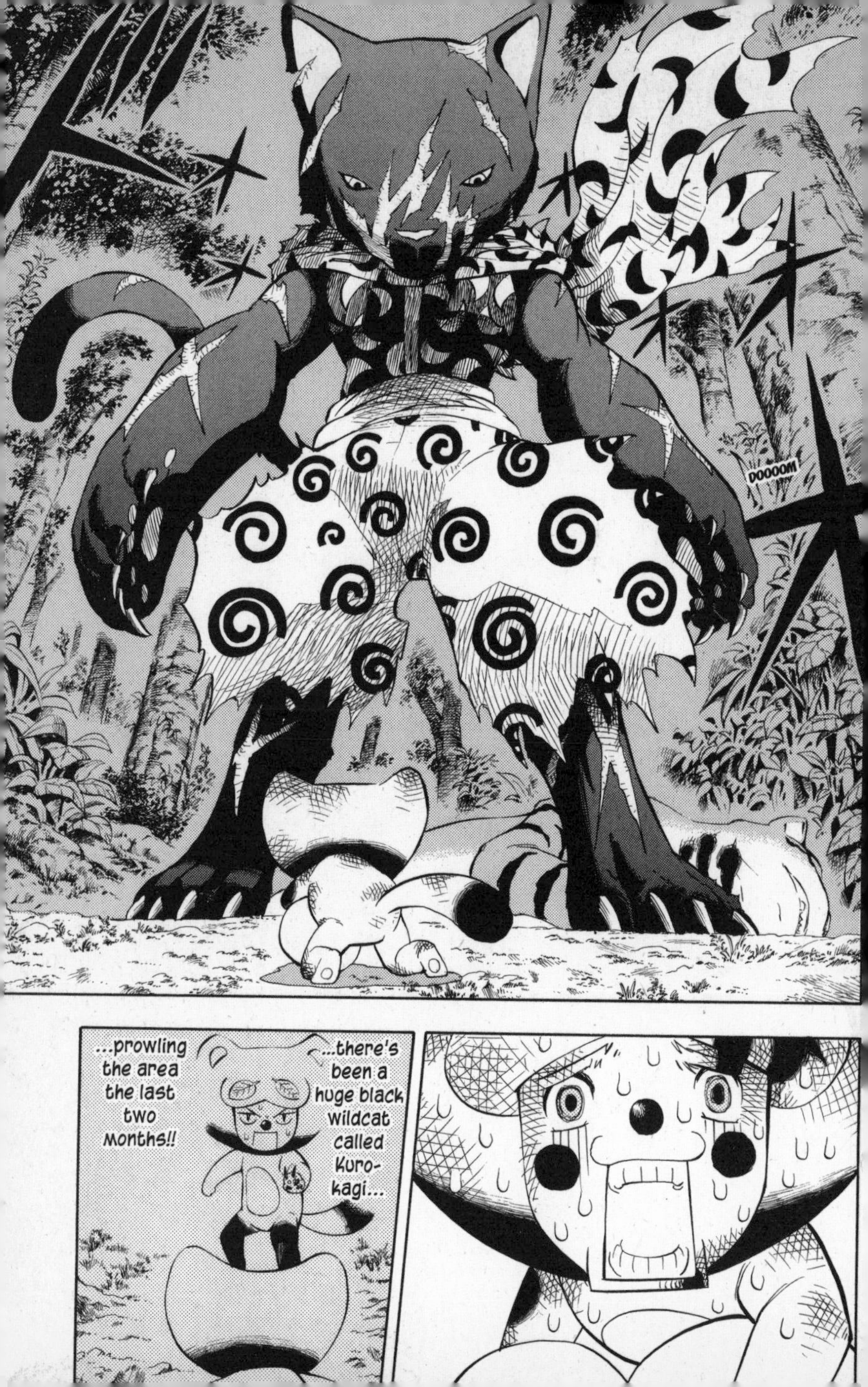
DOOOOM
...there's been a huge black wildcat called Kuro-kagi...
...prowling the area the last two months!!

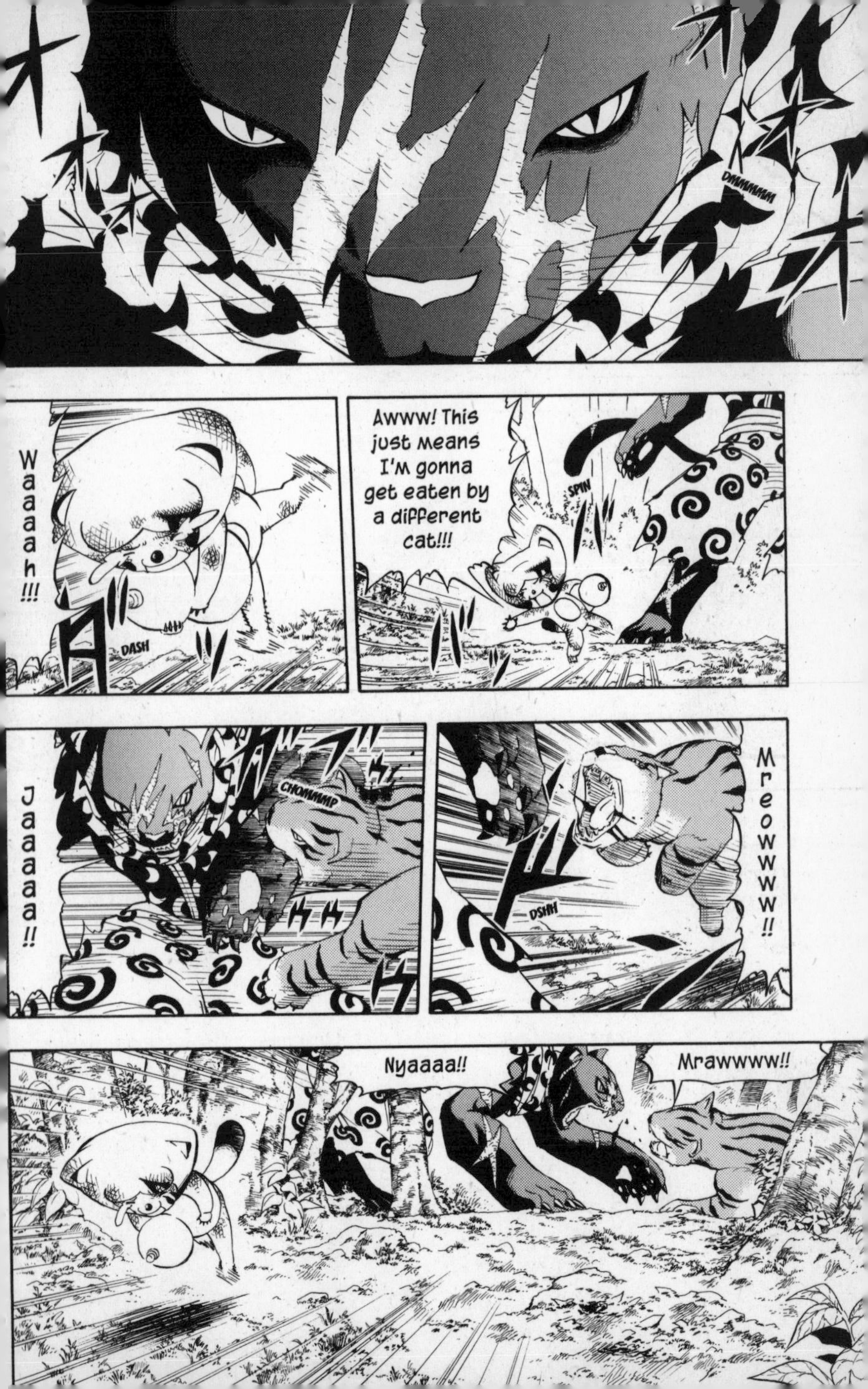
DMMMMM
SPIN
Awww! This just means I'm gonna get eaten by a different cat!!!
Waaaah!!!
DASH
Mreowwww!!
DSHH
CHOMMMP
Jaaaaaa!!
Mrawwww!!
Nyaaaa!!

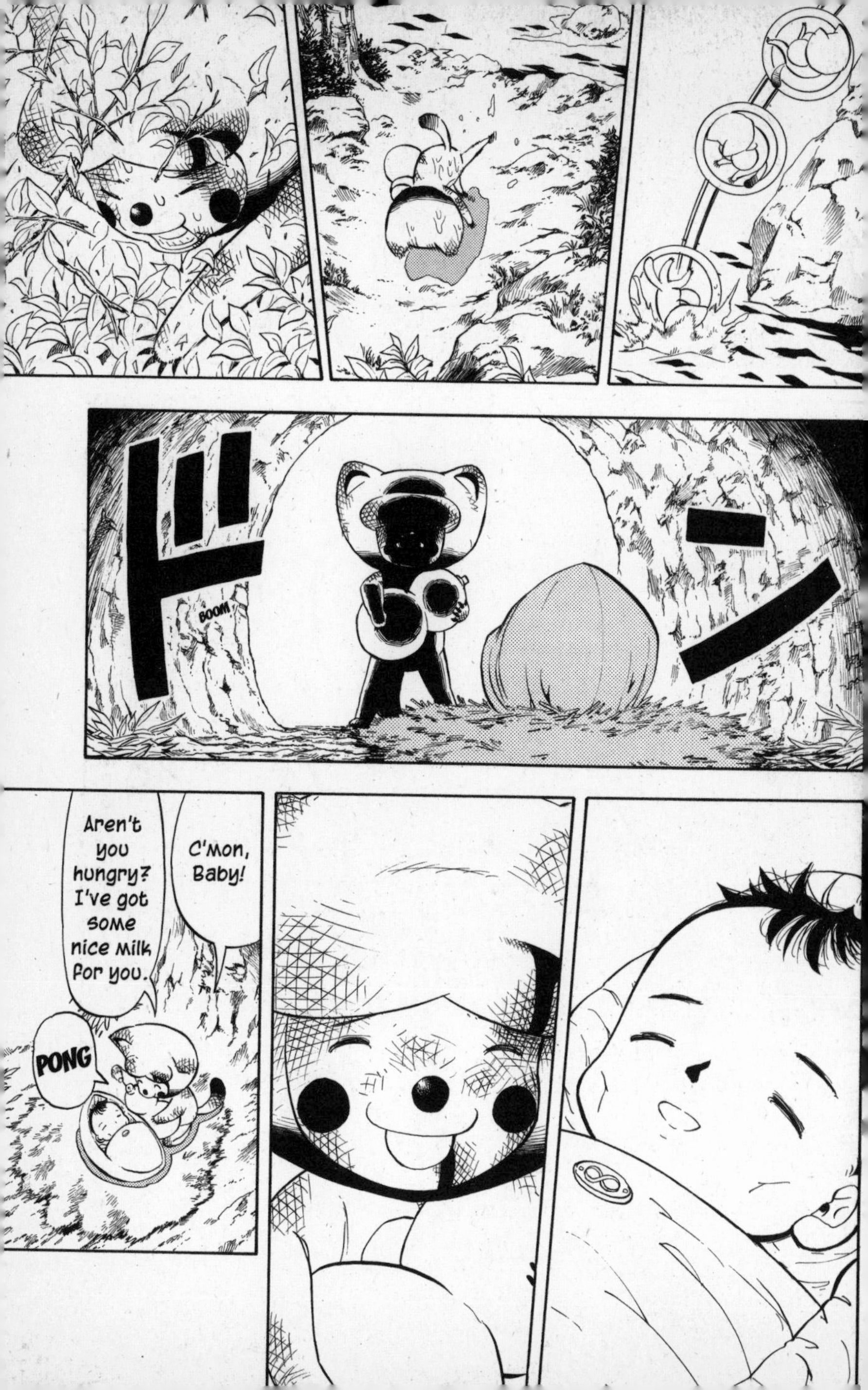
ドーン
BOOM
C'mon, Baby!
Aren't you hungry? I've got some nice milk for you.
PONG

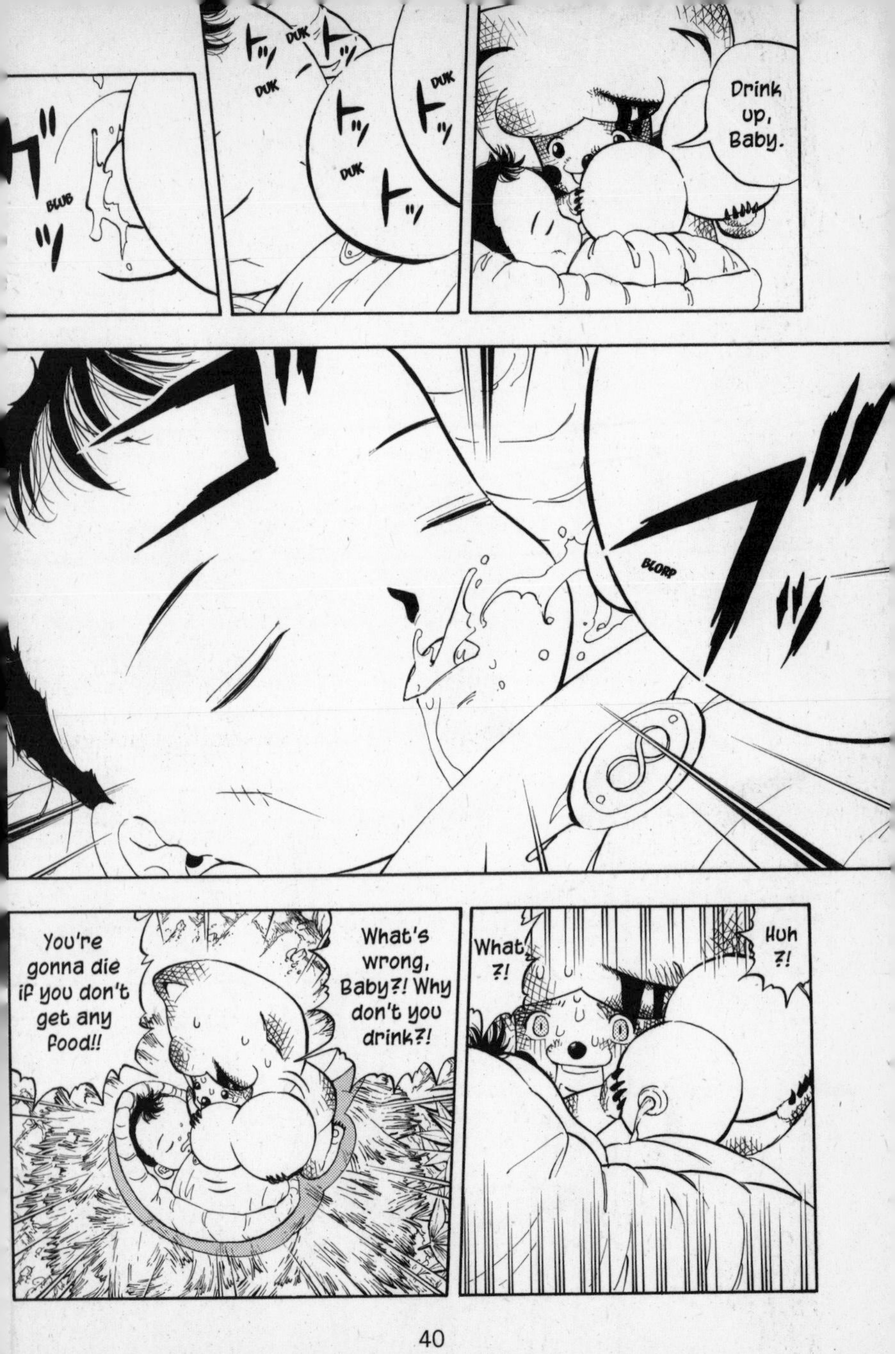
Drink up, Baby.
DUK
DUK
DUK
DUK
BLUB
BLORP
Huh ?!
What ?!
What's wrong, Baby?! Why don't you drink?!
You're gonna die if you don't get any food!!

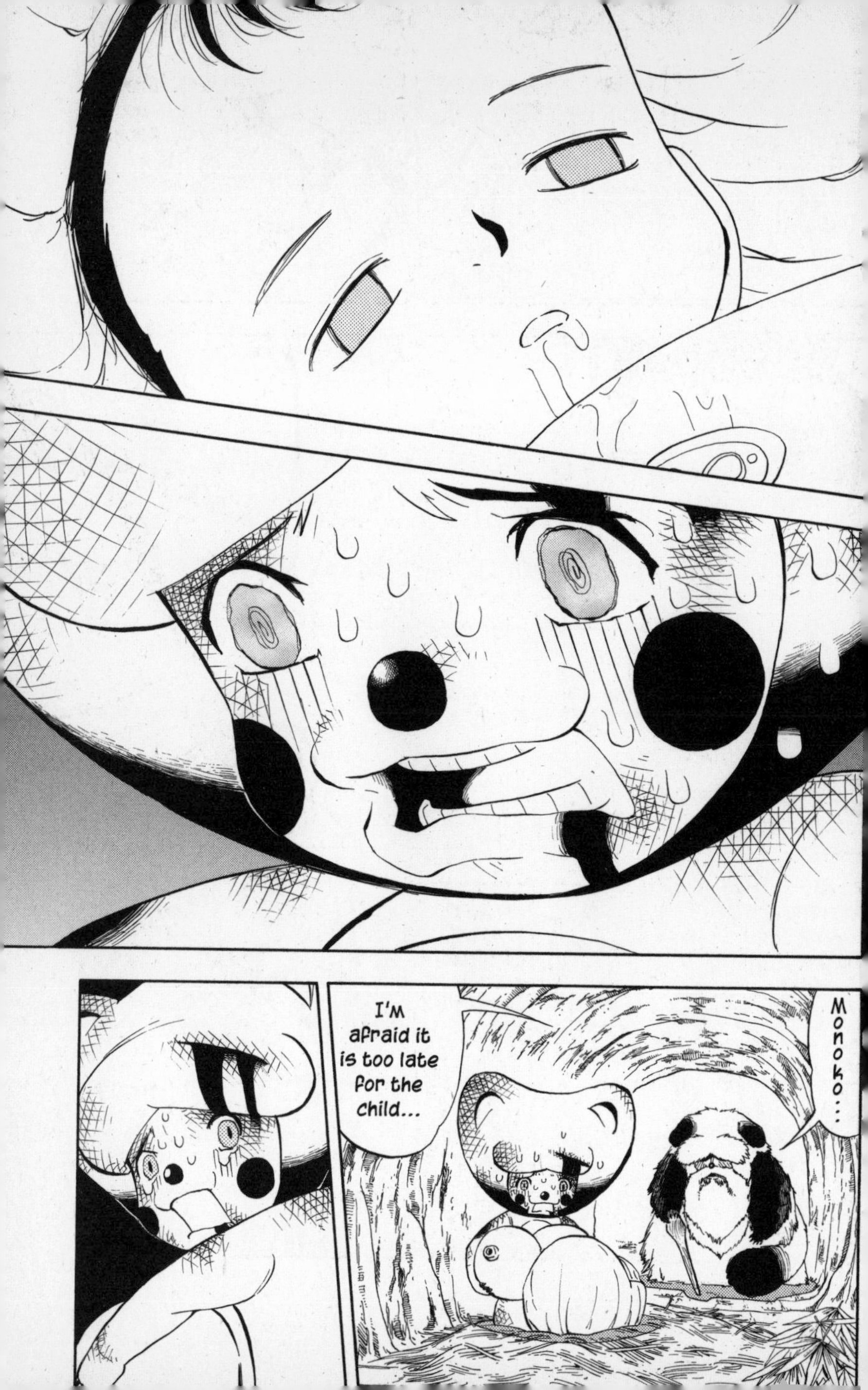
Monoko...
I'M afraid it is too late for the child...

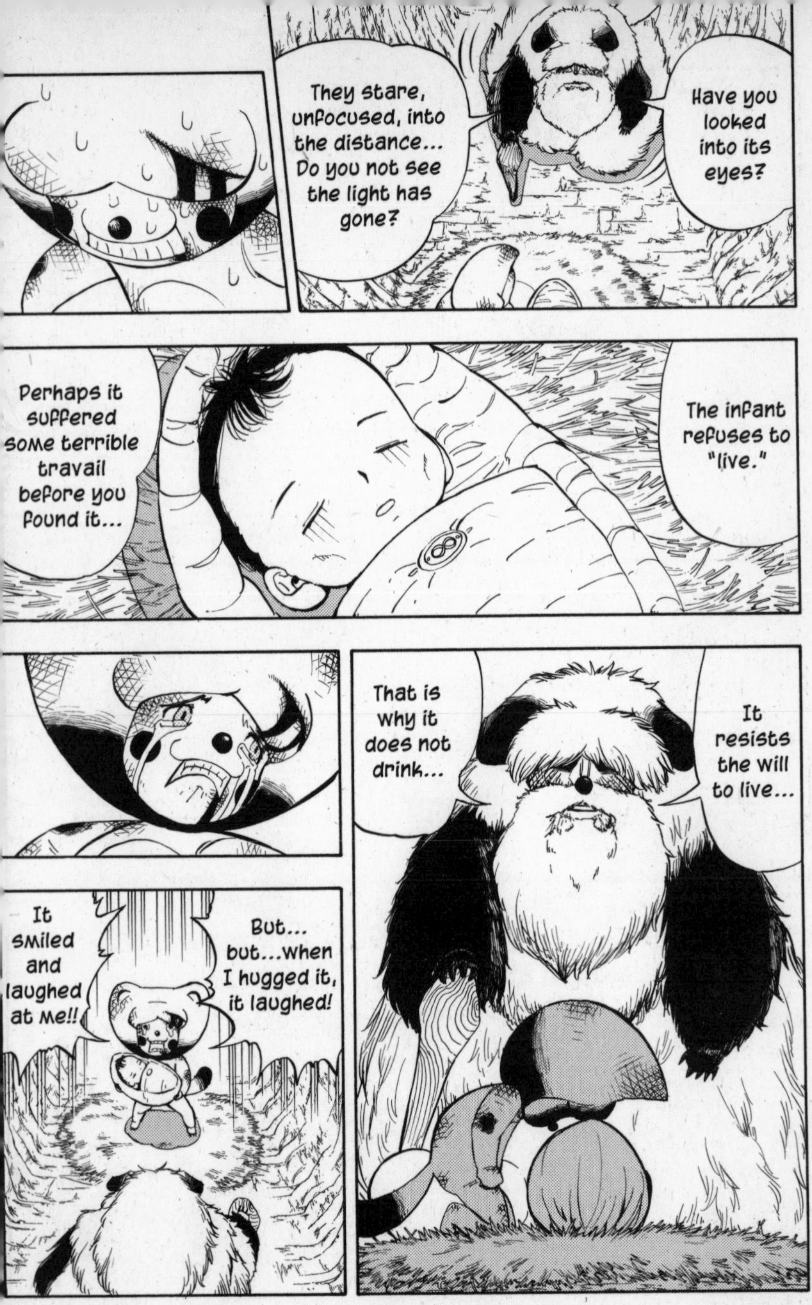
Have you looked into its eyes?
They stare, unfocused, into the distance... Do you not see the light has gone?
The infant refuses to "live."
Perhaps it suffered some terrible travail before you found it...
It resists the will to live...
That is why it does not drink...
But... but...when I hugged it, it laughed!
It smiled and laughed at me!!

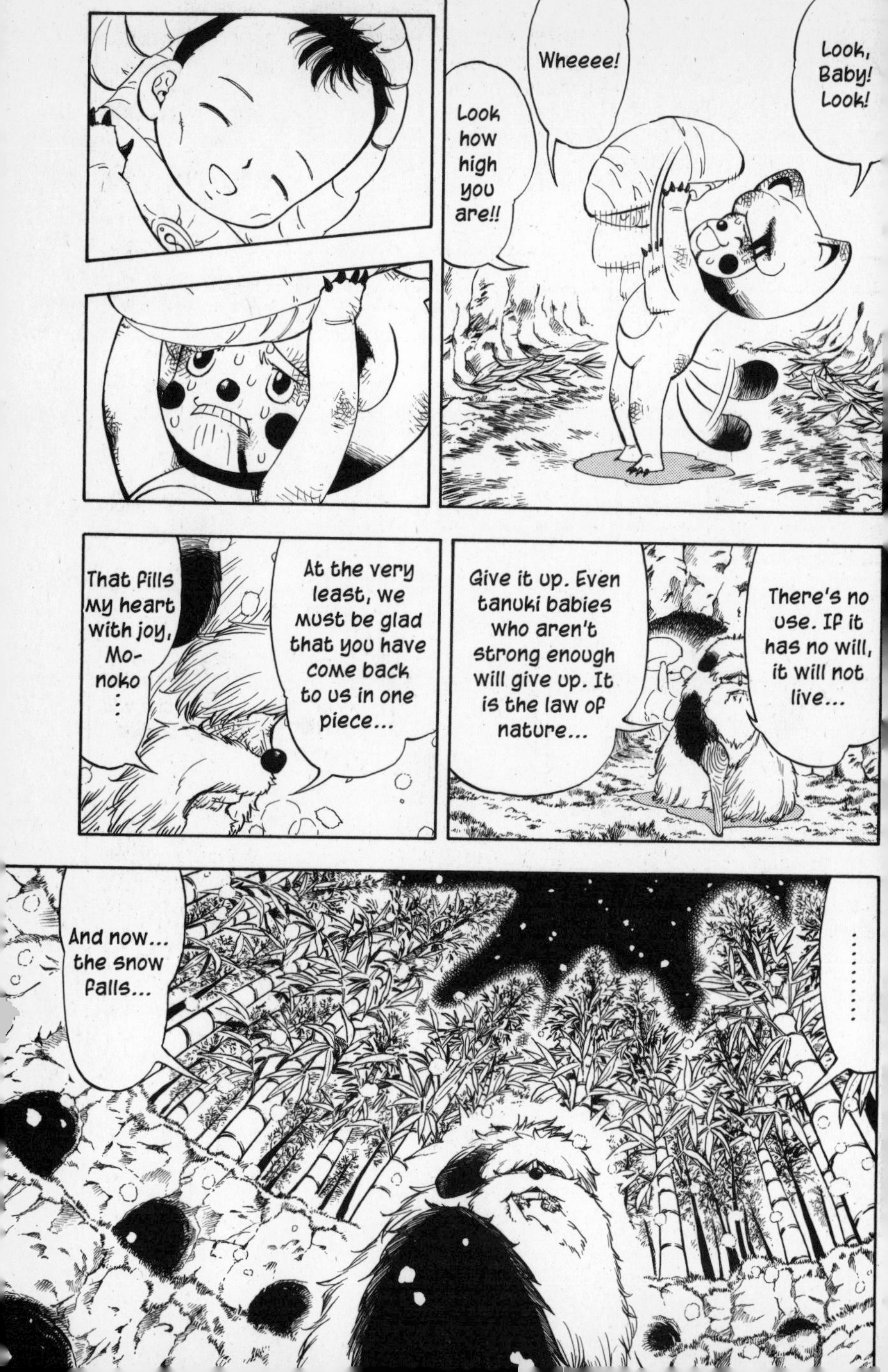
Look, Baby! Look!
Wheeee!
Look how high you are!!
There's no use. If it has no will, it will not live...
Give it up. Even tanuki babies who aren't strong enough will give up. It is the law of nature...
At the very least, we must be glad that you have come back to us in one piece...
That fills my heart with joy, Mo-noko...
......
And now... the snow falls...

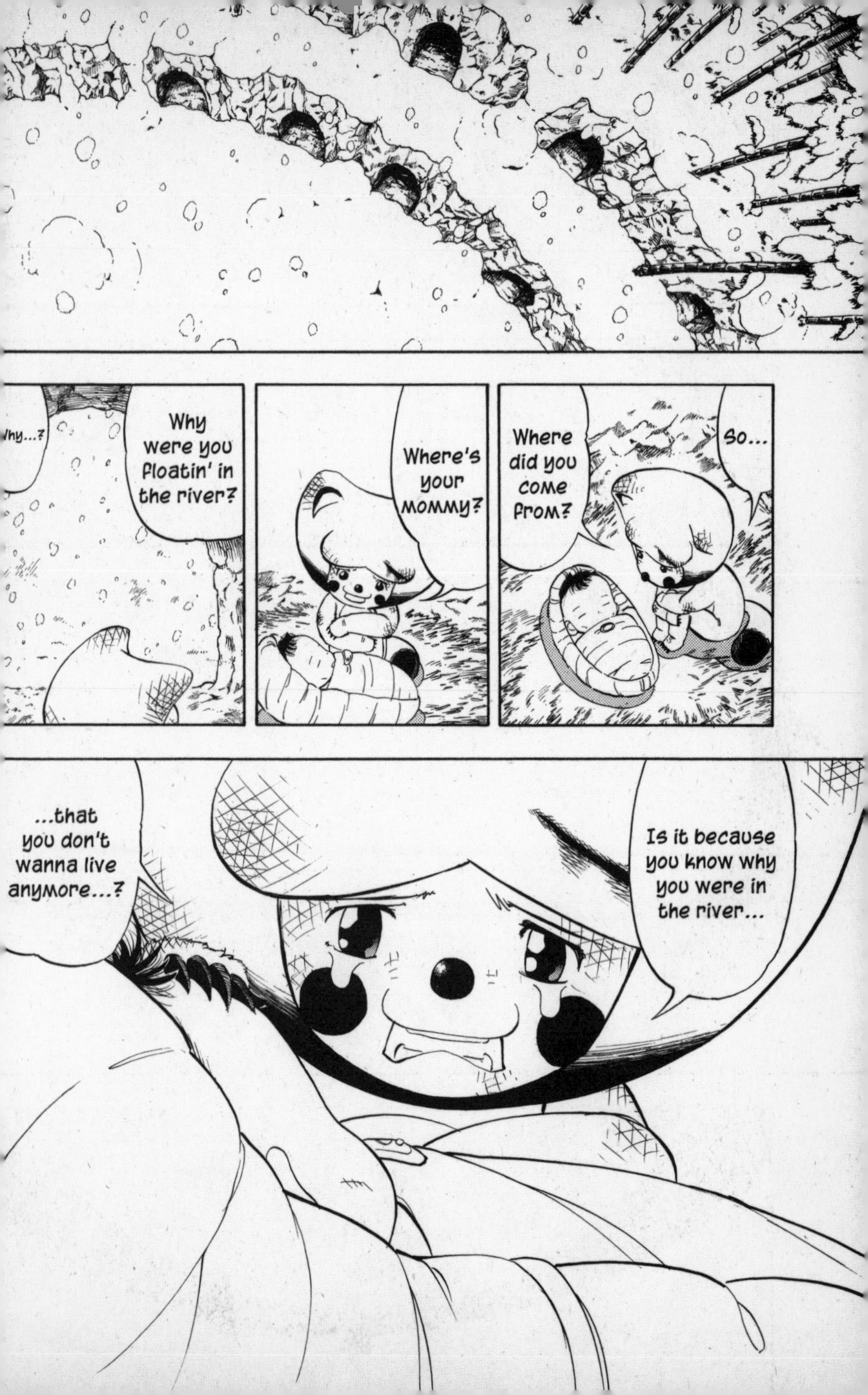
So...
Where did you come from?
Where's your mommy?
Why were you floatin' in the river?
hy...?
Is it because you know why you were in the river...
...that you don't wanna live anymore...?

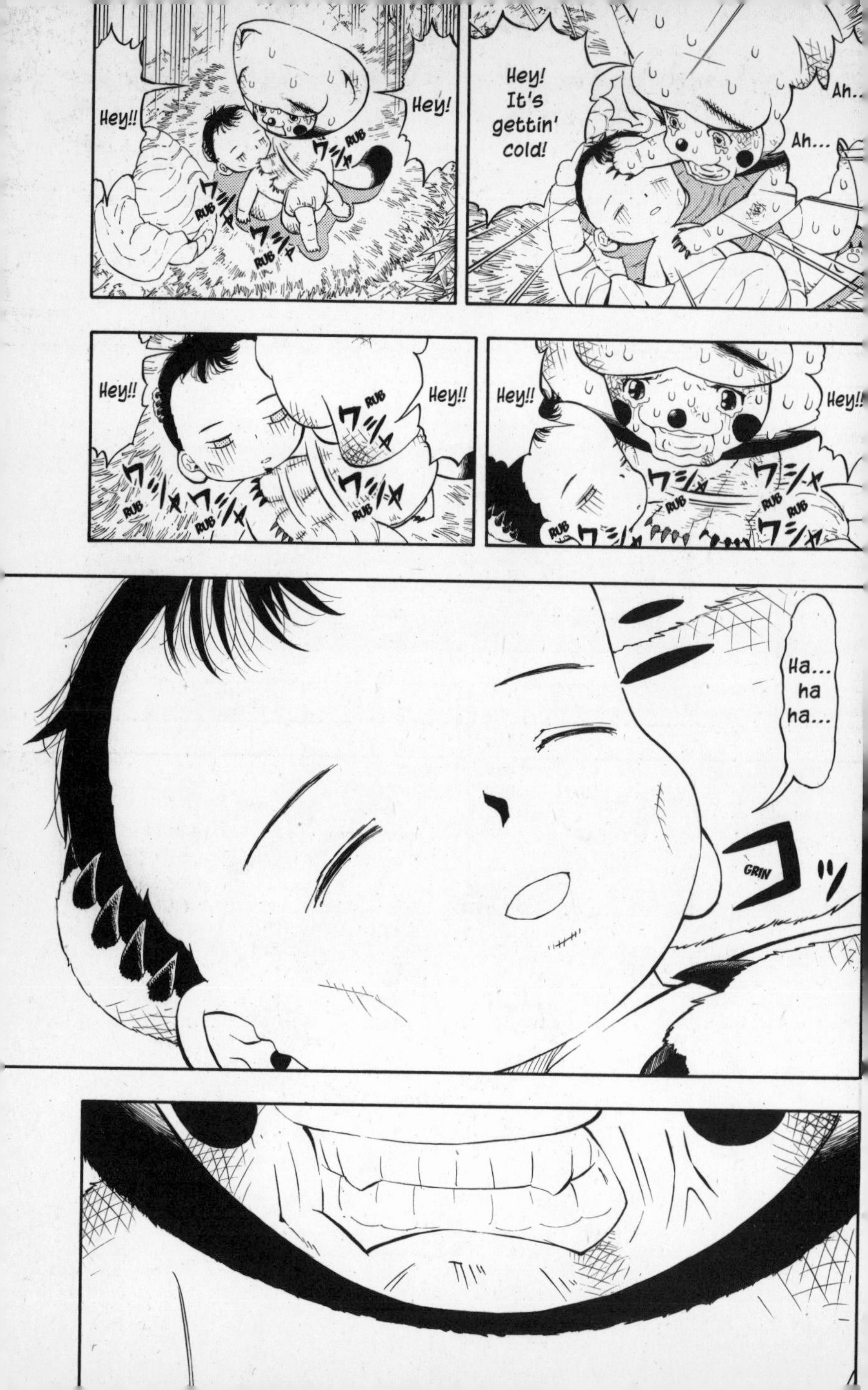

Ah..
Ah...
Hey! It's gettin' cold!
Hey!
RUB
RUB
RUB
Hey!!
Hey!!
Hey!!
RUB
RUB
RUB
RUB
Hey!!
RUB
RUB
RUB
Hey!!
Ha... ha ha...
GRIN

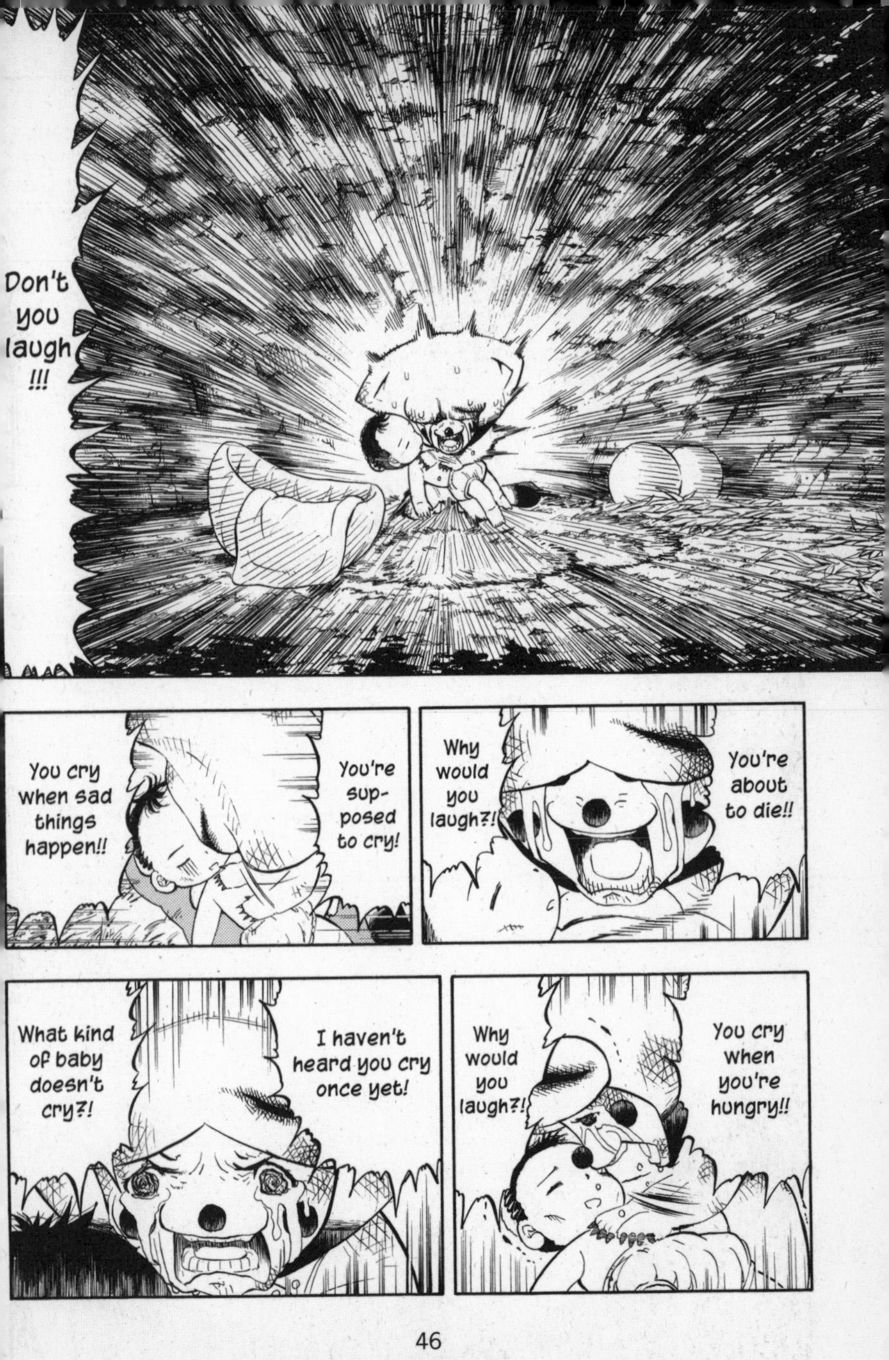
Don't you laugh!!!
You're about to die!!
Why would you laugh?!
You're sup-posed to cry!
You cry when sad things happen!!
You cry when you're hungry!!
Why would you laugh?!
I haven't heard you cry once yet!
What kind of baby doesn't cry?!

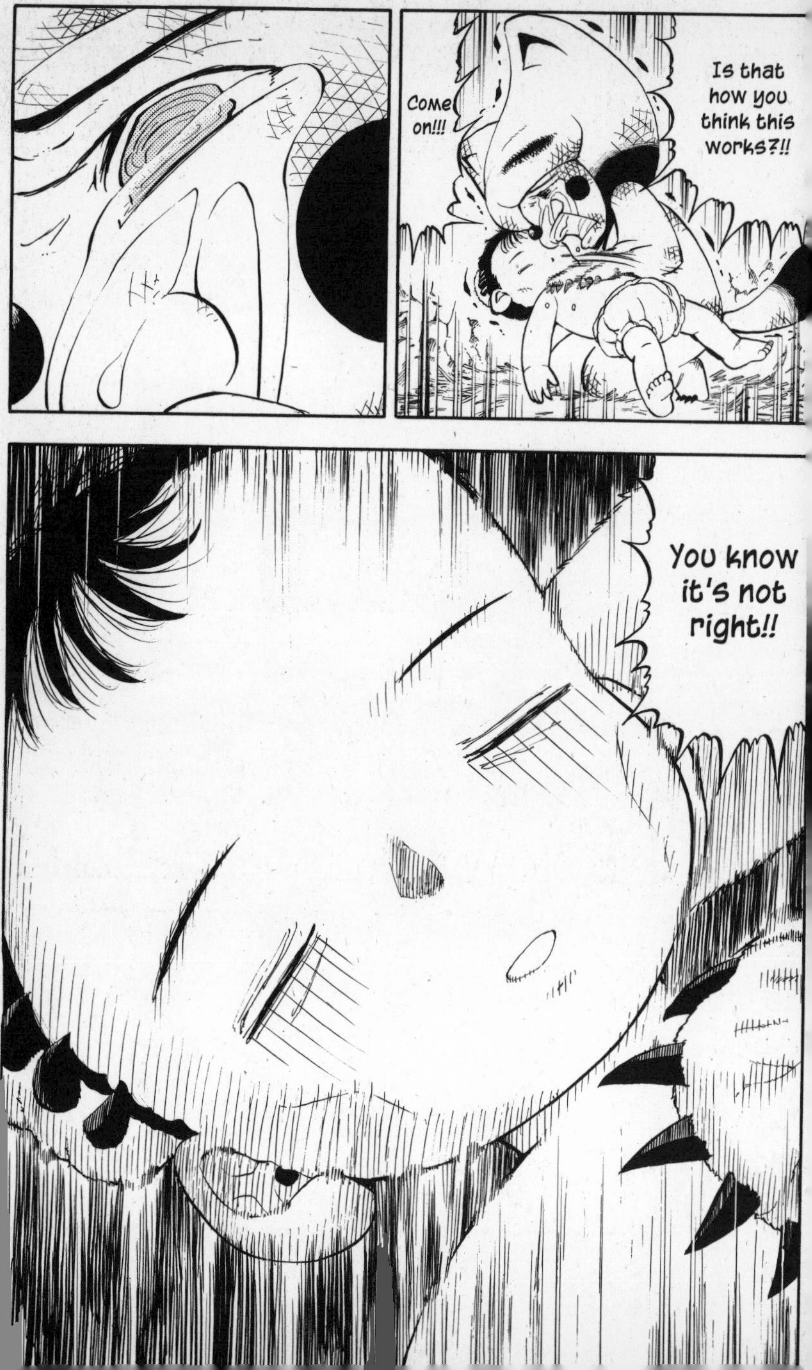
Is that how you think this works?!!
Come on!!!
You know it's not right!!

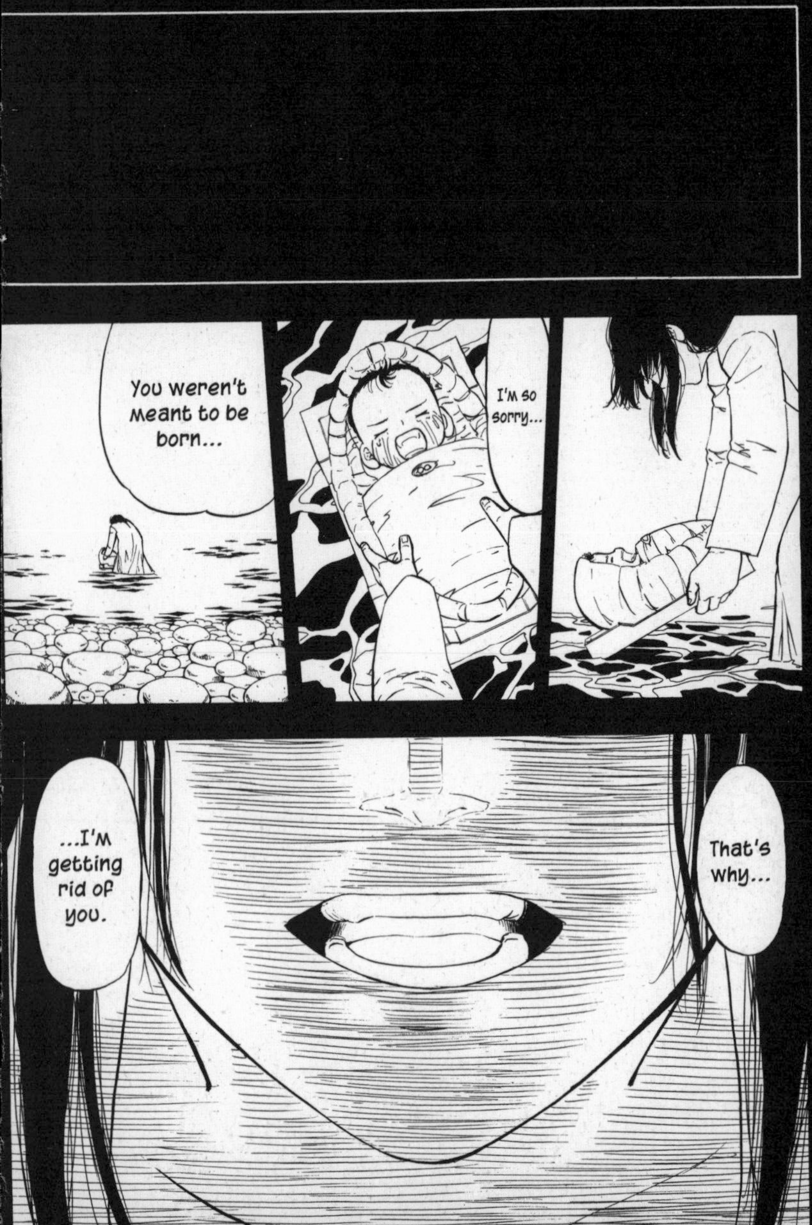
I'm so sorry...
You weren't meant to be born...
That's why...
...I'm getting rid of you.

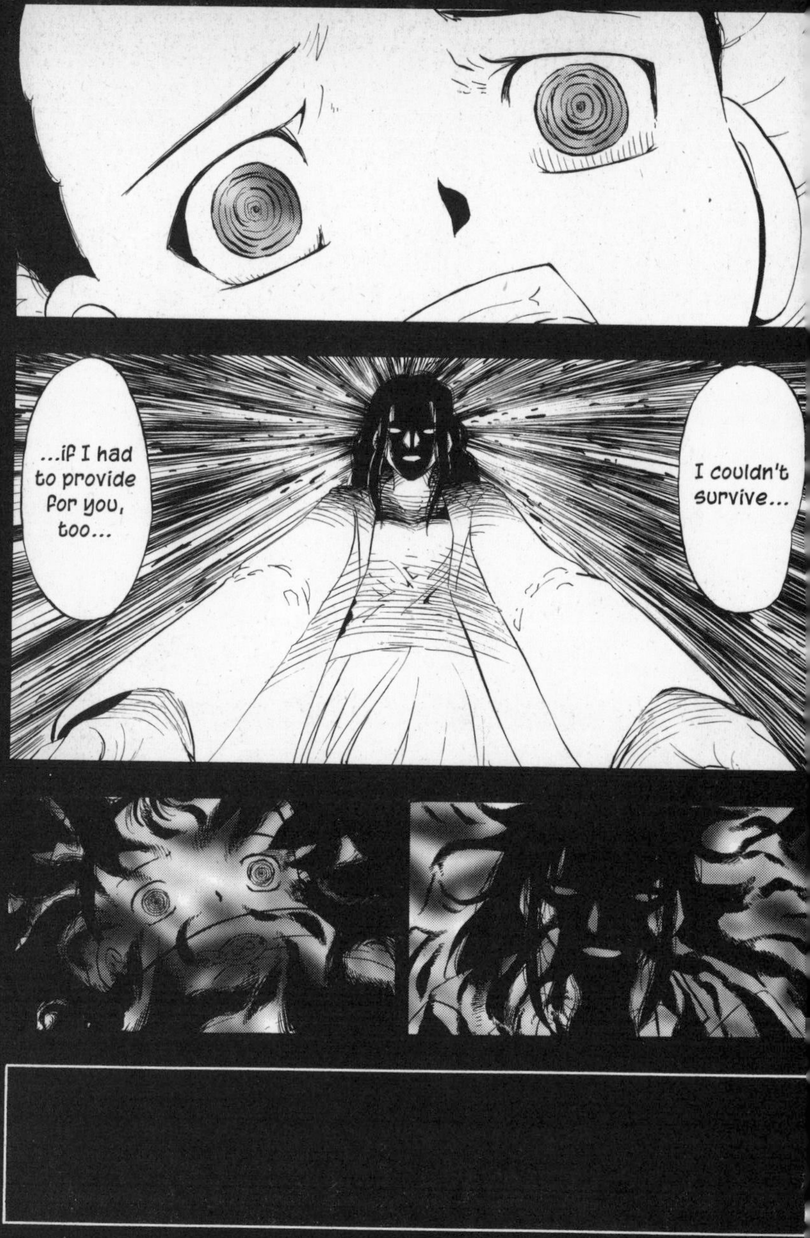
I couldn't survive...
...if I had to provide for you, too...

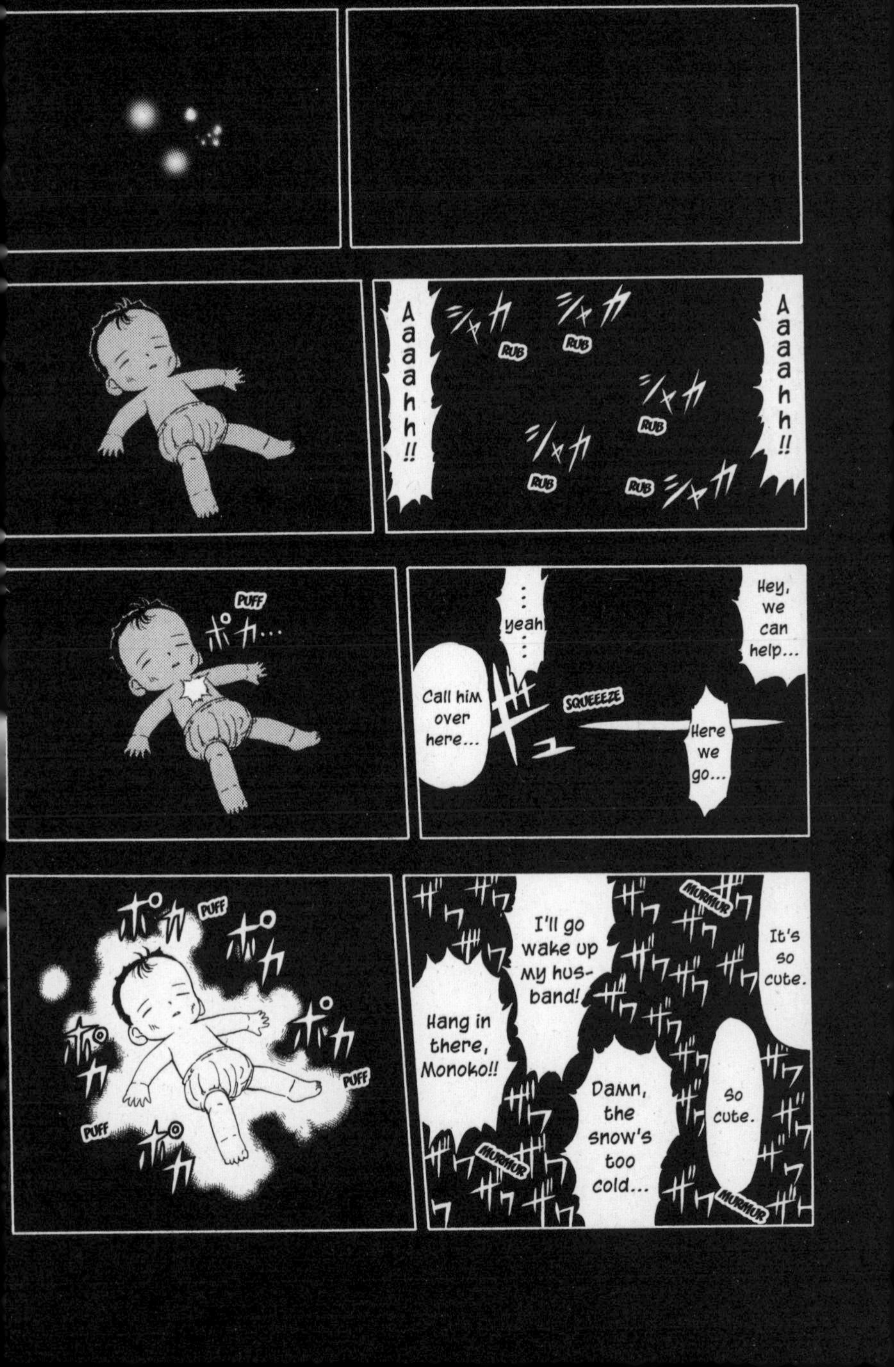

Aaaahh!!
RUB
RUB
RUB
RUB
RUB
Aaaahh!!
Hey, we can help...
...yeah...
Here we go...
SQUEEEZE
Call him over here...
PUFF
It's so cute.
MURMUR
I'll go wake up my hus-band!
So cute.
Damn, the snow's too cold...
Hang in there, Monoko!!
MURMUR
MURMUR
PUFF
PUFF
PUFF

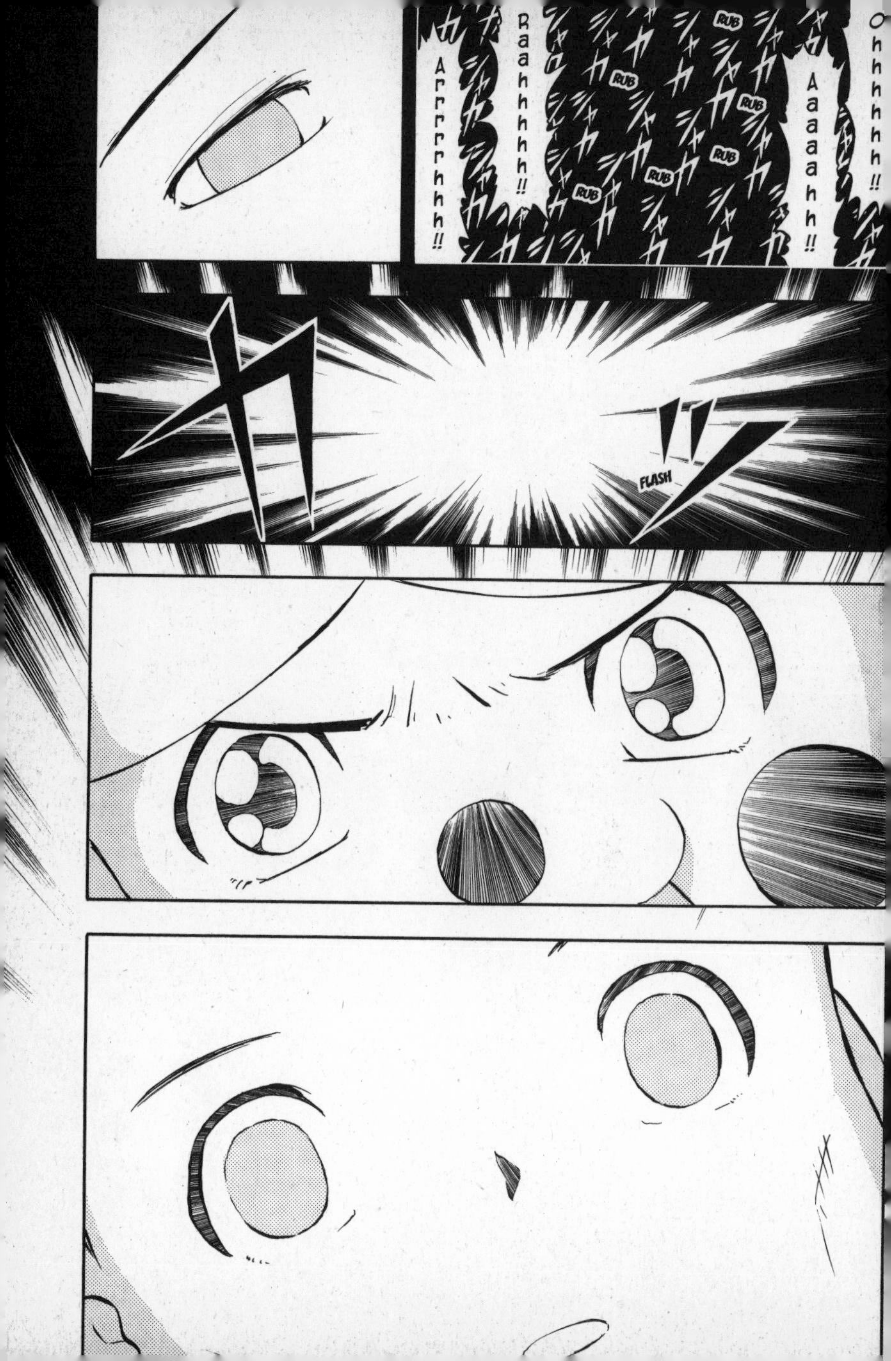
Ohhhhhh!!
Aaaaahh!!
RUB
RUB
RUB
RUB
RUB
RUB
Raahhhhh!!
Arrrrhhh!!
FLASH

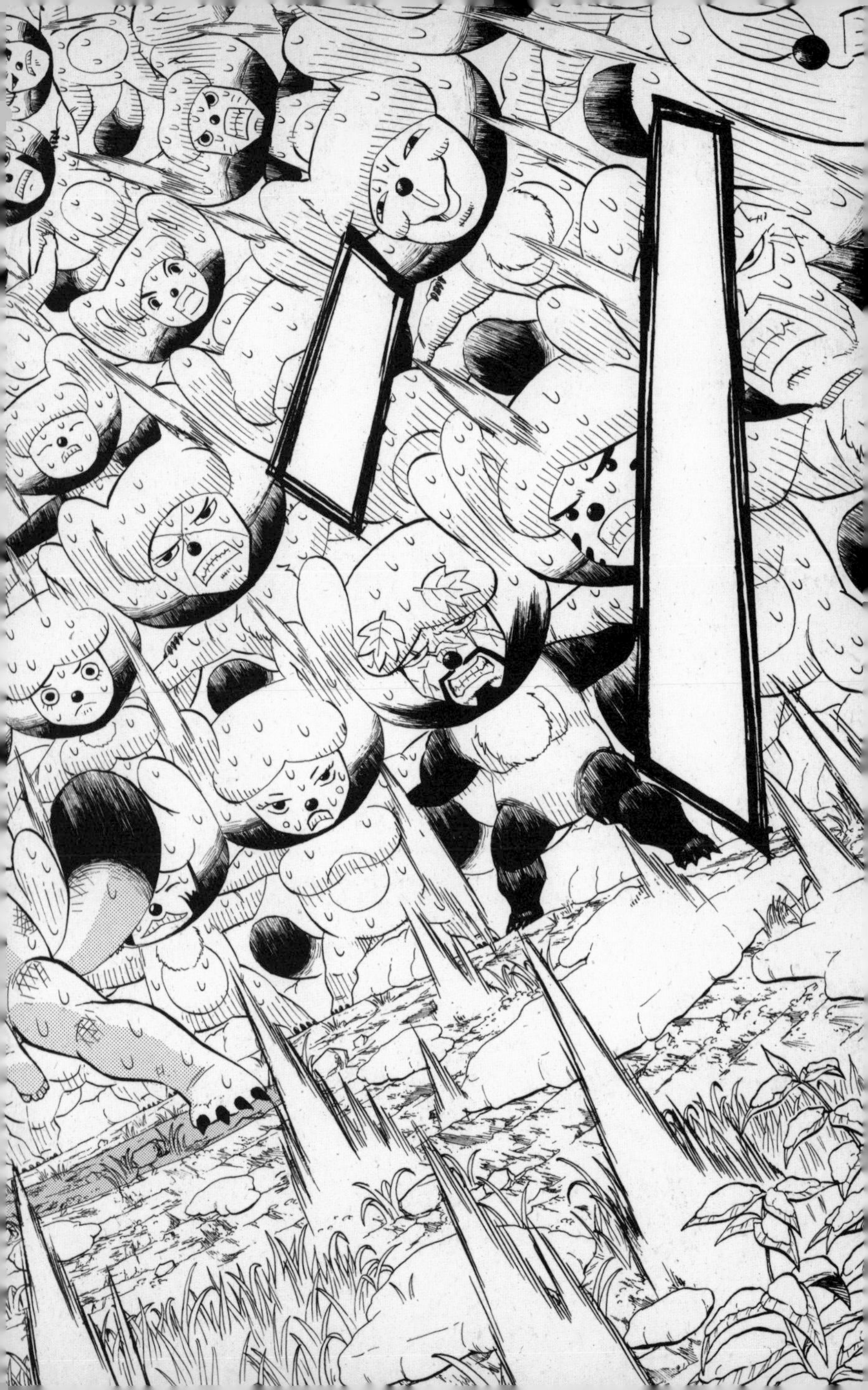

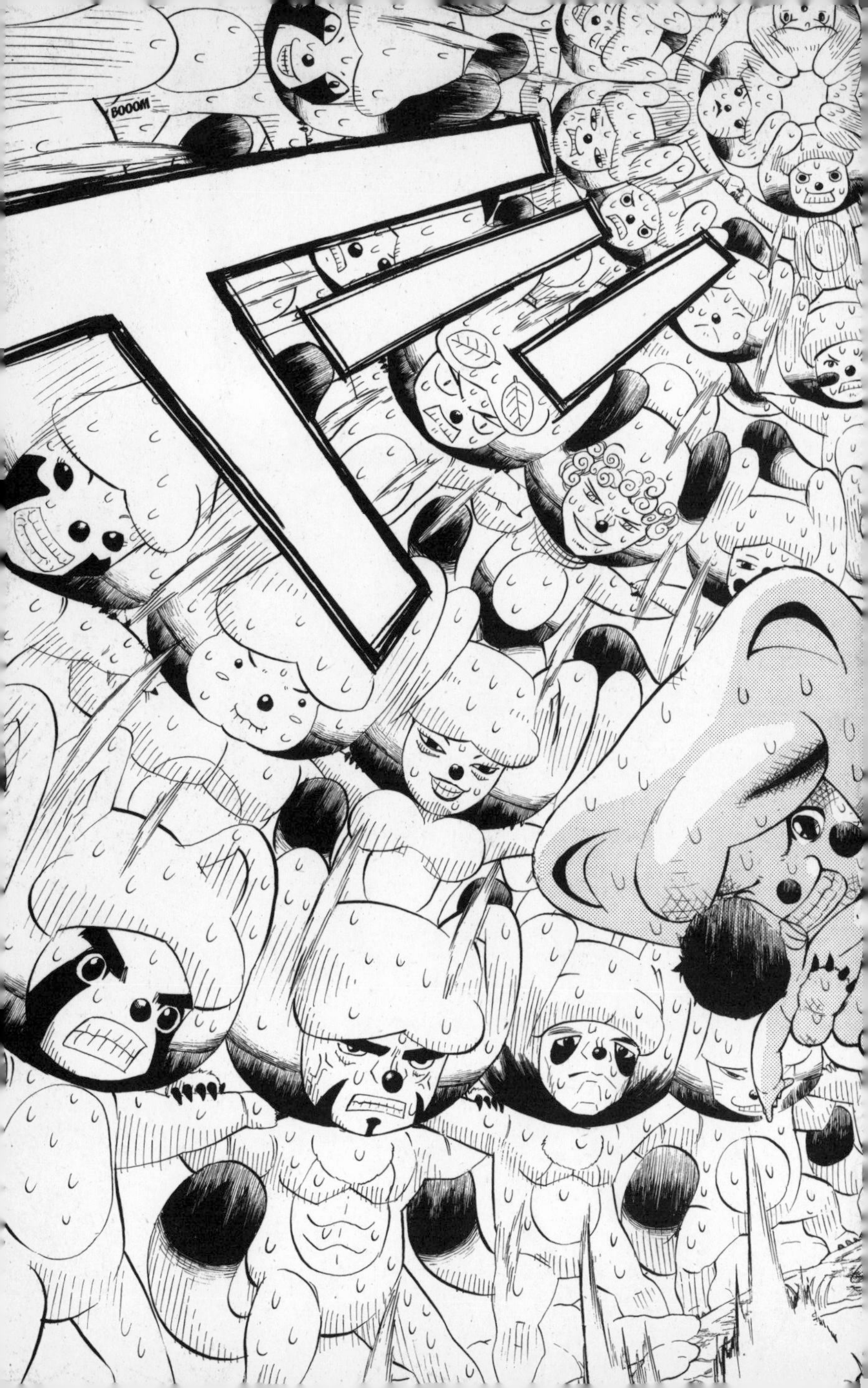
BOOOM

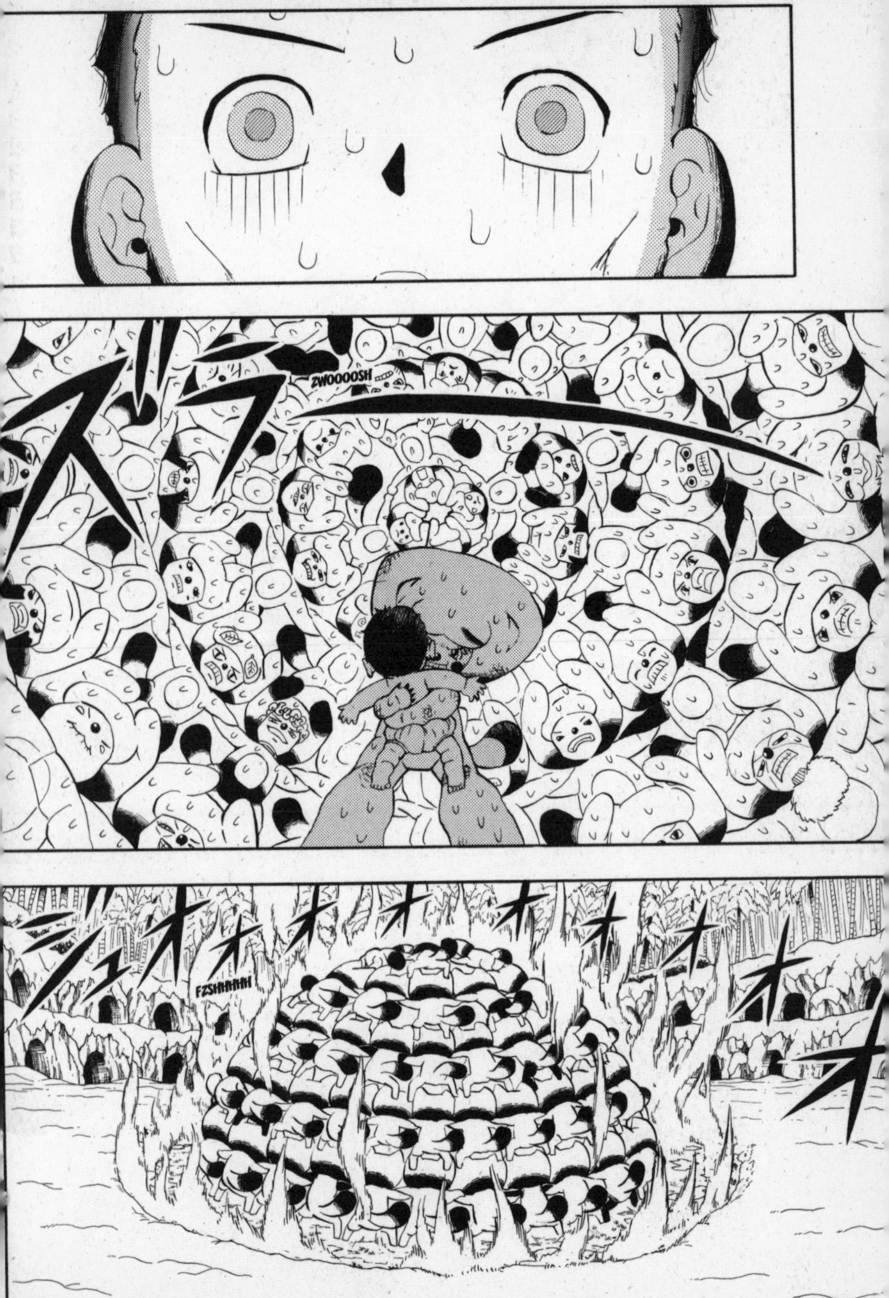
ZWOOOOSH
FZSHHHHH

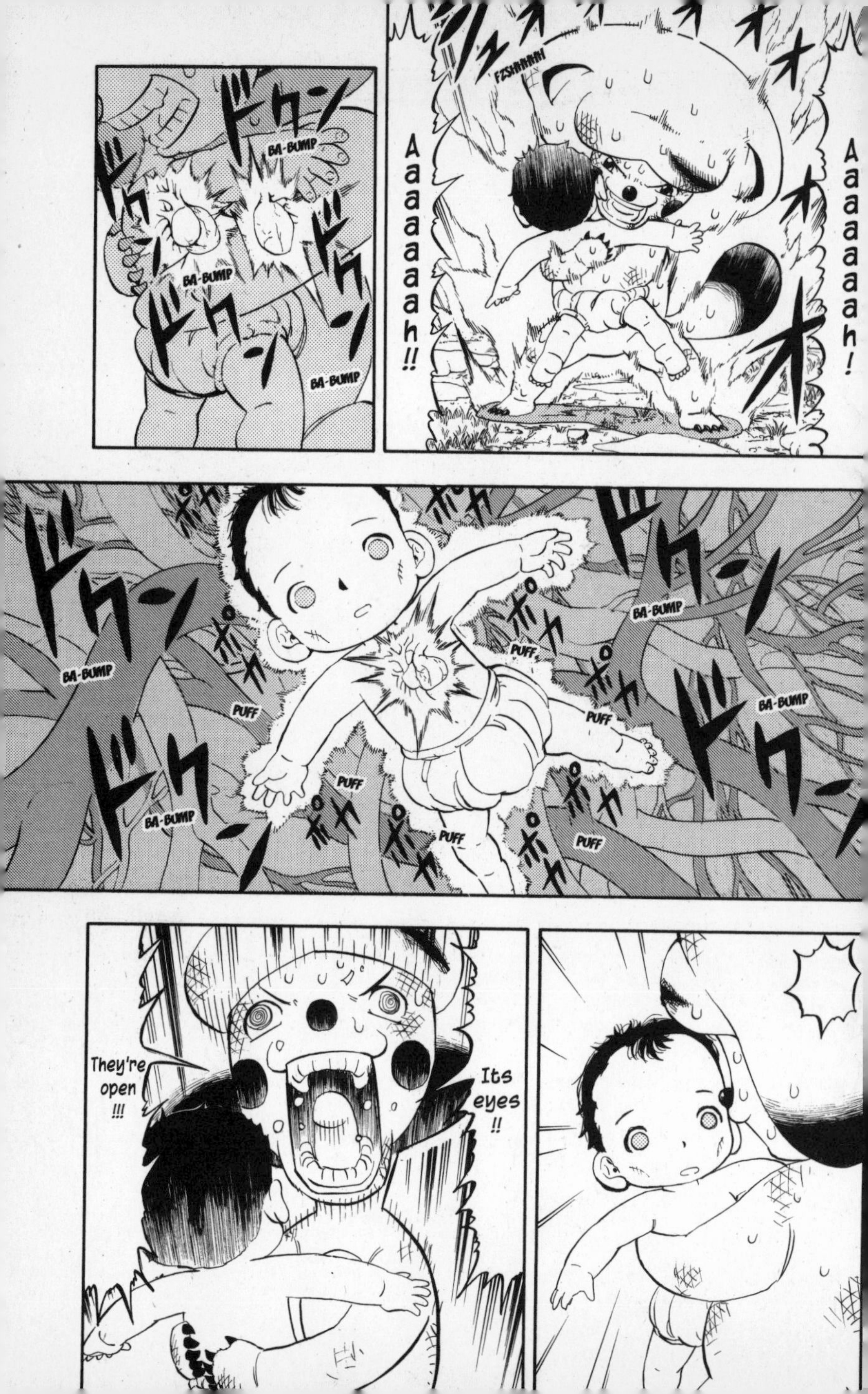

FZSHHHHH
Aaaaaaaaah!
Aaaaaaaaah!!
BA-BUMP
BA-BUMP
BA-BUMP
BA-BUMP
BA-BUMP
PUFF
PUFF
PUFF
BA-BUMP
PUFF
PUFF
PUFF
BA-BUMP
Its eyes !!
They're open !!!

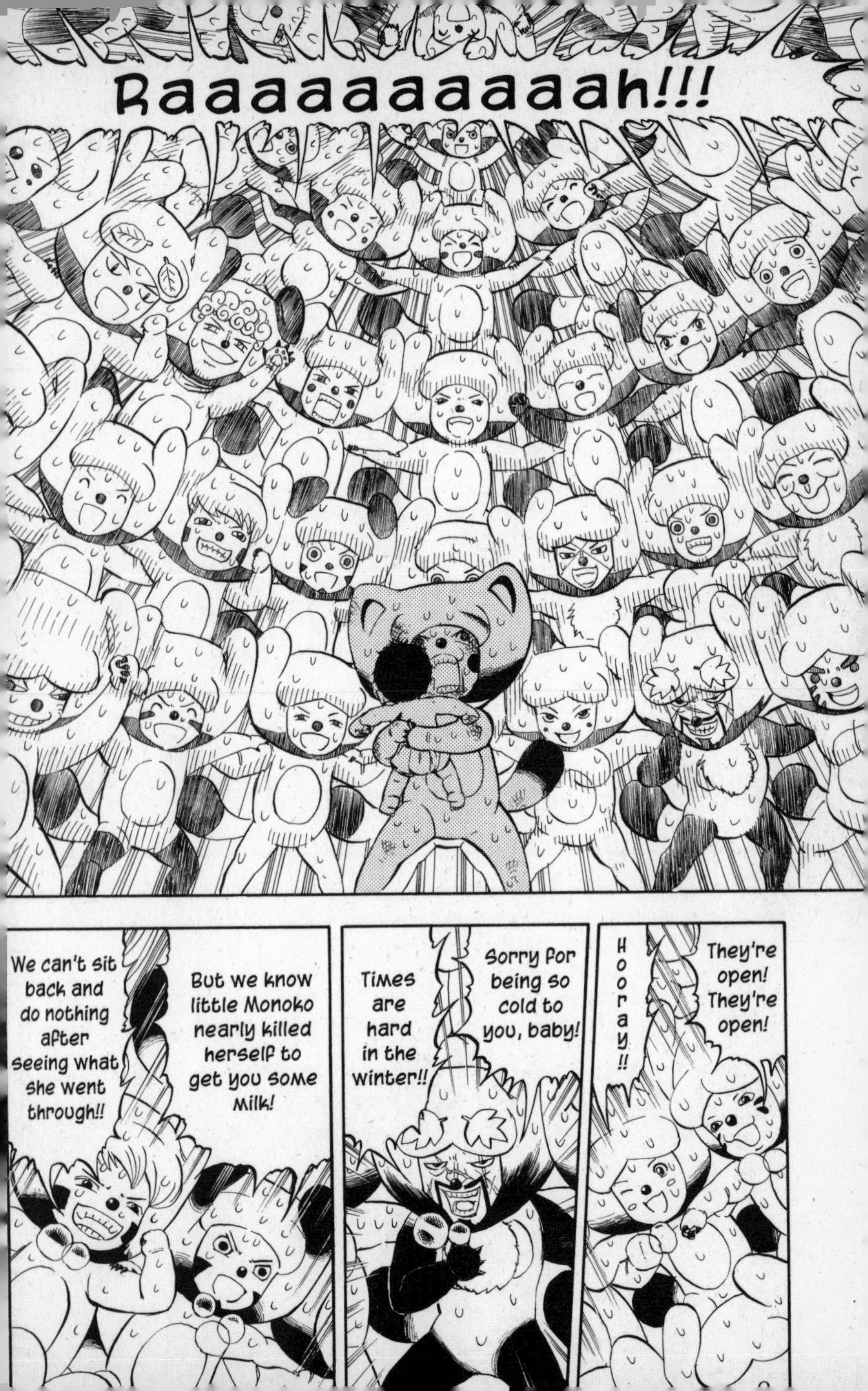
Raaaaaaaaaaah!!!
They're open! They're open!
Hooray!!
Sorry for being so cold to you, baby!
Times are hard in the winter!!
But we know little Monoko nearly killed herself to get you some milk!
We can't sit back and do nothing after seeing what she went through!!

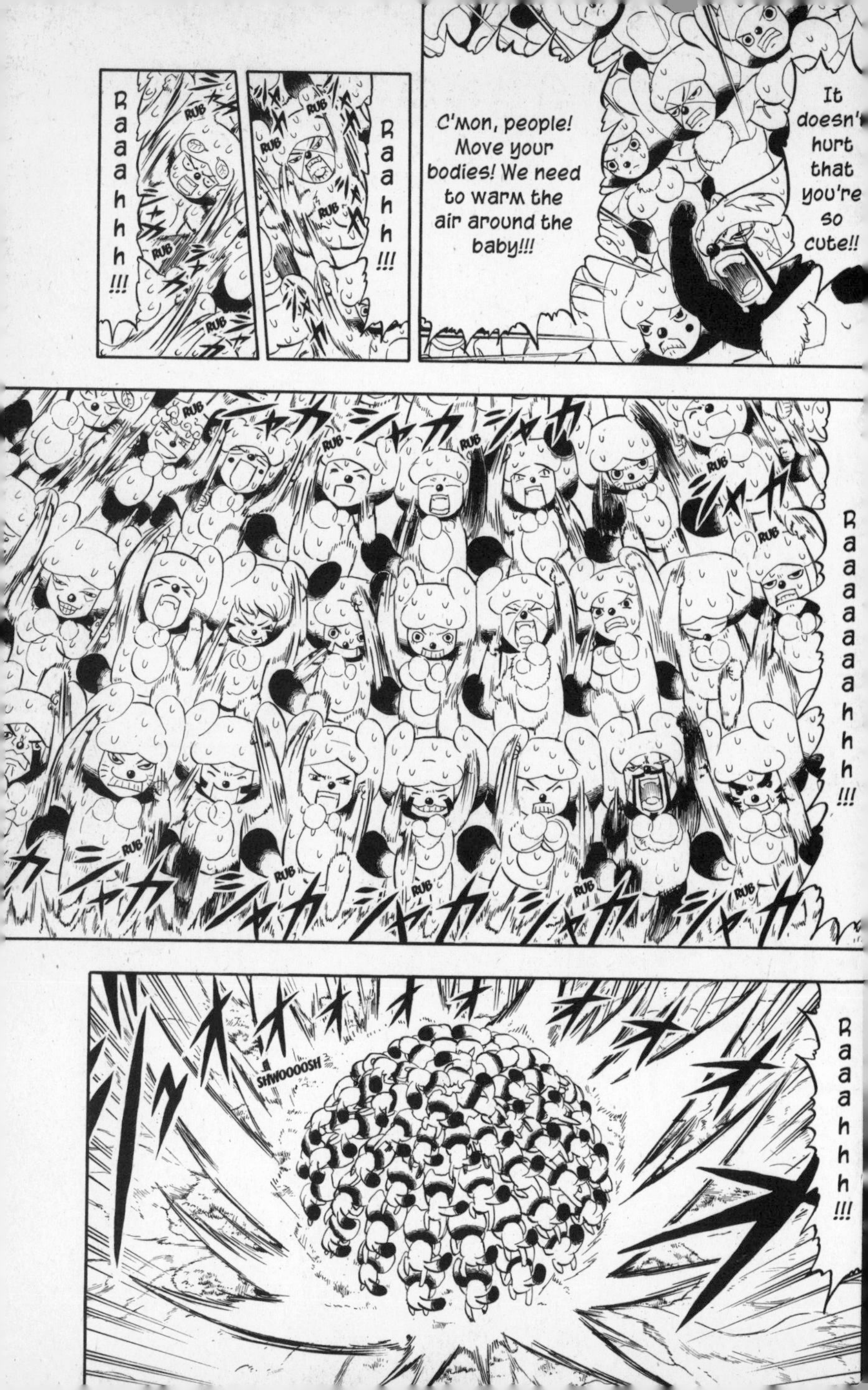
It doesn't hurt that you're so cute!!
C'mon, people! Move your bodies! We need to warm the air around the baby!!!
Raahh!!!
RUB
RUB
RUB
Raaahhhh!!!
RUB
RUB
RUB
Raaaaaaahhh!!!
RUB
RUB
RUB
RUB
RUB
RUB
RUB
RUB
RUB
Raaahhh!!!
SHWOOOOSH

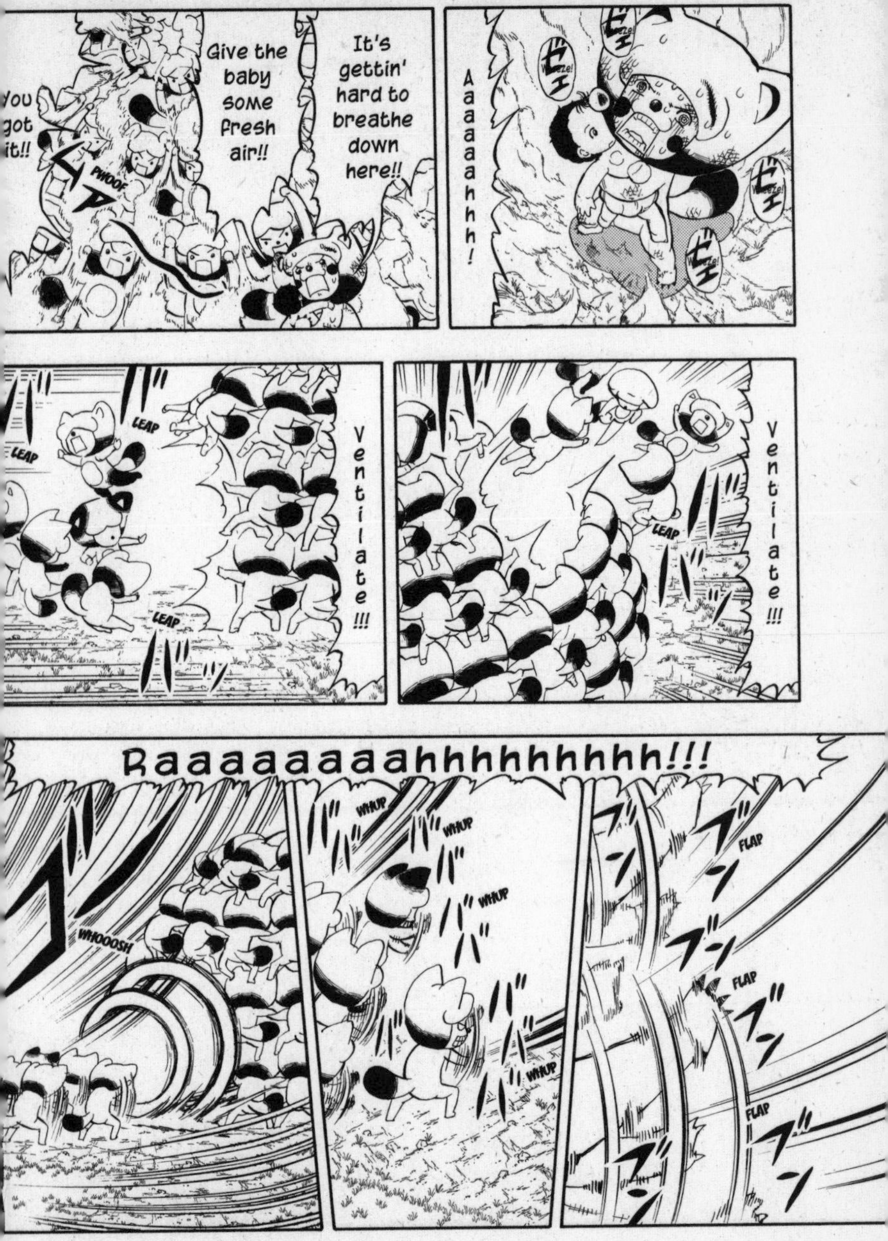
Aaaaaahhh!
It's gettin' hard to breathe down here!!
Give the baby some fresh air!!
PHOOF
You got it!!
Ventilate!!!
LEAP
Ventilate!!!
LEAP
LEAP
LEAP
Raaaaaaaahhhhhhhh!!!
FLAP
FLAP
FLAP
WHUP
WHUP
WHUP
WHUP
WHOOOSH

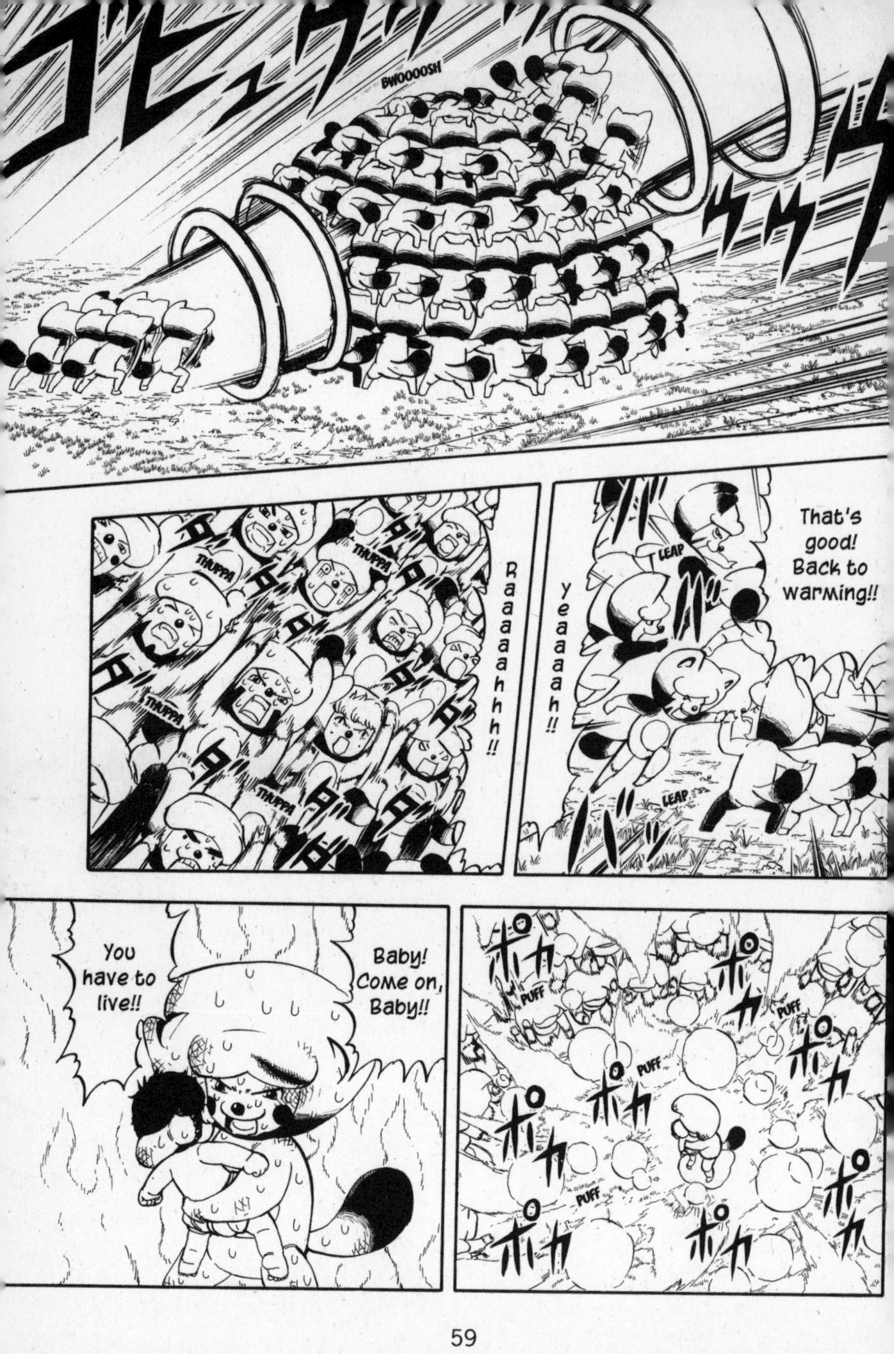
BWOOOOSH
That's good! Back to warming!!
LEAP
yeaaaaah!!
LEAP
Raaaaaahhh!!
THUPPA
THUPPA
THUPPA
THUPPA
PUFF
PUFF
PUFF
PUFF
ポカ
Baby! Come on, Baby!!
You have to live!!

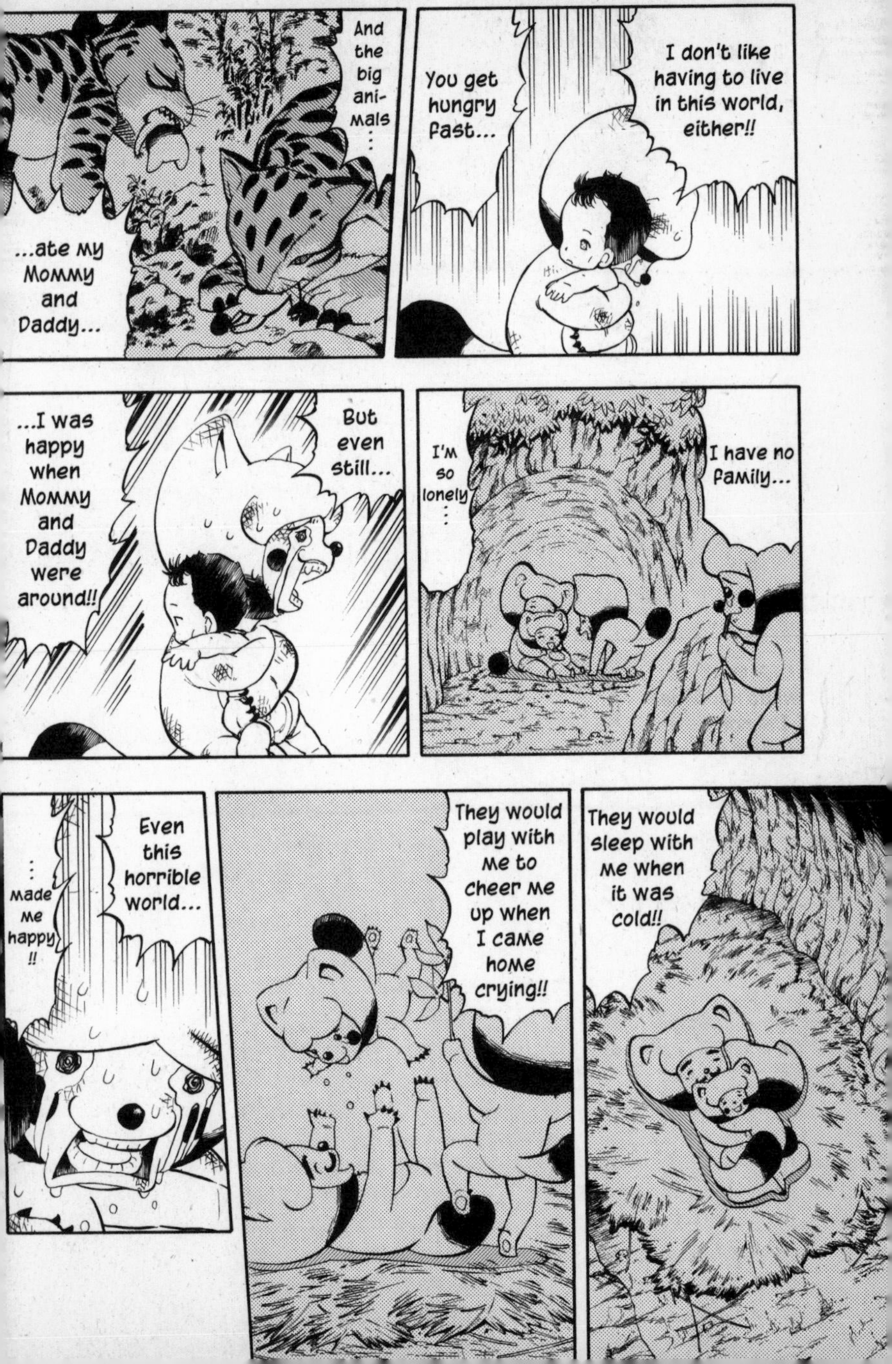
I don't like having to live in this world, either!!
You get hungry fast...
And the big ani-mals...
...ate my Mommy and Daddy...
I have no family...
I'm so lonely...
But even still...
...I was happy when Mommy and Daddy were around!!
They would sleep with me when it was cold!!
They would play with me to cheer me up when I came home crying!!
Even this horrible world...
...made me happy!!

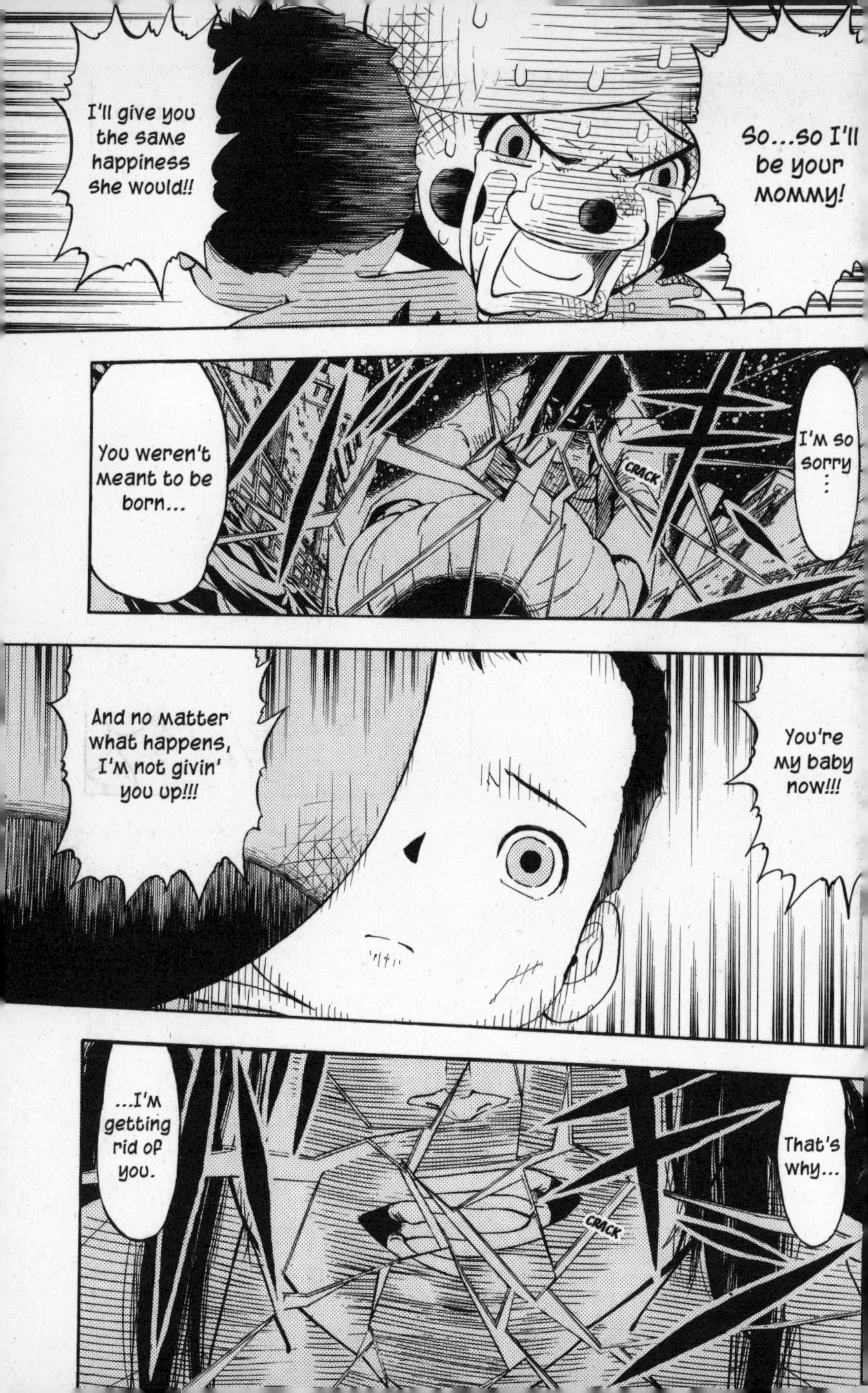
So...so I'll be your MOMMY!
I'll give you the same happiness she would!!
I'm so sorry...
CRACK
You weren't meant to be born...
You're my baby now!!!
And no matter what happens, I'm not givin' you up!!!
That's why...
CRACK
...I'm getting rid of you.

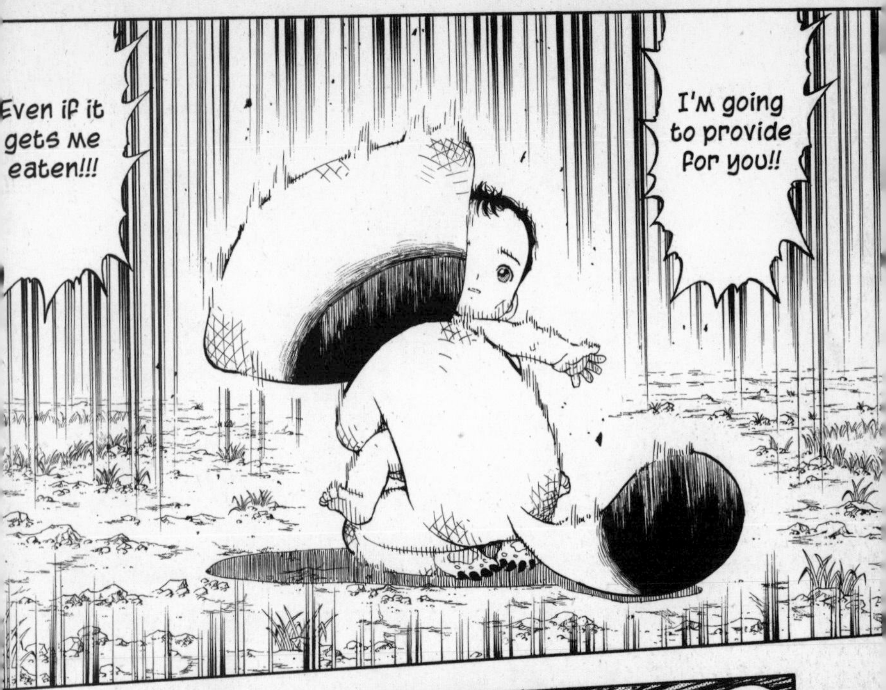
I'm going to provide for you!!
Even if it gets me eaten!!!

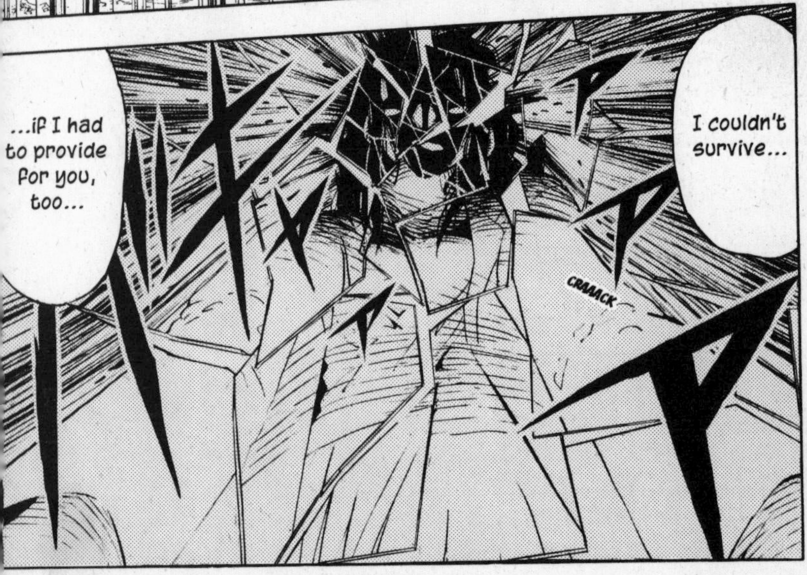
I couldn't survive...
...if I had to provide for you, too...
CRAAACK

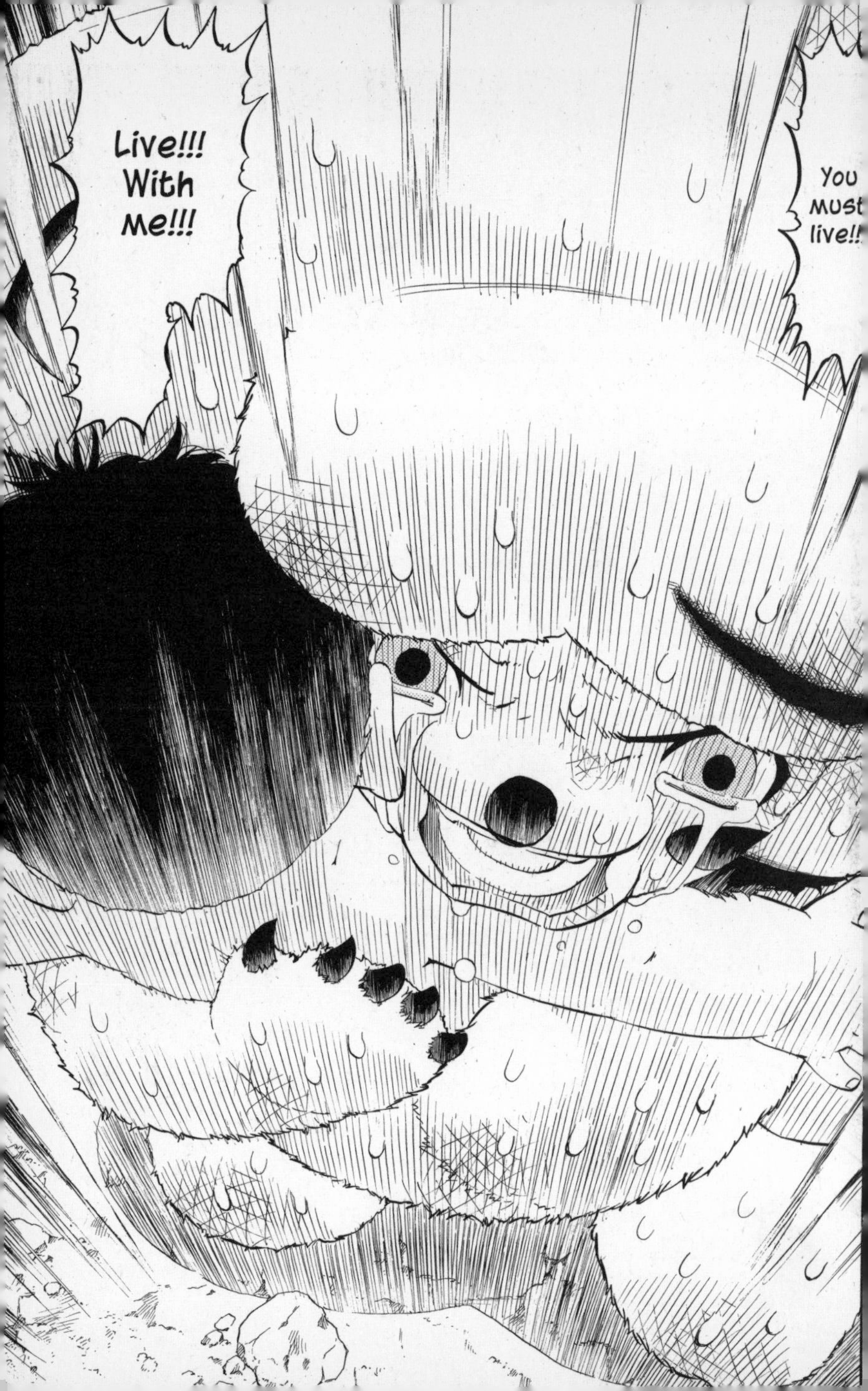

You must live!!
Live!!! With Me!!!

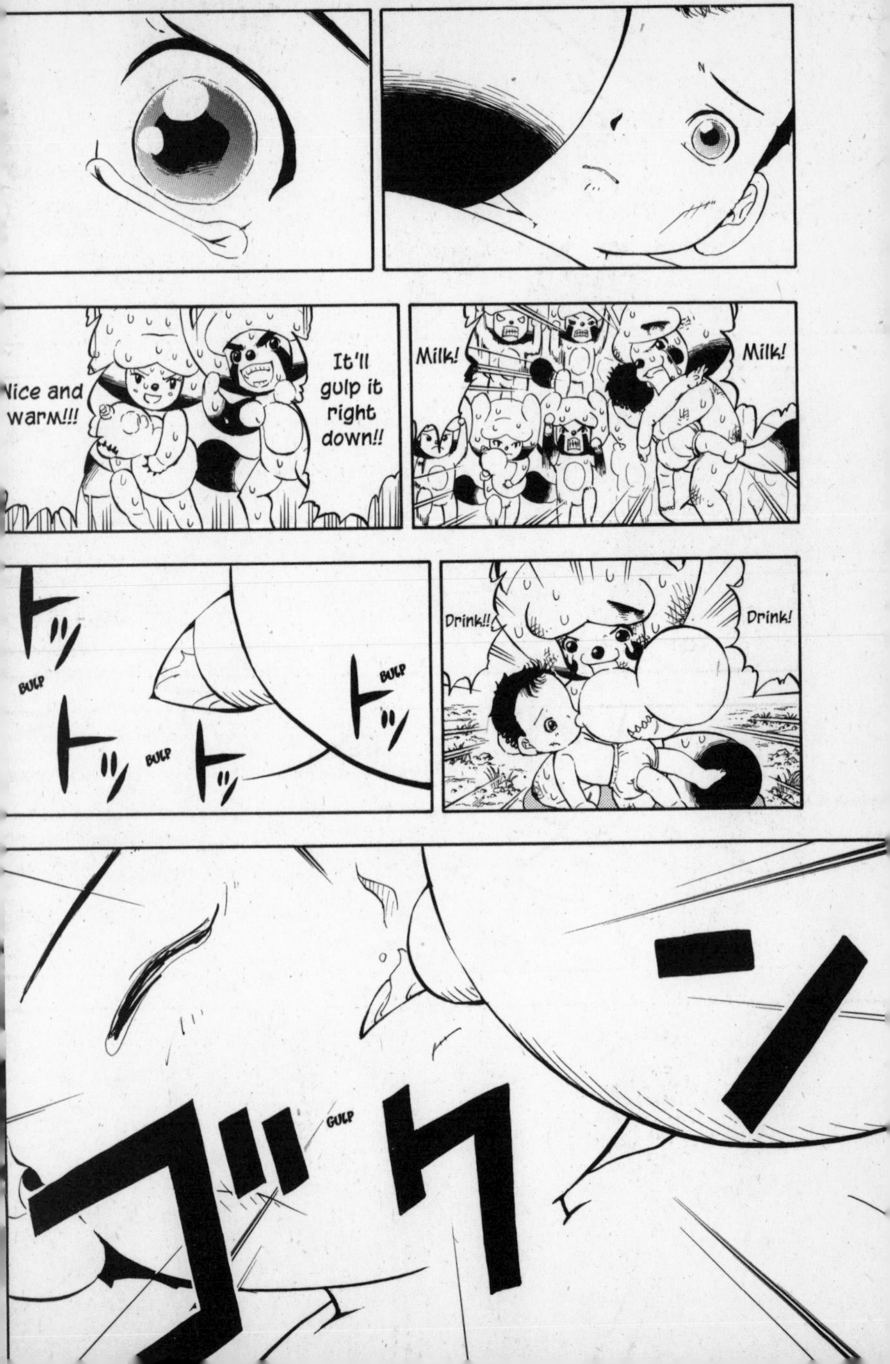
Milk!
Milk!
It'll gulp it right down!!
Nice and warm!!!
Drink!
Drink!!
トッ
BULP
トッ
トッ
BULP
トッ
BULP
ゴクー
GULP

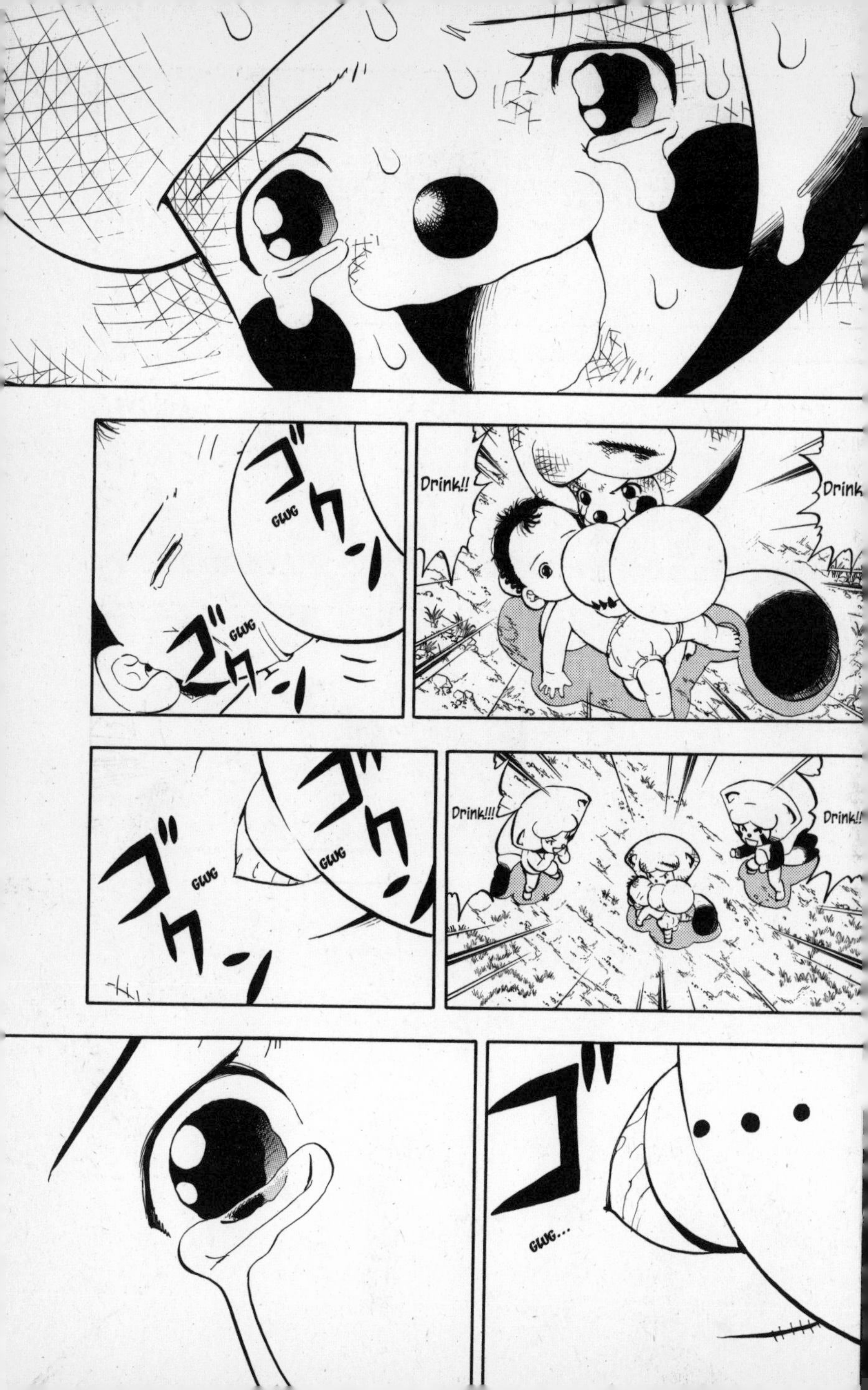
Drink!!
Drink
ゴクッ
GUG
ゴクッ
GUG
Drink!!
Drink!!!
ゴクッ
GUG
ゴクッ
GUG
ゴ
GUG...
...

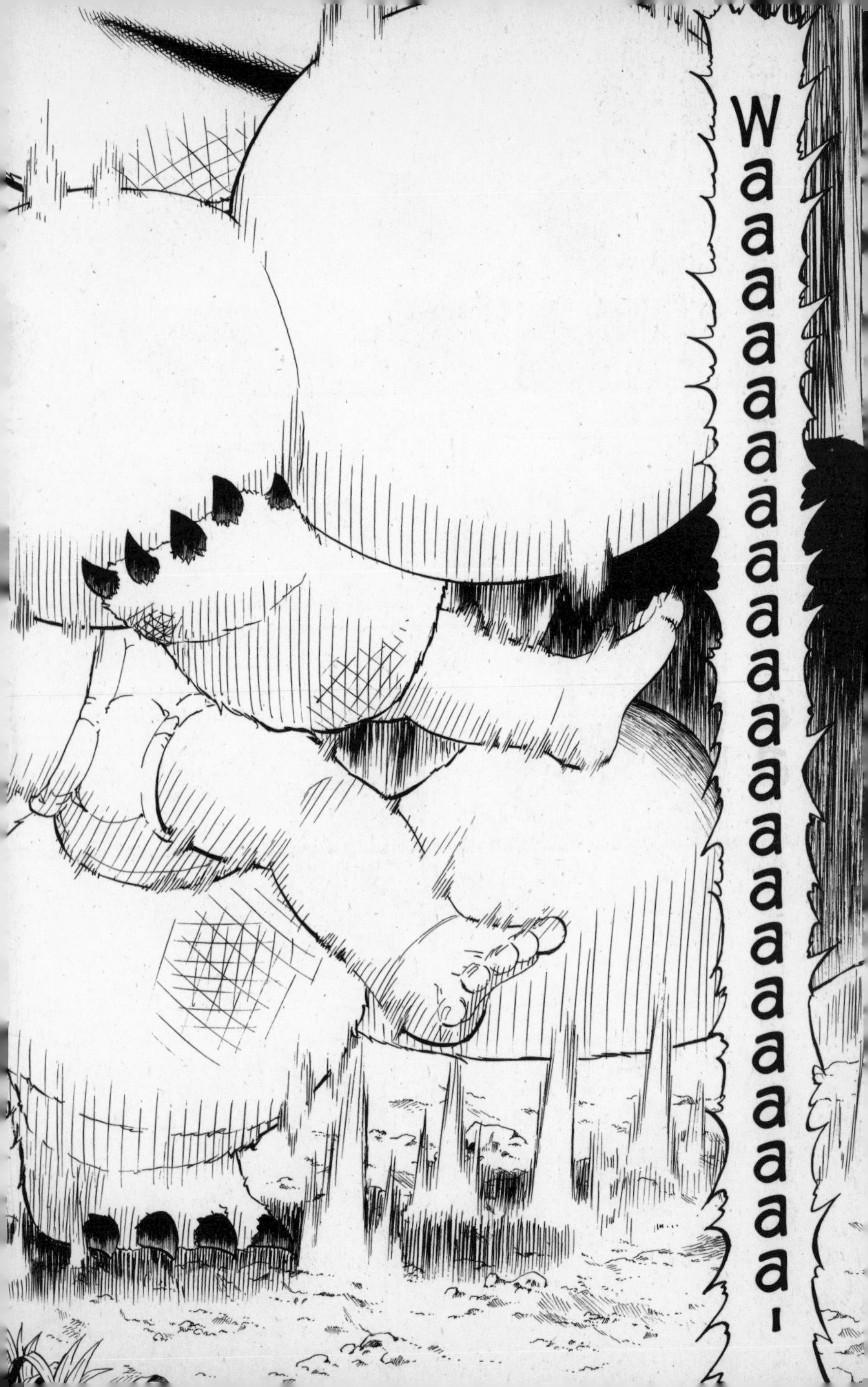
Waaaaaaaaaaaaaaaaaaaaaaa!

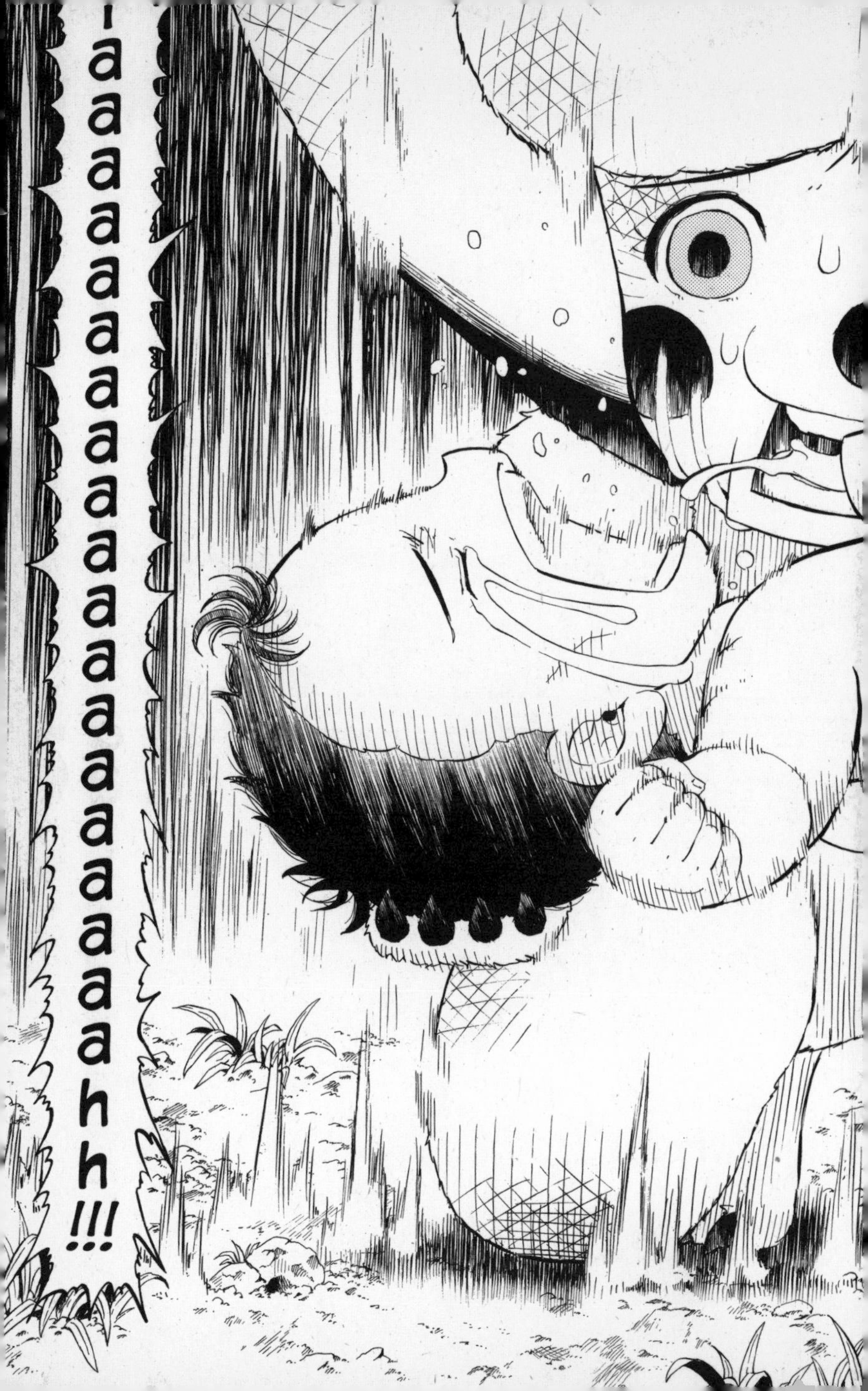
Iaaaaaaaaaaaaaaaaaaaaaaahh!!!

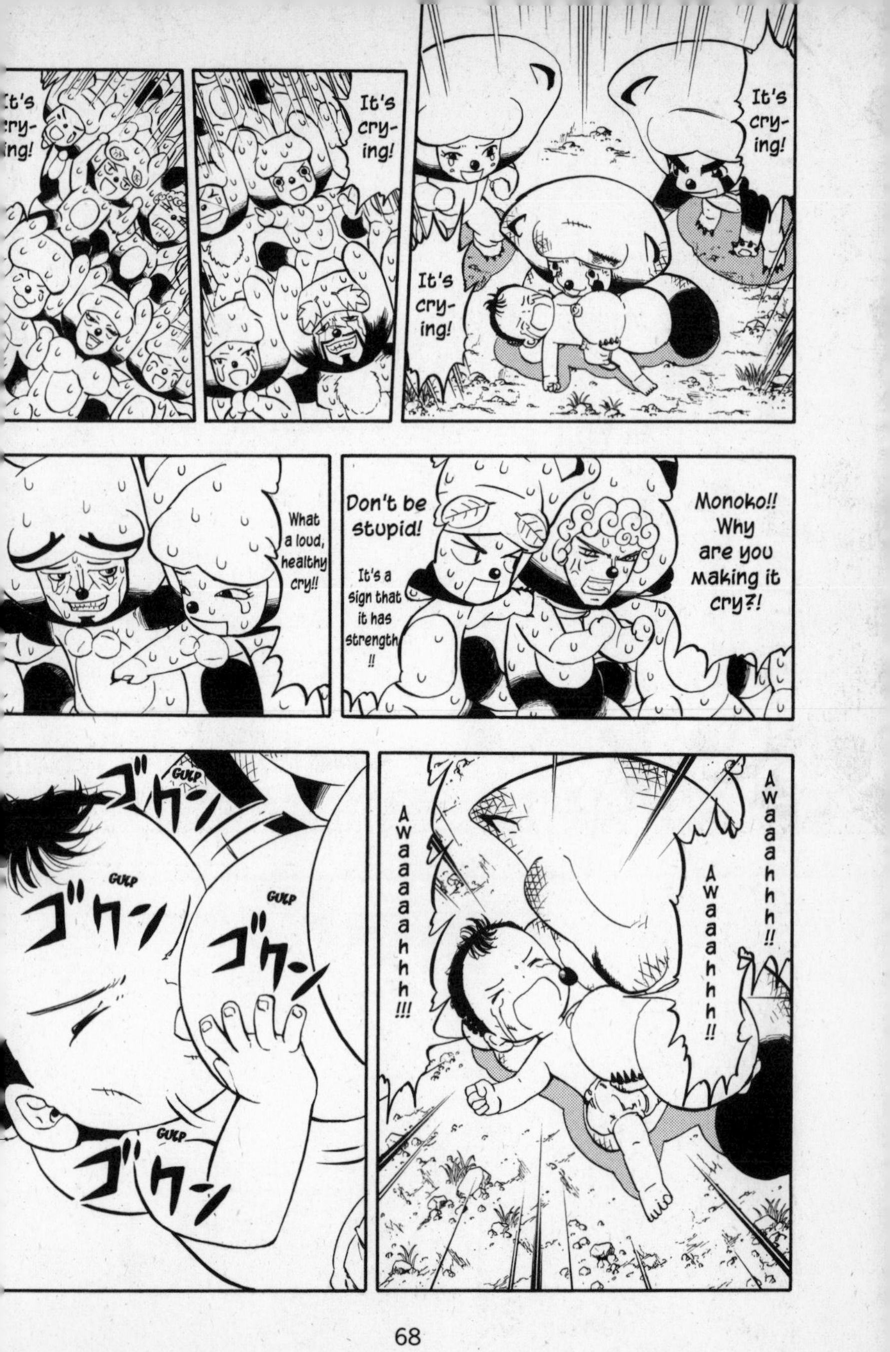

It's cry-ing!
It's cry-ing!
It's cry-ing!
t's ry- ing!
Monoko!! Why are you making it cry?!
Don't be stupid!
It's a sign that it has strength!!
What a loud, healthy cry!!
Awaaaahhhh!!
Awaaahhhh!!
Awaaaaahhhh!!!
ゴクン GULP
ゴクン GULP
ゴクン GULP
ゴクン GULP

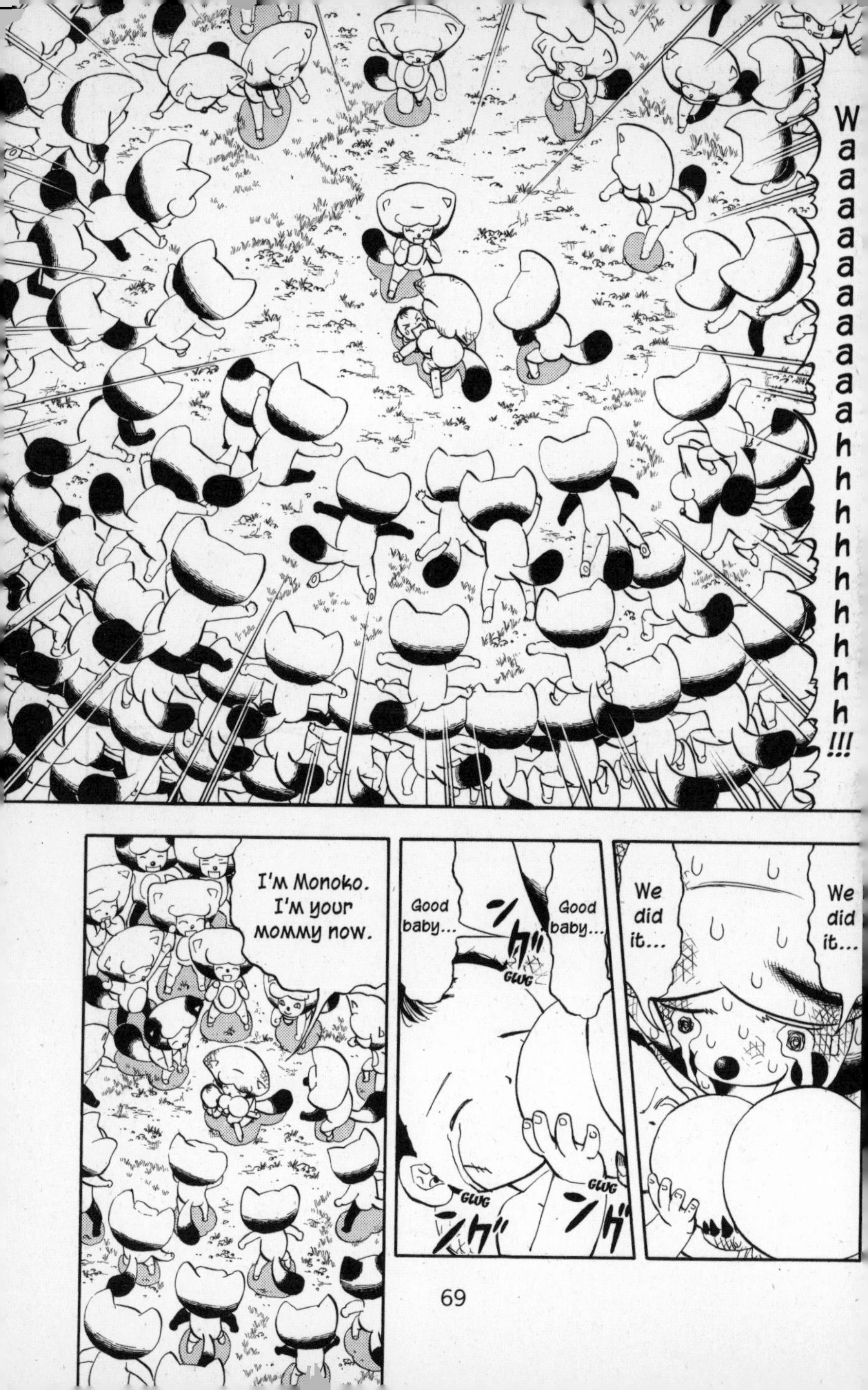
Waaaaaaaaaahhhhhhhhhh!!!
We did it...
We did it...
Good baby...
Good baby...
GLUG
GLUG
GLUG
I'm Monoko. I'm your mommy now.

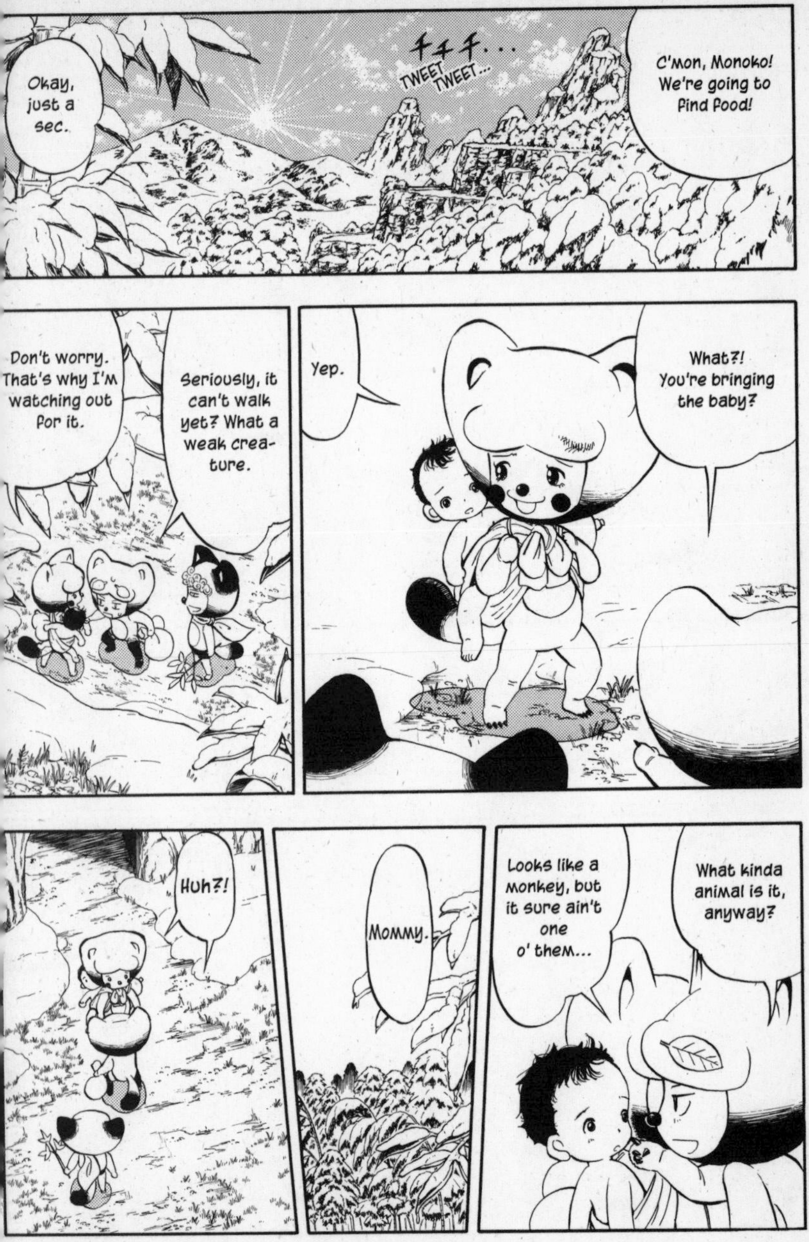
C'mon, Monoko! We're going to find food!
チチチ...
TWEET TWEET...
Okay, just a sec.
What?! You're bringing the baby?
Yep.
Seriously, it can't walk yet? What a weak creature.
Don't worry. That's why I'm watching out for it.
What kinda animal is it, anyway?
Looks like a monkey, but it sure ain't one o' them...
Mommy.
Huh?!

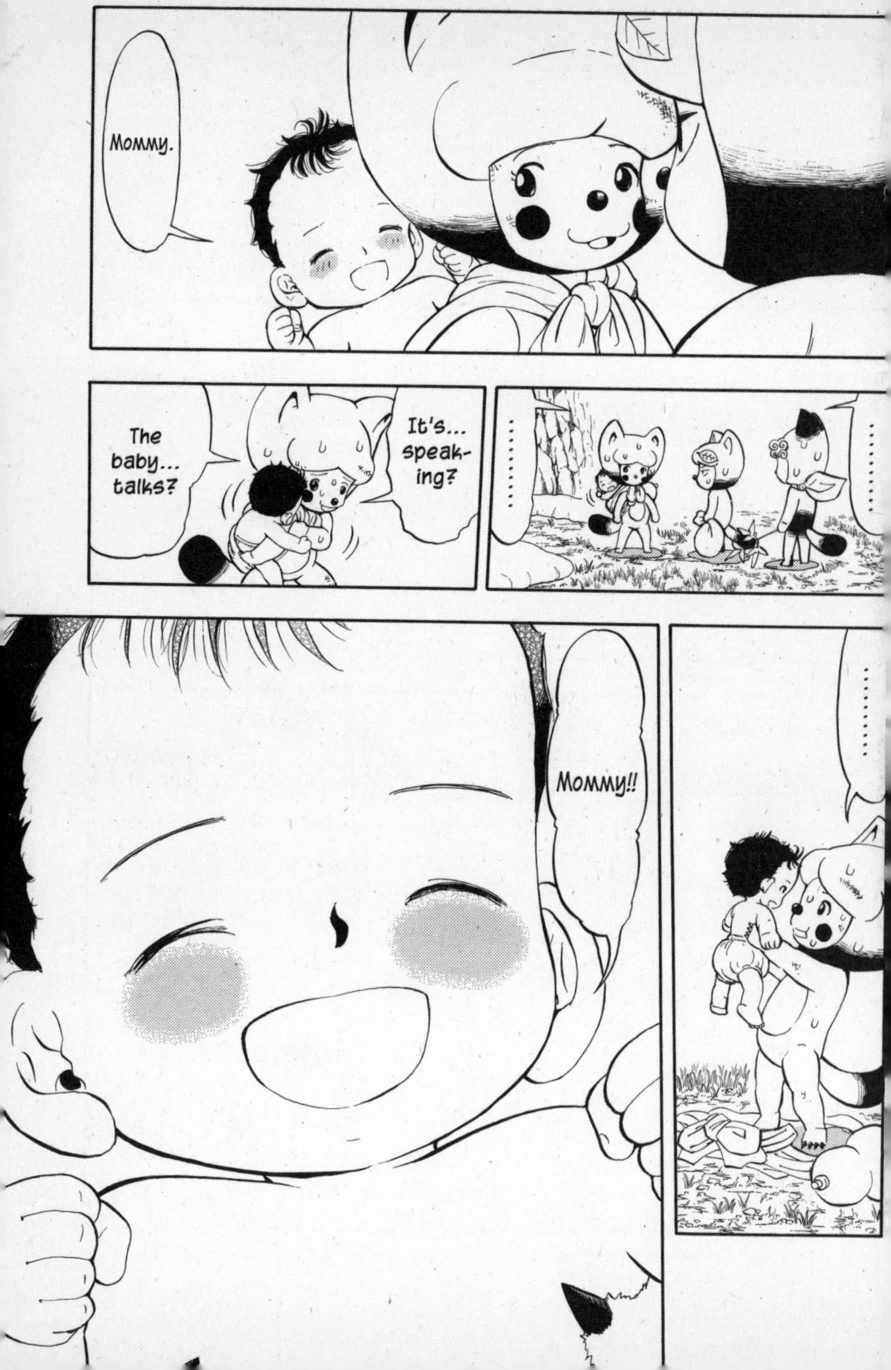
Mommy.
......
......
It's... speak-ing?
The baby... talks?
......
Mommy!!

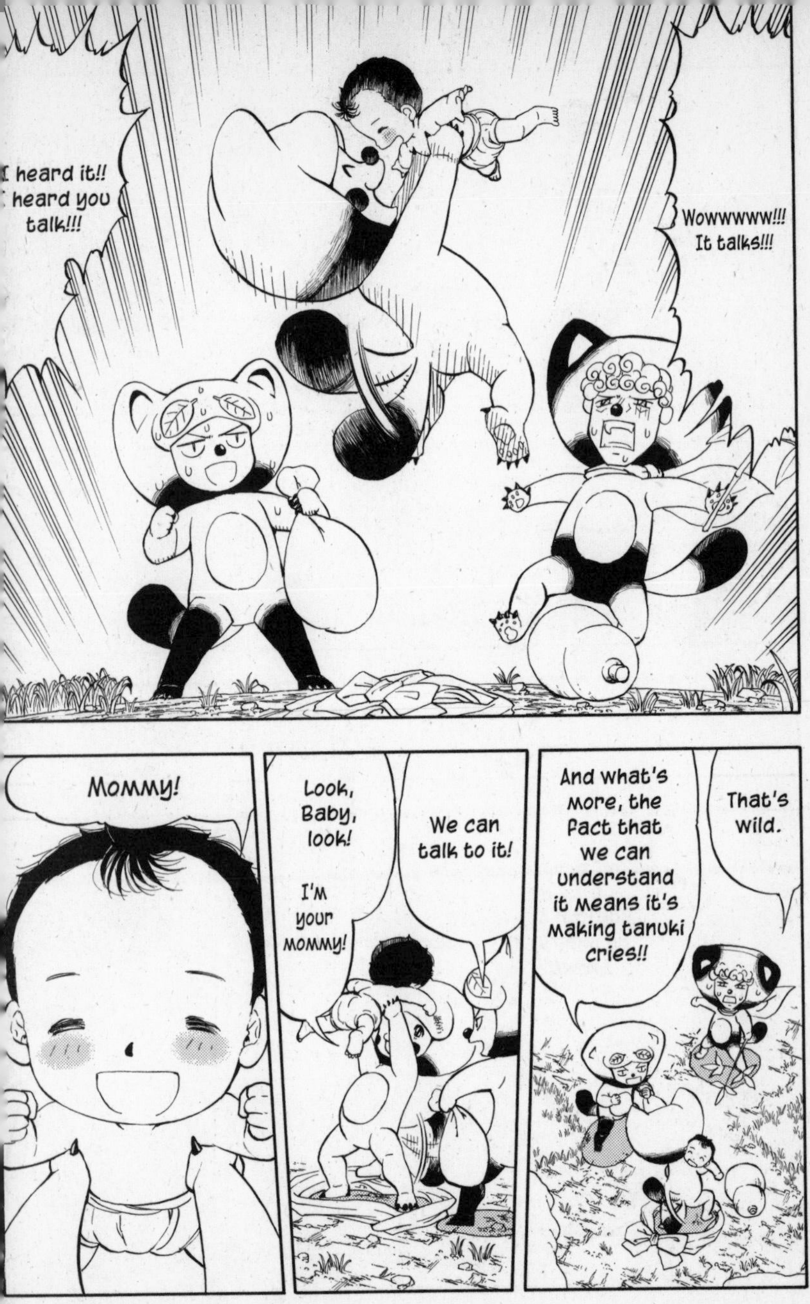
Wowwwww!!! It talks!!!
I heard it!! heard you talk!!!
That's wild.
And what's more, the fact that we can understand it means it's making tanuki cries!!
We can talk to it!
Look, Baby, look!
I'm your mommy!
Mommy!

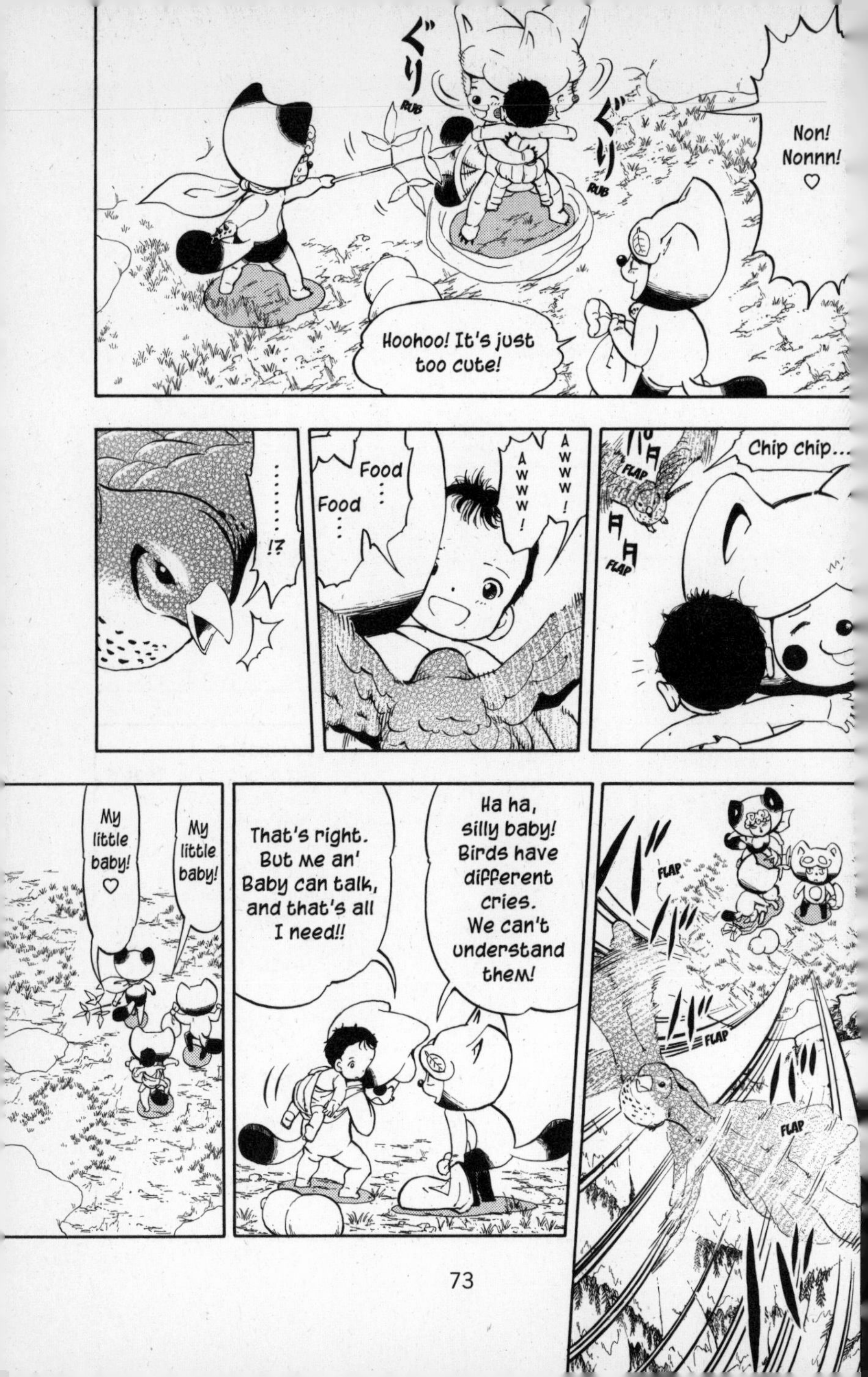
ぐり
RUB
ぐり
RUB
Non! Nonnn! ♡
Hoohoo! It's just too cute!
Chip chip...
パタ
FLAP
タタ
FLAP
AWWW!
AWWW!
Food...
Food...
......!?
FLAP
FLAP
FLAP
Ha ha, silly baby! Birds have different cries. We can't understand them!
That's right. But me an' Baby can talk, and that's all I need!!
My little baby!
My little baby! ♡

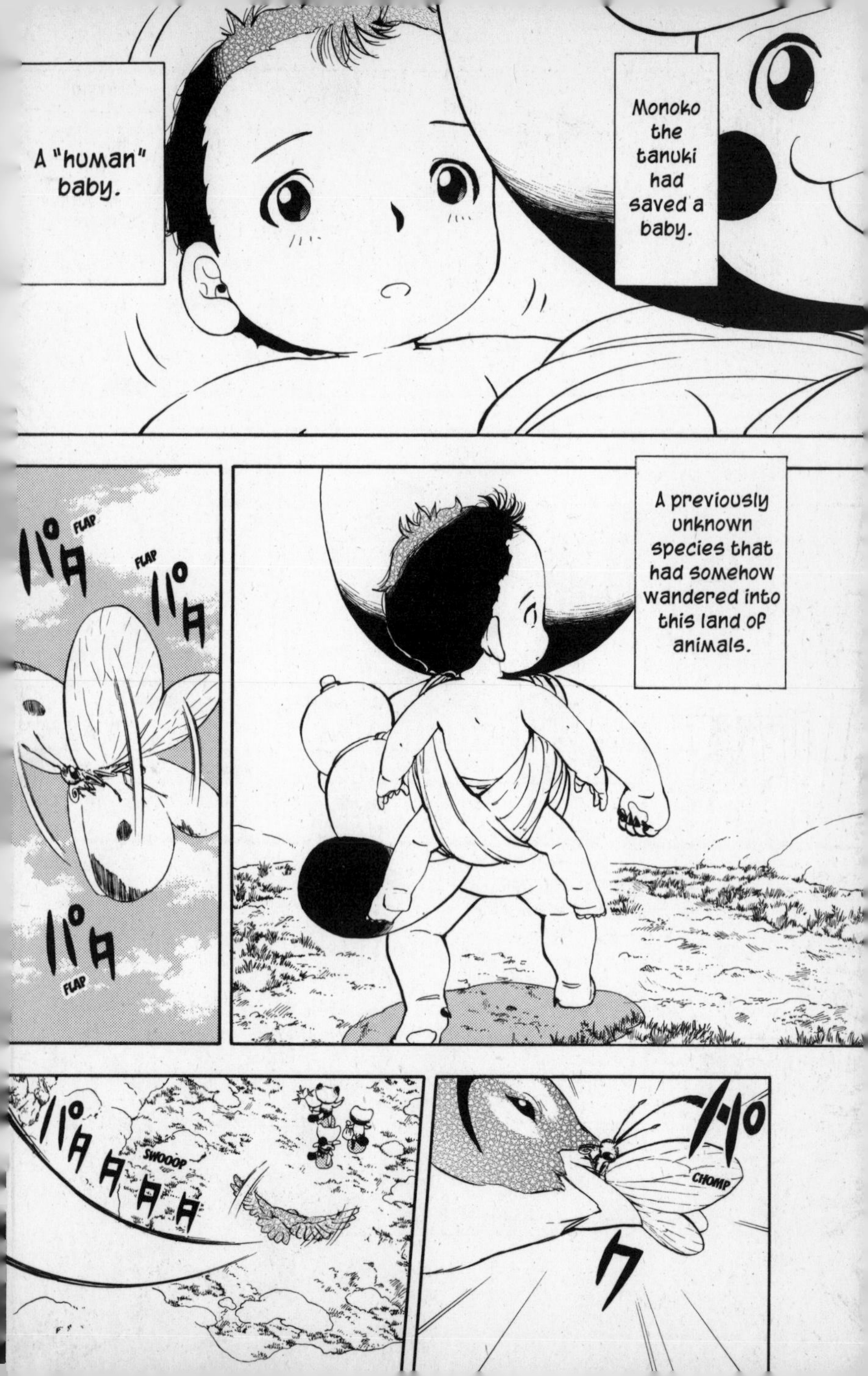
Monoko the tanuki had saved a baby.
A "human" baby.
A previously unknown species that had somehow wandered into this land of animals.
パタ
FLAP
パタ
FLAP
パタ
FLAP
パク
CHOMP
パタタタタ
SWOOOP

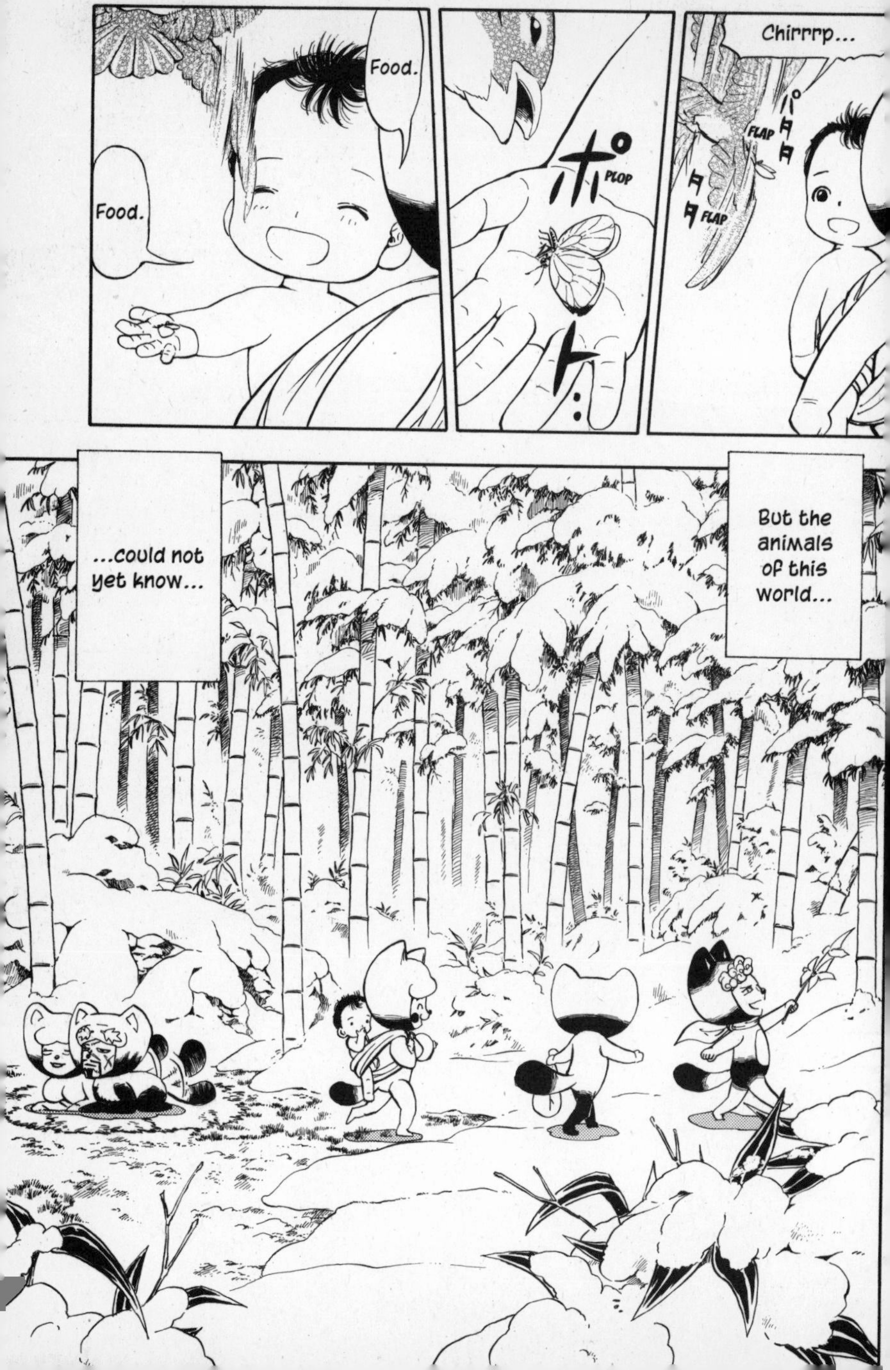
Chirrrp...
パタタ
FLAP
タタ
FLAP
ポ
PLOP
ト
Food.
Food.
But the animals of this world...
...could not yet know...

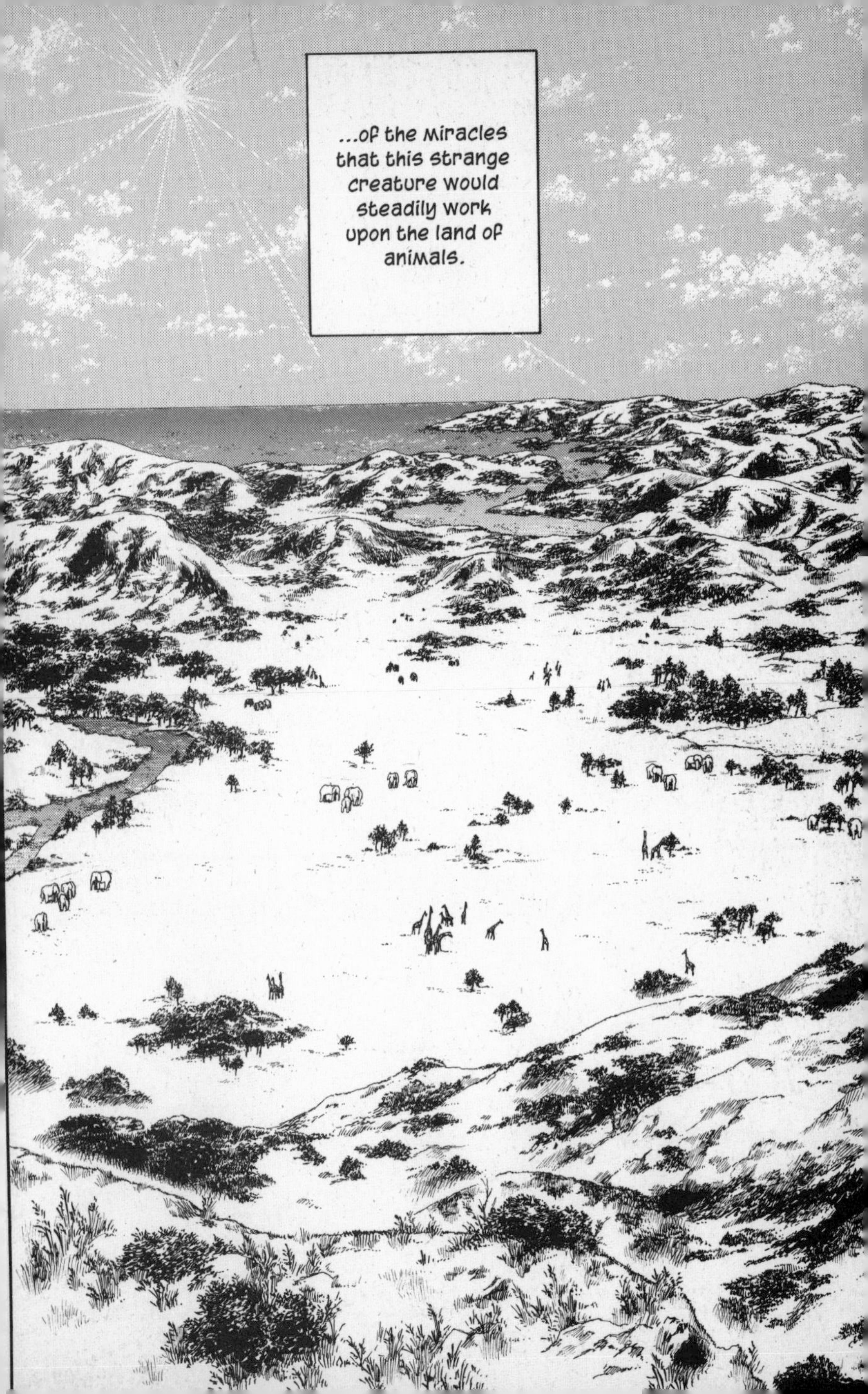
...of the miracles that this strange creature would steadily work upon the land of animals.

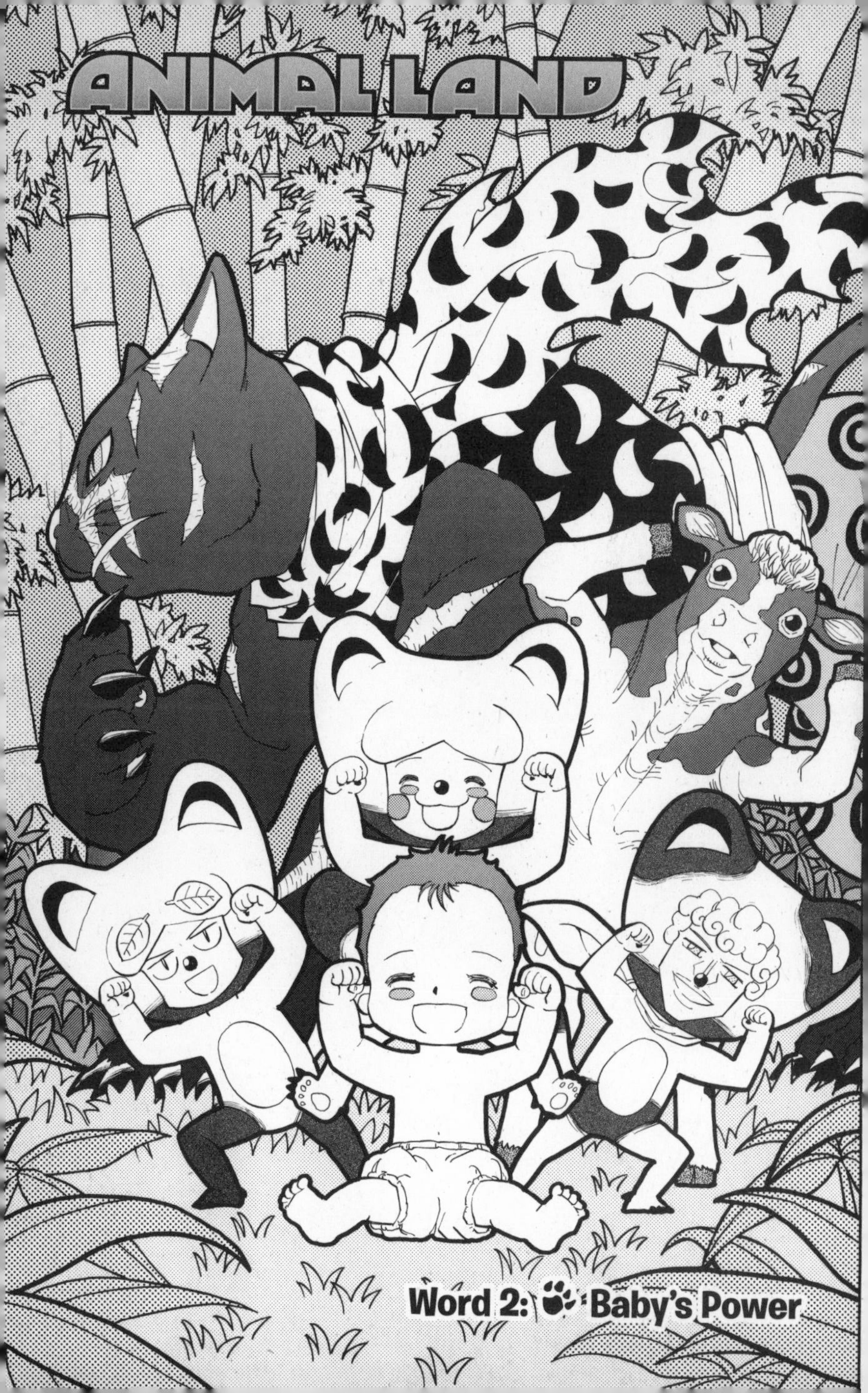
ANIMAL LAND
Word 2: Baby's Power

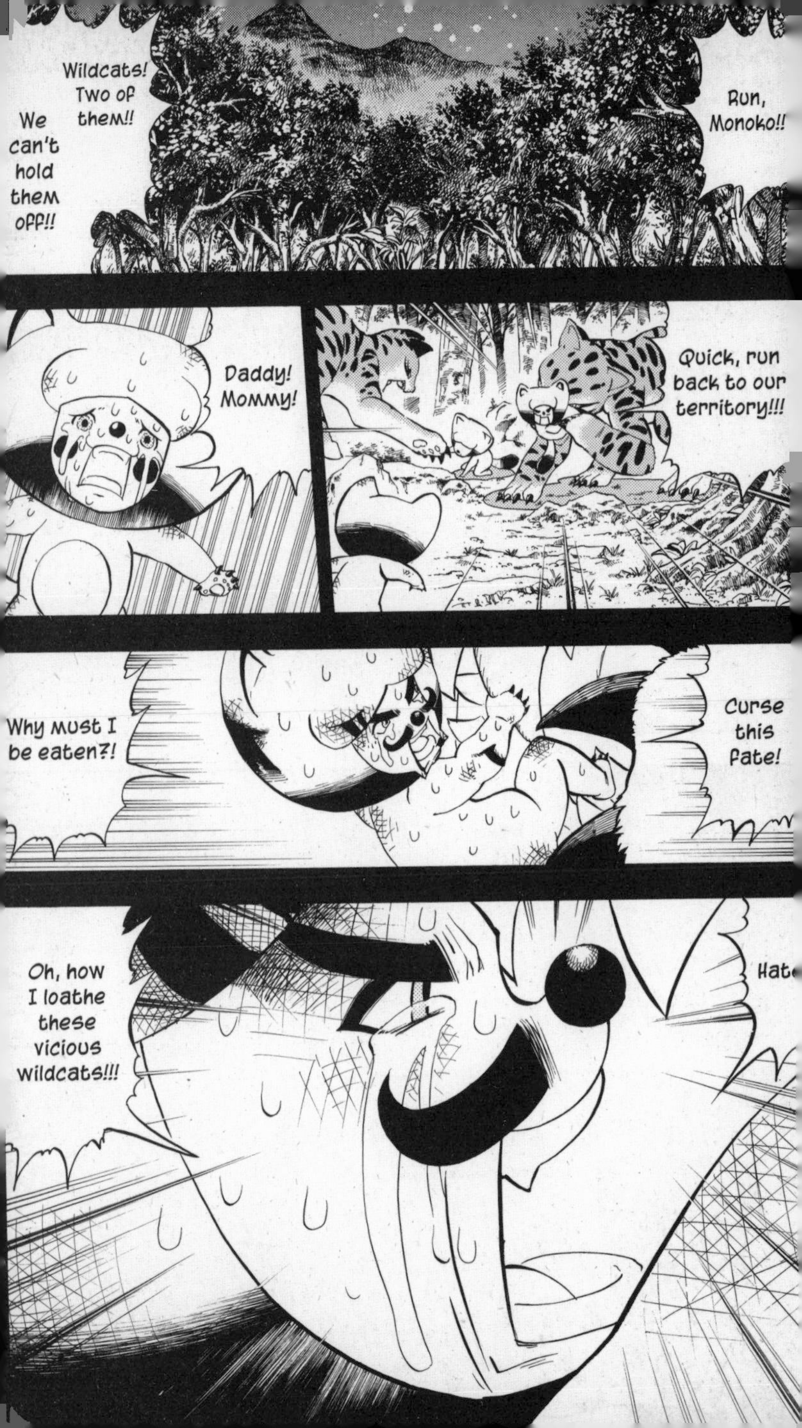
Run, Monoko!!
Wildcats! Two of them!!
We can't hold them off!!
Quick, run back to our territory!!!
Daddy! Mommy!
Curse this fate!
Why must I be eaten?!
Hat
Oh, how I loathe these vicious wildcats!!!

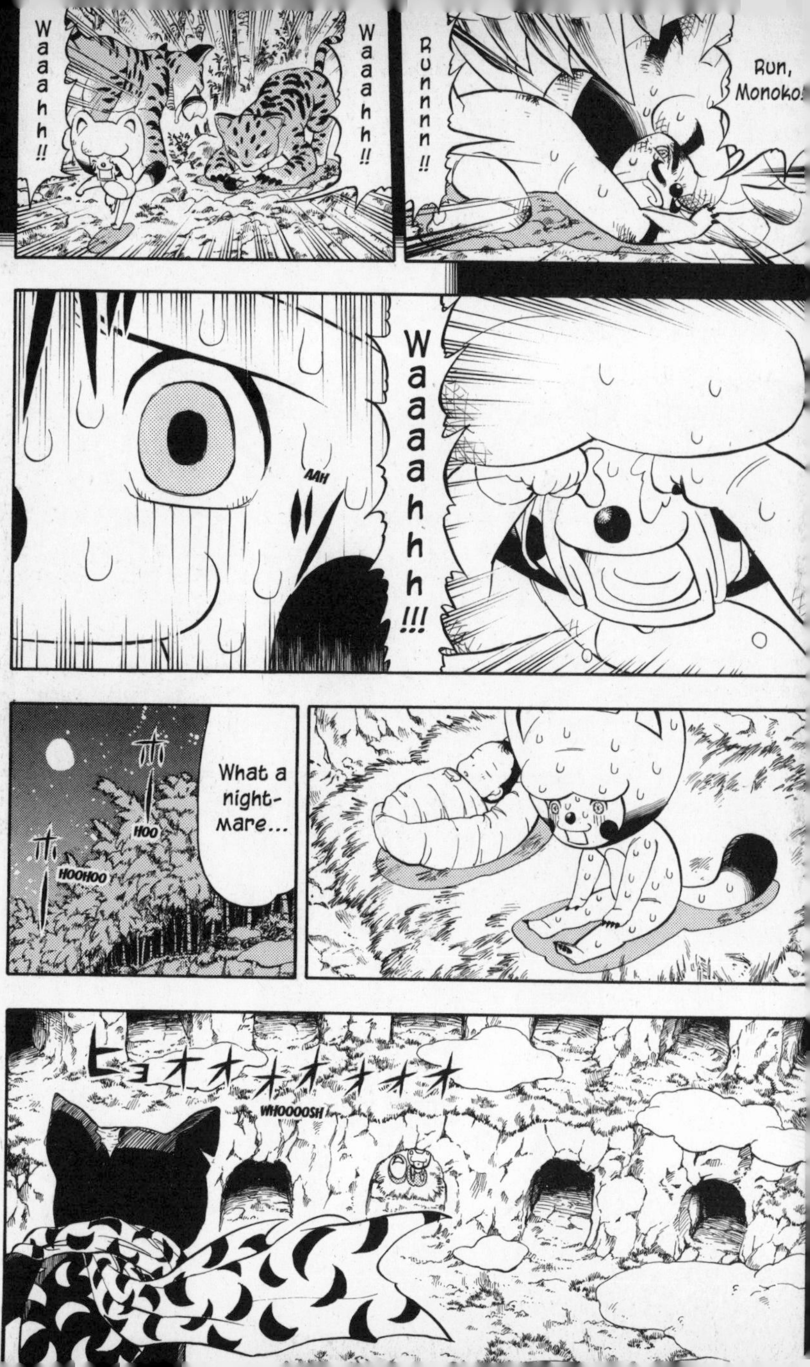
Run, Monoko!
Runnnn!!
Waaahh!!
Waaahh!!
Waaaaahhh!!!
AAH
What a nightmare...
ホー
HOO
ホー
HOOHOO
ヒョオオオオオオオ
WHOOOOSH

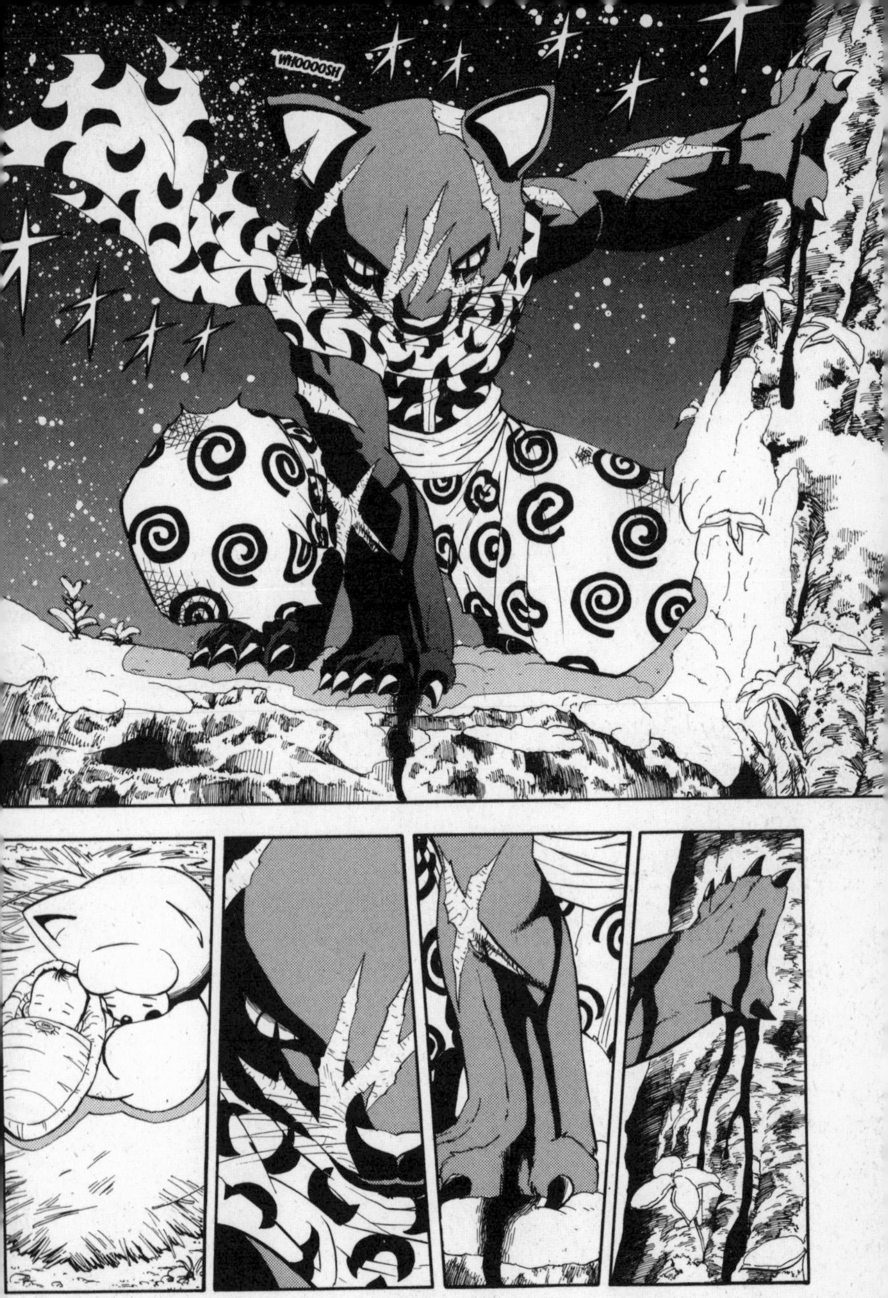
WHOOOOSH

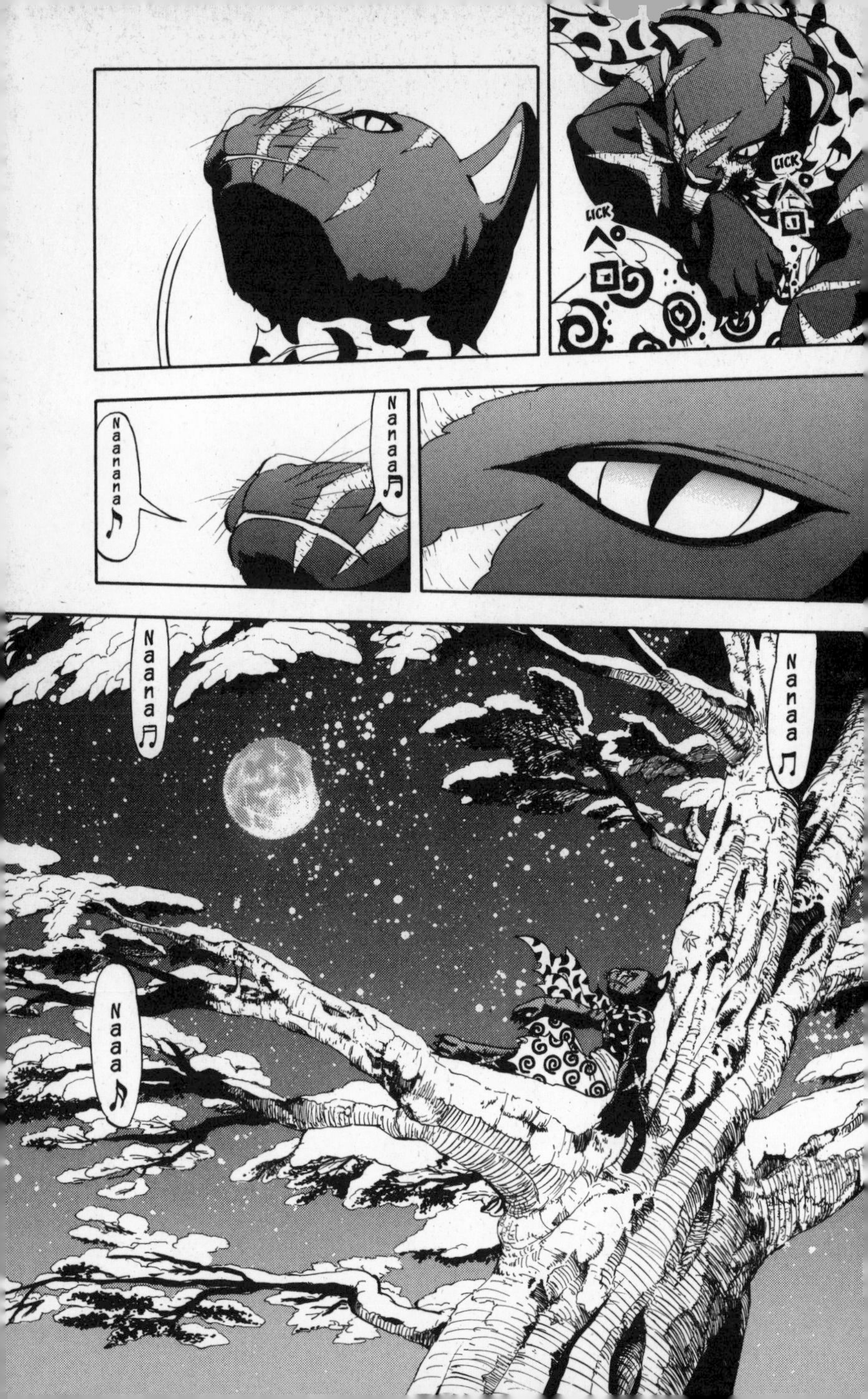
LICK
ペロ
LICK
ペロ
Nanaa♫
Naanana♪
Nanaa♫
Naanana♫
Naaa♪

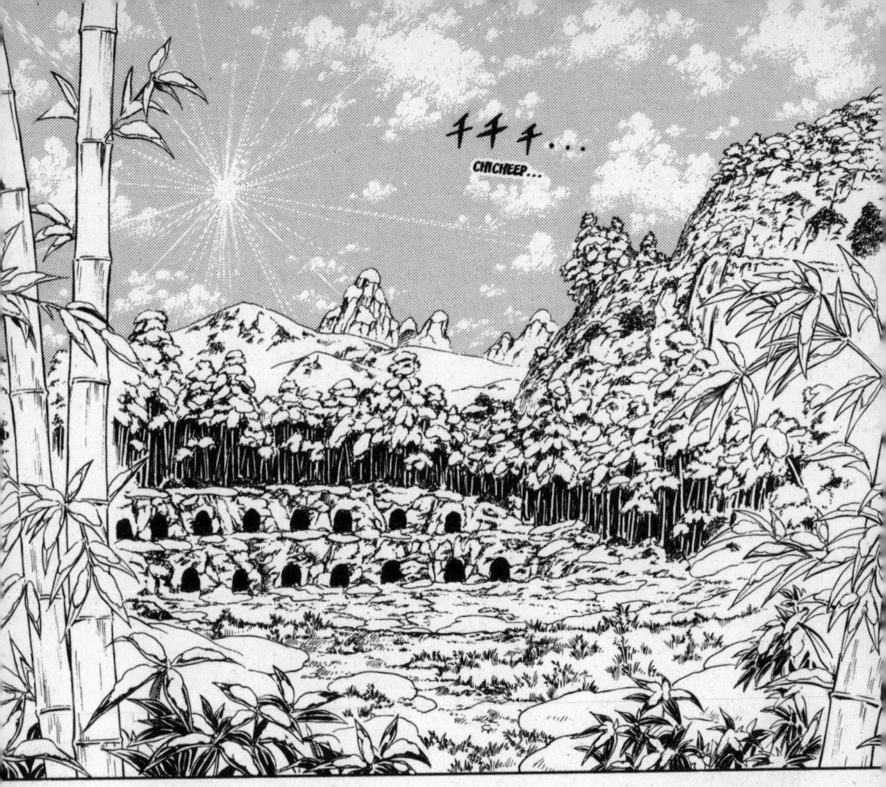
チチチ...
CHICHEEP...

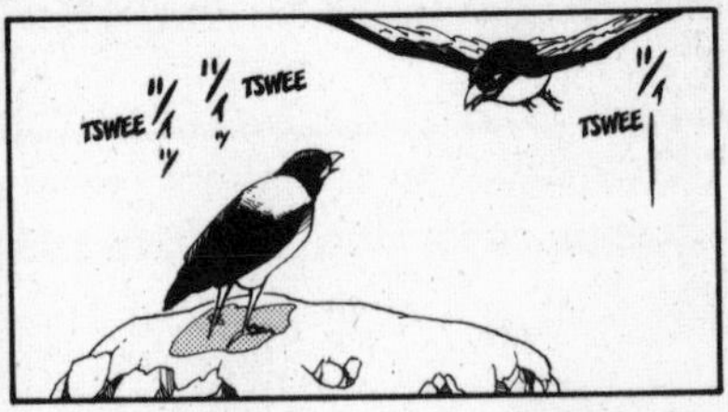
ツイッ
TSWEE
TSWEE
TSWEE

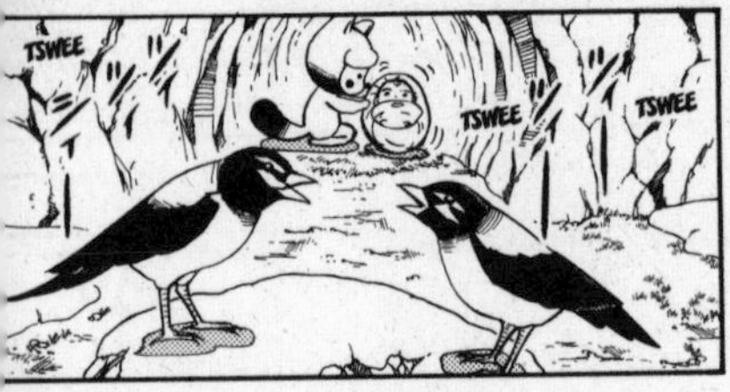
TSWEE
TSWEE
TSWEE

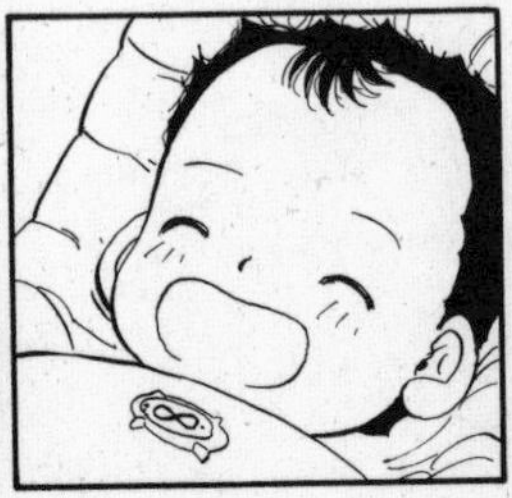

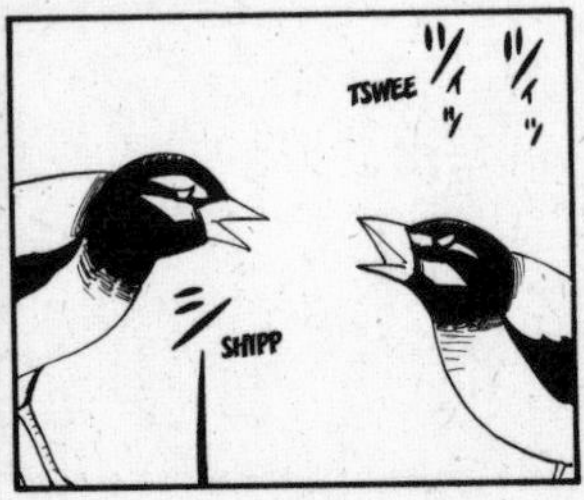
ツイッ
ツイッ
TSWEE
SHIPP

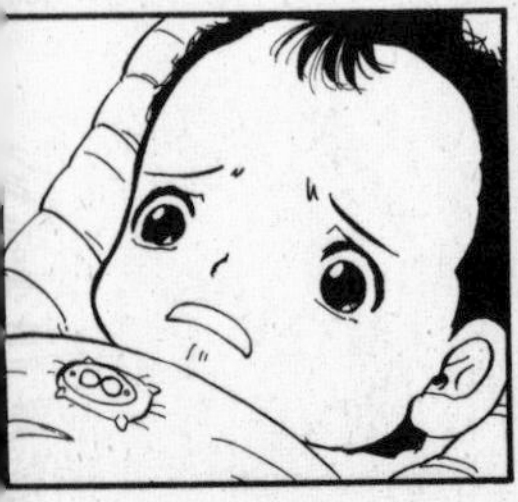

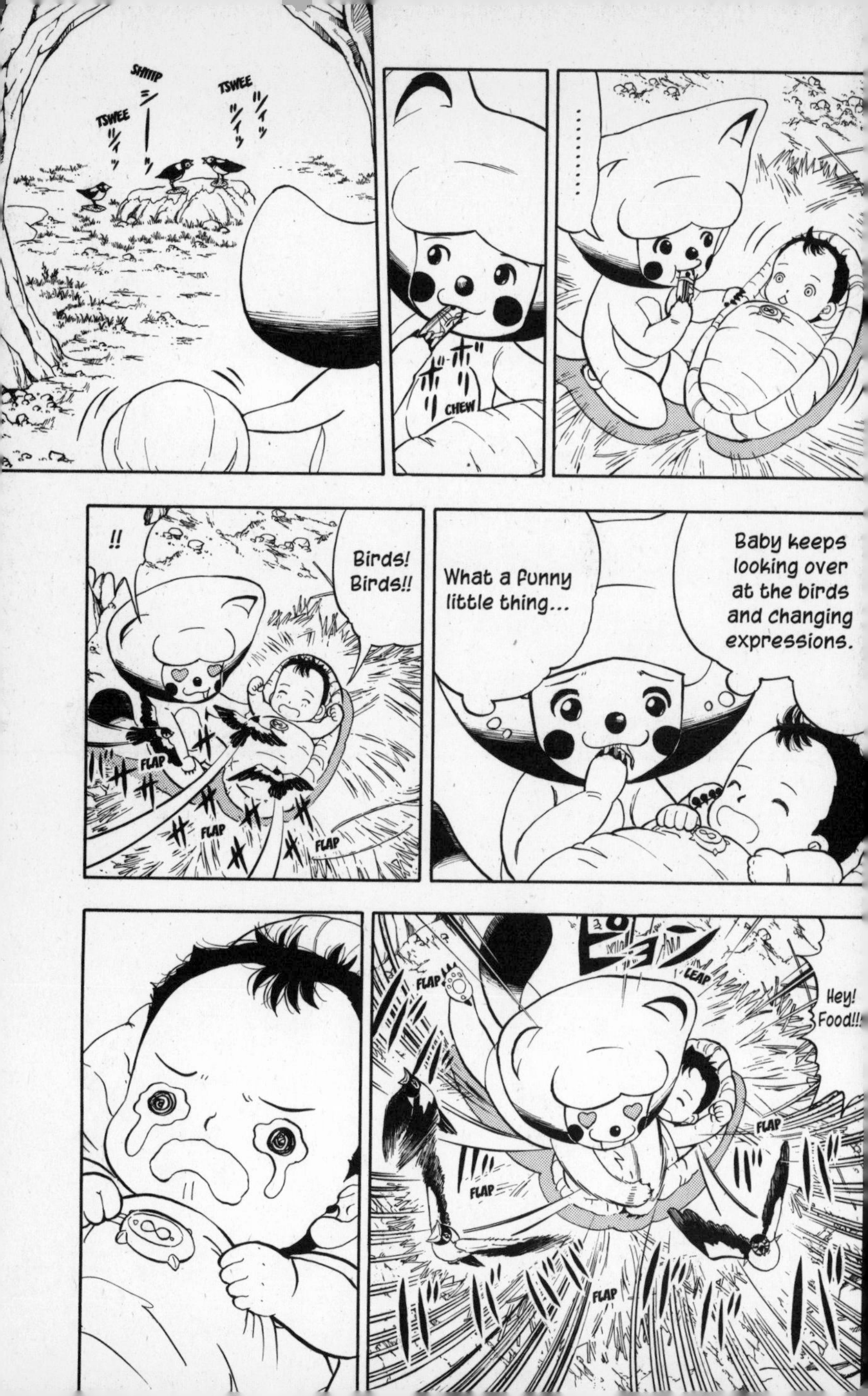
......
CHEW
TSWEE
SHIIIP
TSWEE
Baby keeps looking over at the birds and changing expressions.
What a funny little thing...
Birds! Birds!!
!!
FLAP
FLAP
FLAP
Hey! Food!!
LEAP
FLAP
FLAP
FLAP
FLAP

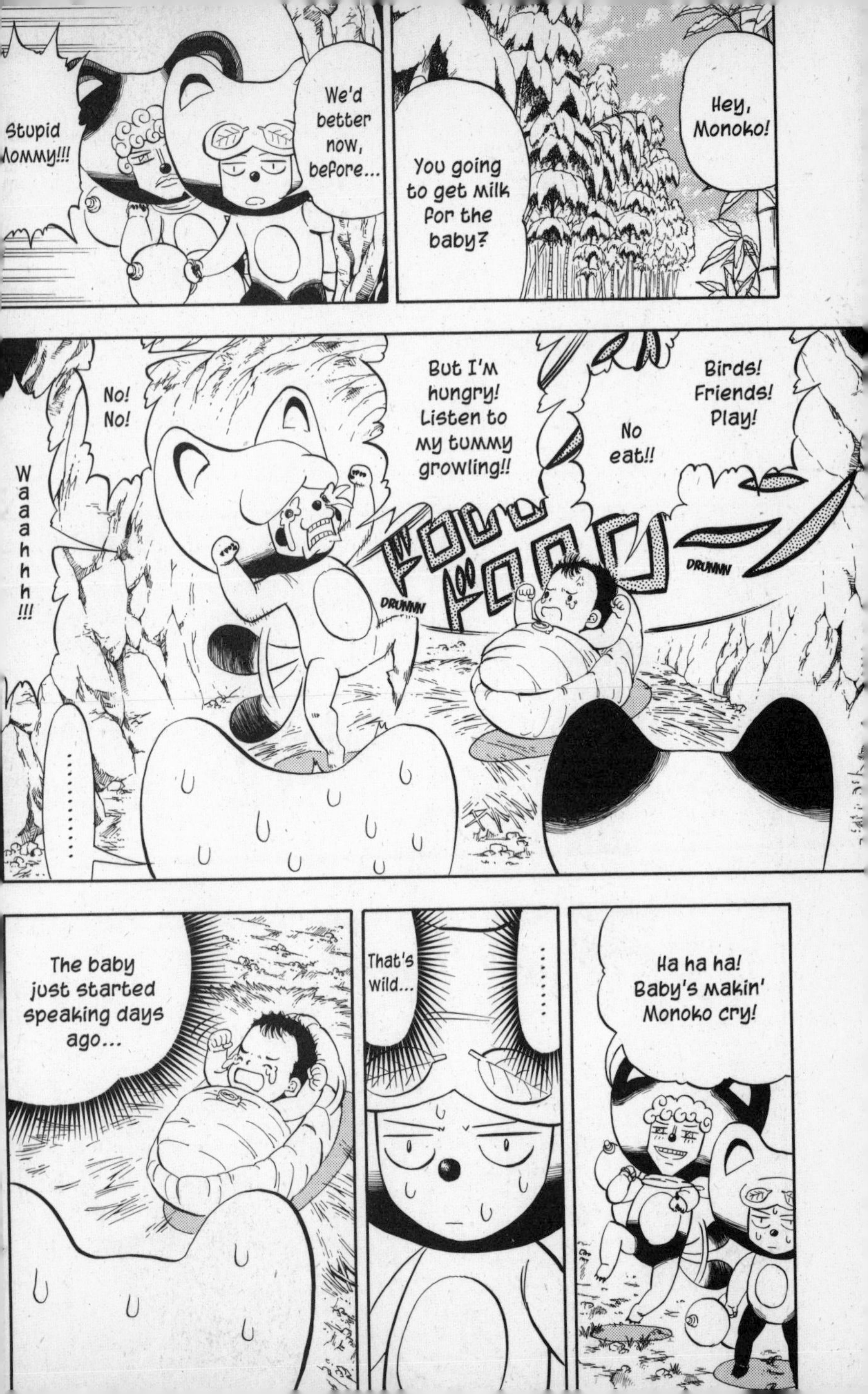
Hey, Monoko!
You going to get milk for the baby?
We'd better now, before...
Stupid Mommy!!!
Birds! Friends! Play!
No eat!!
But I'm hungry! Listen to my tummy growling!!
No! No!
Waaahhh!!!
DRUNNN
DRUNNN
......
Ha ha ha! Baby's makin' Monoko cry!
......
That's wild...
The baby just started speaking days ago...

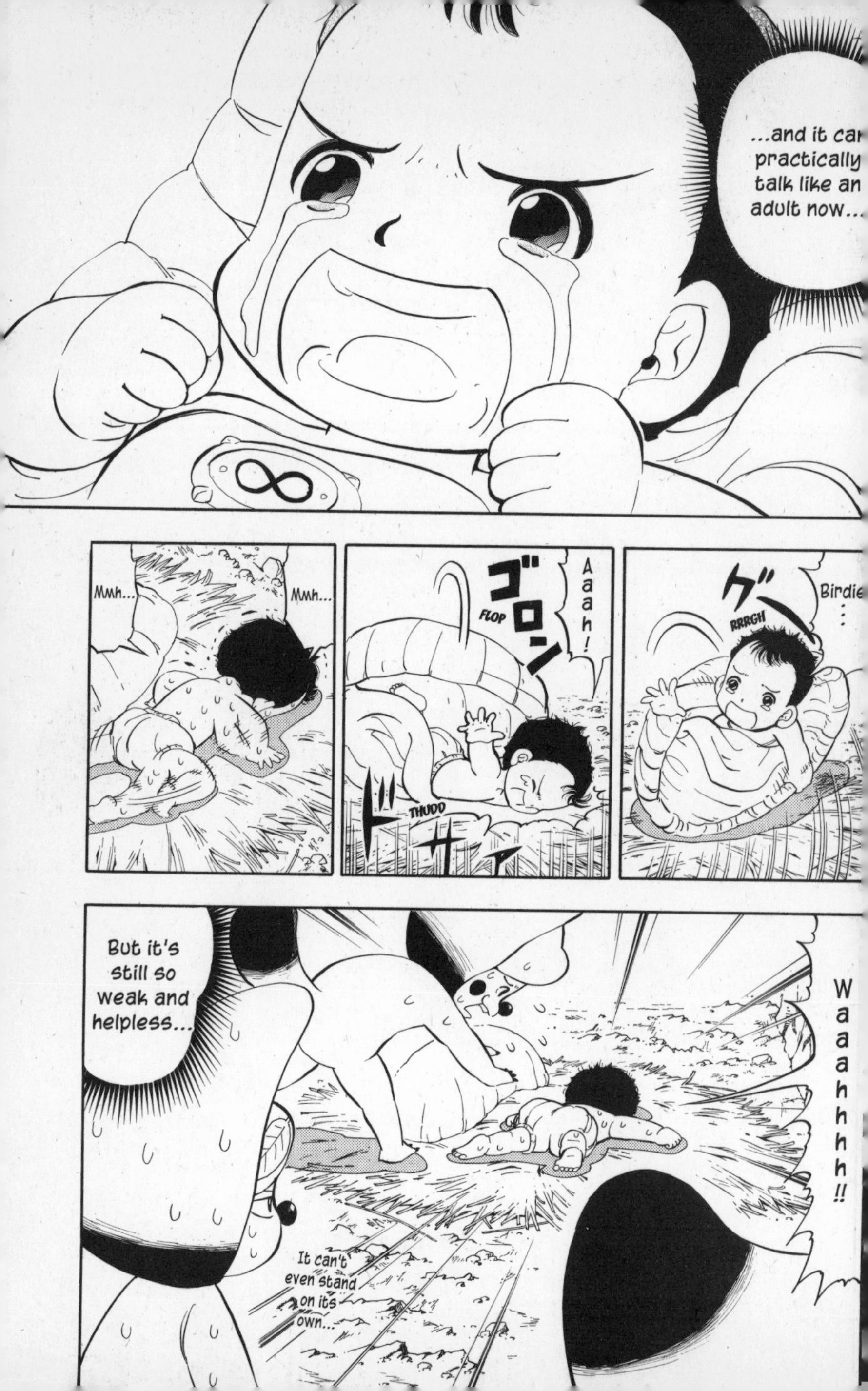
...and it can practically talk like an adult now...
Birdie...
グ
RRRGH
Aaah!
ゴロン
FLOP
ドサァ
THUDD
Mmh...
Mmh...
Waaaahhhh!!
But it's still so weak and helpless...
It can't even stand on its own...

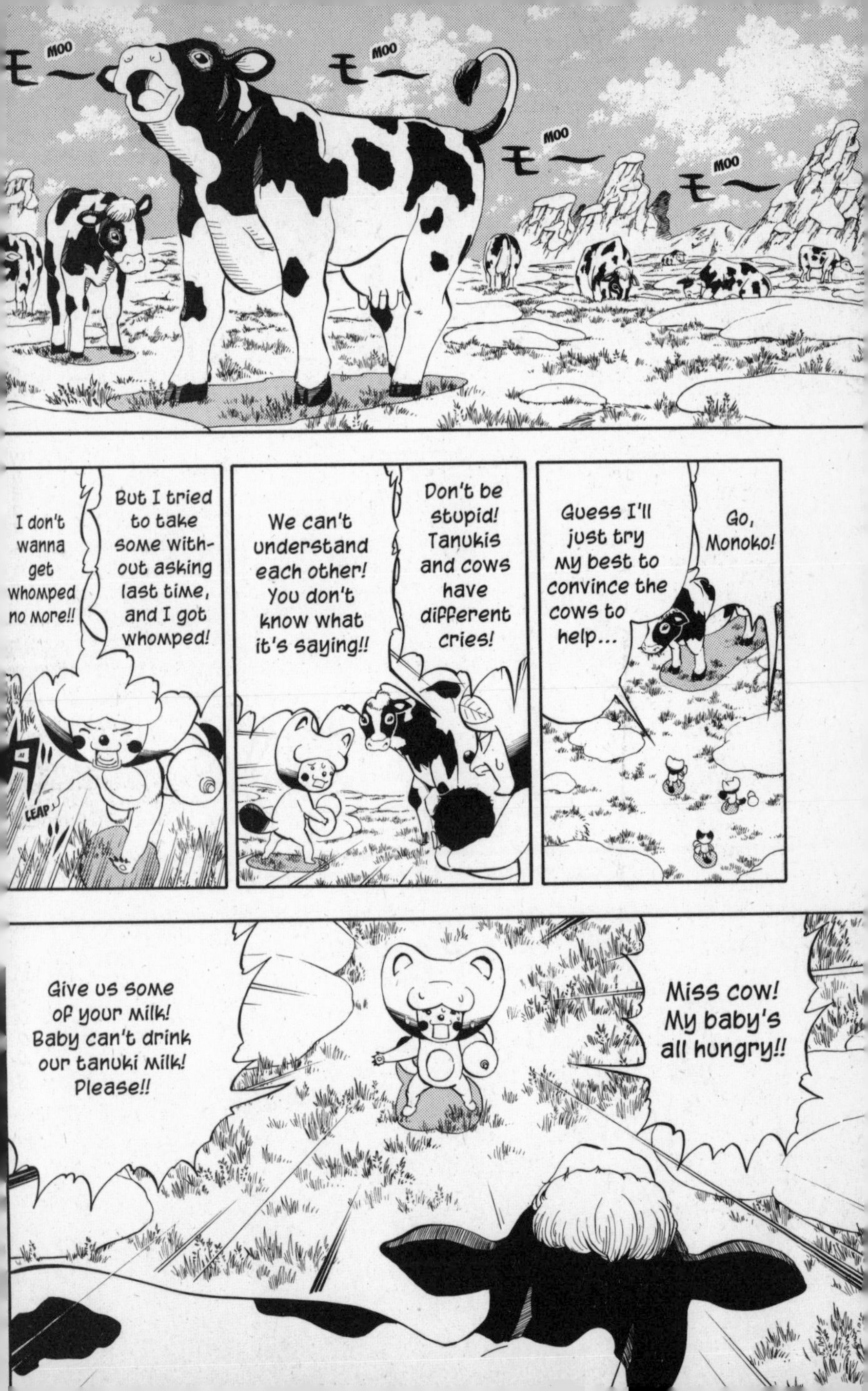

MOO
MOO
MOO
MOO
Go, Monoko!
Guess I'll just try my best to convince the cows to help...
Don't be stupid! Tanukis and cows have different cries!
We can't understand each other! You don't know what it's saying!!
But I tried to take some without asking last time, and I got whomped!
I don't wanna get whomped no more!!
LEAP
Miss cow! My baby's all hungry!!
Give us some of your milk! Baby can't drink our tanuki milk! Please!!

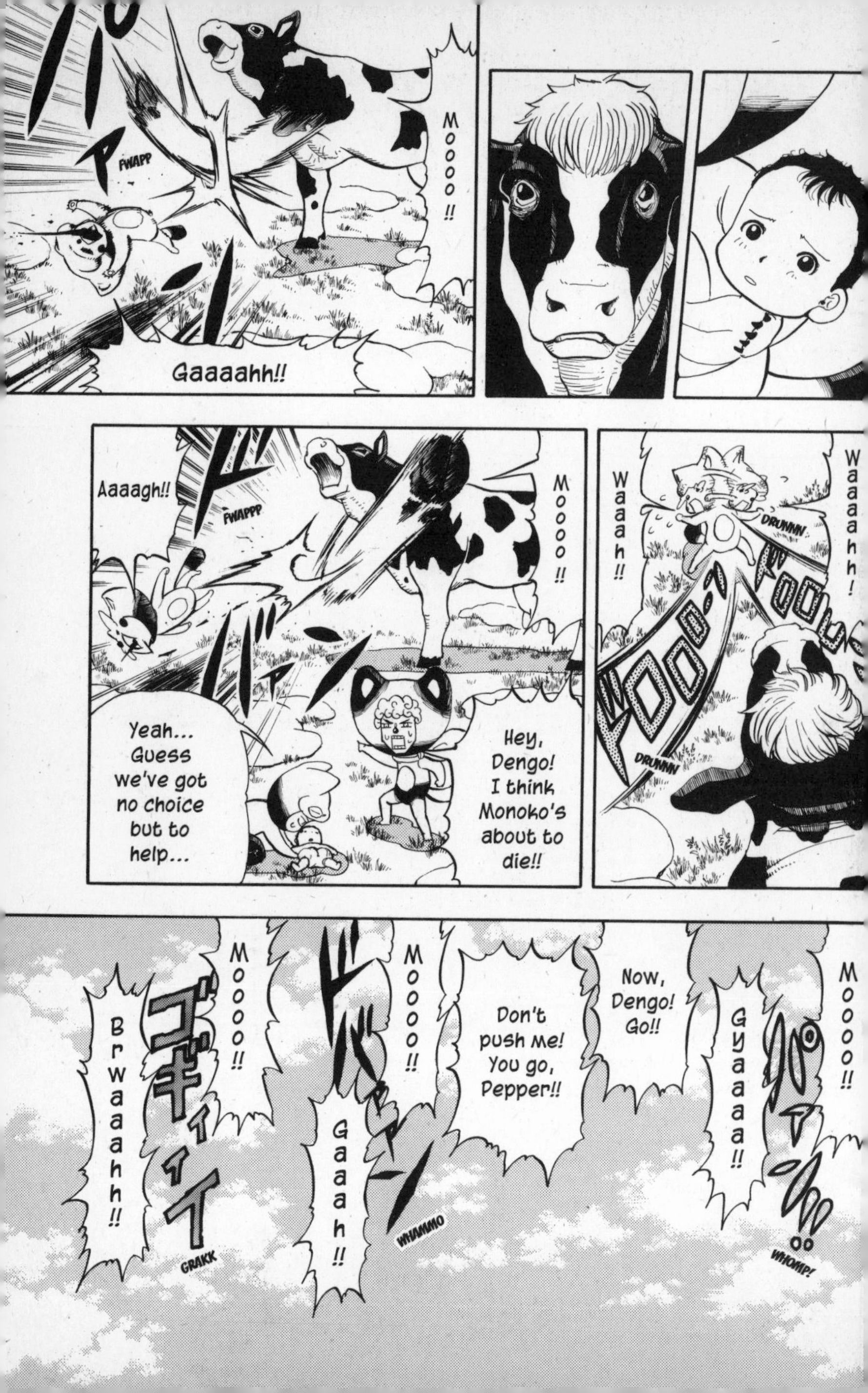
Moooo!!
FWAPP
Gaaaahh!!
Waaaahh!
Waaah!!
DRUNNN
DRUNNN
Moooo!!
Aaaagh!!
FWAPPP
Hey, Dengo! I think Monoko's about to die!!
Yeah... Guess we've got no choice but to help...
Moooo!!
Gyaaaaa!!
WHOMP!
Now, Dengo! Go!!
Don't push me! You go, Pepper!!
Moooo!!
Gaaah!!
WHAMMO
Moooo!!
Brwaaahh!!
GRAKK

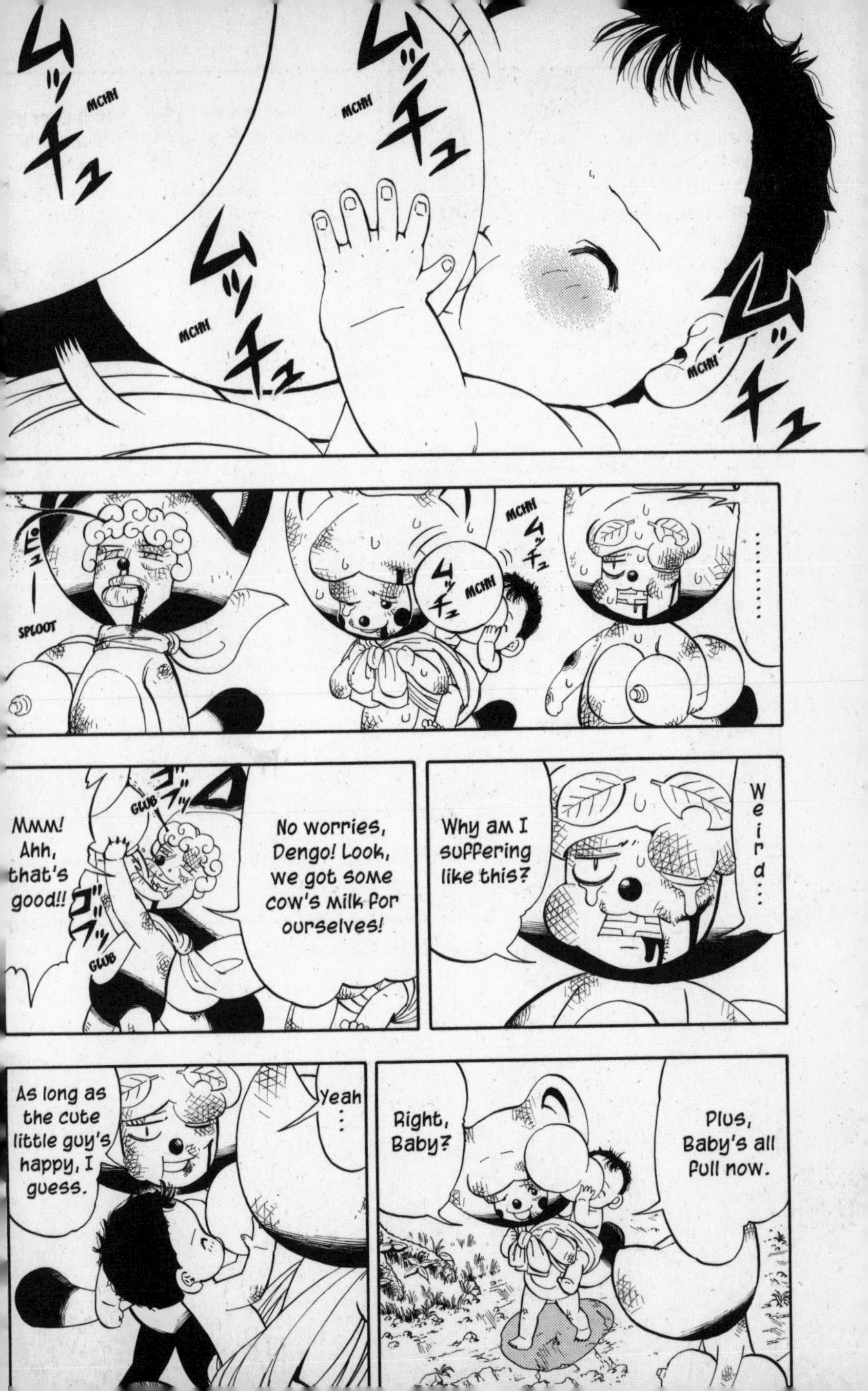
ムッチュ
MCHH
ムッチュ
MCHH
ムッチュ
MCHH
MCHH
....
MCHH
ムッチュ
ムッチュ
MCHH
SPLOOT
Weird...
Why am I suffering like this?
No worries, Dengo! Look, we got some cow's milk for ourselves!
Mmm! Ahh, that's good!!
GLUB
GLUB
Plus, Baby's all full now.
Right, Baby?
Yeah...
As long as the cute little guy's happy, I guess.

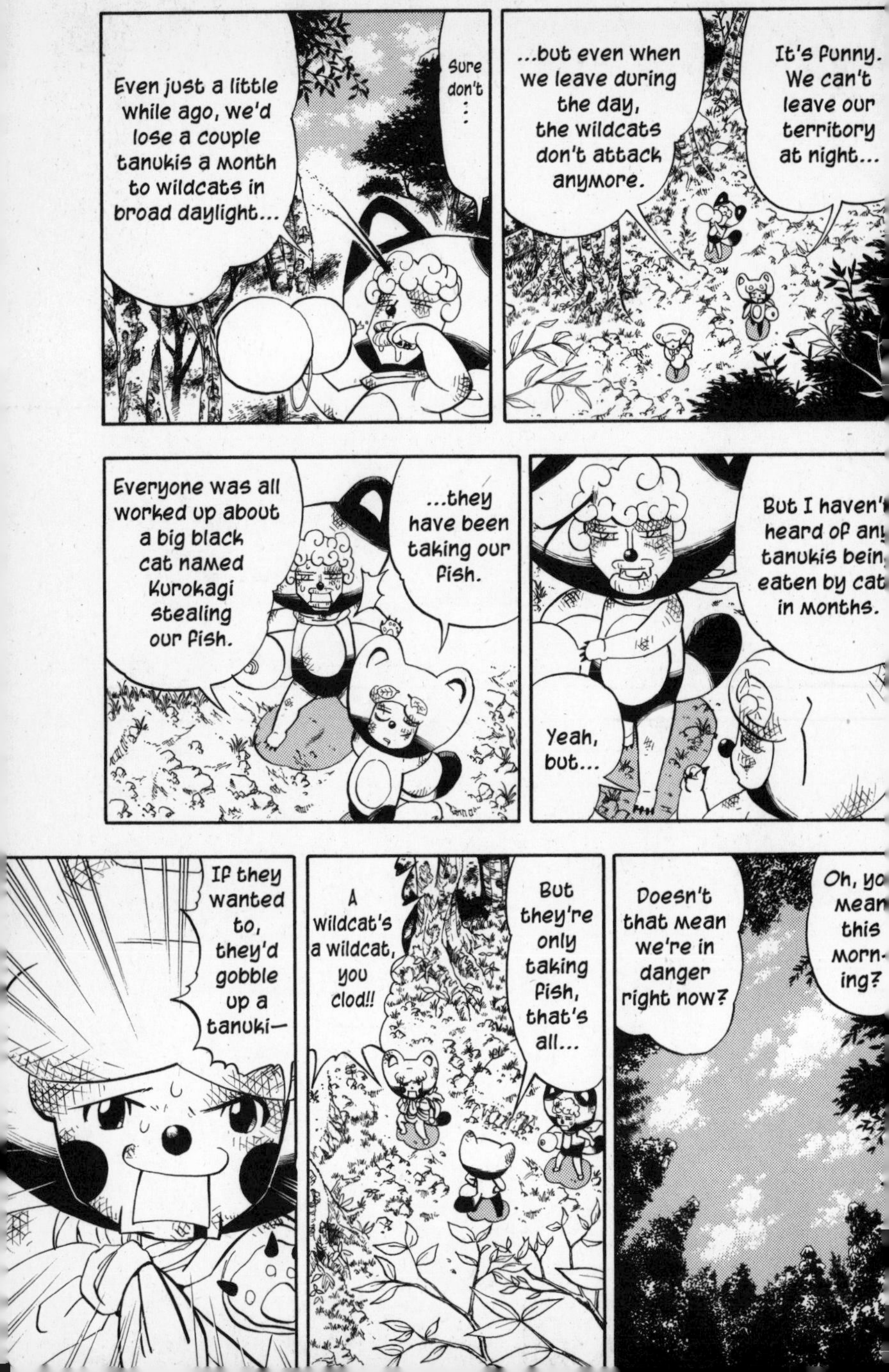
It's funny. We can't leave our territory at night...
...but even when we leave during the day, the wildcats don't attack anymore.
Sure don't...
Even just a little while ago, we'd lose a couple tanukis a month to wildcats in broad daylight...
But I haven' heard of an tanukis bein eaten by cat in months.
Yeah, but...
...they have been taking our fish.
Everyone was all worked up about a big black cat named Kurokagi stealing our fish.
Oh, yo mean this morn-ing?
Doesn't that mean we're in danger right now?
But they're only taking fish, that's all...
A wildcat's a wildcat, you clod!!
If they wanted to, they'd gobble up a tanuki—

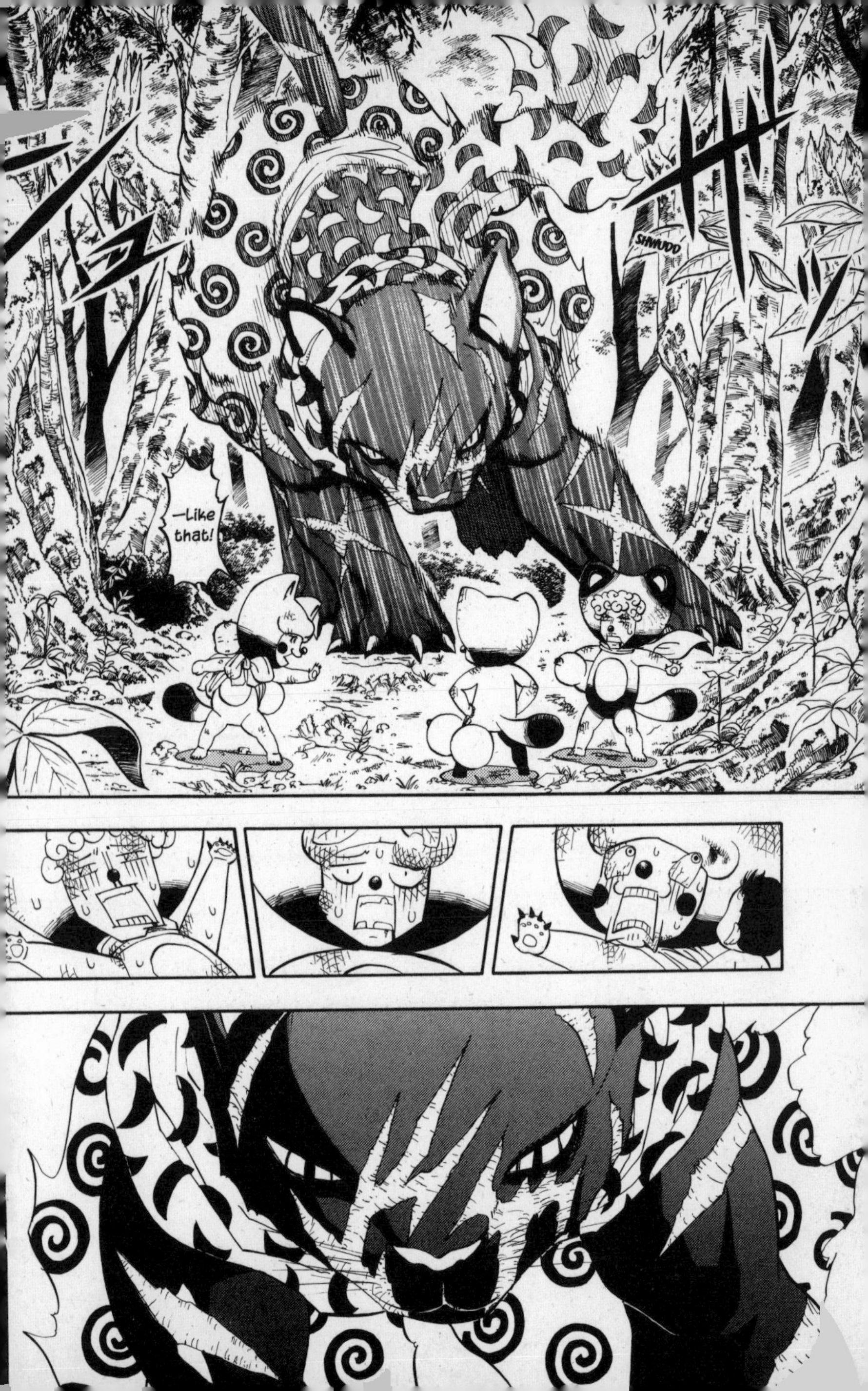
SHWUDD
—Like that!

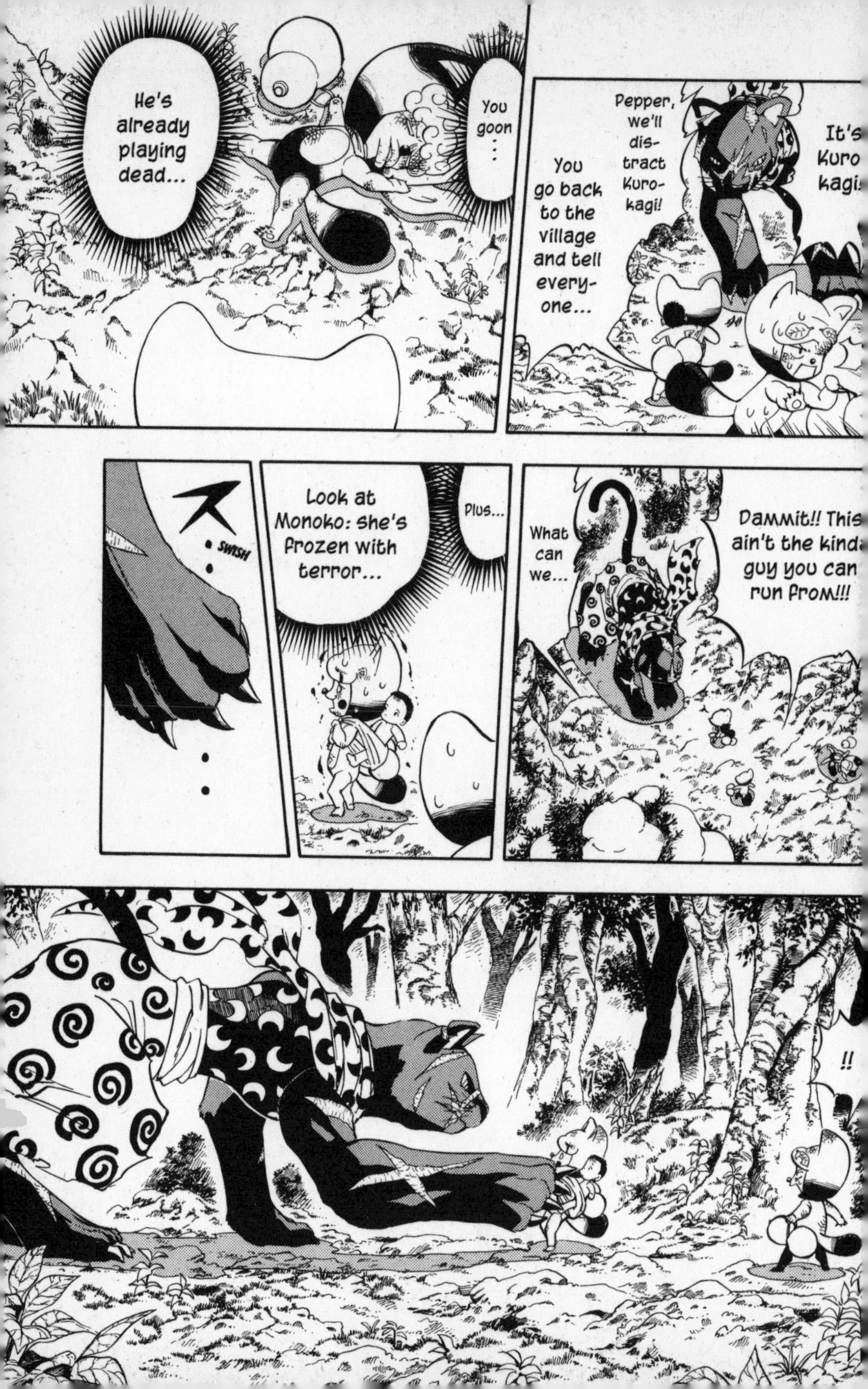
It's Kurokagi!
Pepper, we'll distract Kurokagi!
You go back to the village and tell everyone...
You goon...
He's already playing dead...
Dammit!! This ain't the kinda guy you can run from!!!
What can we...
Plus...
Look at Monoko: she's frozen with terror...
ス
SWISH
!!

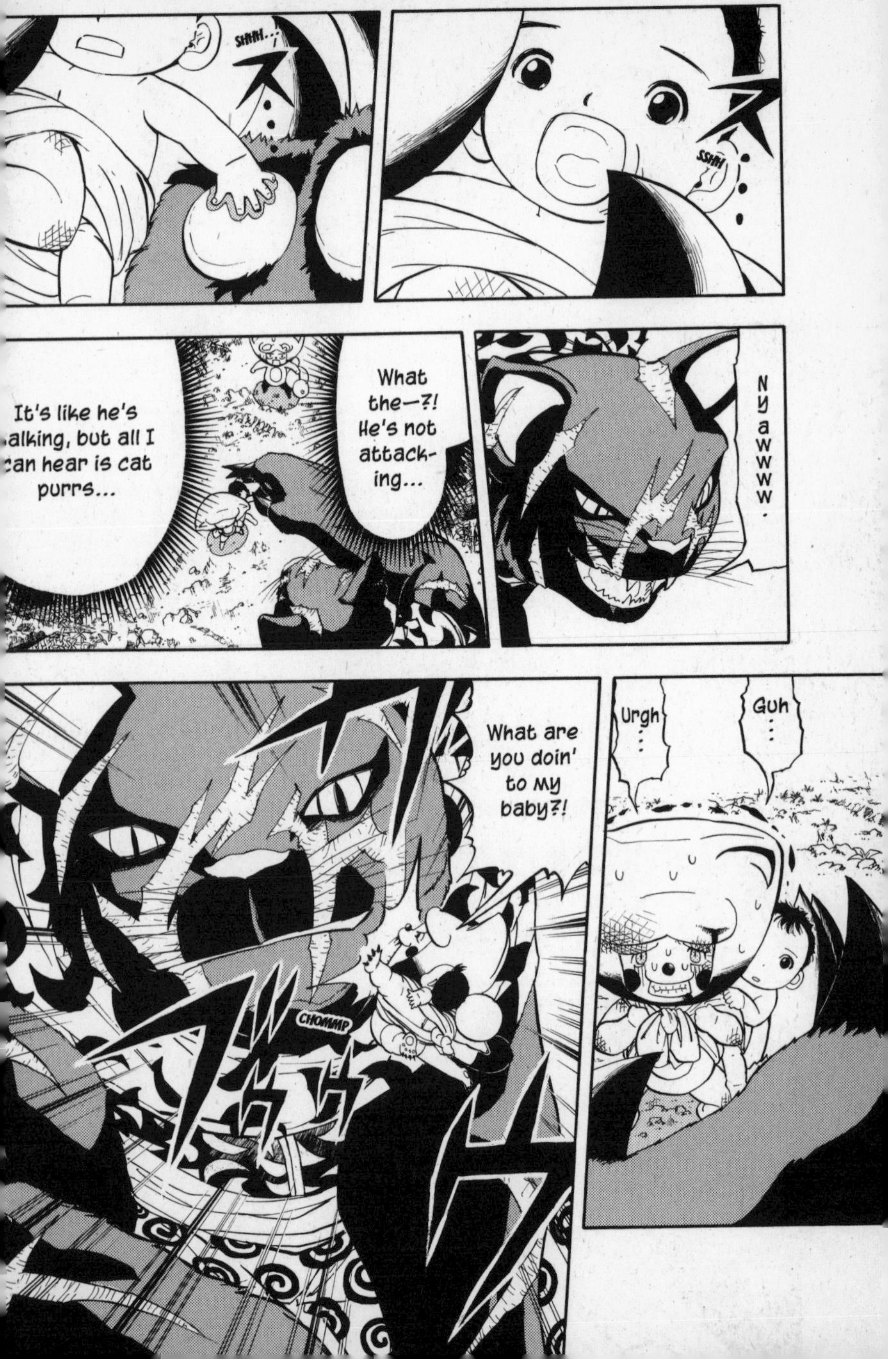
SSHH
SHHH...
Nyawwww.
What the—?! He's not attacking...
It's like he's alking, but all I an hear is cat purrs...
Guh...
Urgh...
What are you doin' to my baby?!
CHOMMP

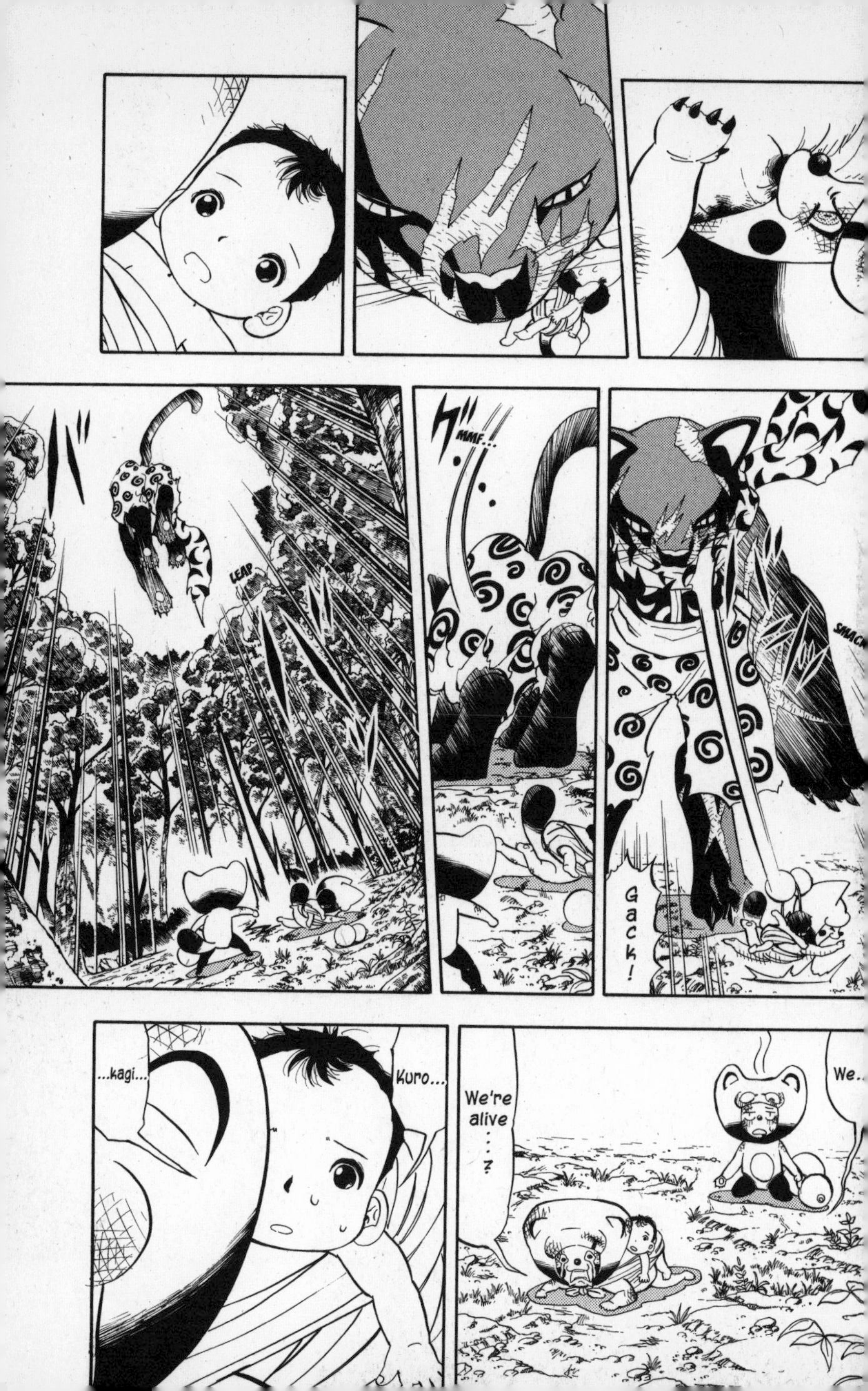
SMAC
Gack!
MMF...
LEAP
We...
We're alive...?
Kuro...
...kagi...

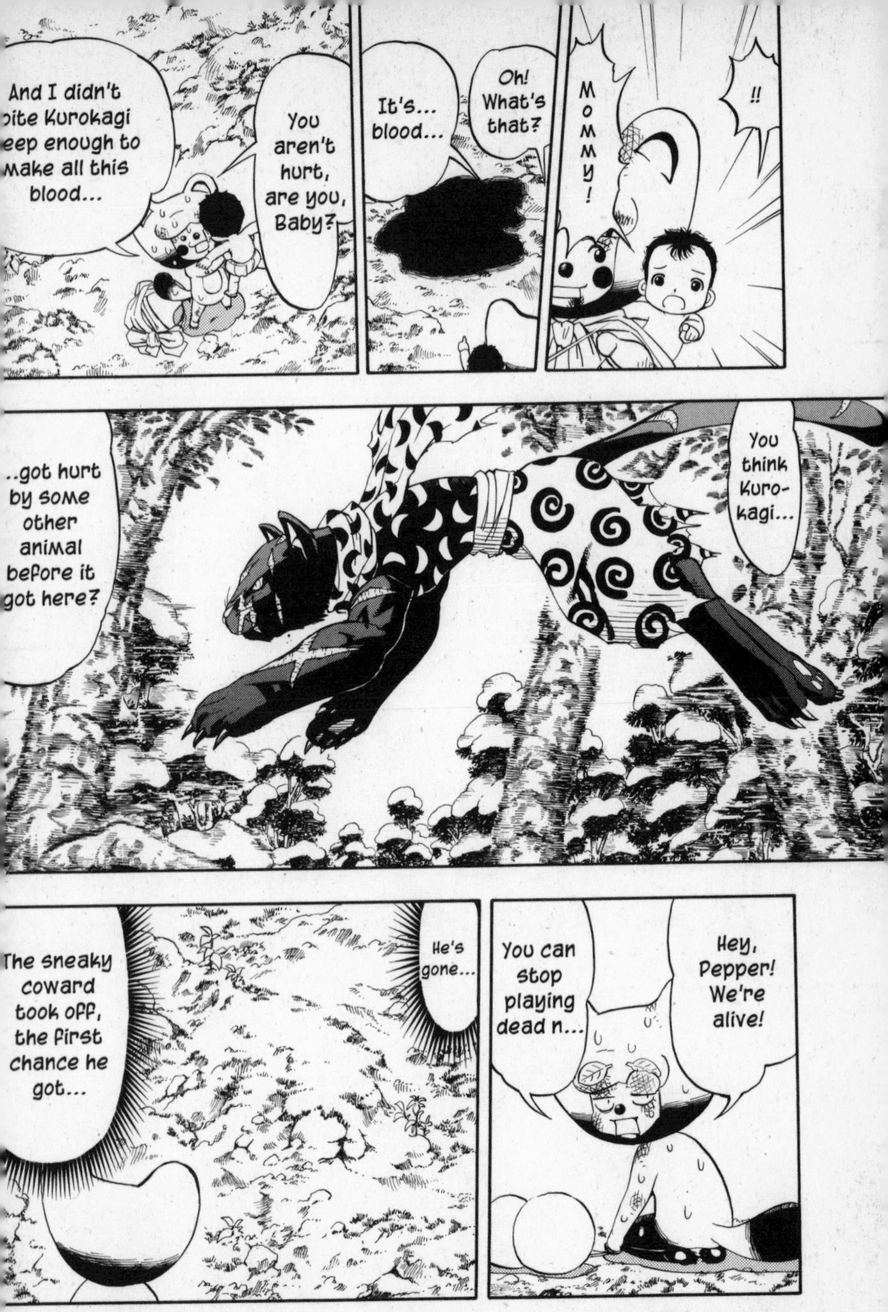
!!
MOMMY!
Oh! What's that?
It's... blood...
You aren't hurt, are you, Baby?
And I didn't oite Kurokagi eep enough to make all this blood...
You think Kuro-kagi...
..got hurt by some other animal before it got here?
Hey, Pepper! We're alive!
You can stop playing dead n...
He's gone...
The sneaky coward took off, the first chance he got...

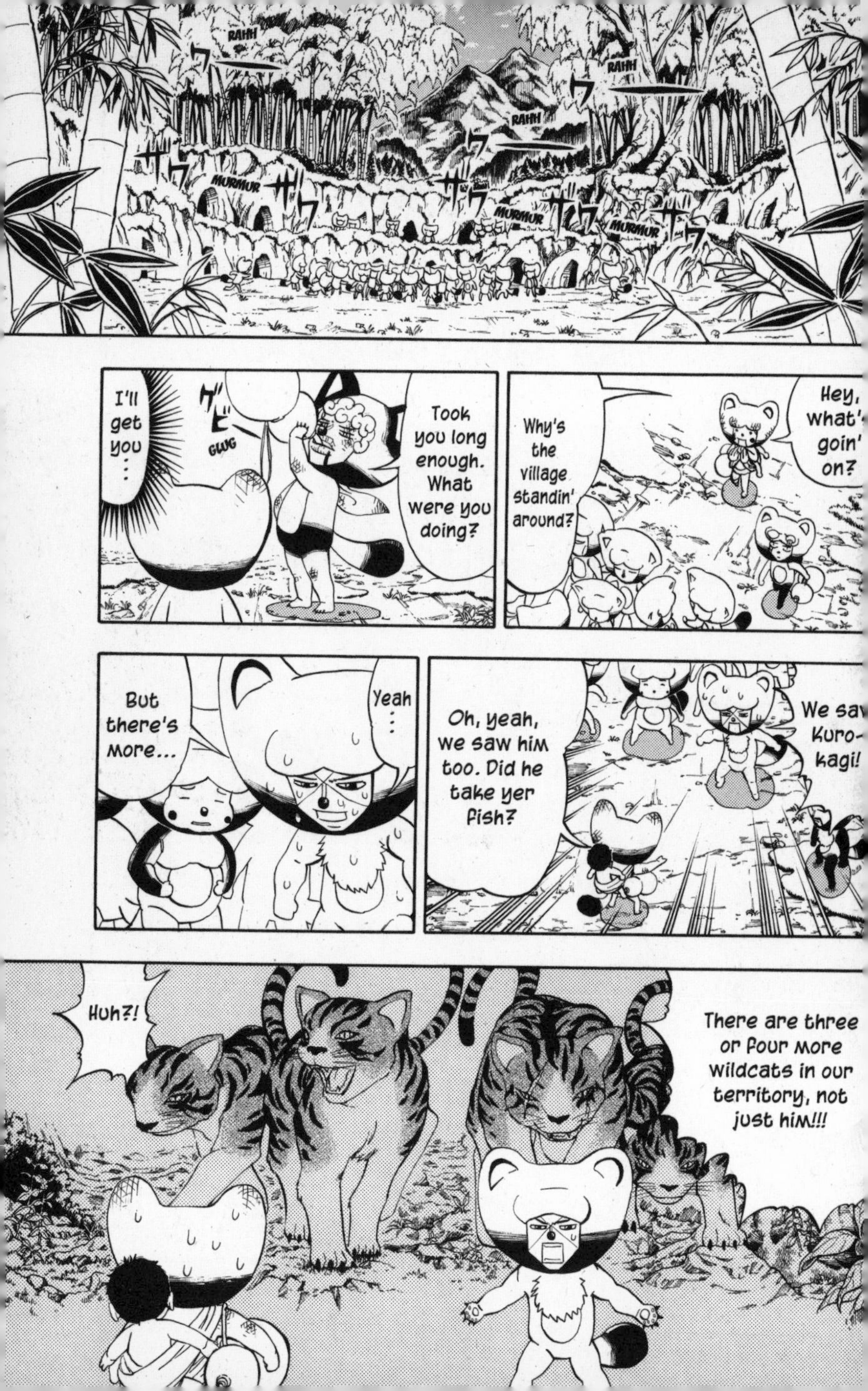
RAHH
RAHH
RAHH
MURMUR
MURMUR
MURMUR
Hey, what's goin' on?
Why's the village standin' around?
Took you long enough. What were you doing?
GUG
I'll get you...
We saw Kuro-kagi!
Oh, yeah, we saw him too. Did he take yer fish?
Yeah...
But there's more...
There are three or four more wildcats in our territory, not just him!!!
Huh?!

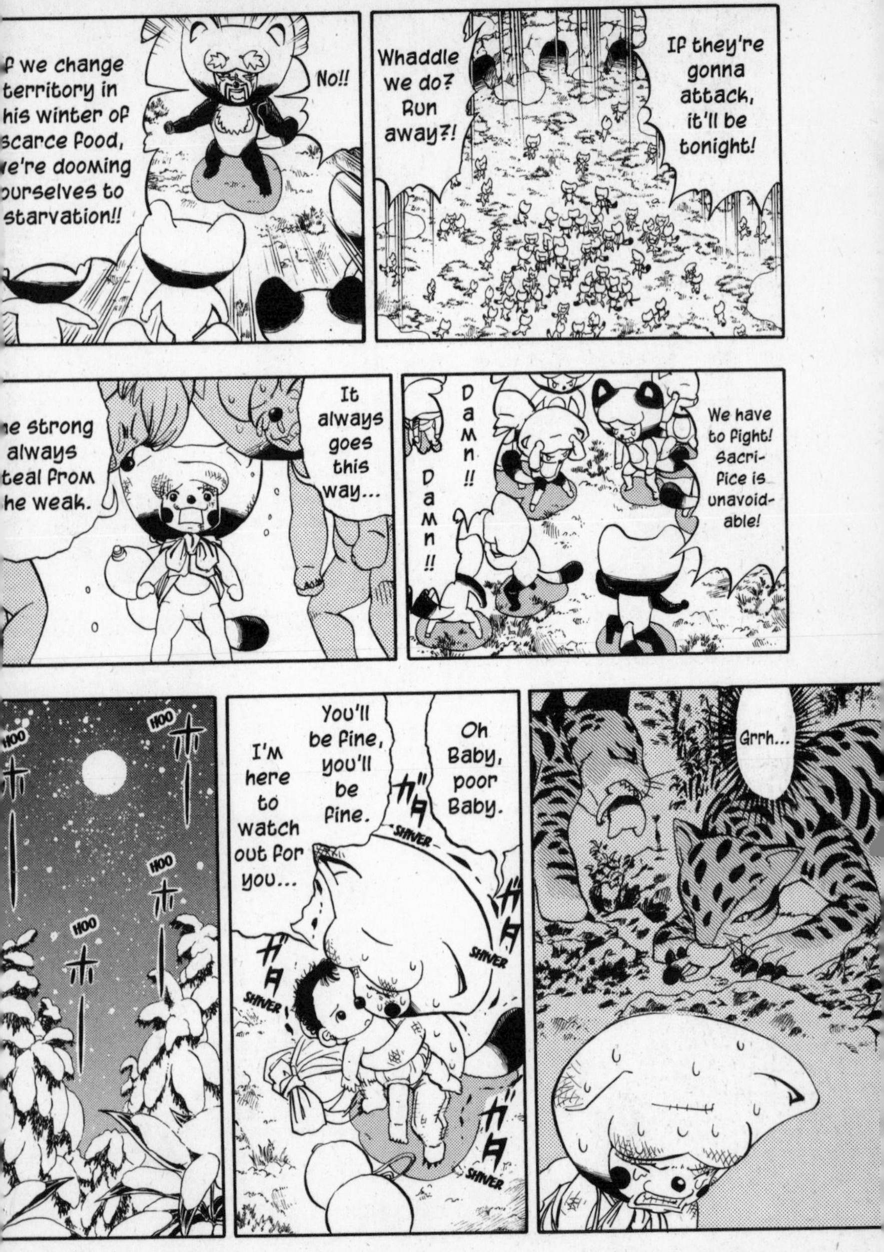
If they're gonna attack, it'll be tonight!
Whaddle we do? Run away?!
No!!
f we change territory in his winter of scarce food, e're dooming ourselves to starvation!!
We have to fight! Sacrifice is unavoidable!
Damn!!
Damn!!
It always goes this way...
e strong always teal from he weak.
Grrh...
Oh Baby, poor Baby.
ガタ
SHIVER
You'll be fine, you'll be fine.
I'm here to watch out for you...
ガタ
SHIVER
ガタ
SHIVER
ガタ
SHIVER
ホー
HOO
ホー
HOO
ホー
HOO
ホー
HOO

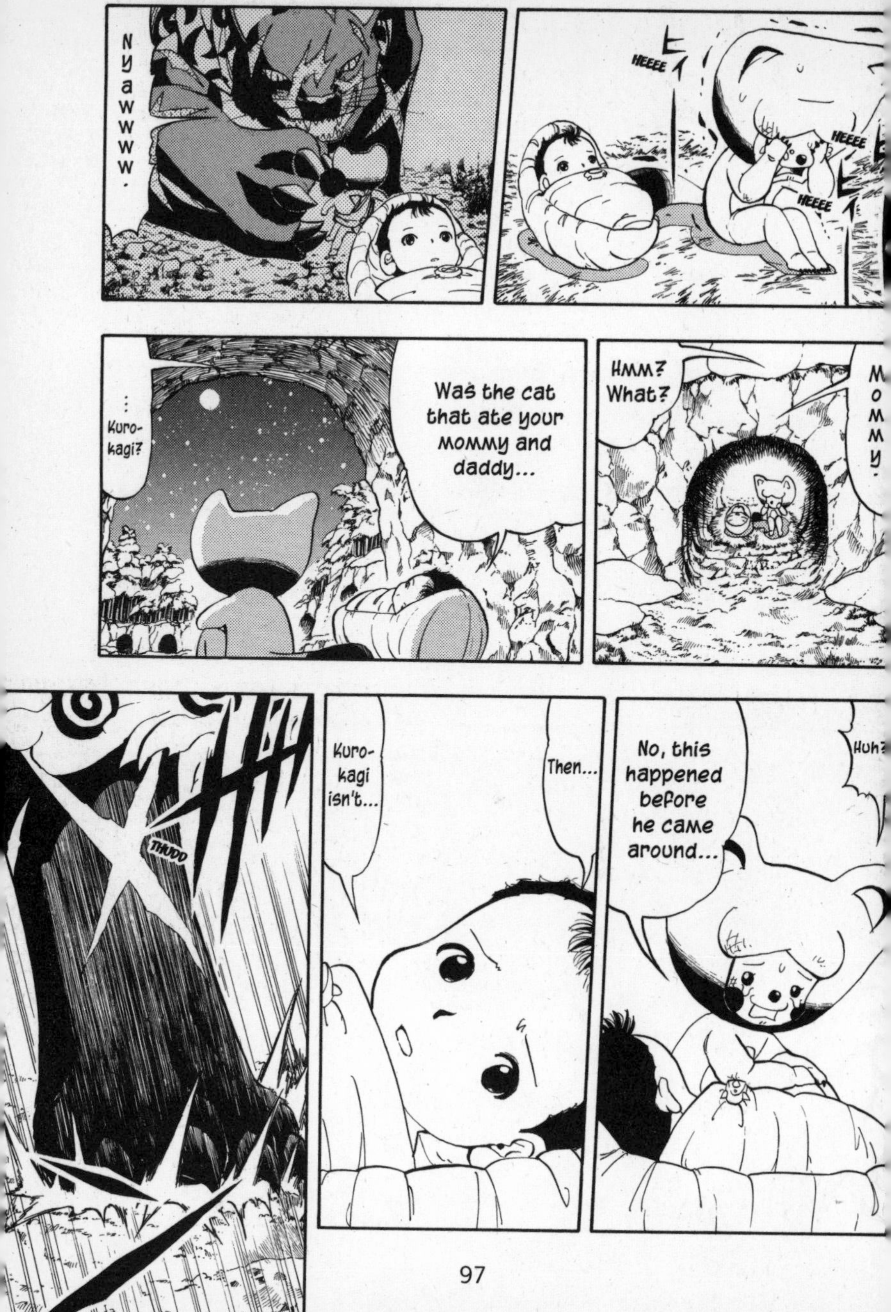
HEEEE
HEEEE
HEEEE
Nyawwww.
Mommy.
HMM? What?
Was the cat that ate your mommy and daddy...
...Kuro-kagi?
Huh?
No, this happened before he came around...
Then...
Kuro-kagi isn't...
THUDD

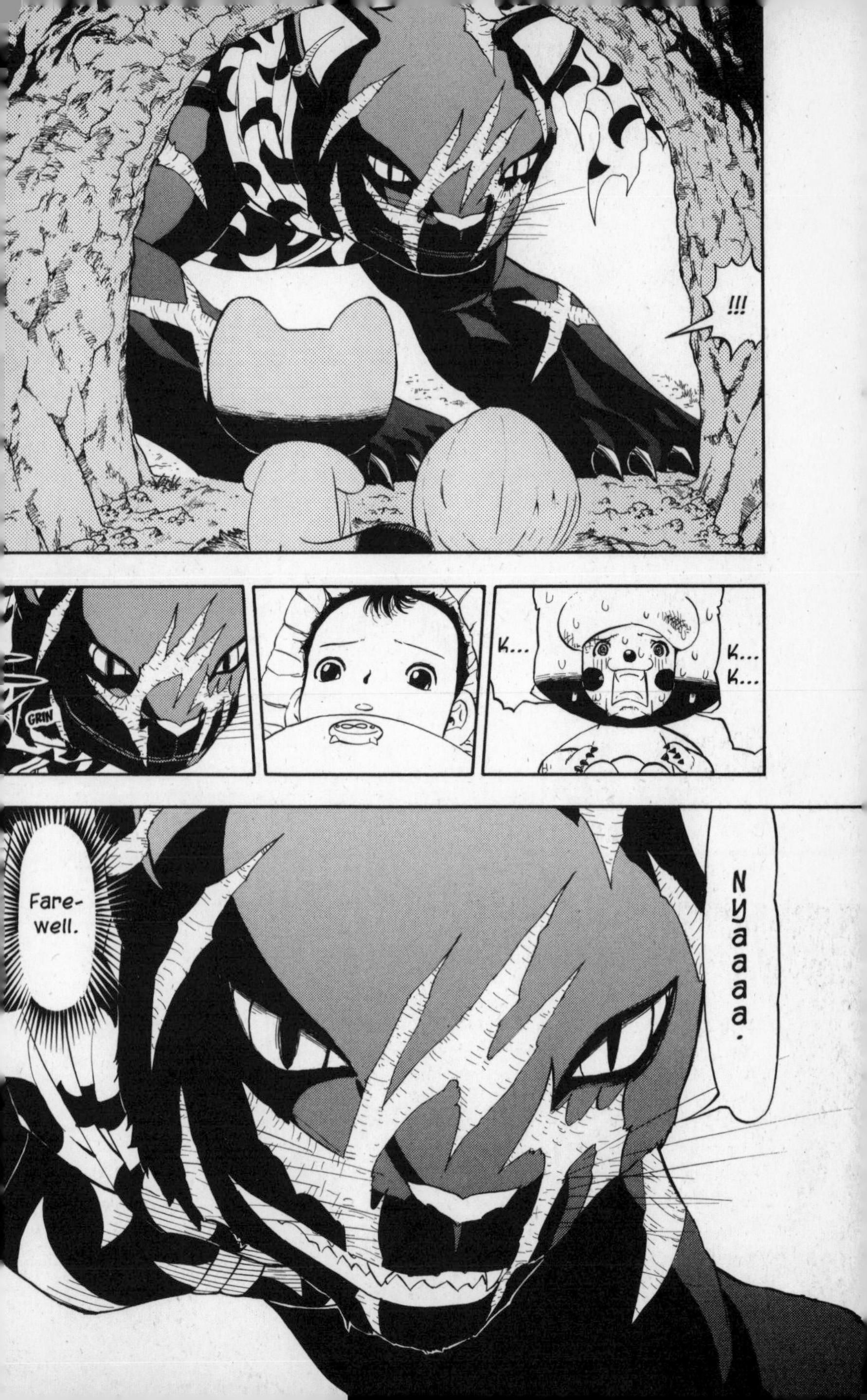
!!!
K...
K...
K...
GRIN
Nyaaaa.
Fare-well.

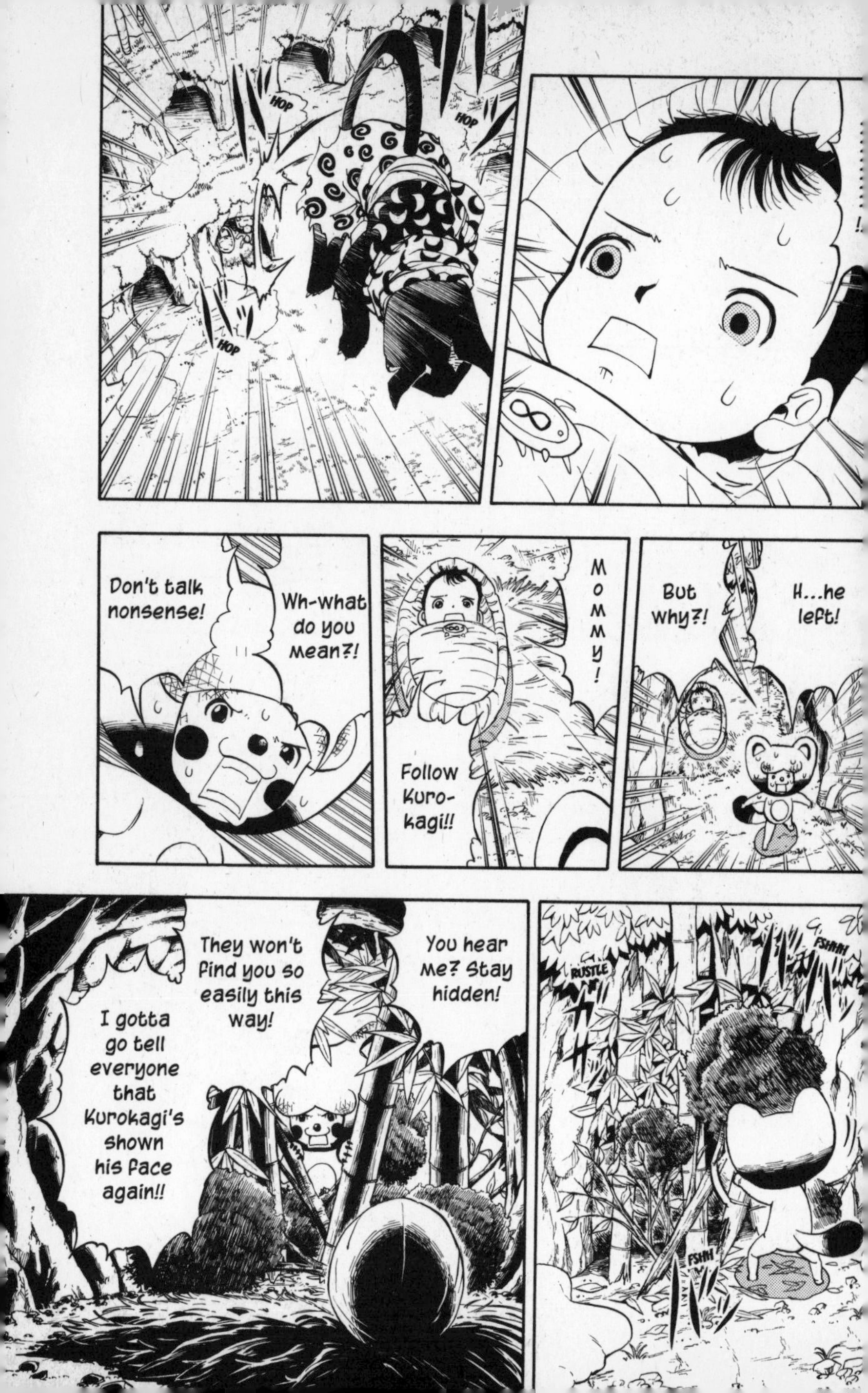
!
HOP
HOP
HOP
H...he left!
But why?!
Mommy!
Follow Kuro-kagi!!
Wh-what do you mean?!
Don't talk nonsense!
FSHHH
RUSTLE
FSHH
You hear me? Stay hidden!
They won't find you so easily this way!
I gotta go tell everyone that Kurokagi's shown his face again!!

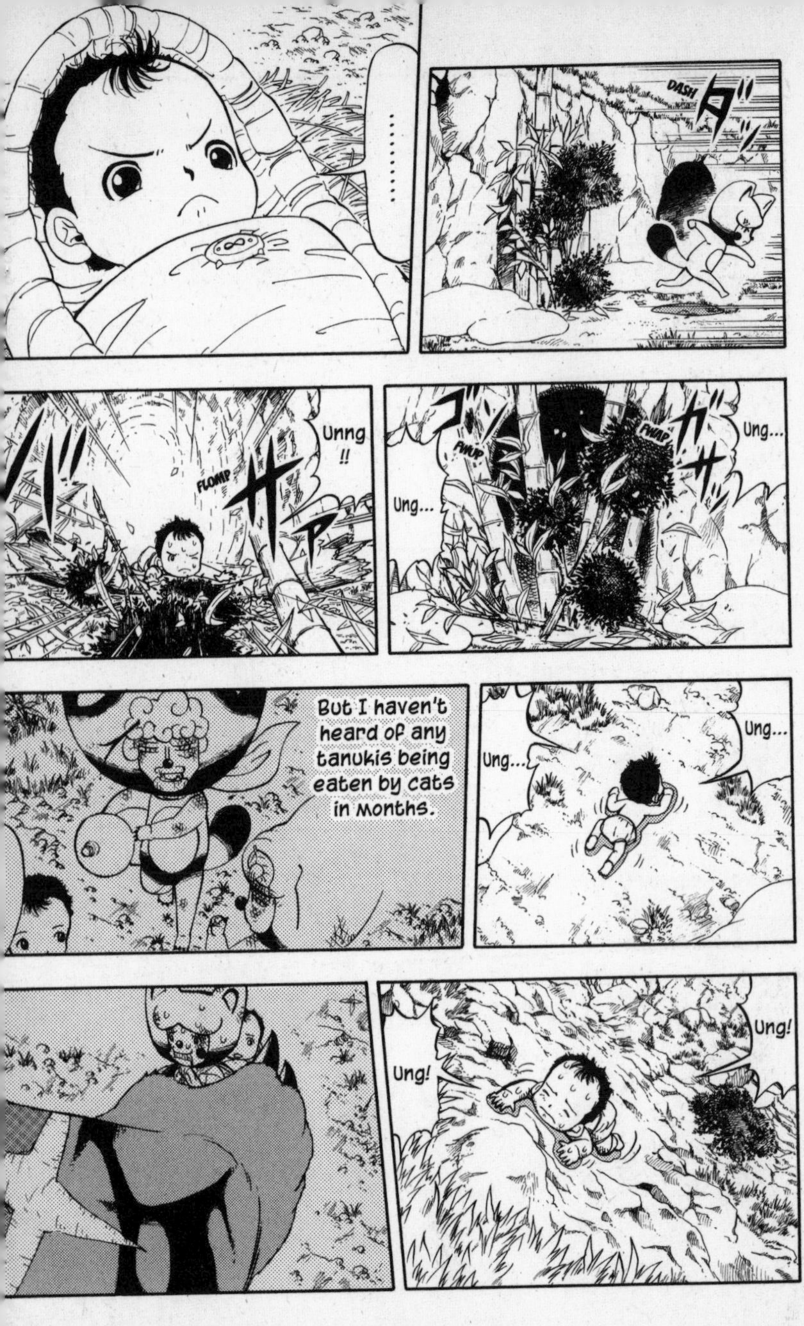
DASH
......
Ung...
FWAP
FWUP
Ung...
Unng !!
FLOMP
Ung...
Ung...
But I haven't heard of any tanukis being eaten by cats in months.
Ung!
Ung!

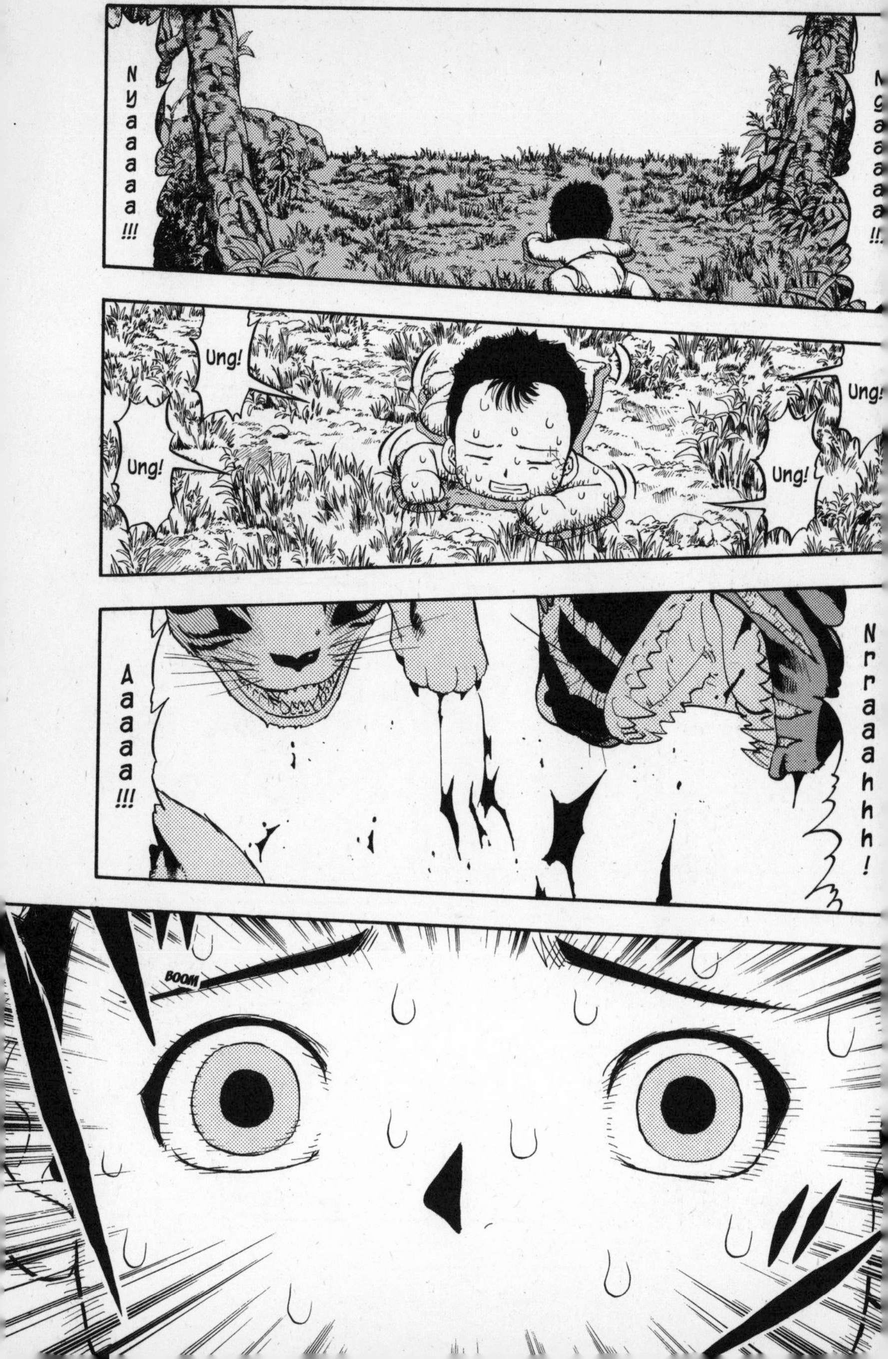
Ngaaaaaa!!
Nyaaaaa!!!
Ung!
Ung!
Ung!
Ung!
Nrraaahhh!
Aaaaa!!!
BOOM

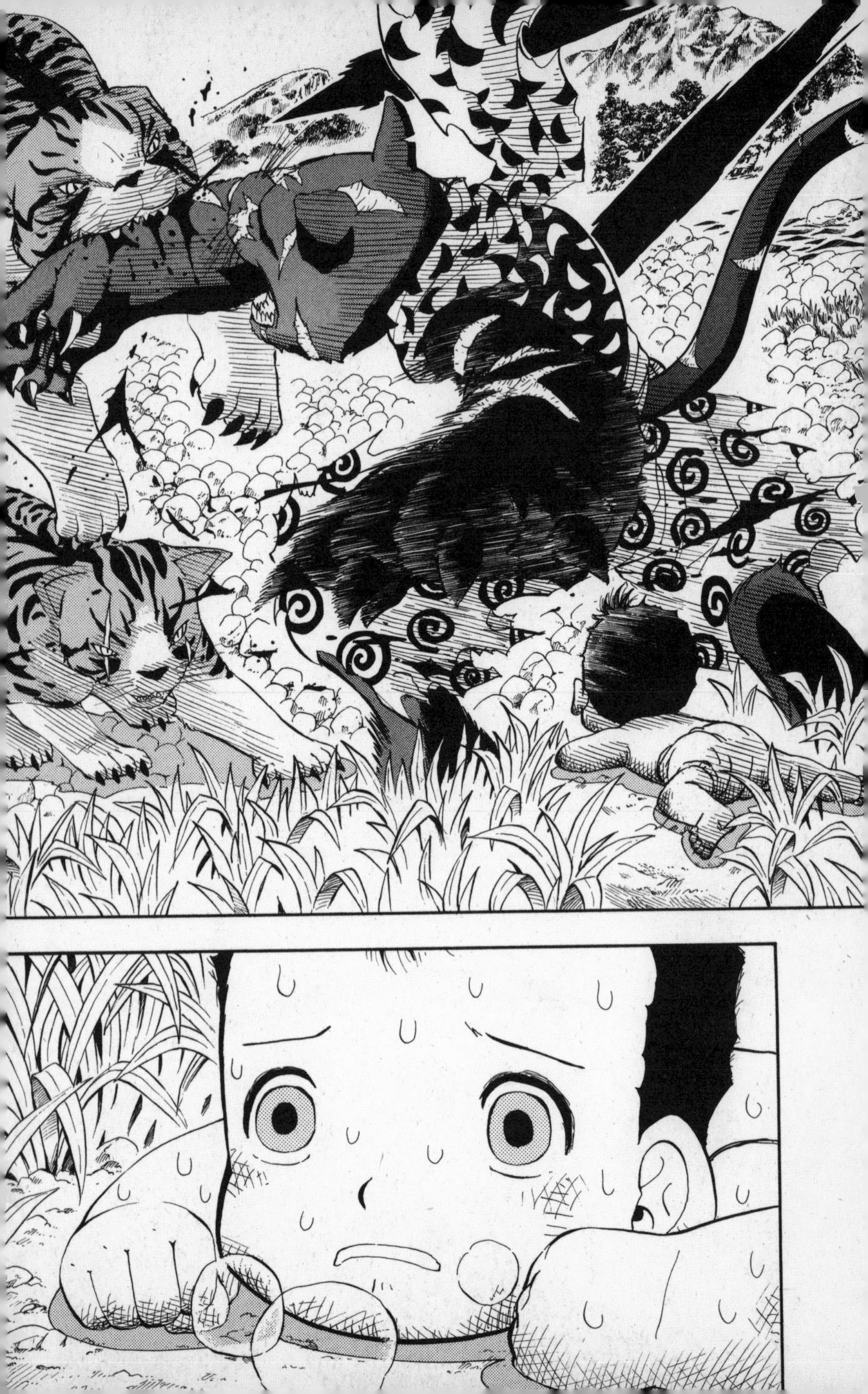

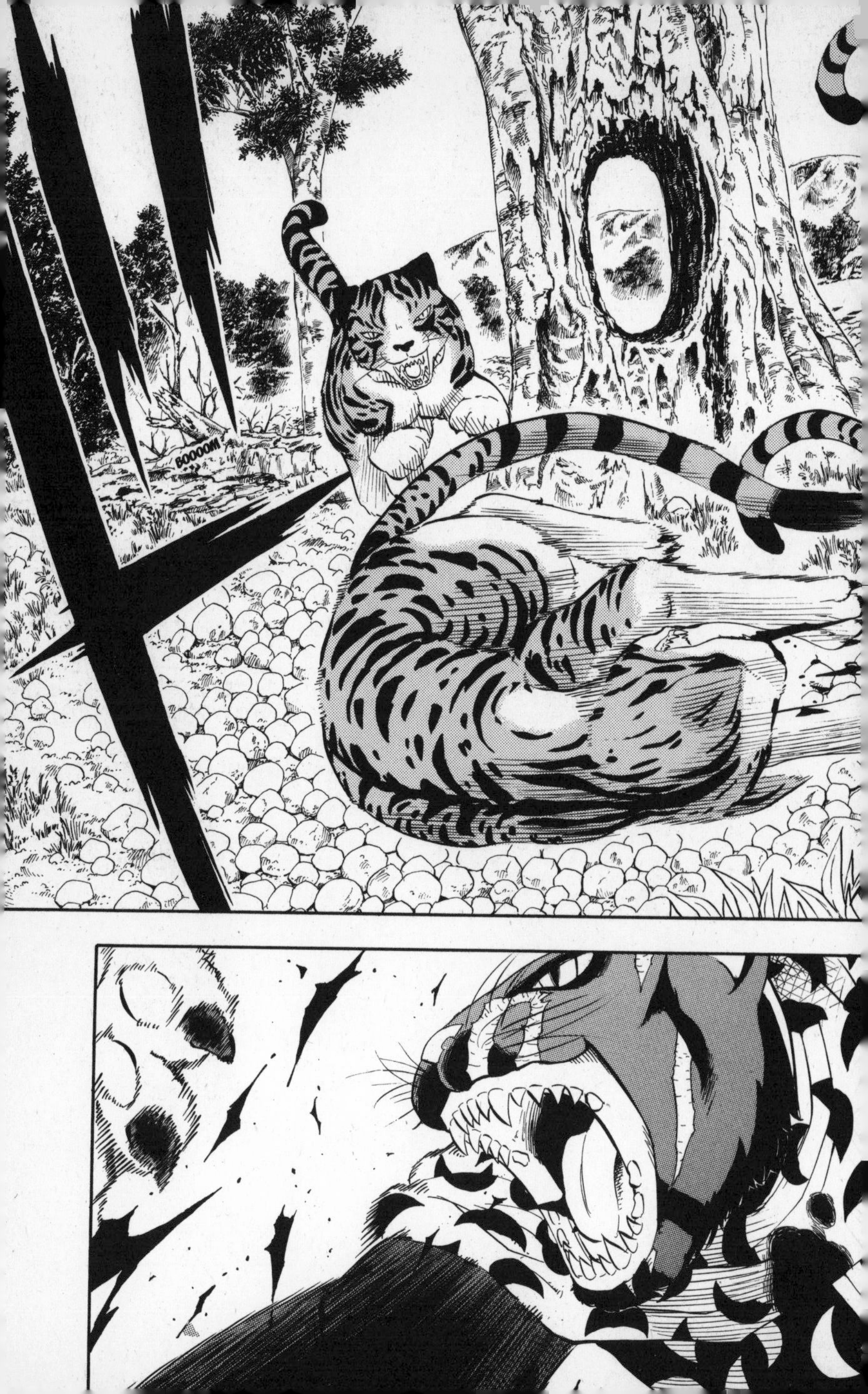
BOOOOM

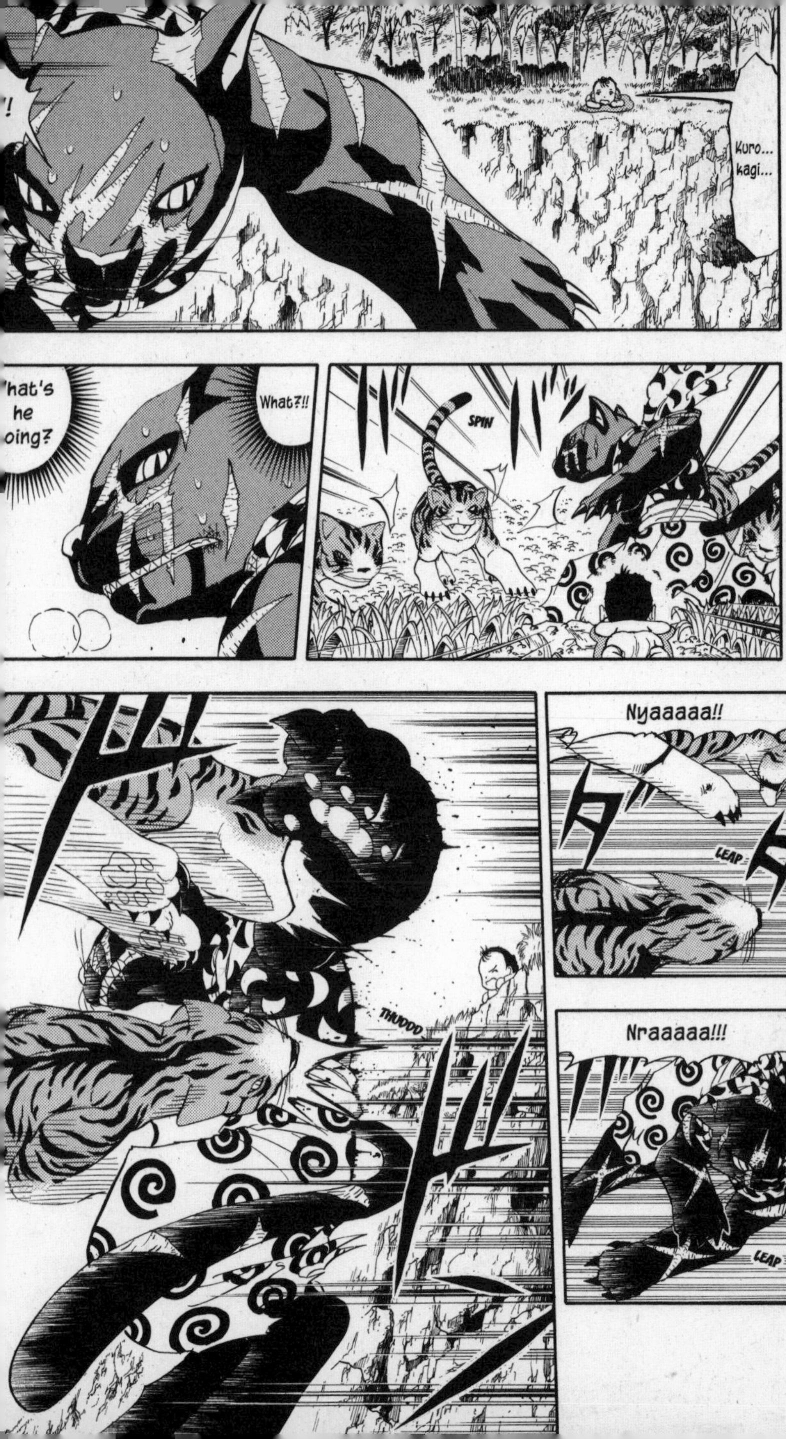
Kuro... kagi...
SPIN
What?!!
hat's he oing?
Nyaaaaa!!
LEAP
Nraaaaa!!!
LEAP
THUDD

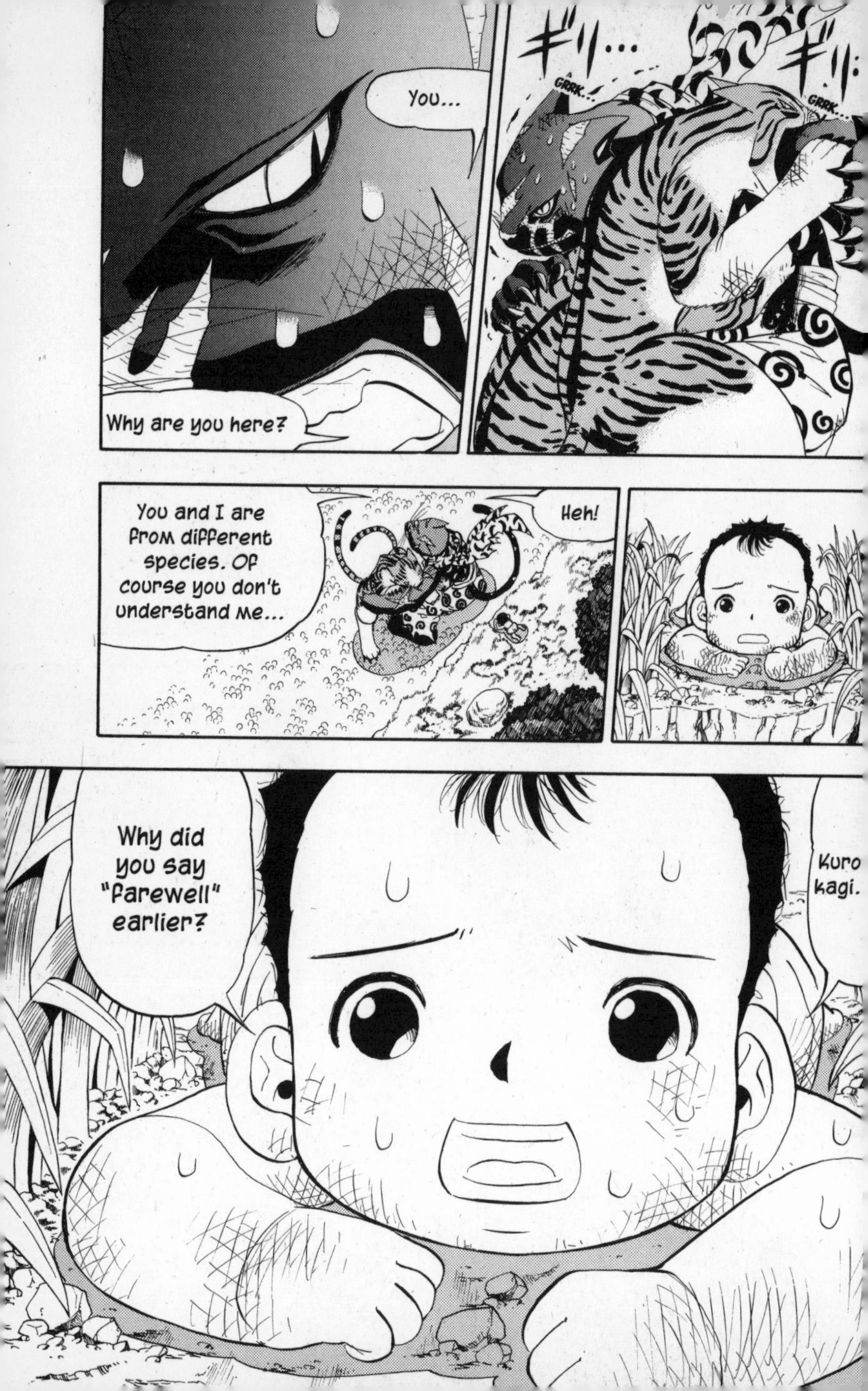
ギリ!!
GRRK...
ギリ…
GRRK...
You...
Why are you here?
Heh!
You and I are from different species. Of course you don't understand me...
Kuro kagi.
Why did you say "farewell" earlier?

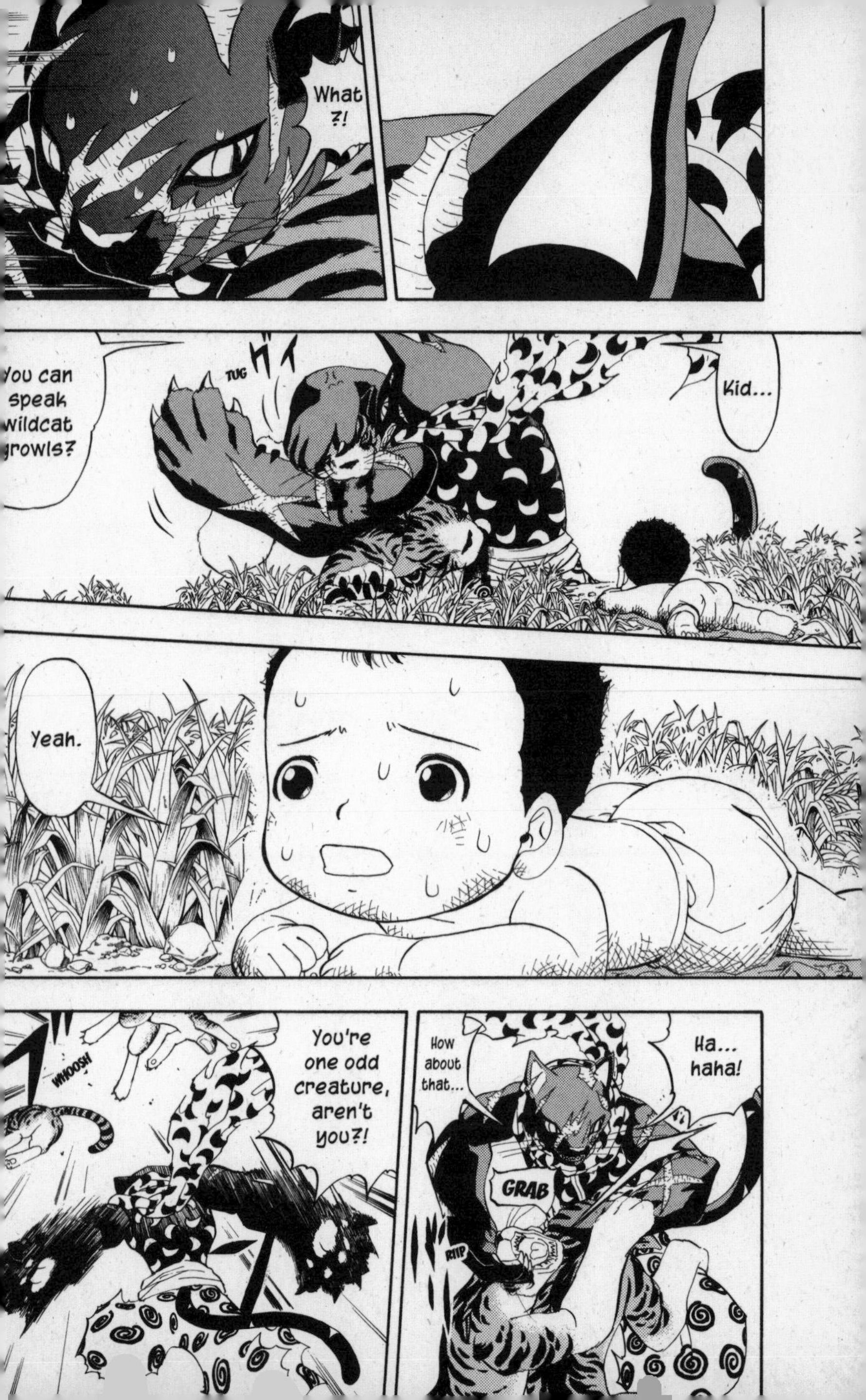
What?!
Kid...
TUG
You can speak wildcat growls?
Yeah.
Ha... haha!
How about that...
GRAB
RIP
You're one odd creature, aren't you?!
WHOOSH

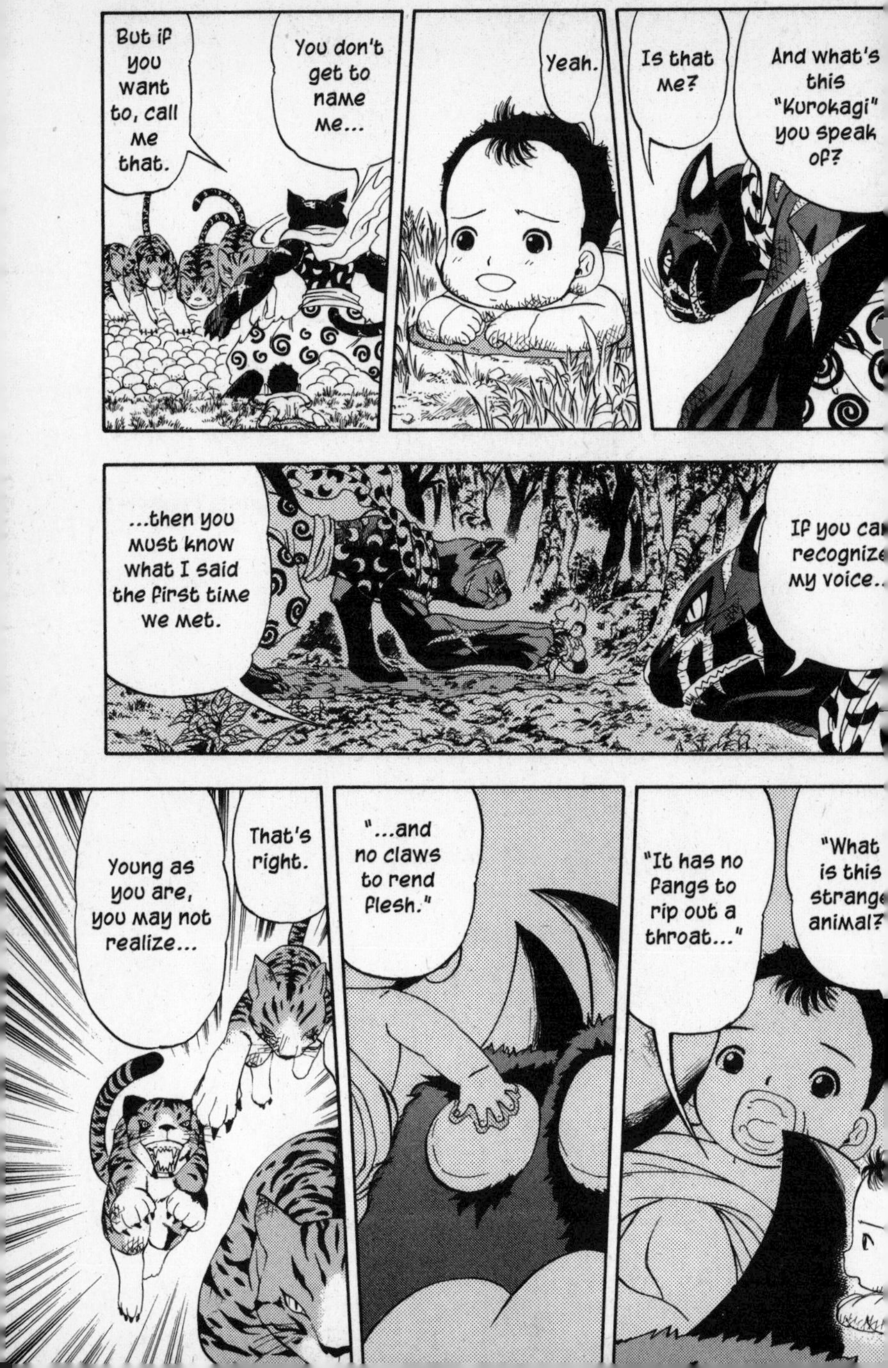
And what's this "Kurokagi" you speak of?
Is that me?
Yeah.
You don't get to name me...
But if you want to, call me that.
If you can recognize my voice...
...then you must know what I said the first time we met.
"What is this strange animal?
"It has no fangs to rip out a throat..."
"...and no claws to rend flesh."
That's right.
Young as you are, you may not realize...

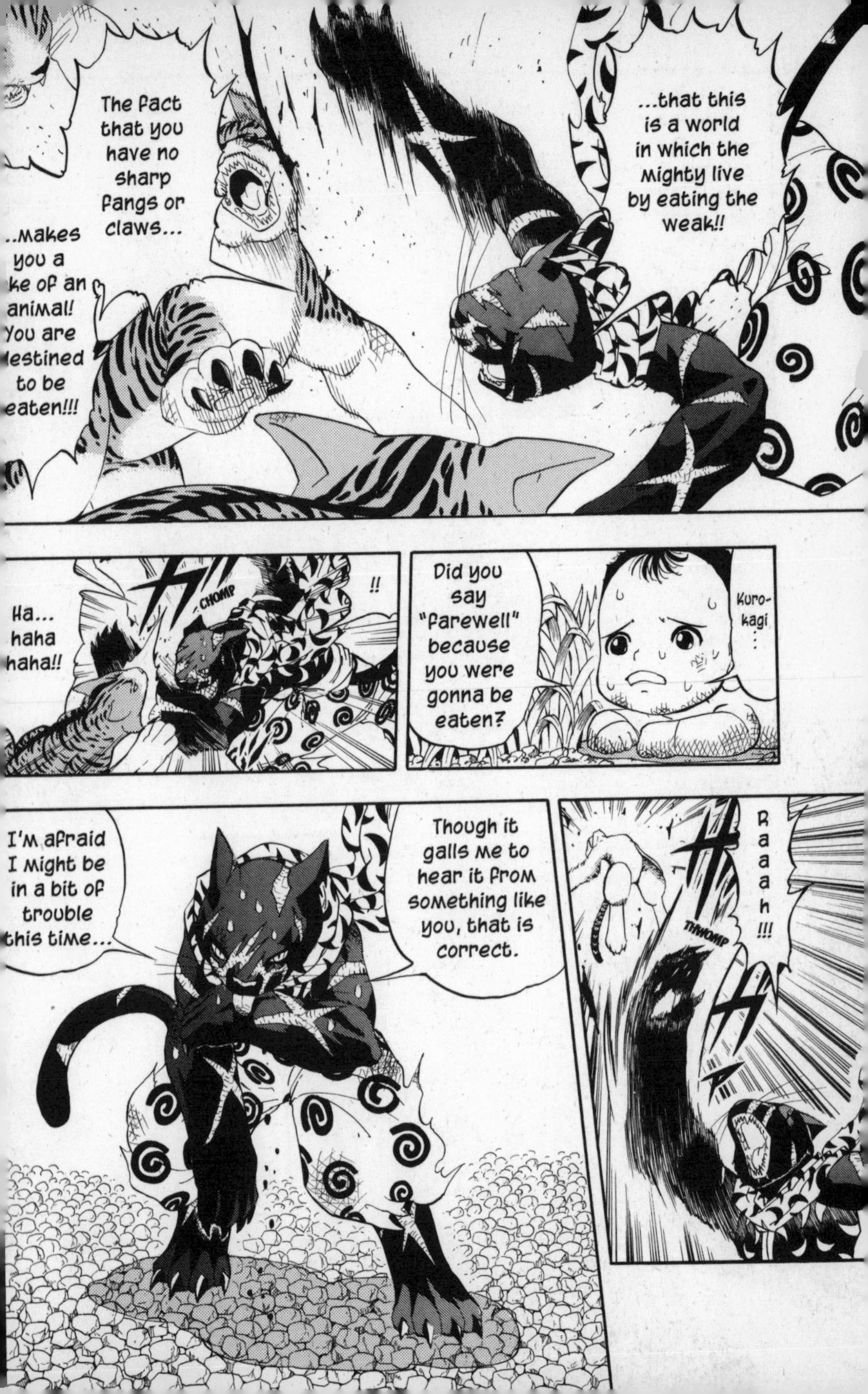
...that this is a world in which the mighty live by eating the weak!!
The fact that you have no sharp fangs or claws...
..makes you a ke of an animal! You are estined to be eaten!!!
Kuro-kagi...
Did you say "farewell" because you were gonna be eaten?
!!
CHOMP
Ha... haha haha!!
Raaah!!!
THWOMP
Though it galls me to hear it from something like you, that is correct.
I'm afraid I might be in a bit of trouble this time...

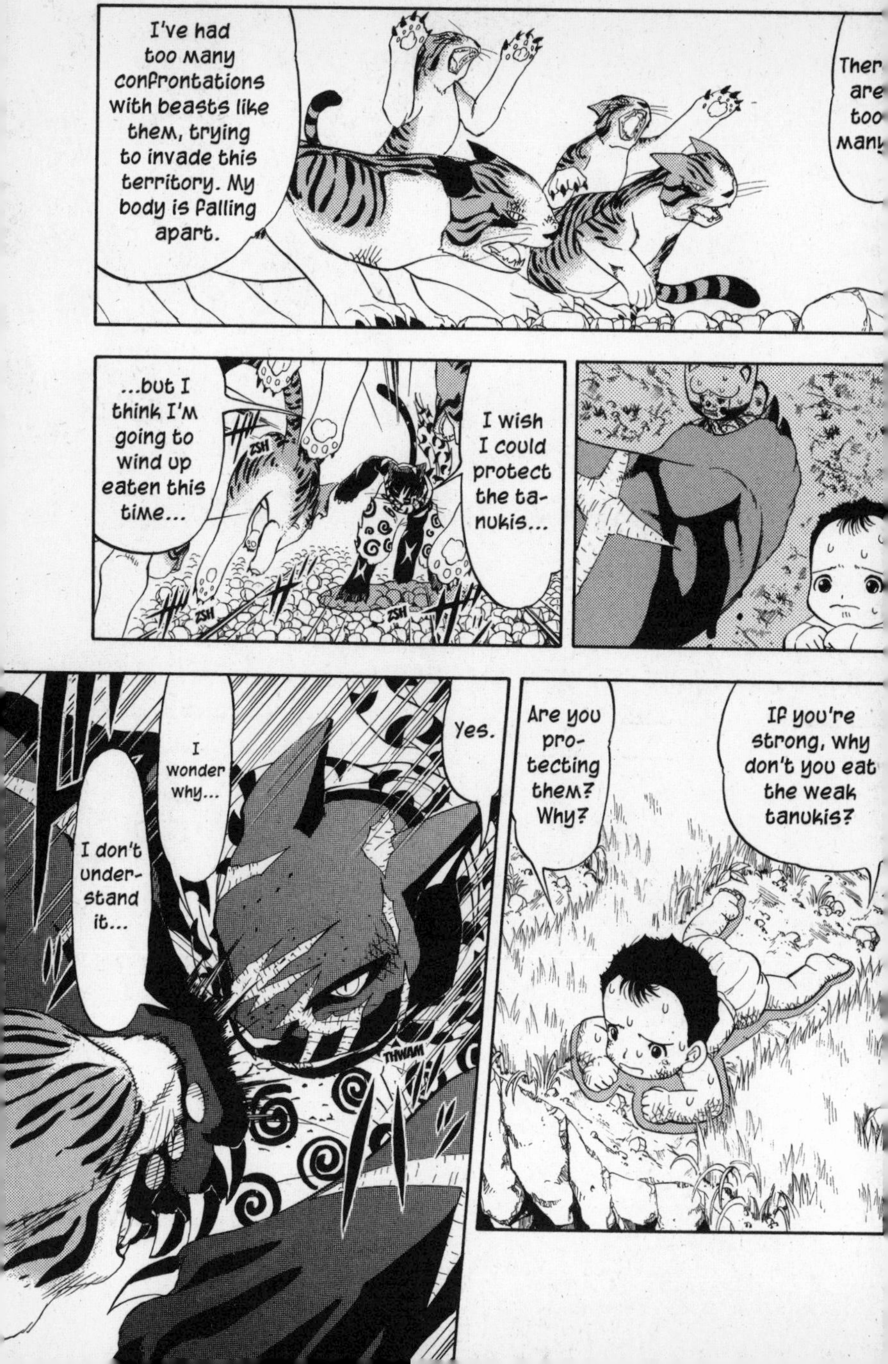
Ther are too many
I've had too many confrontations with beasts like them, trying to invade this territory. My body is falling apart.
I wish I could protect the tanukis...
...but I think I'm going to wind up eaten this time...
ZSH
ZSH
ZSH
If you're strong, why don't you eat the weak tanukis?
Are you protecting them? Why?
Yes.
I wonder why...
I don't understand it...
THWAM

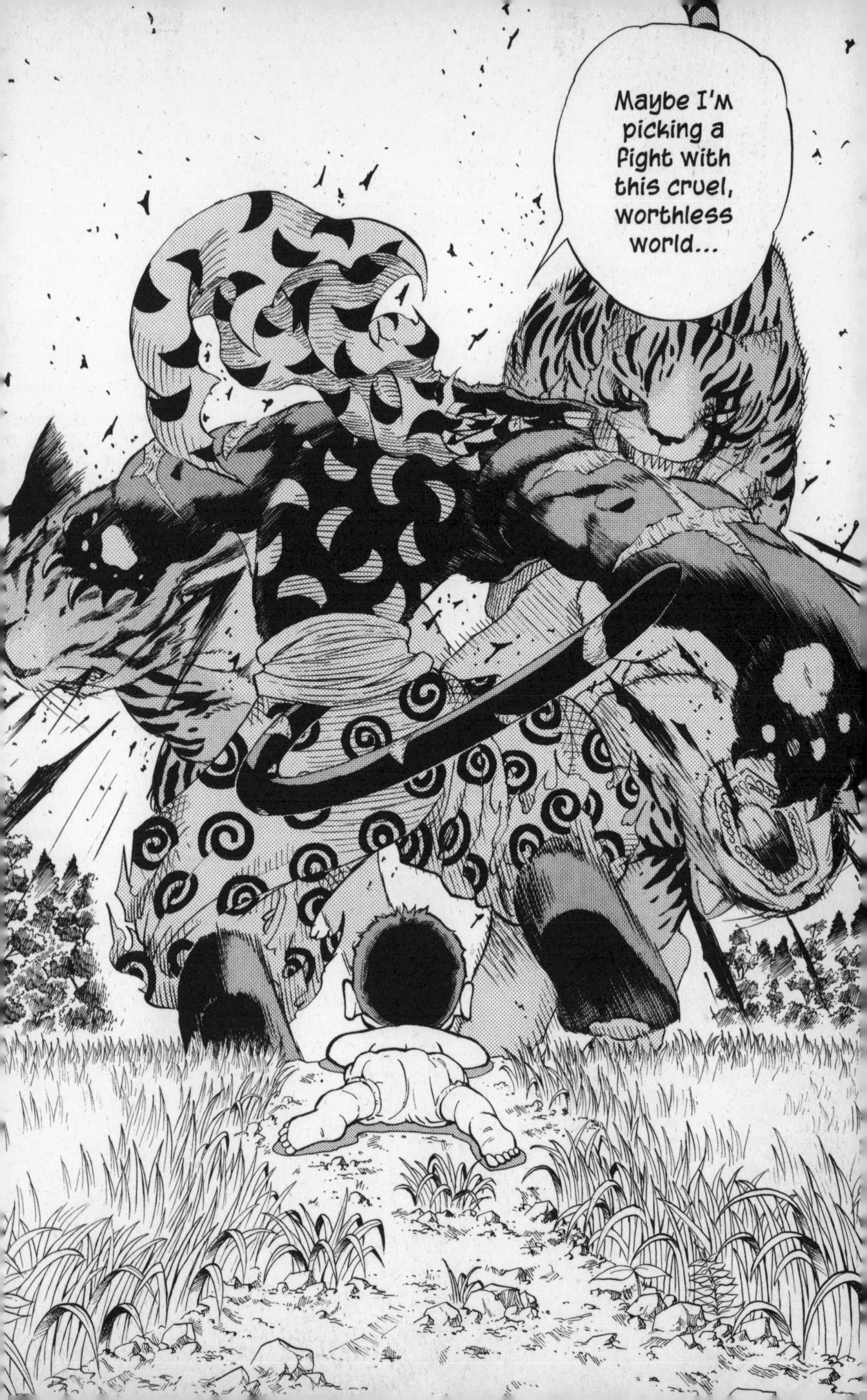
Maybe I'm picking a fight with this cruel, worthless world...

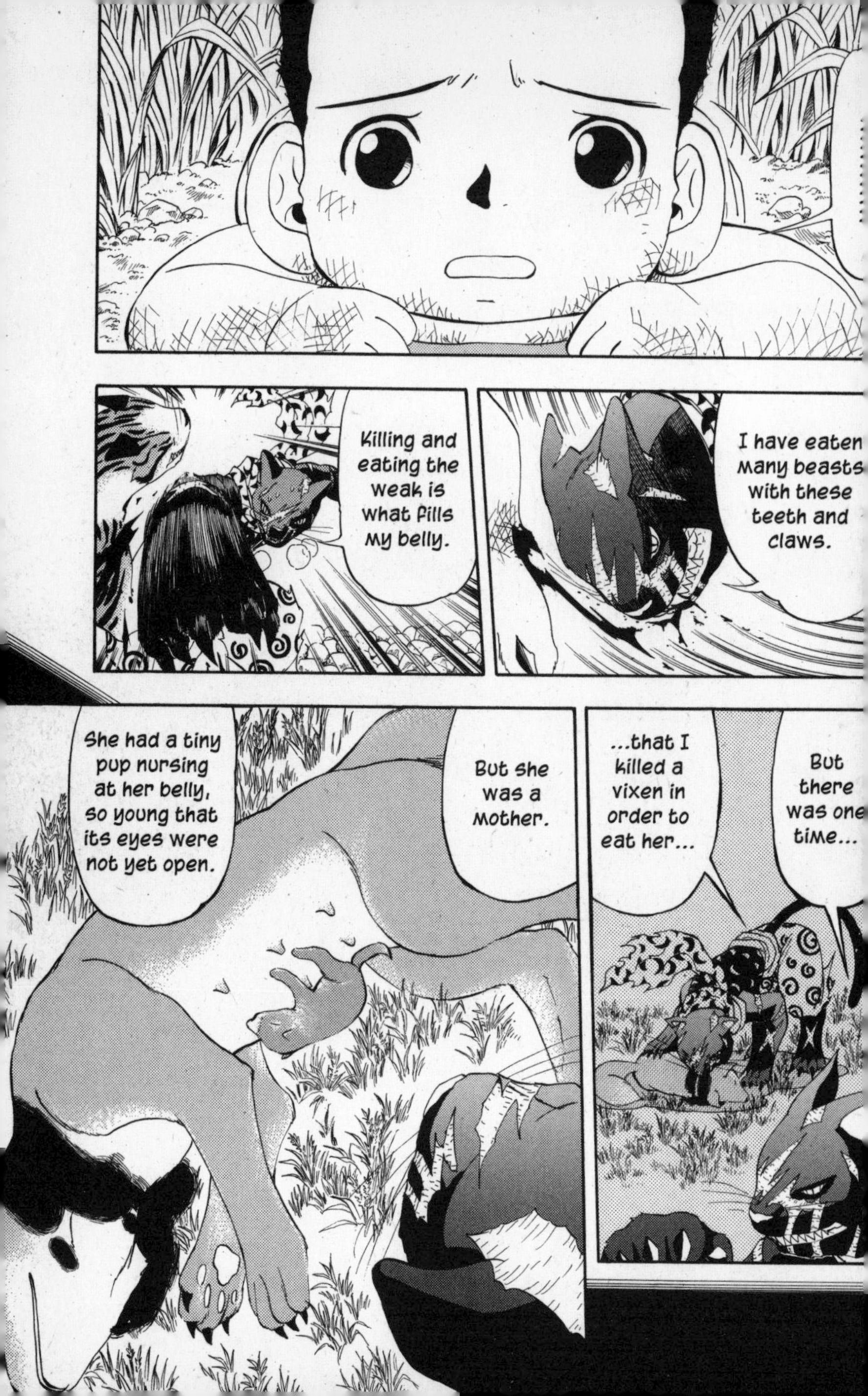
I have eaten many beasts with these teeth and claws.
Killing and eating the weak is what fills my belly.
But there was one time...
...that I killed a vixen in order to eat her...
But she was a mother.
She had a tiny pup nursing at her belly, so young that its eyes were not yet open.

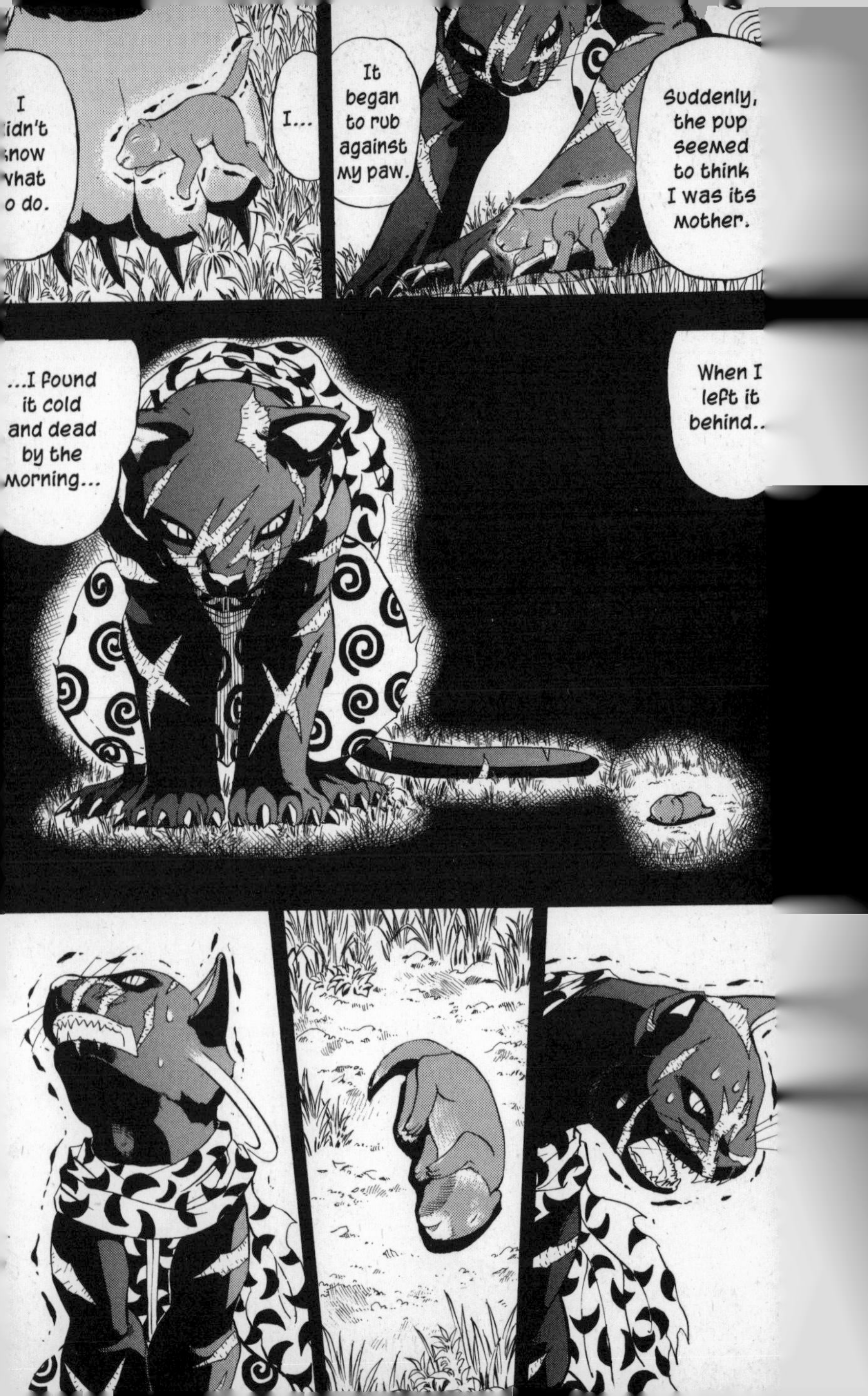
Suddenly, the pup seemed to think I was its mother.
It began to rub against my paw.
I...
I idn't now vhat o do.
When I left it behind...
...I found it cold and dead by the morning...

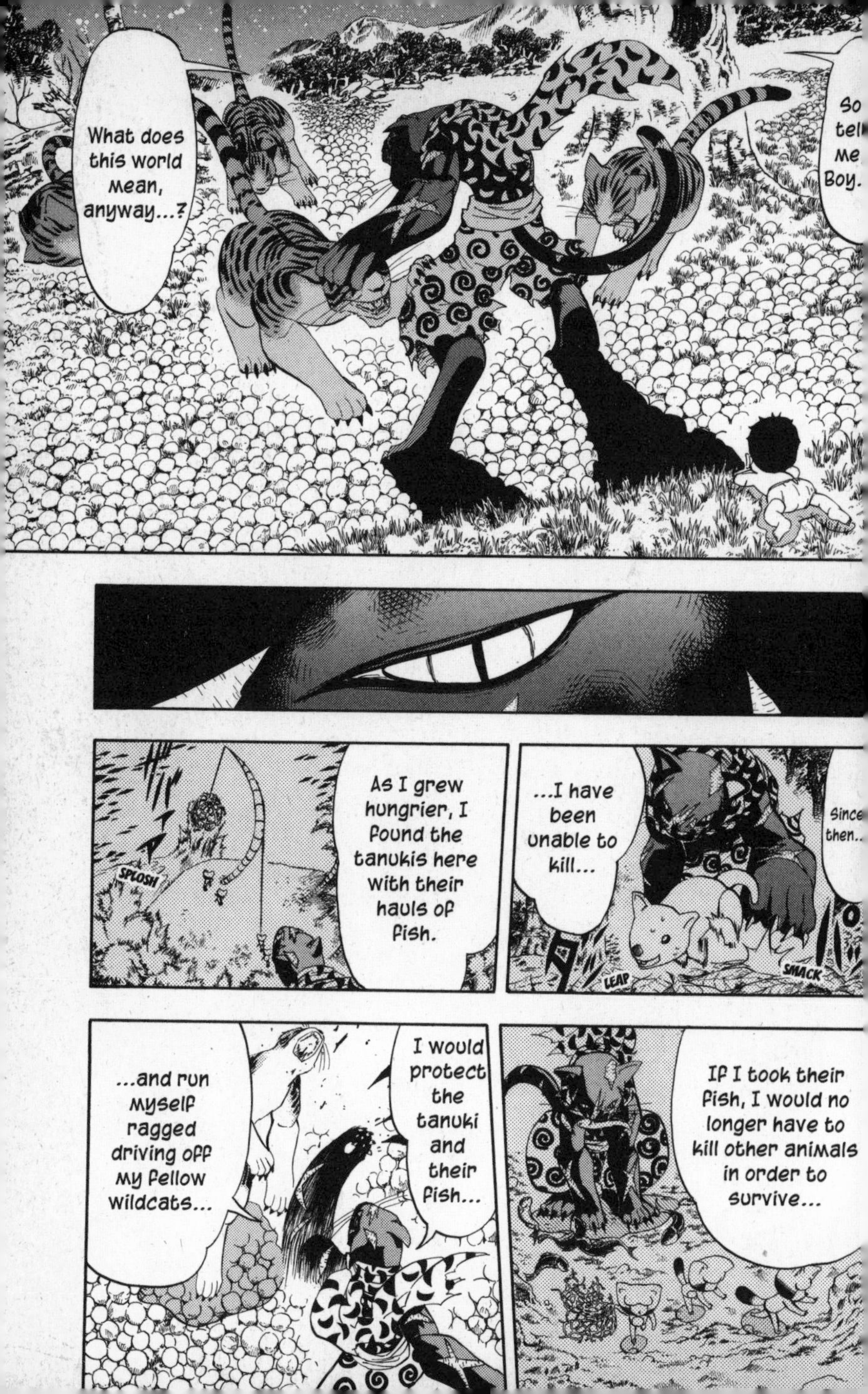
So tel me Boy.
What does this world mean, anyway...?
Since then...
...I have been unable to kill...
SMACK
LEAP
As I grew hungrier, I found the tanukis here with their hauls of fish.
SPLOSH
If I took their fish, I would no longer have to kill other animals in order to survive...
I would protect the tanuki and their fish...
...and run myself ragged driving off my fellow wildcats...

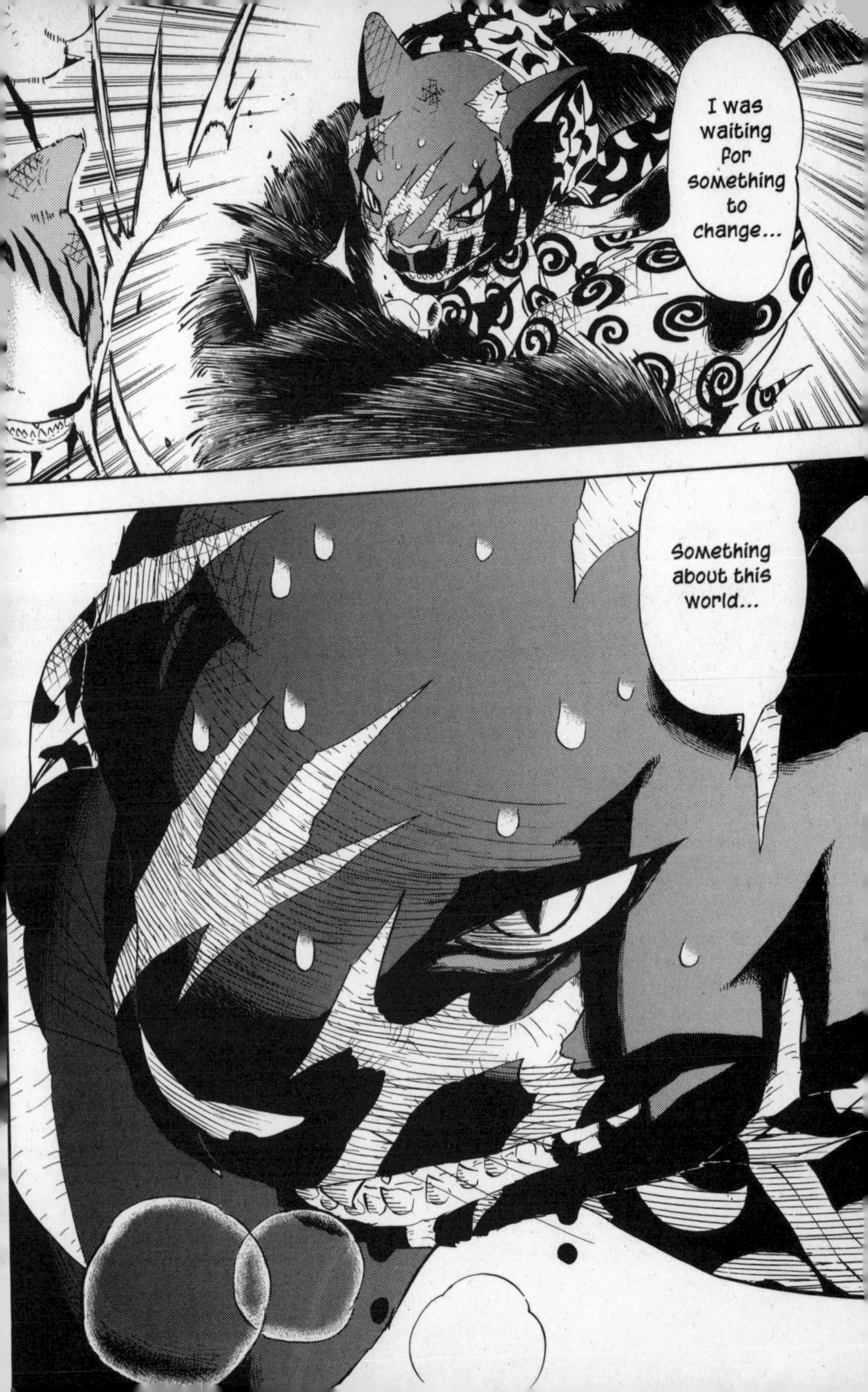
I was waiting for something to change...
Something about this world...

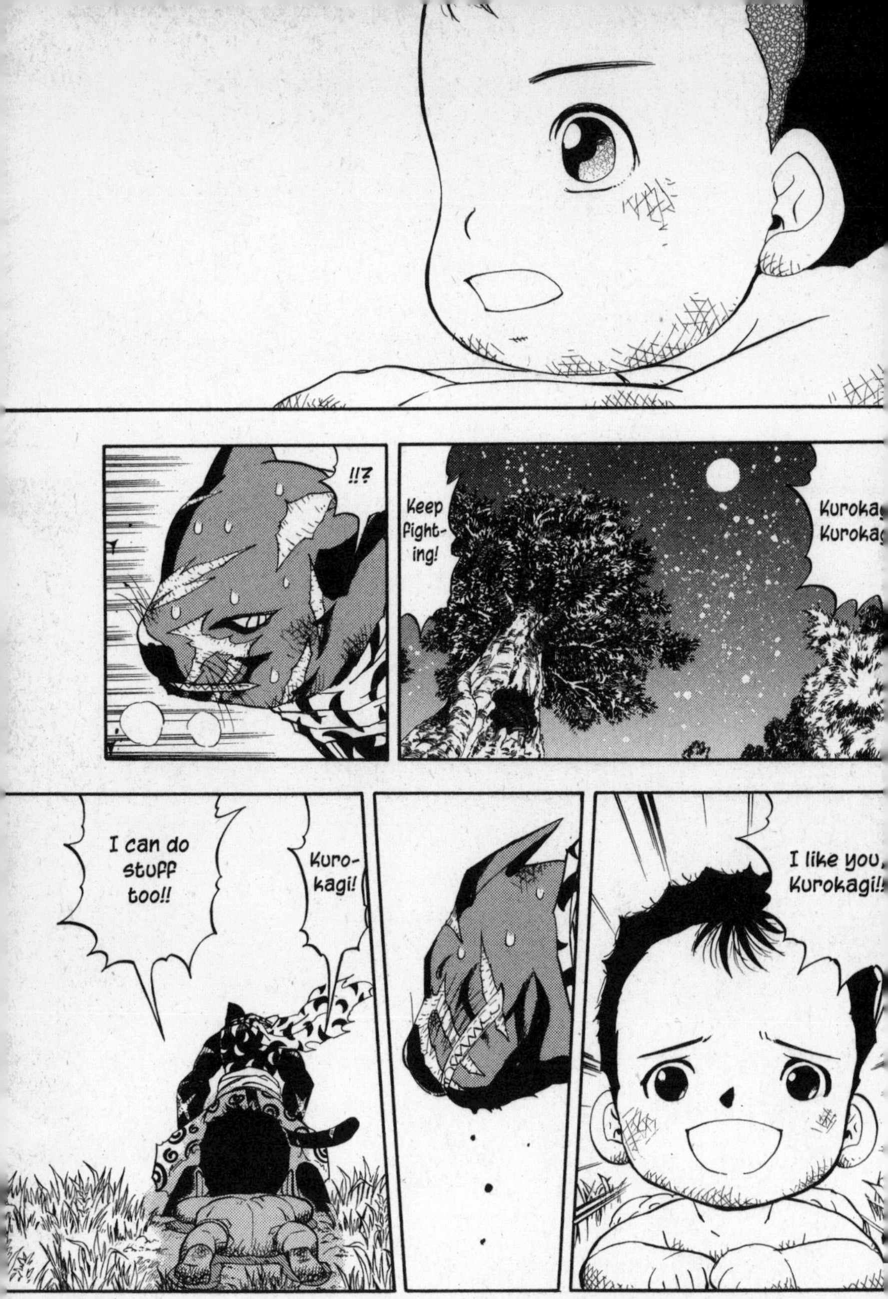
Kurokag
Kurokag
Keep fight-ing!
!!?
I like you, Kurokagi!!
Kuro-kagi!
I can do stuff too!!

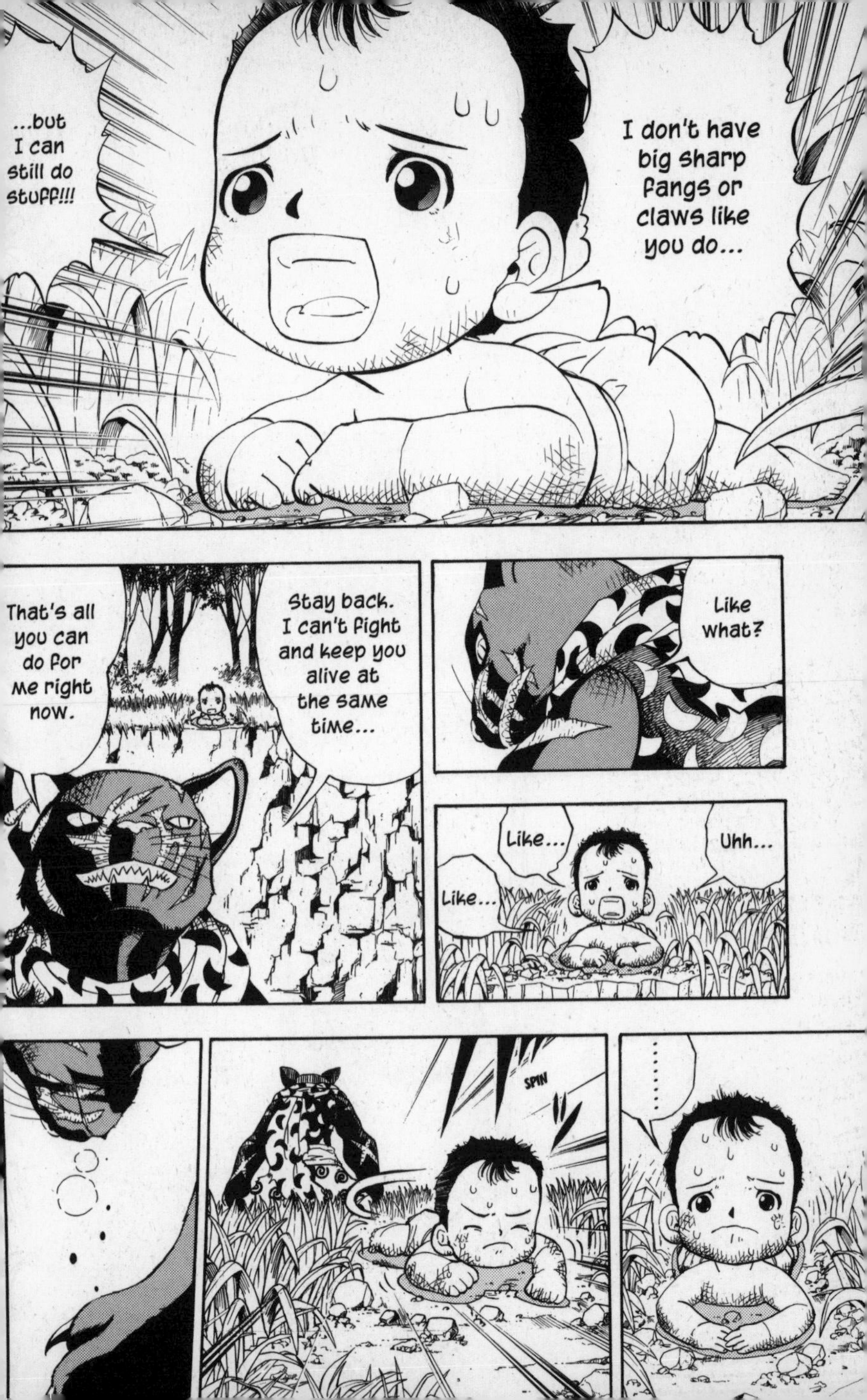
I don't have big sharp fangs or claws like you do...
...but I can still do stuff!!!
Like what?
Uhh...
Like...
Like...
Stay back. I can't fight and keep you alive at the same time...
That's all you can do for me right now.
......
SPIN

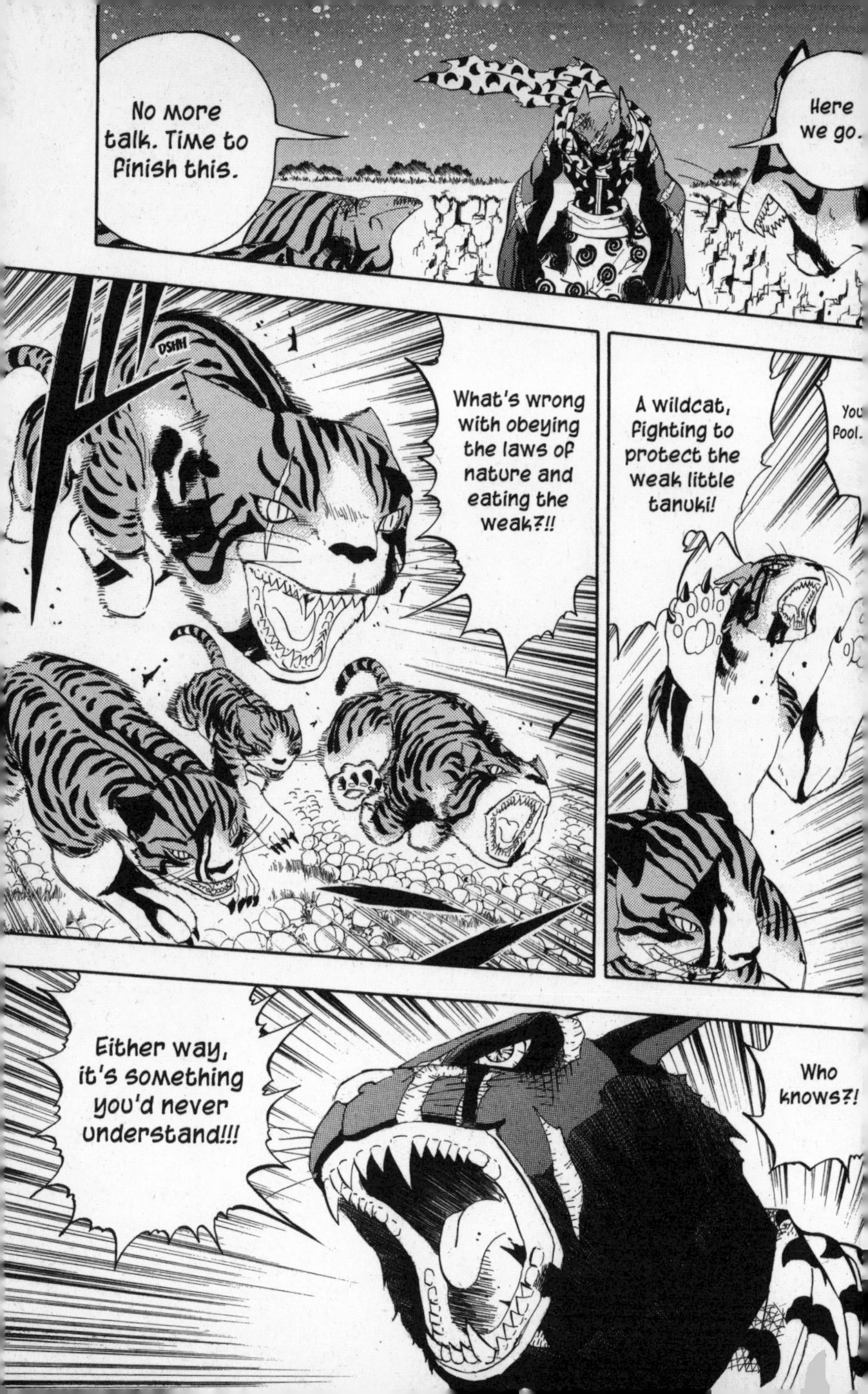
Here we go.
No more talk. Time to finish this.
You fool.
A wildcat, fighting to protect the weak little tanuki!
What's wrong with obeying the laws of nature and eating the weak?!!
DSHH
Who knows?!
Either way, it's something you'd never understand!!!

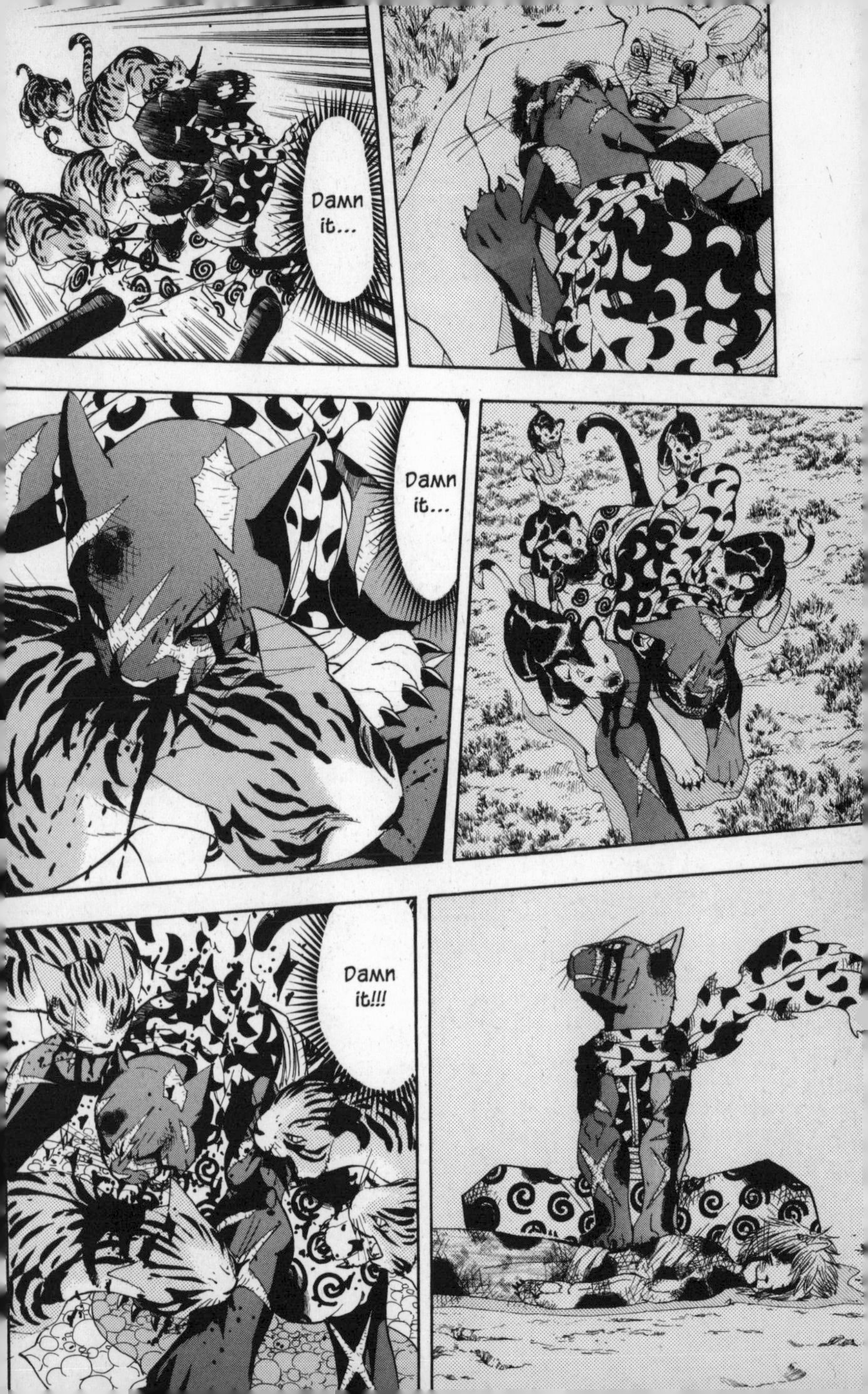
Damn it...
Damn it...
Damn it!!!

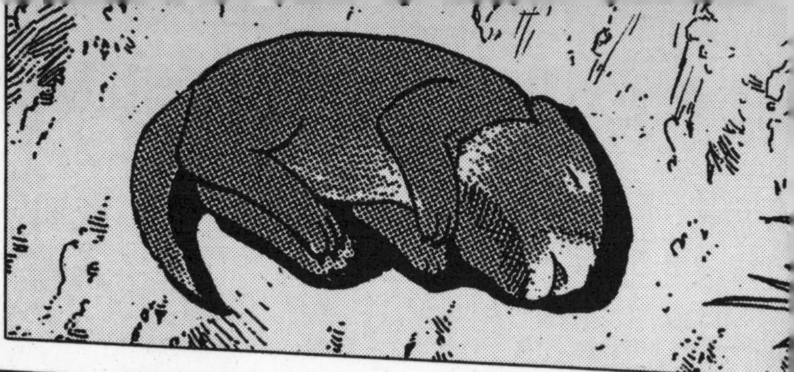

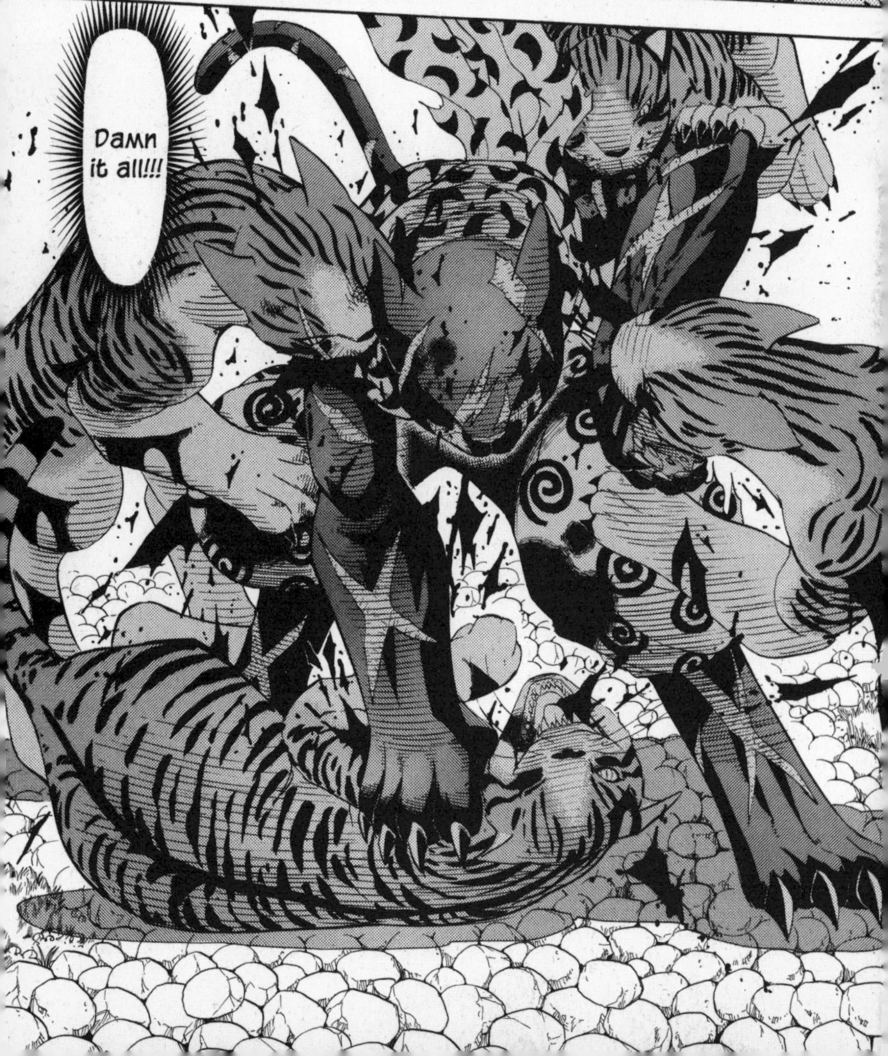
Damn it all!!!

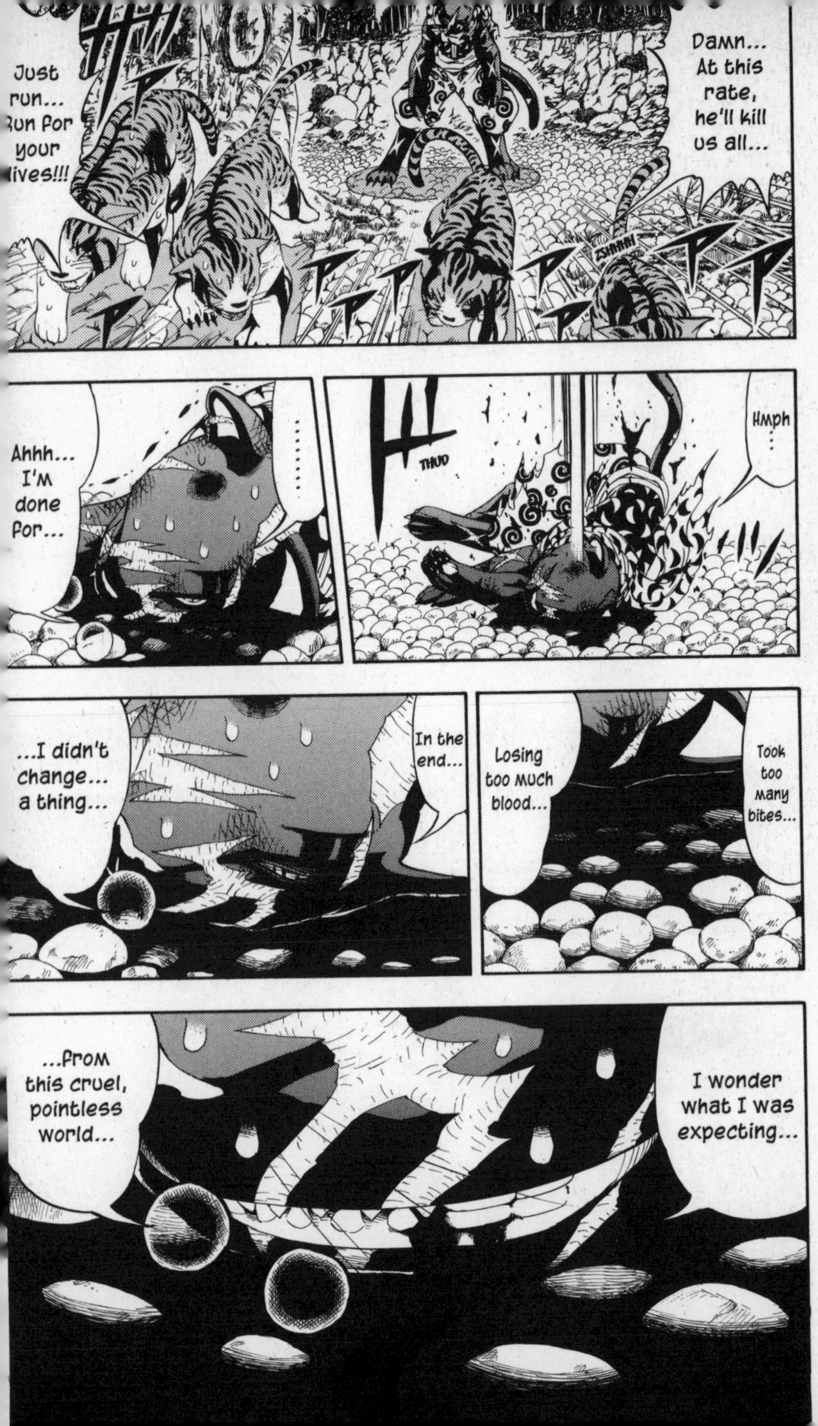
Damn... At this rate, he'll kill us all...
Just run... Run for your lives!!!
ZSHHHH
Hmph...
THUD
......
Ahhh... I'm done for...
Took too many bites...
Losing too much blood...
In the end...
...I didn't change... a thing...
I wonder what I was expecting...
...from this cruel, pointless world...

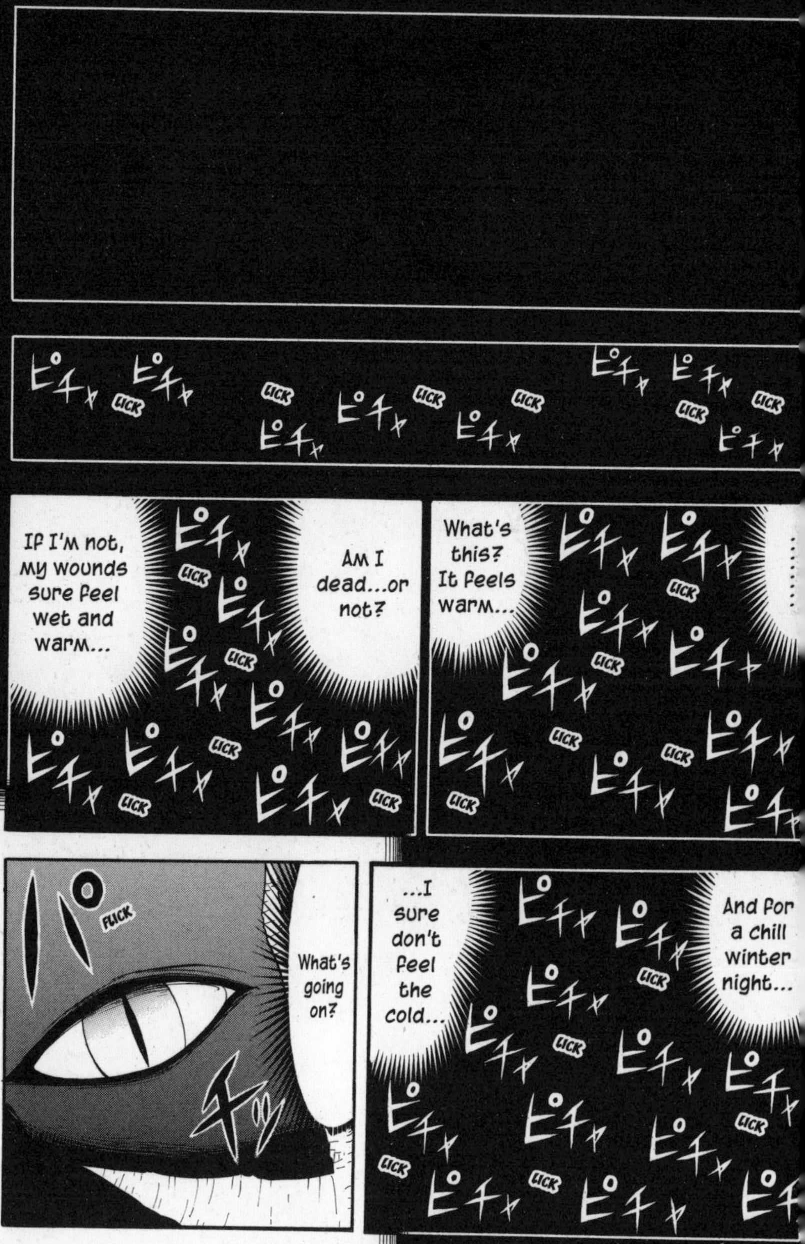
LICK
What's this? It feels warm...
Am I dead...or not?
If I'm not, my wounds sure feel wet and warm...
And for a chill winter night...
...I sure don't feel the cold...
What's going on?
FLICK

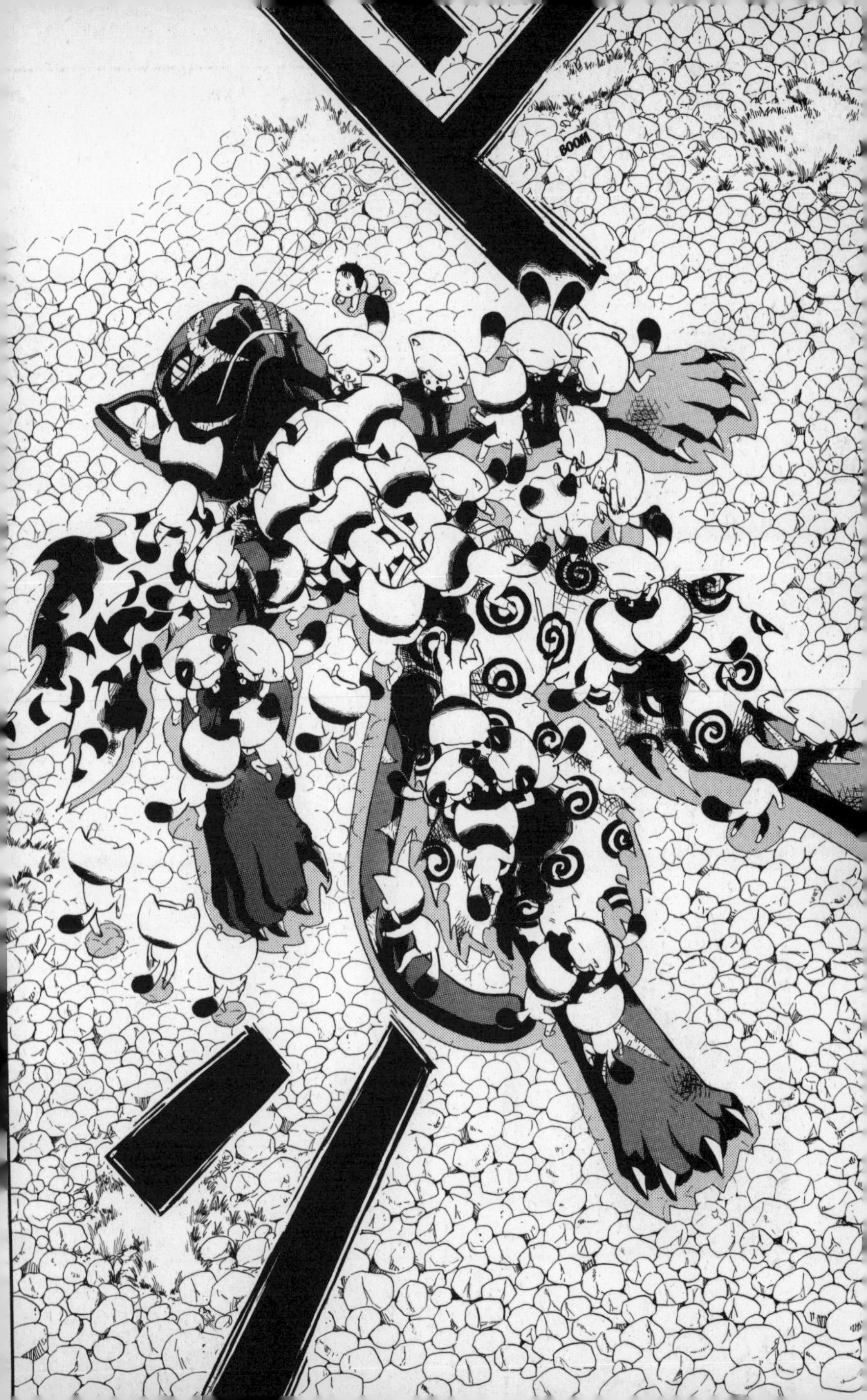
BOOM

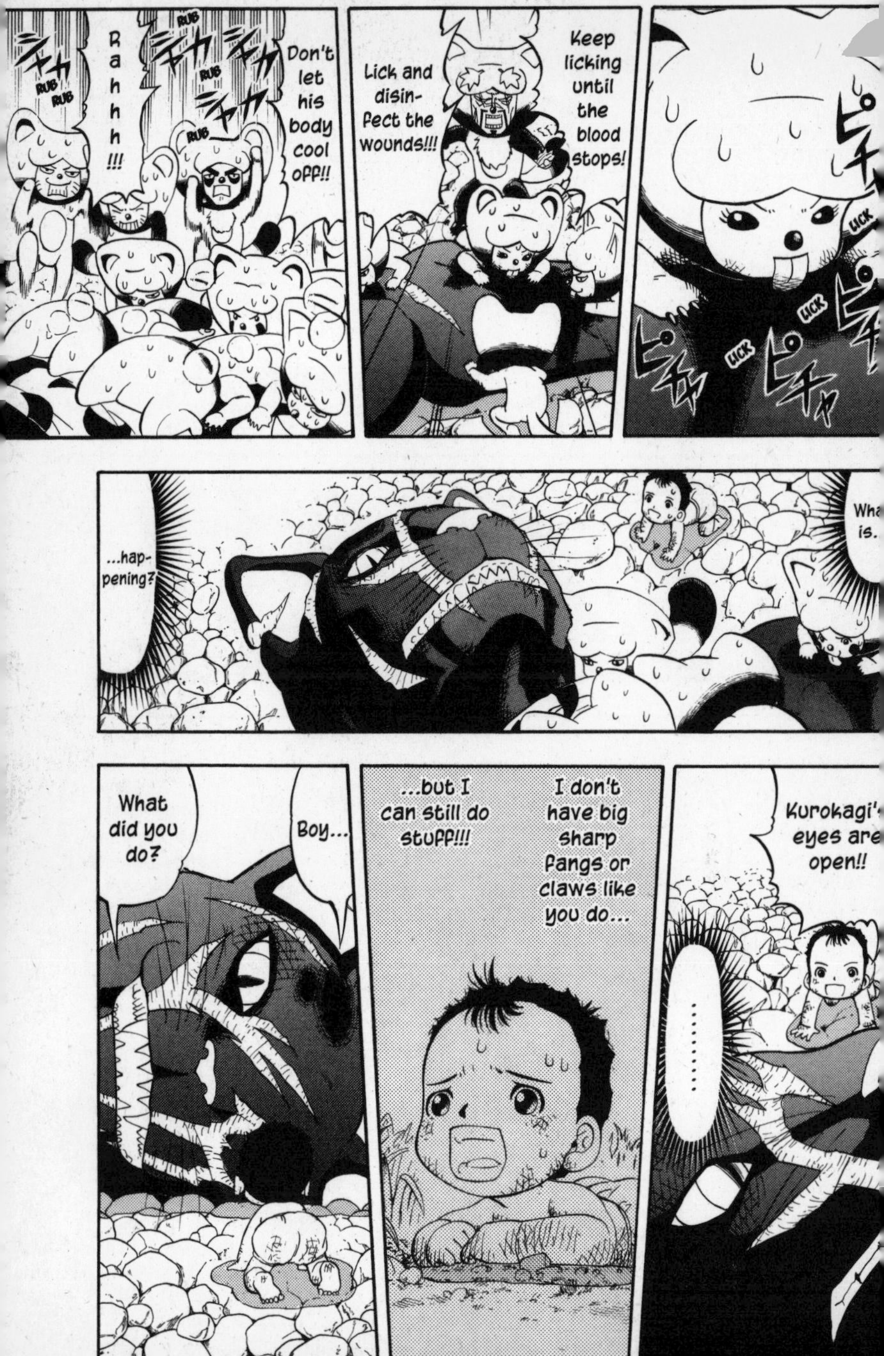
ピチャ
LICK
LICK
LICK
ピチャ
ピチャ
ピチャ
Keep licking until the blood stops!
Lick and disinfect the wounds!!!
Don't let his body cool off!!
Rahhh!!!
シャカ
RUB
RUB
RUB
RUB
Wha is.
...happening?
Kurokagi' eyes are open!!
......
I don't have big sharp fangs or claws like you do...
...but I can still do stuff!!!
Boy...
What did you do?

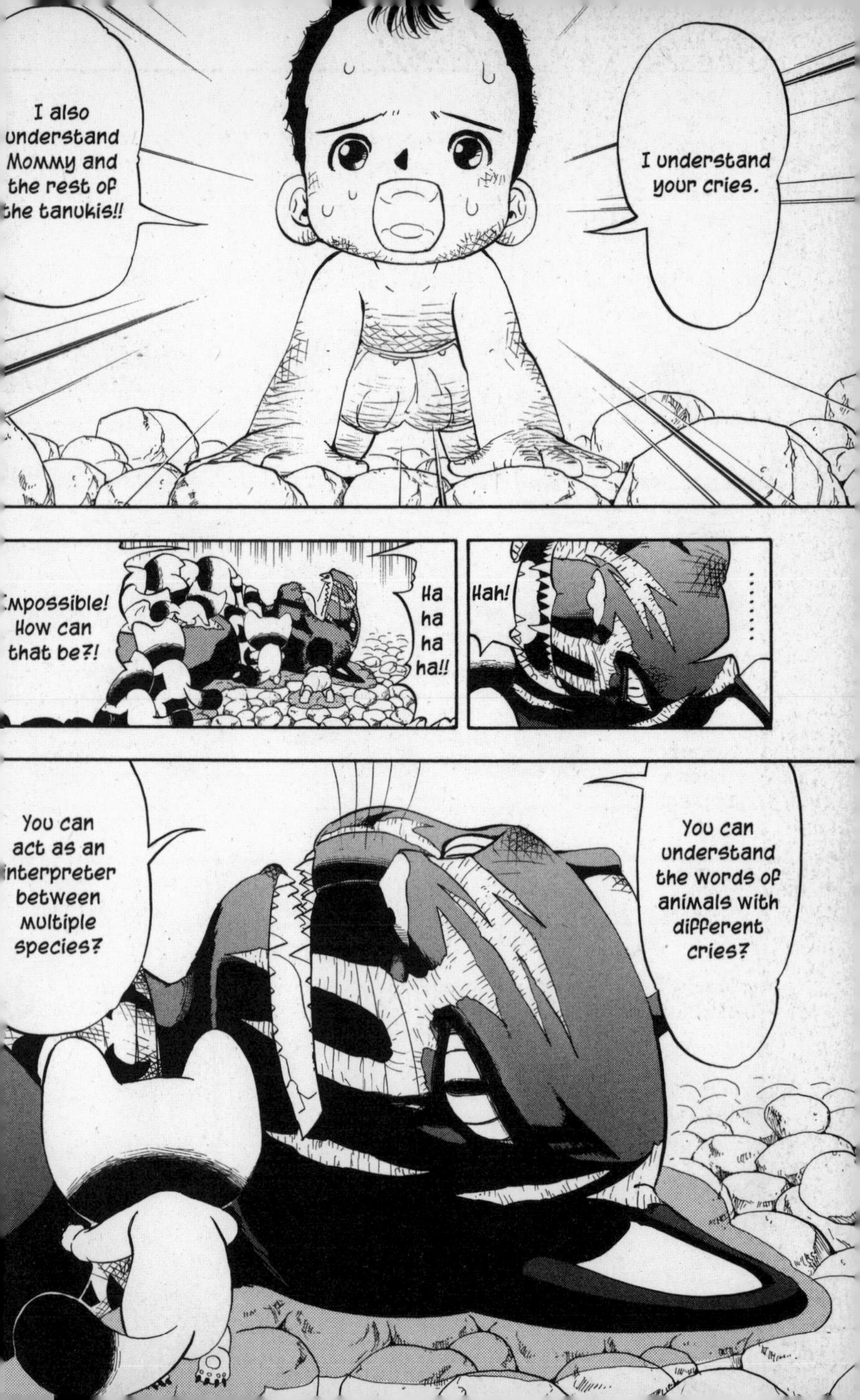
I understand your cries.
I also understand Mommy and the rest of the tanukis!!
......
Hah!
Ha ha ha ha!!
Impossible! How can that be?!
You can understand the words of animals with different cries?
You can act as an interpreter between multiple species?

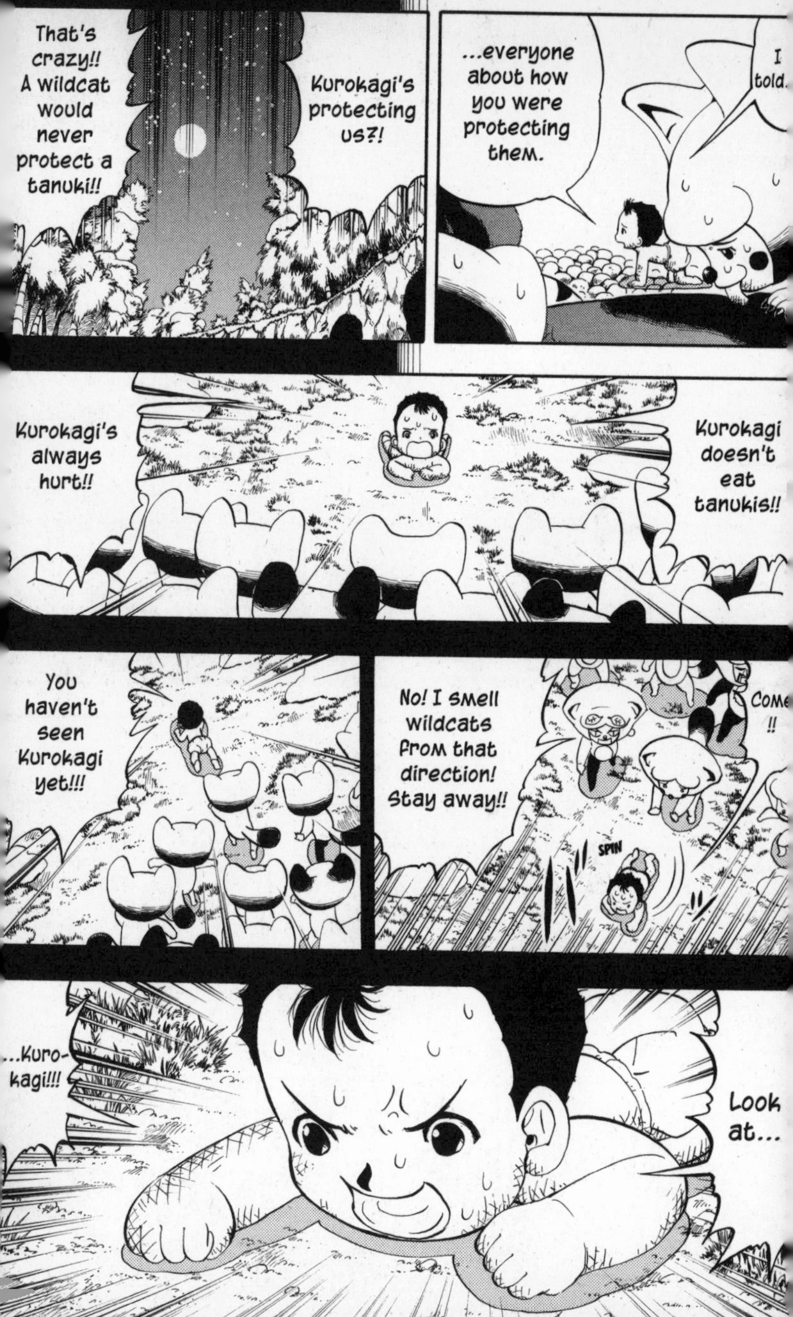
I told.
...everyone about how you were protecting them.
Kurokagi's protecting us?!
That's crazy!! A wildcat would never protect a tanuki!!
Kurokagi doesn't eat tanukis!!
Kurokagi's always hurt!!
Come!!
No! I smell wildcats from that direction! Stay away!!
SPIN
You haven't seen Kurokagi yet!!!
Look at...
...Kuro-kagi!!!

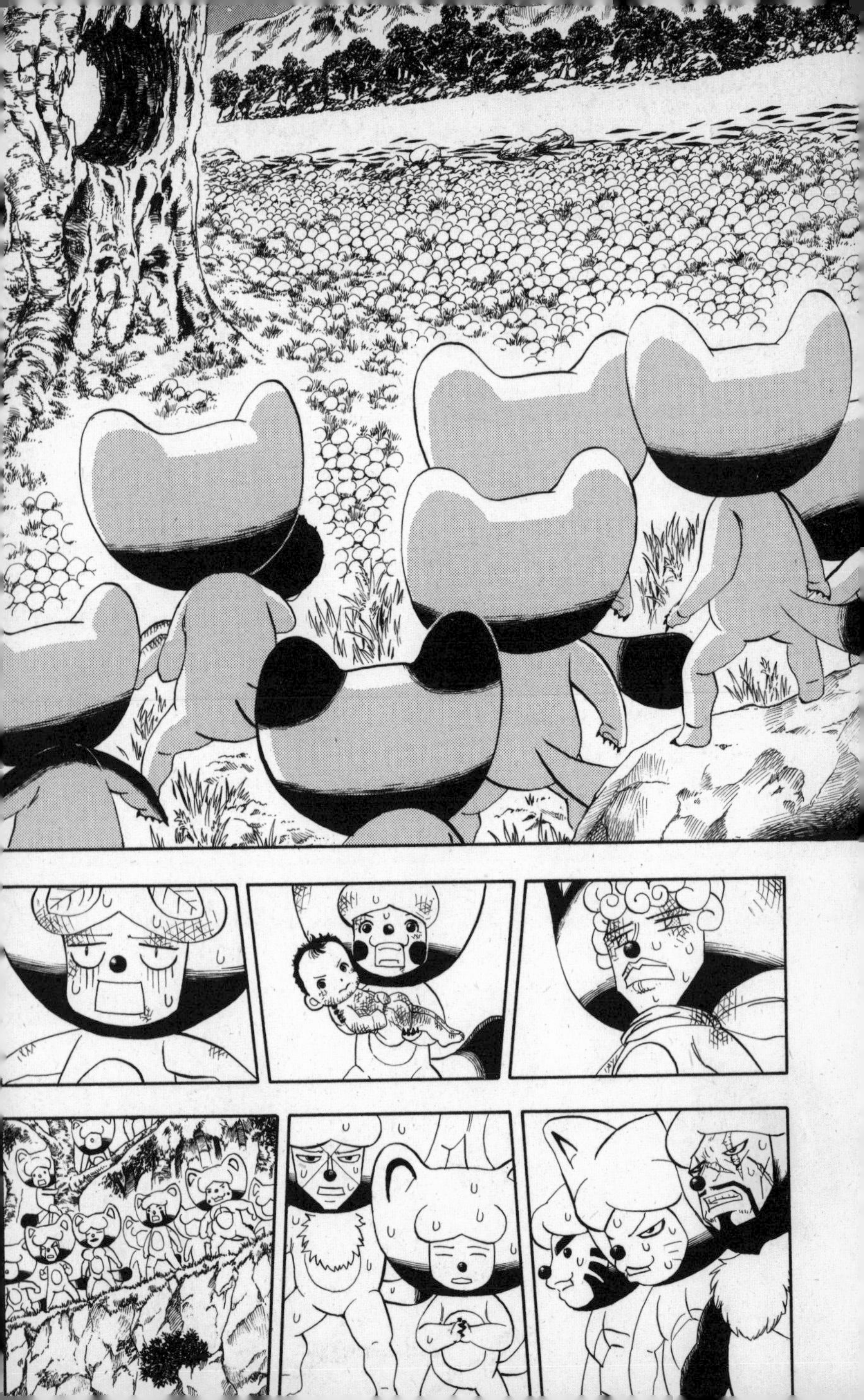

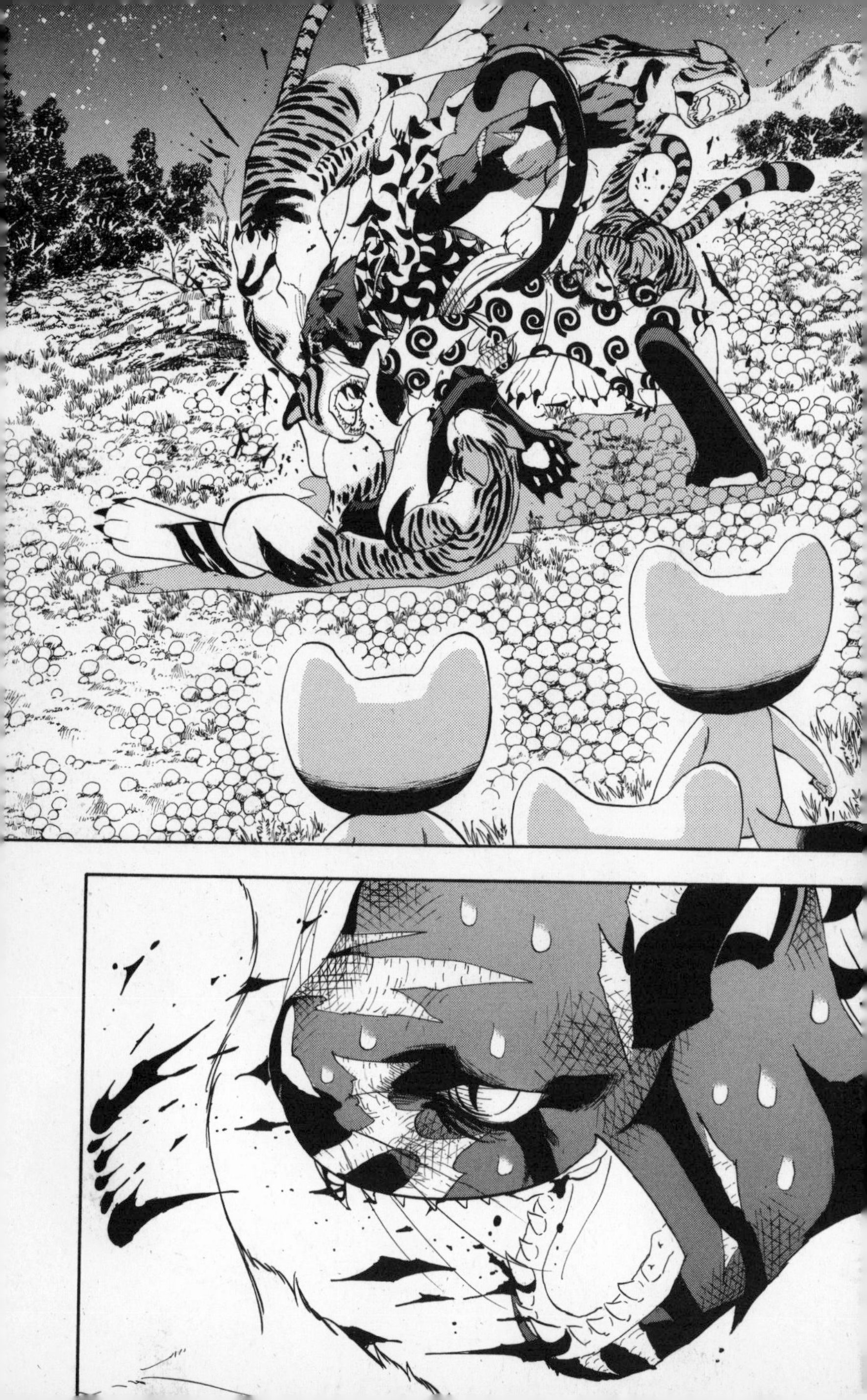

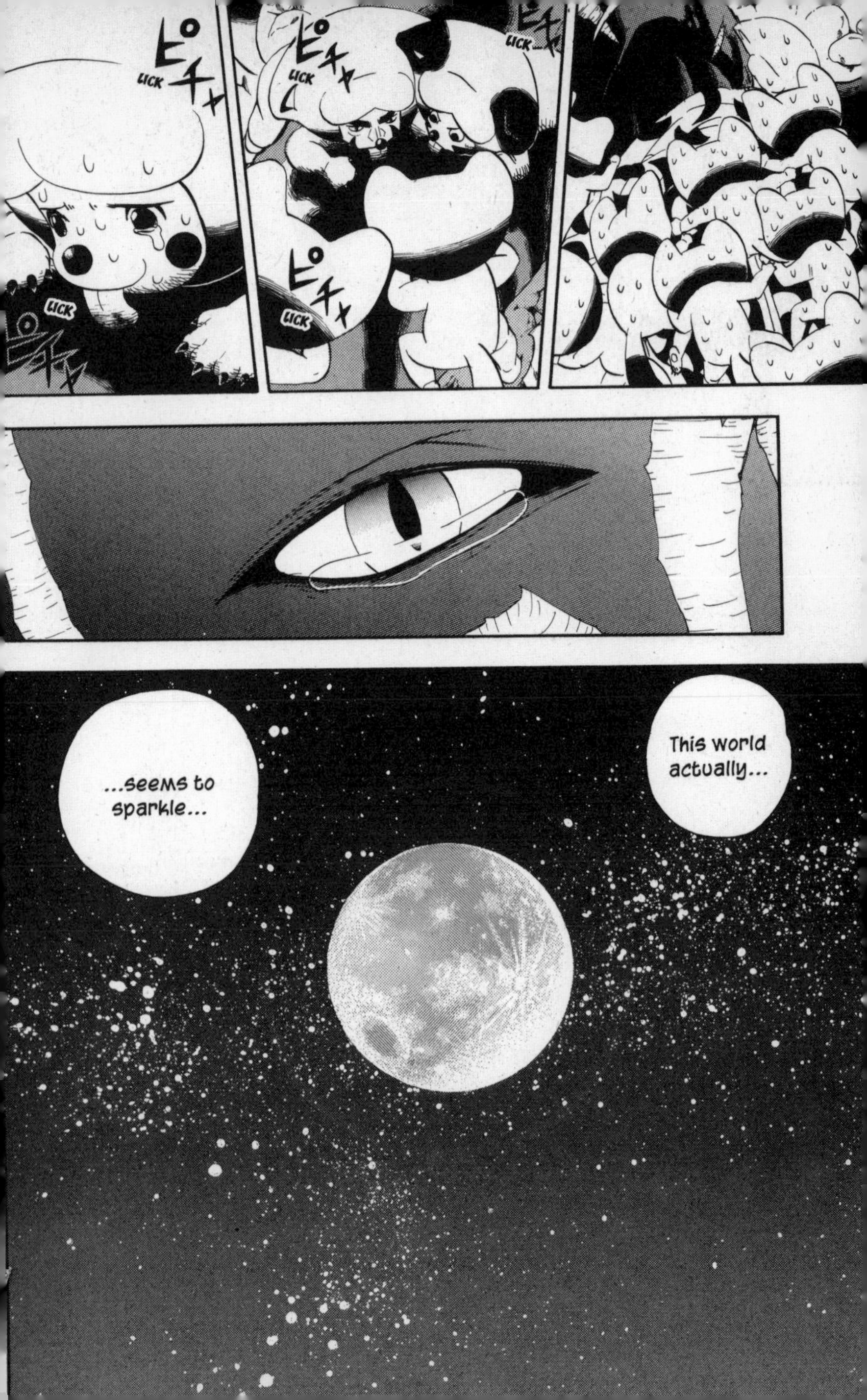
ピチャ
LICK
ピチャ
LICK
ピチャ
LICK
ピチャ
LICK
LICK
ピチャ
This world actually...
...seems to sparkle...

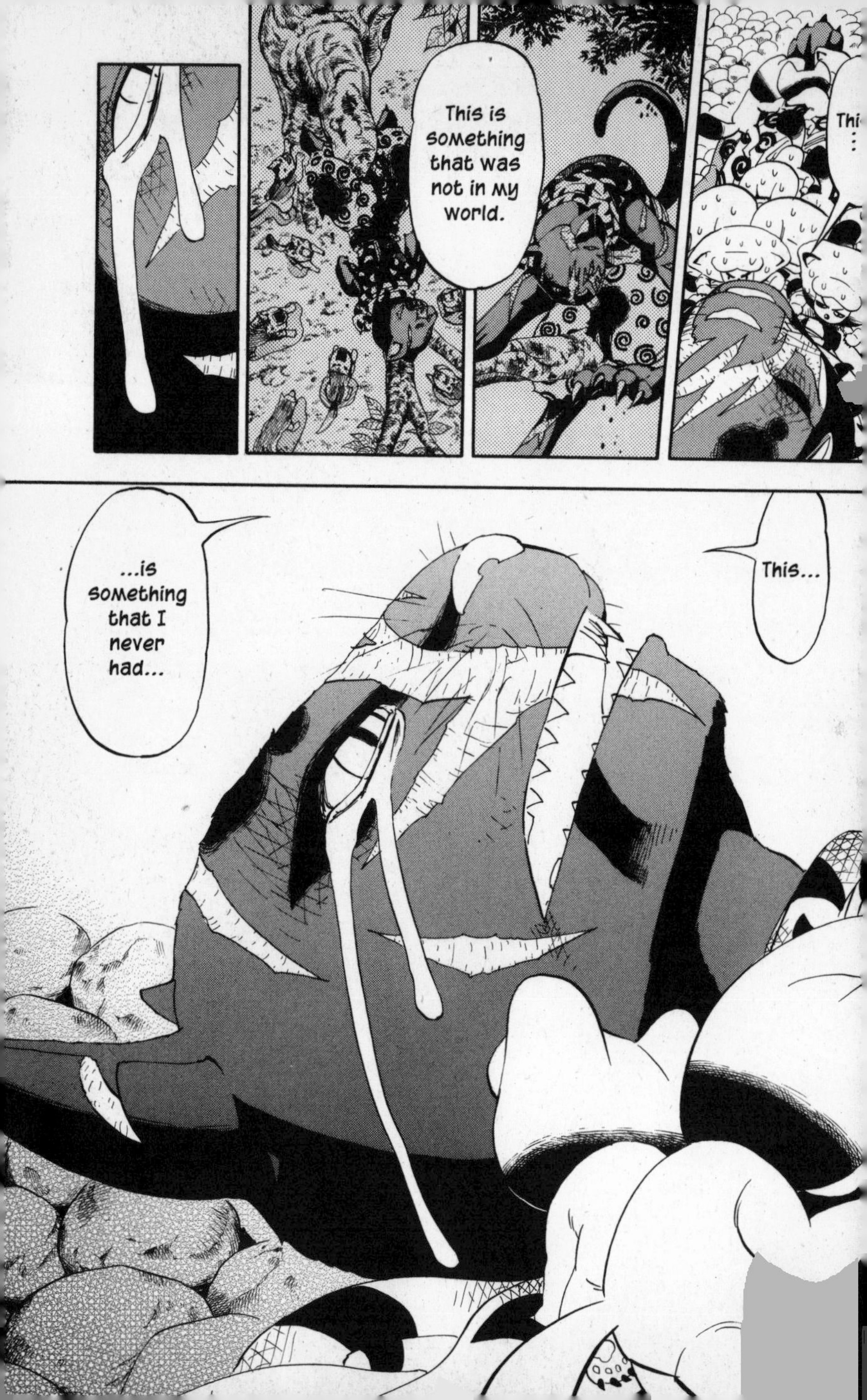
Thi...
This is something that was not in my world.
This...
...is something that I never had...

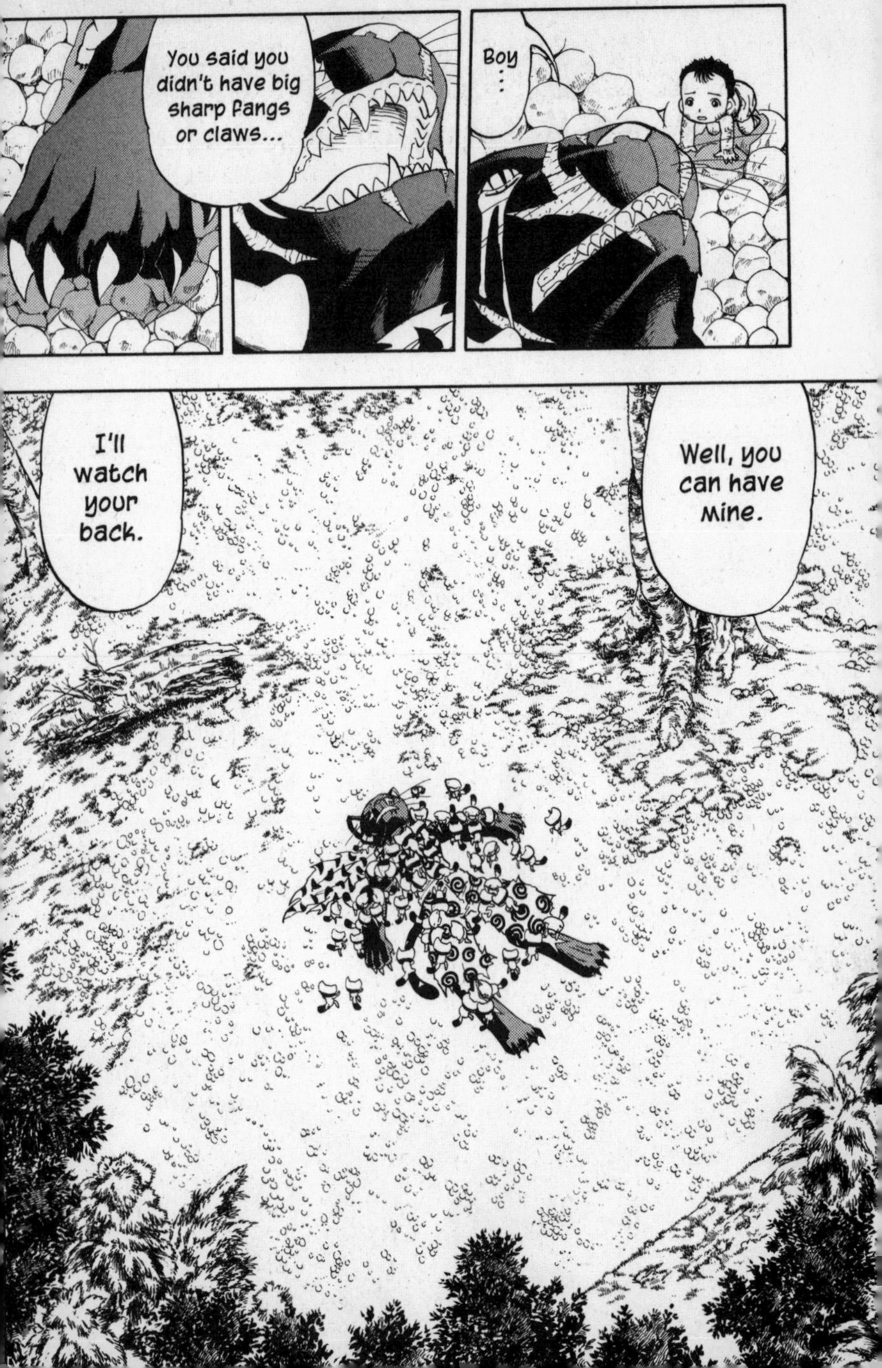
Boy ...
You said you didn't have big sharp fangs or claws...
Well, you can have mine.
I'll watch your back.

ANIMAL LAND

Word 3: Baby Cries Over His Name!

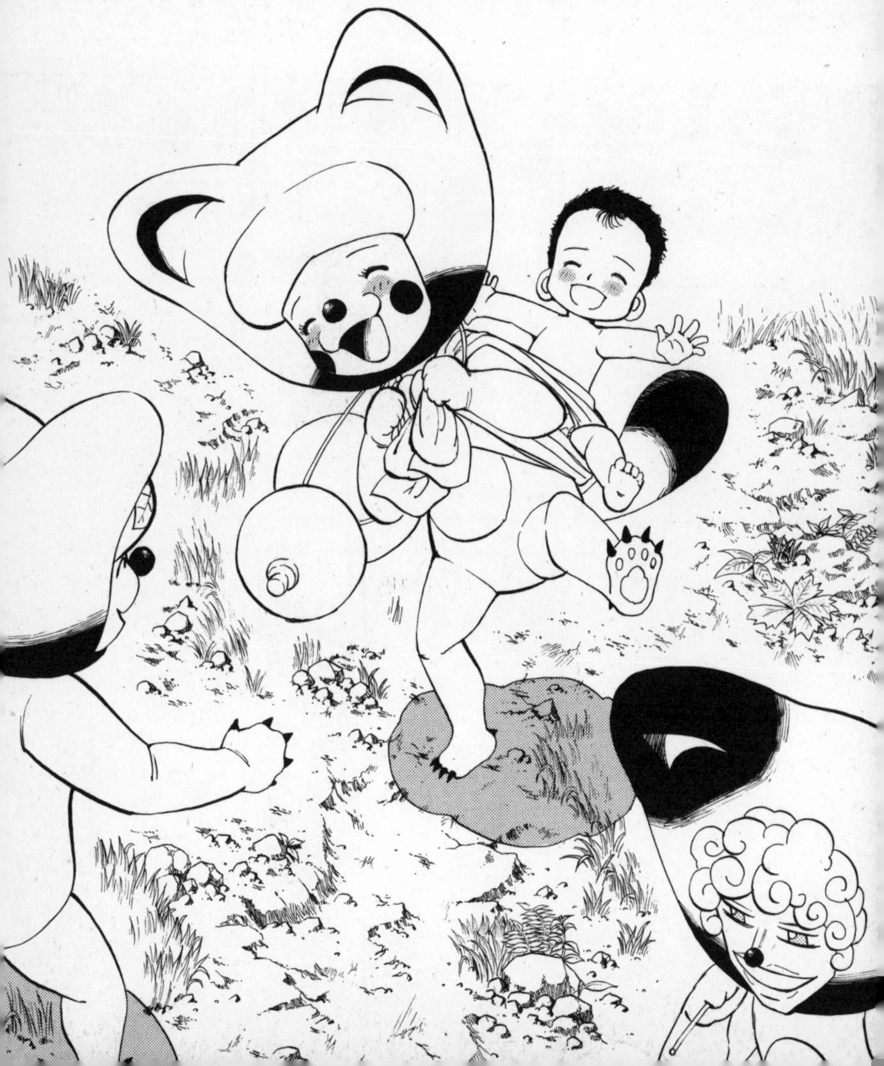

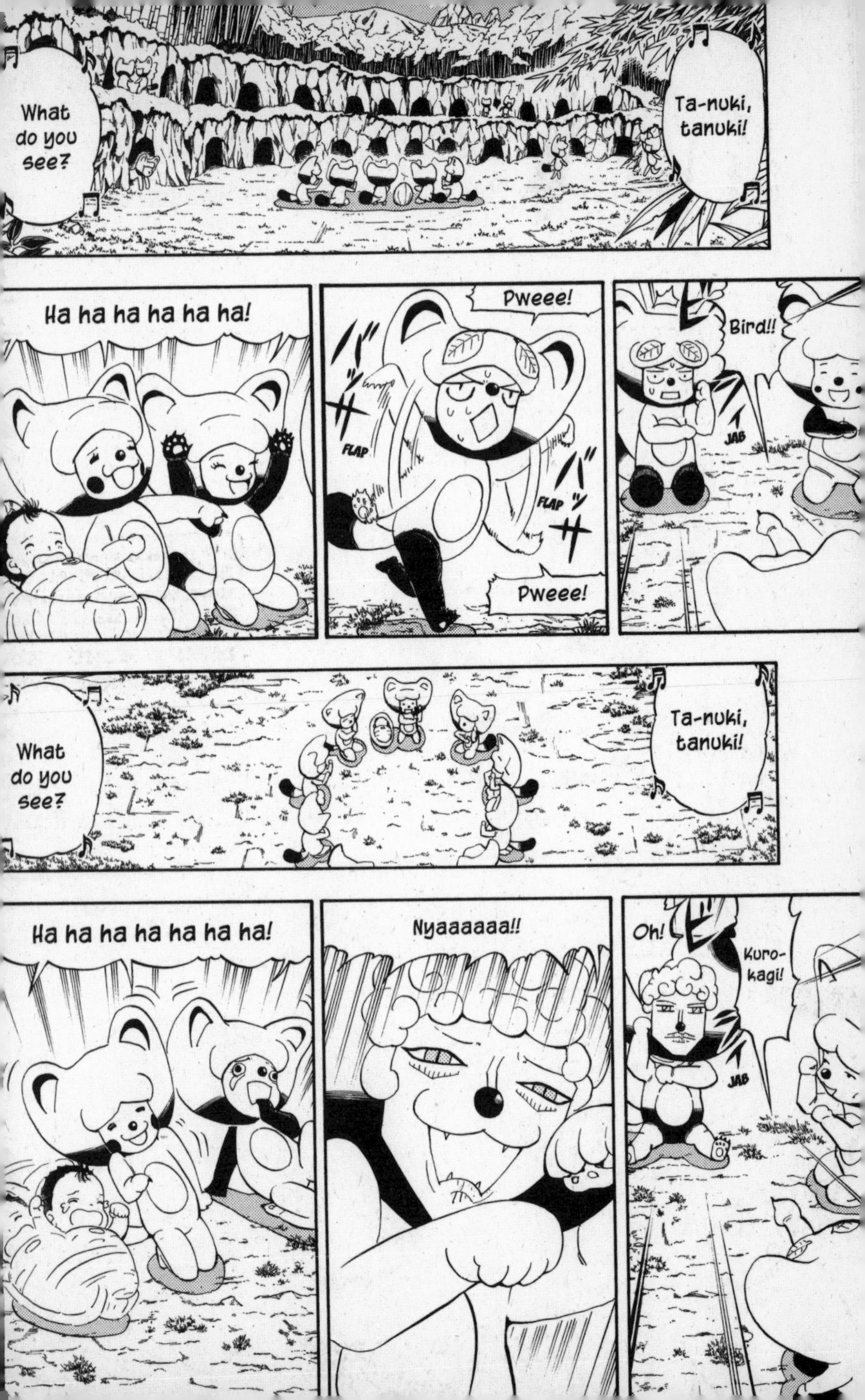
Ta-nuki, tanuki!
What do you see?
Bird!!
JAB
Pweee!
FLAP
FLAP
Pweee!
Ha ha ha ha ha ha!
Ta-nuki, tanuki!
What do you see?
Oh!
Kuro-kagi!
JAB
Nyaaaaaa!!
Ha ha ha ha ha ha ha!

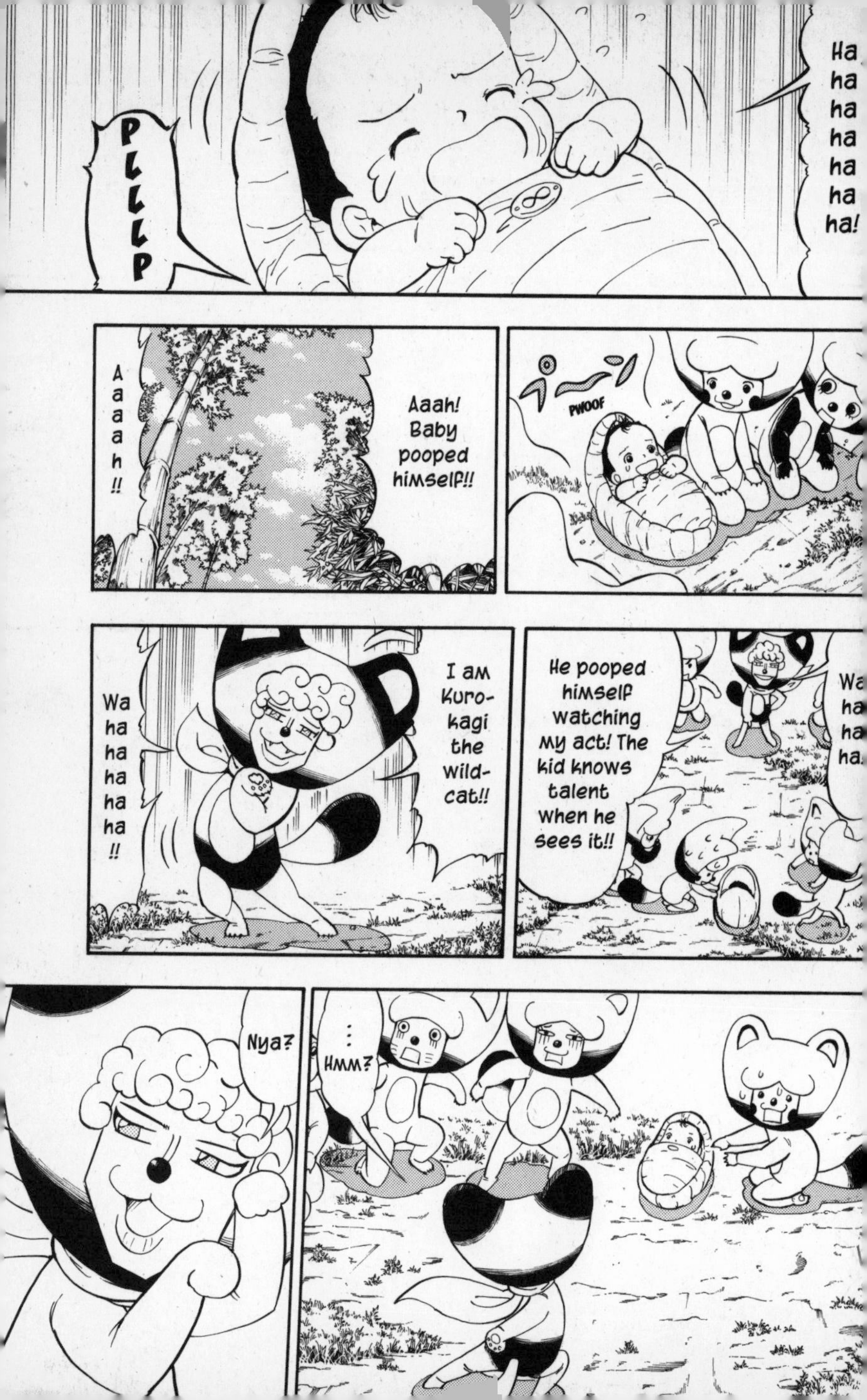
Ha ha ha ha ha ha ha!
PLLLP
PWOOF
Aaah! Baby pooped himself!!
Aaaah!!
Wa ha ha ha.
He pooped himself watching my act! The kid knows talent when he sees it!!
I am Kuro-kagi the wild-cat!!
Wa ha ha ha ha ha!!
...
Hmm?
Nya?

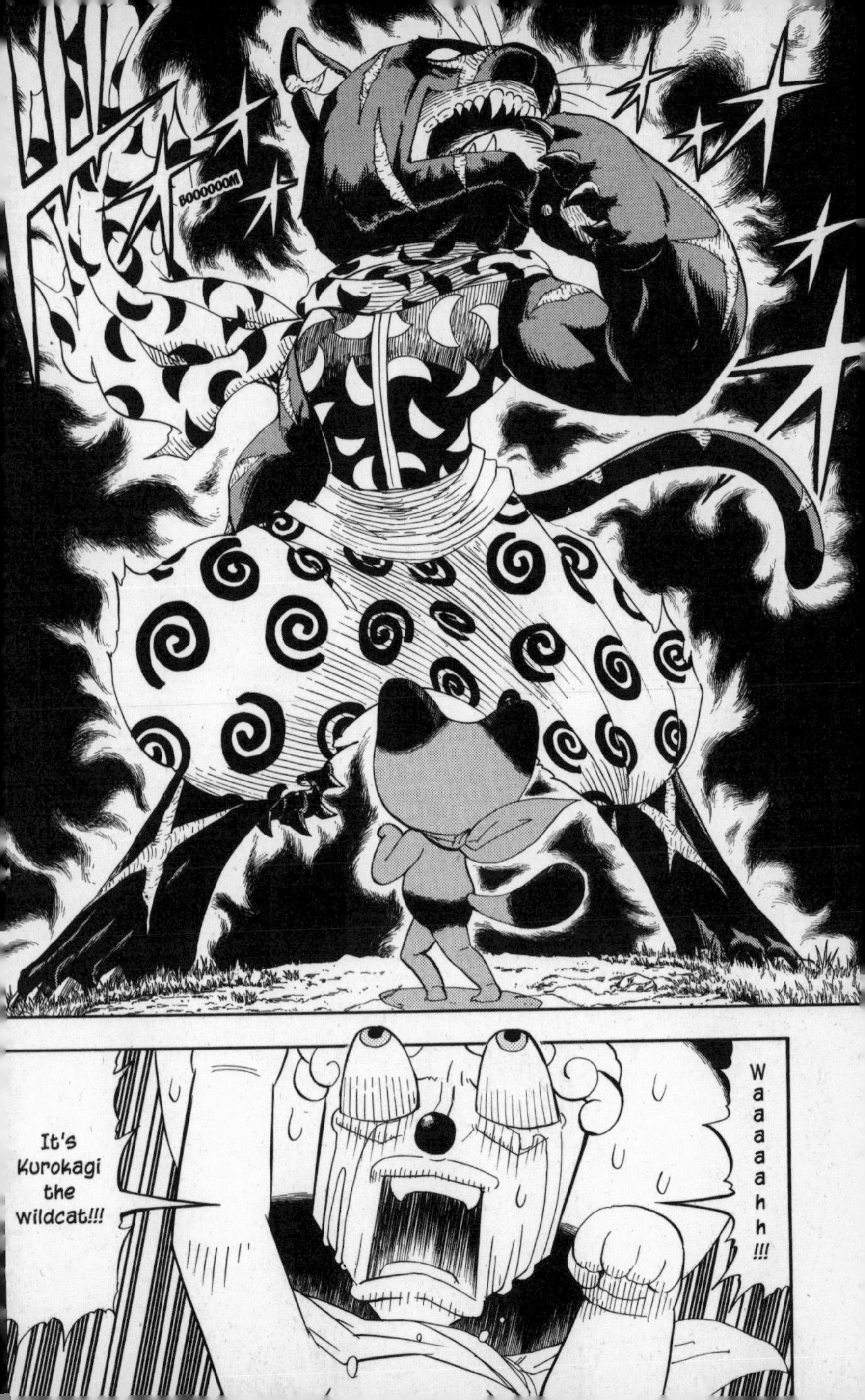
BOOOOOOM
Waaaaahh!!!
It's Kurokagi the wildcat!!!

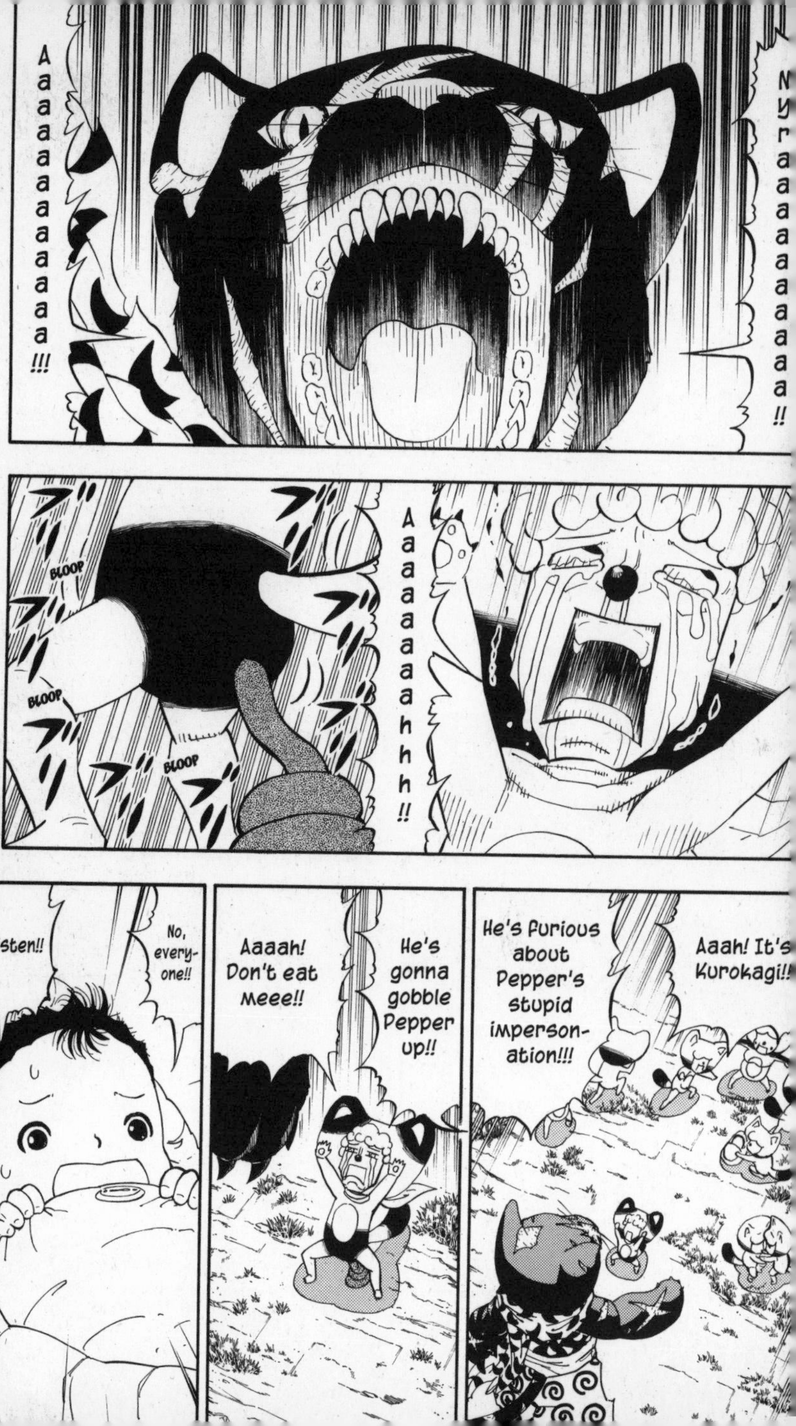
Nyraaaaaaaaaaaaaa!!
Aaaaaaaaaaaaa!!!
Aaaaaaaaaaaaaahhh!!
BLOOP
BLOOP
BLOOP
Aaah! It's Kurokagi!!
He's furious about Pepper's stupid imperson-ation!!!
He's gonna gobble Pepper up!!
Aaaah! Don't eat Meee!!
No, every-one!!
Listen!!

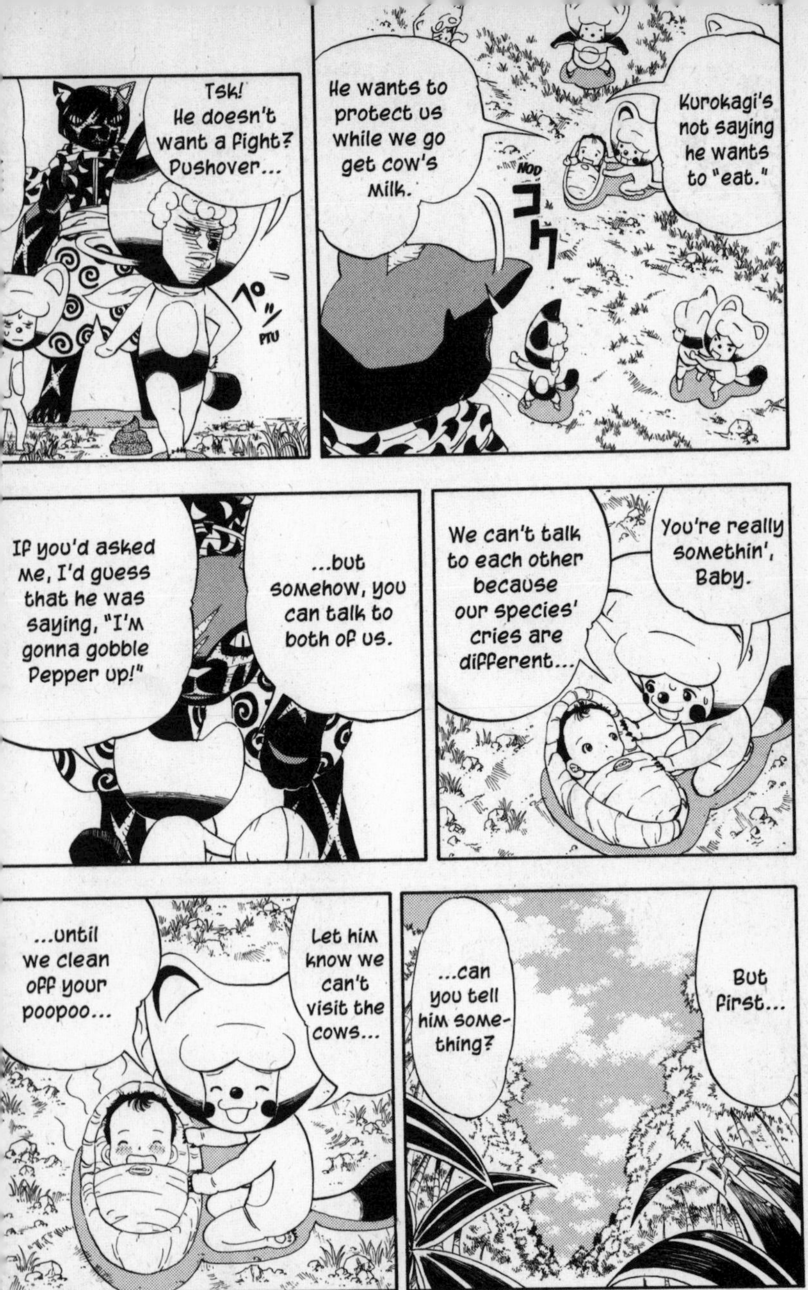
Kurokagi's not saying he wants to "eat."
He wants to protect us while we go get cow's milk.
NOD
Tsk! He doesn't want a fight? Pushover...
PTU
You're really somethin', Baby.
We can't talk to each other because our species' cries are different...
...but somehow, you can talk to both of us.
If you'd asked me, I'd guess that he was saying, "I'm gonna gobble Pepper up!"
But first...
...can you tell him some-thing?
Let him know we can't visit the cows...
...until we clean off your poopoo...

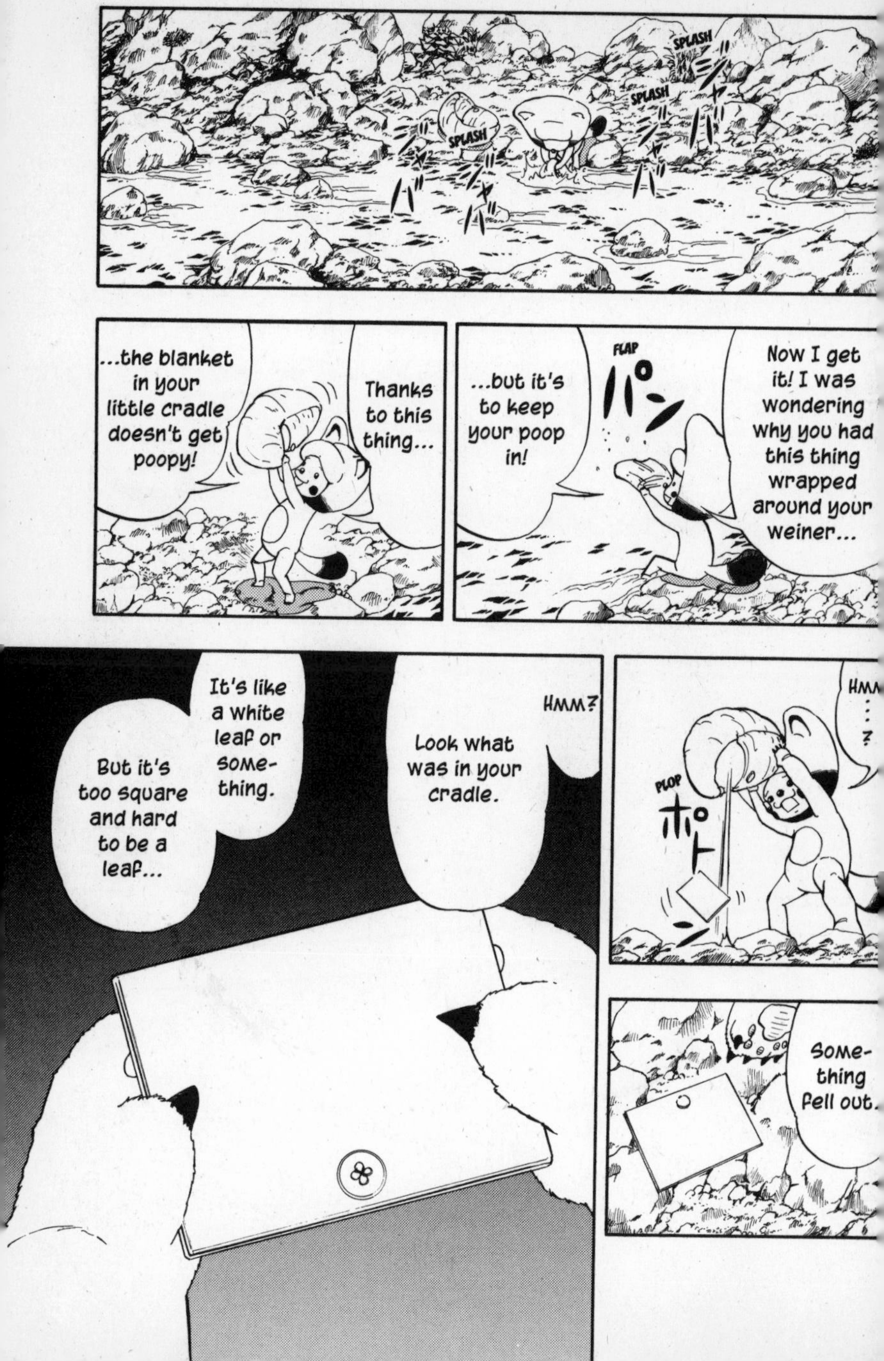
SPLASH
SPLASH
SPLASH
Now I get it! I was wondering why you had this thing wrapped around your weiner...
FLAP
...but it's to keep your poop in!
Thanks to this thing...
...the blanket in your little cradle doesn't get poopy!
PLOP
Something fell out.
HMM?
Look what was in your cradle.
It's like a white leaf or something.
But it's too square and hard to be a leaf...

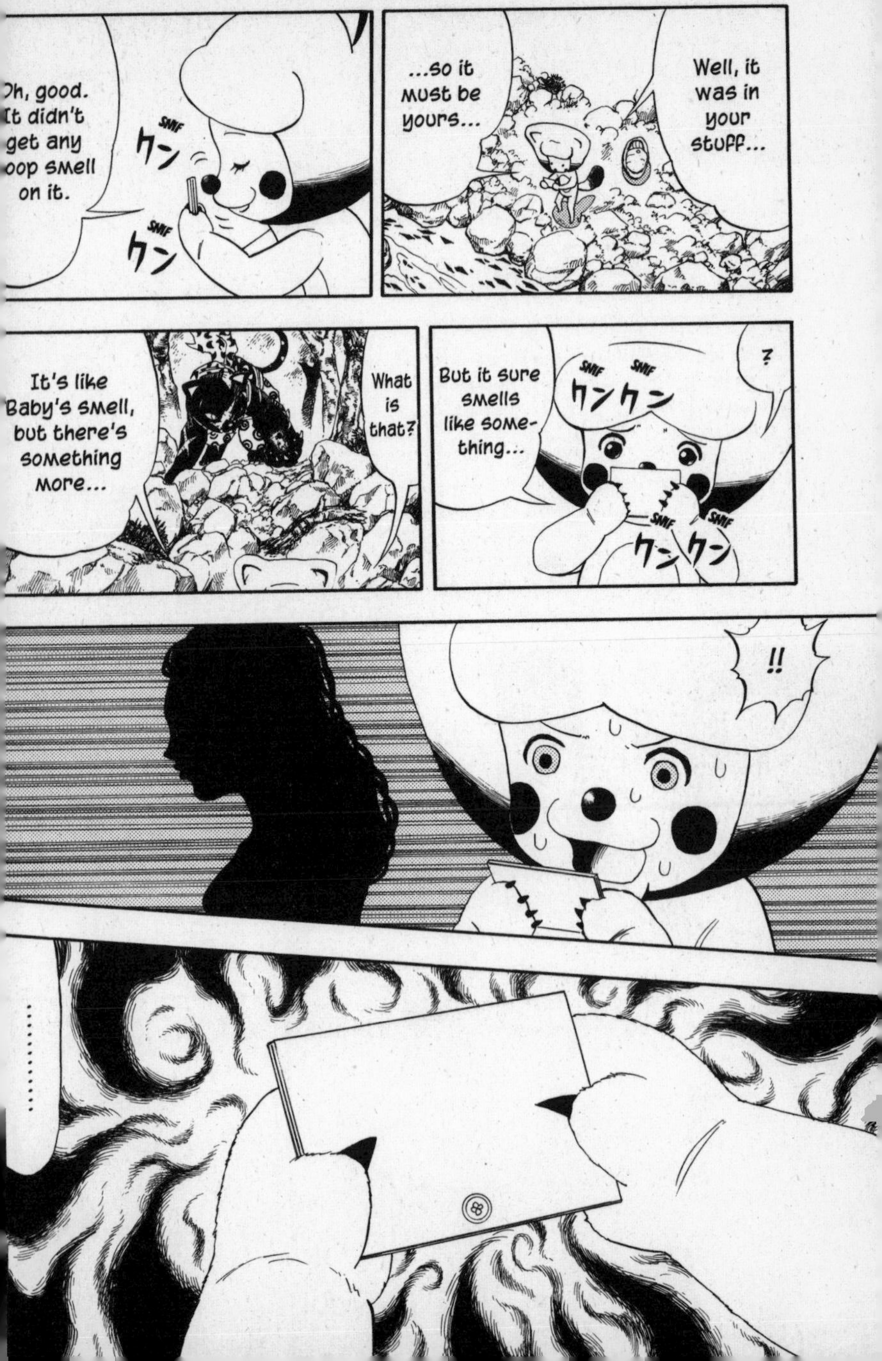
Well, it was in your stuff...
...so it must be yours...
Oh, good. It didn't get any poop smell on it.
SNIF クン
SNIF クン
?
But it sure smells like some-thing...
SNIF SNIF クンクン
SNIF SNIF クンクン
What is that?
It's like Baby's smell, but there's something more...
!!
....

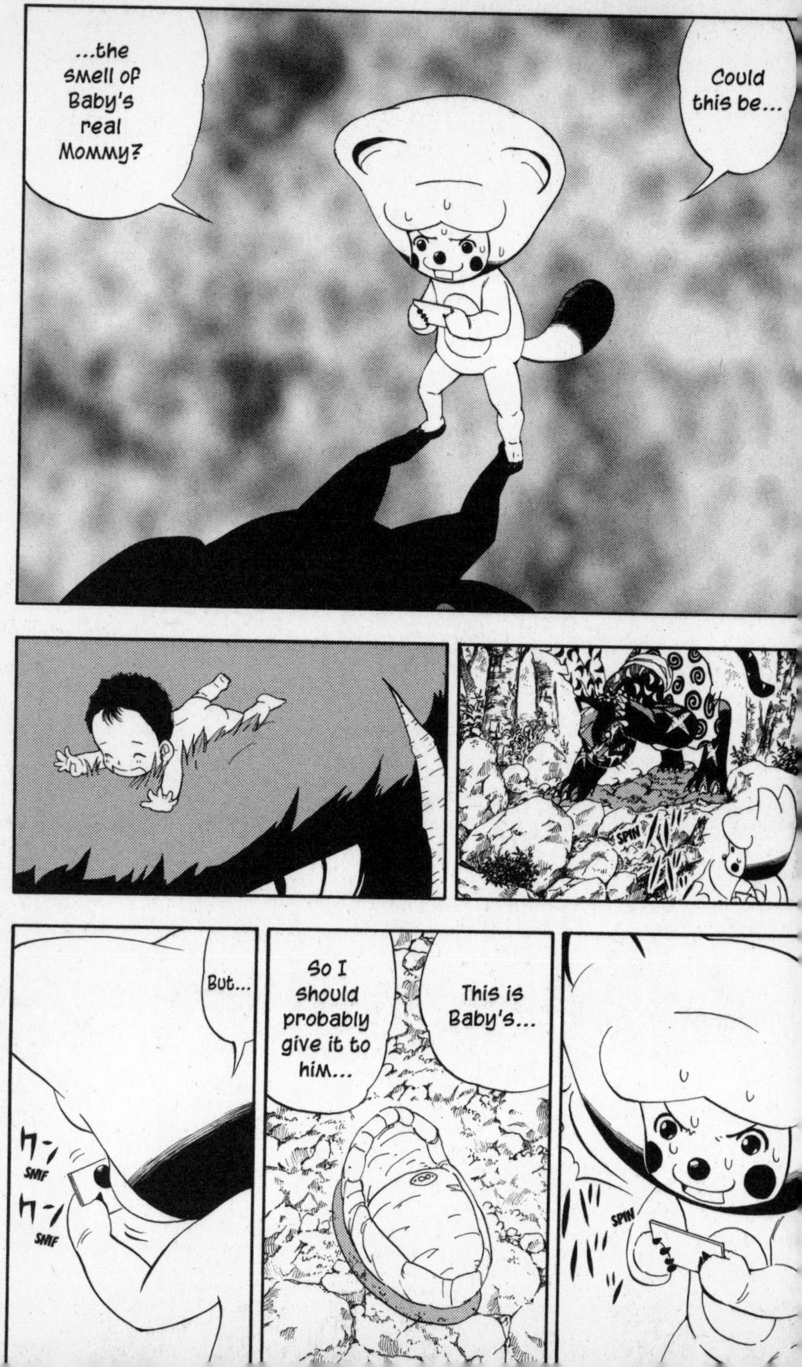

Could this be...
...the smell of Baby's real Mommy?
SPIN
SPIN
This is Baby's...
So I should probably give it to him...
But...
SNIF
SNIF

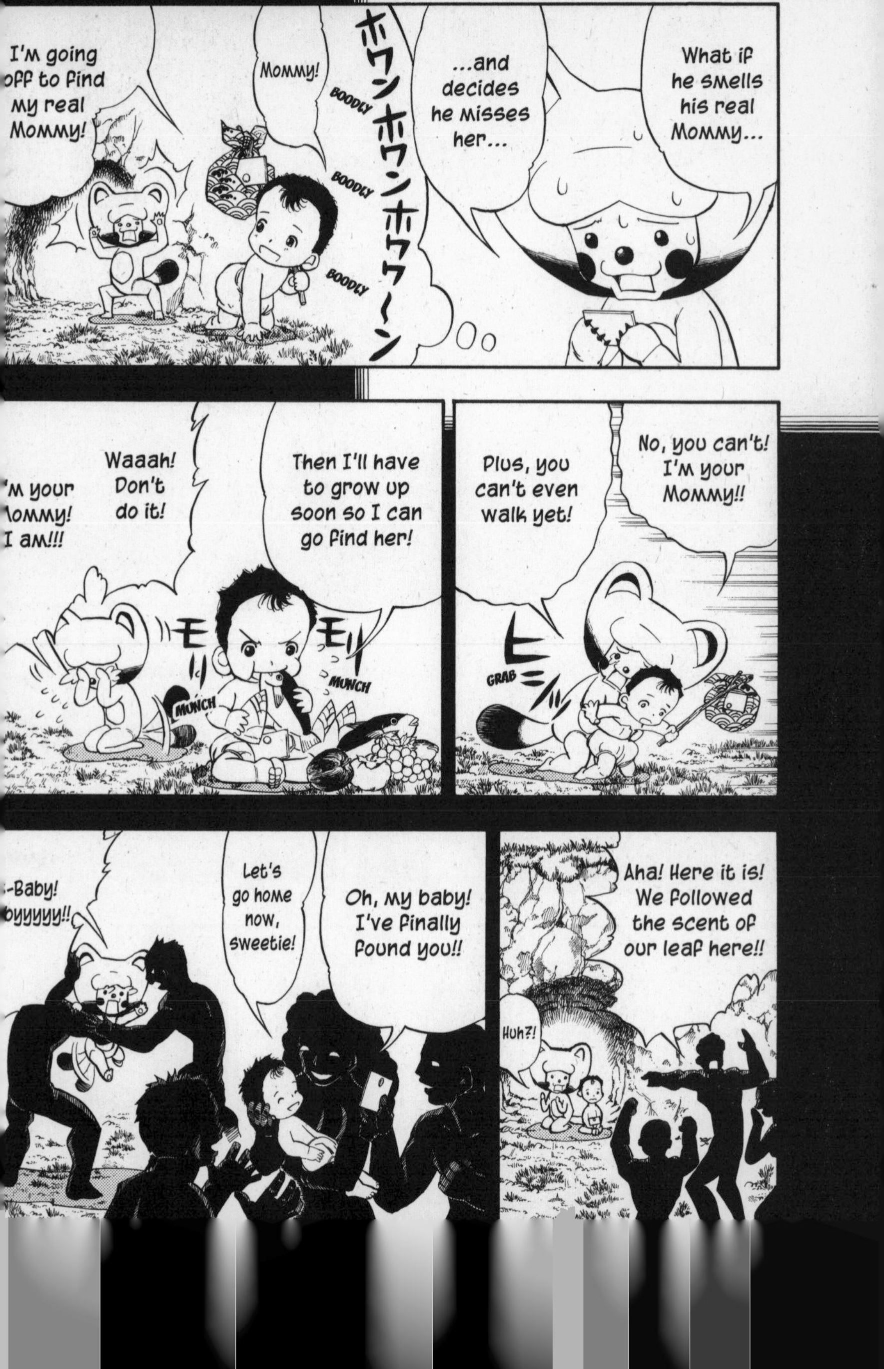
What if he smells his real Mommy...
...and decides he misses her...
ホワンホワンホワ〜ン
BOODLY
BOODLY
BOODLY
Mommy!
I'm going off to find my real Mommy!
No, you can't! I'm your Mommy!!
Plus, you can't even walk yet!
GRAB
Then I'll have to grow up soon so I can go find her!
モリ
MUNCH
モリ
MUNCH
Waaah! Don't do it!
'm your ommy! I am!!!
Aha! Here it is! We followed the scent of our leaf here!!
Huh?!
Oh, my baby! I've finally found you!!
Let's go home now, sweetie!
-Baby! oyyyyy!!

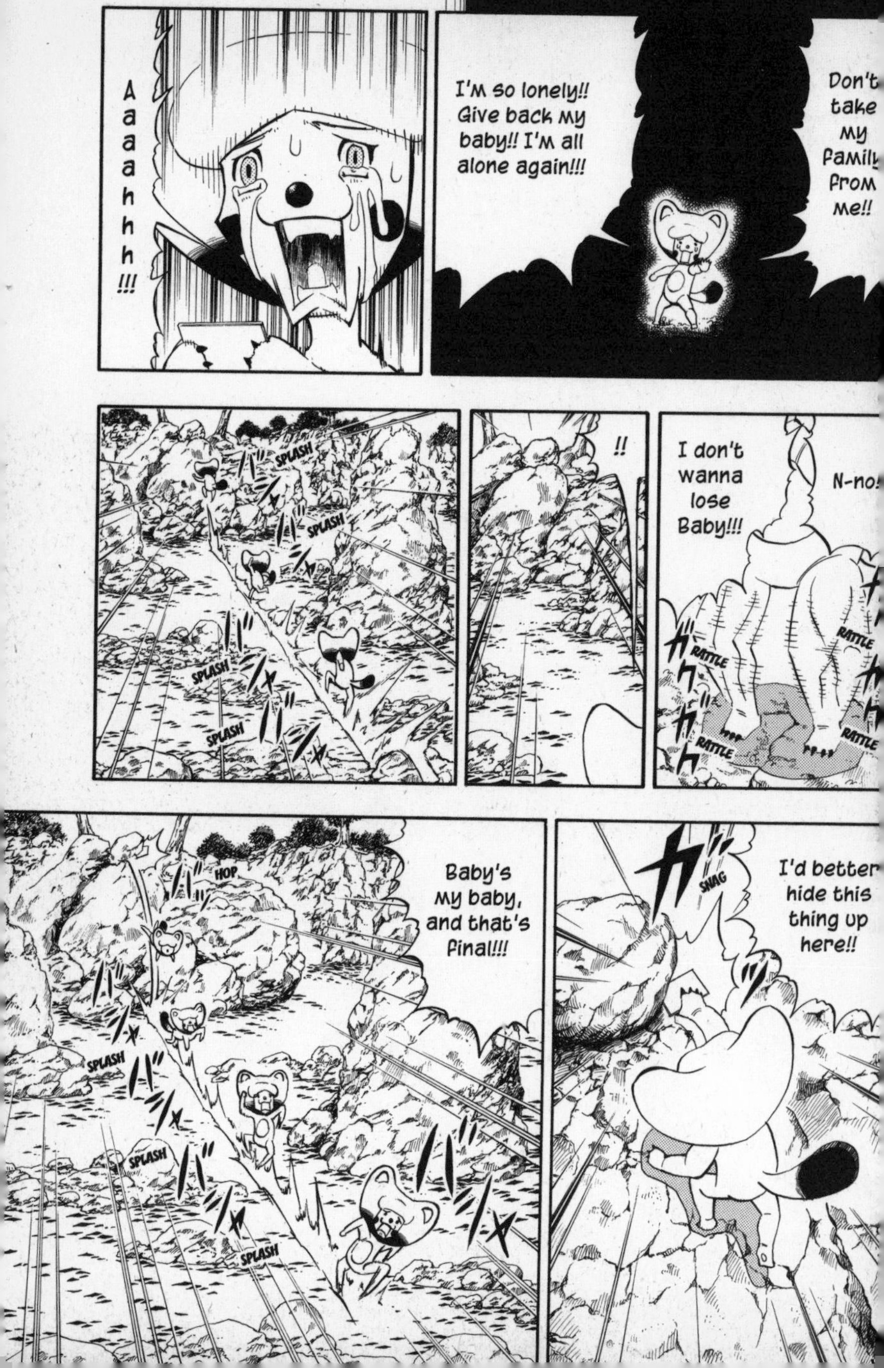
Don't take my family from me!!
I'm so lonely!! Give back my baby!! I'm all alone again!!!
Aaaaahhh!!!
N-no!
I don't wanna lose Baby!!!
RATTLE
RATTLE
RATTLE
RATTLE
!!
SPLASH
SPLASH
SPLASH
SPLASH
I'd better hide this thing up here!!
SNAG
Baby's my baby, and that's final!!!
HOP
SPLASH
SPLASH
SPLASH

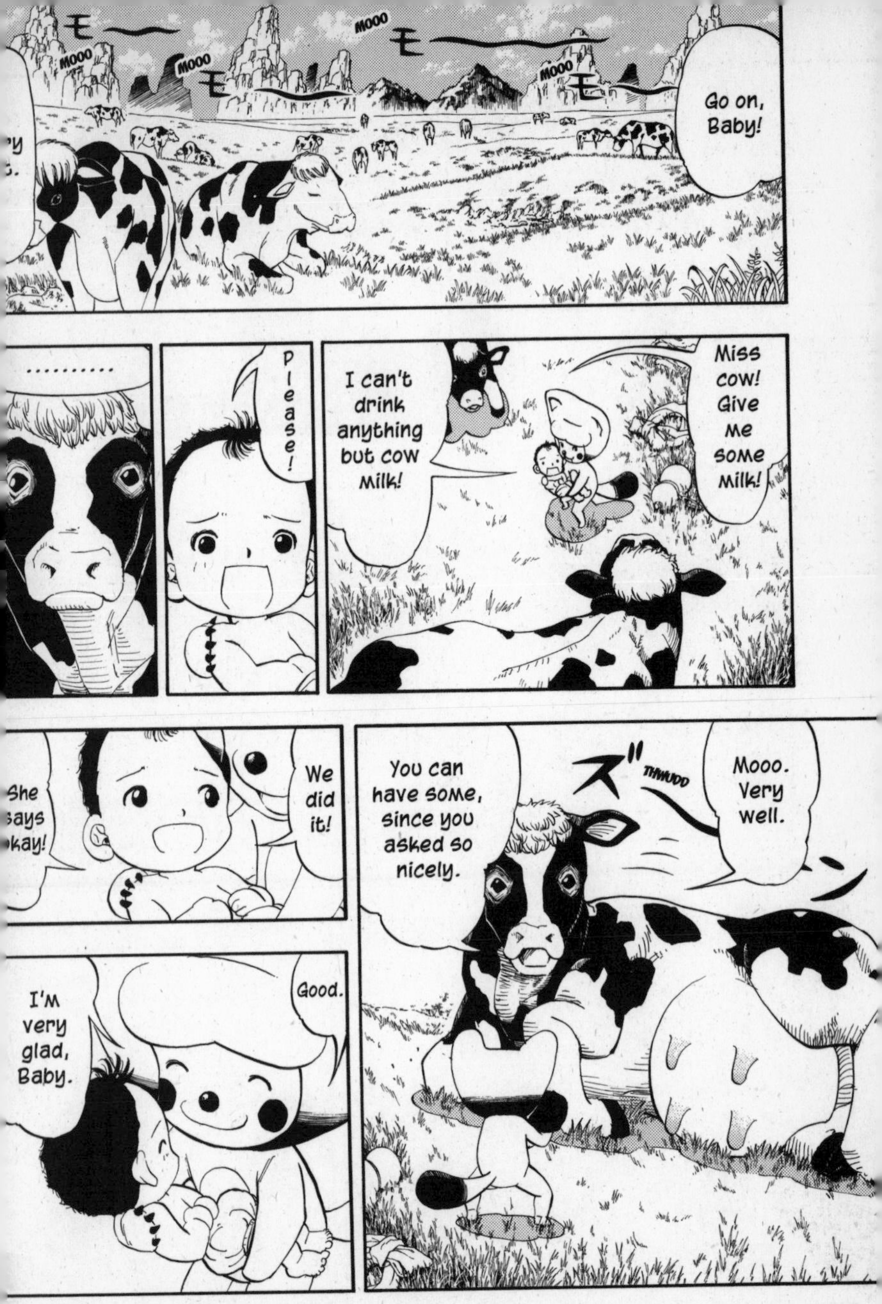
Go on, Baby!
MOOO
MOOO
MOOO
MOOO
Miss cow! Give me some milk!
I can't drink anything but cow milk!
Please!
....
Mooo. Very well.
THWUDD
You can have some, since you asked so nicely.
We did it!
She says okay!
Good.
I'm very glad, Baby.

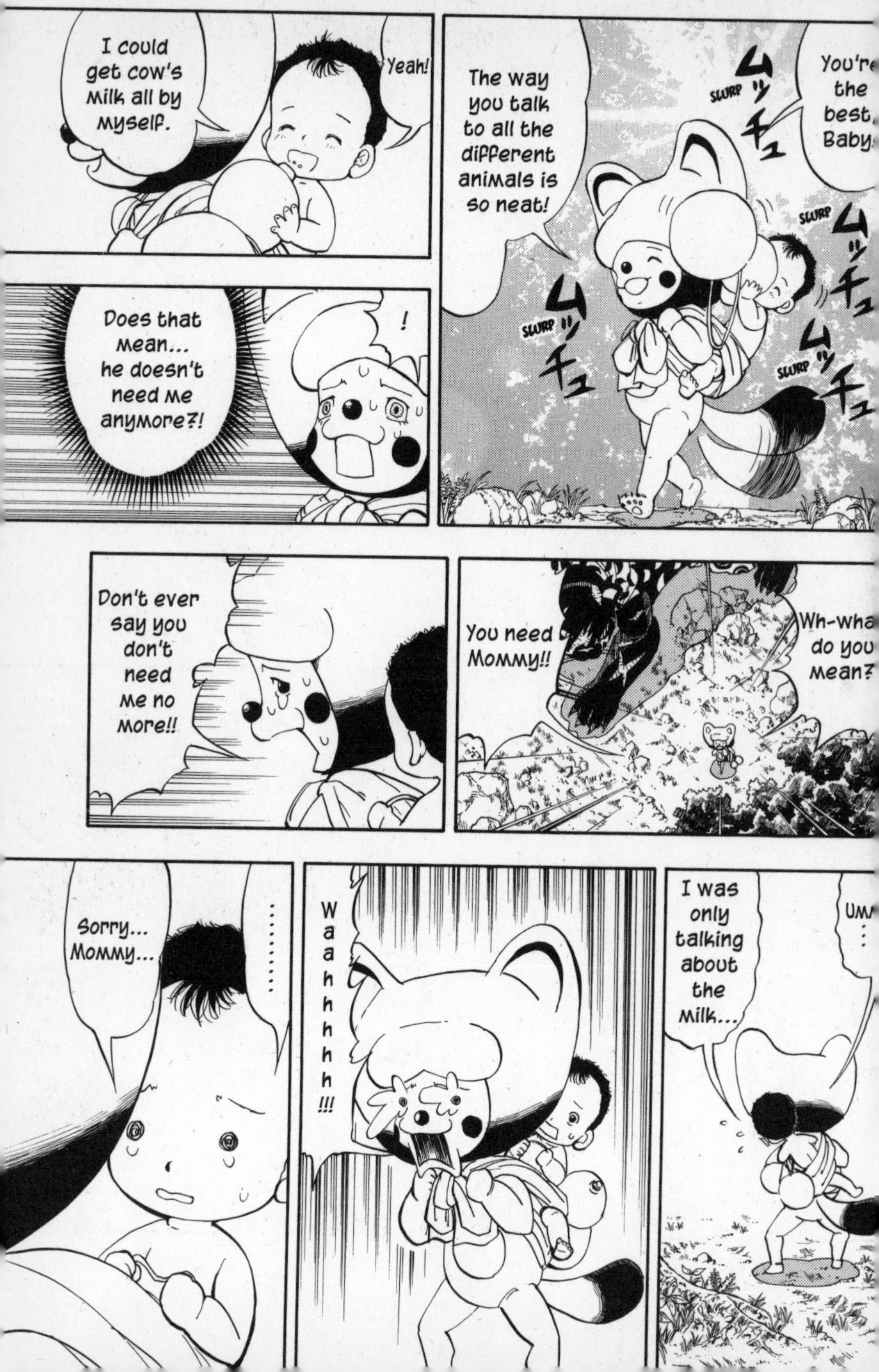

You'r the best, Baby
ムッチュ SLURP
ムッチュ SLURP
ムッチュ SLURP
ムッチュ SLURP
The way you talk to all the different animals is so neat!
Yeah!
I could get cow's milk all by myself.
!
Does that mean... he doesn't need me anymore?!
Wh-wha do you mean?
You need Mommy!!
Don't ever say you don't need me no more!!
UM...
I was only talking about the milk...
Waahhhhhhh!!!
......
Sorry... Mommy...

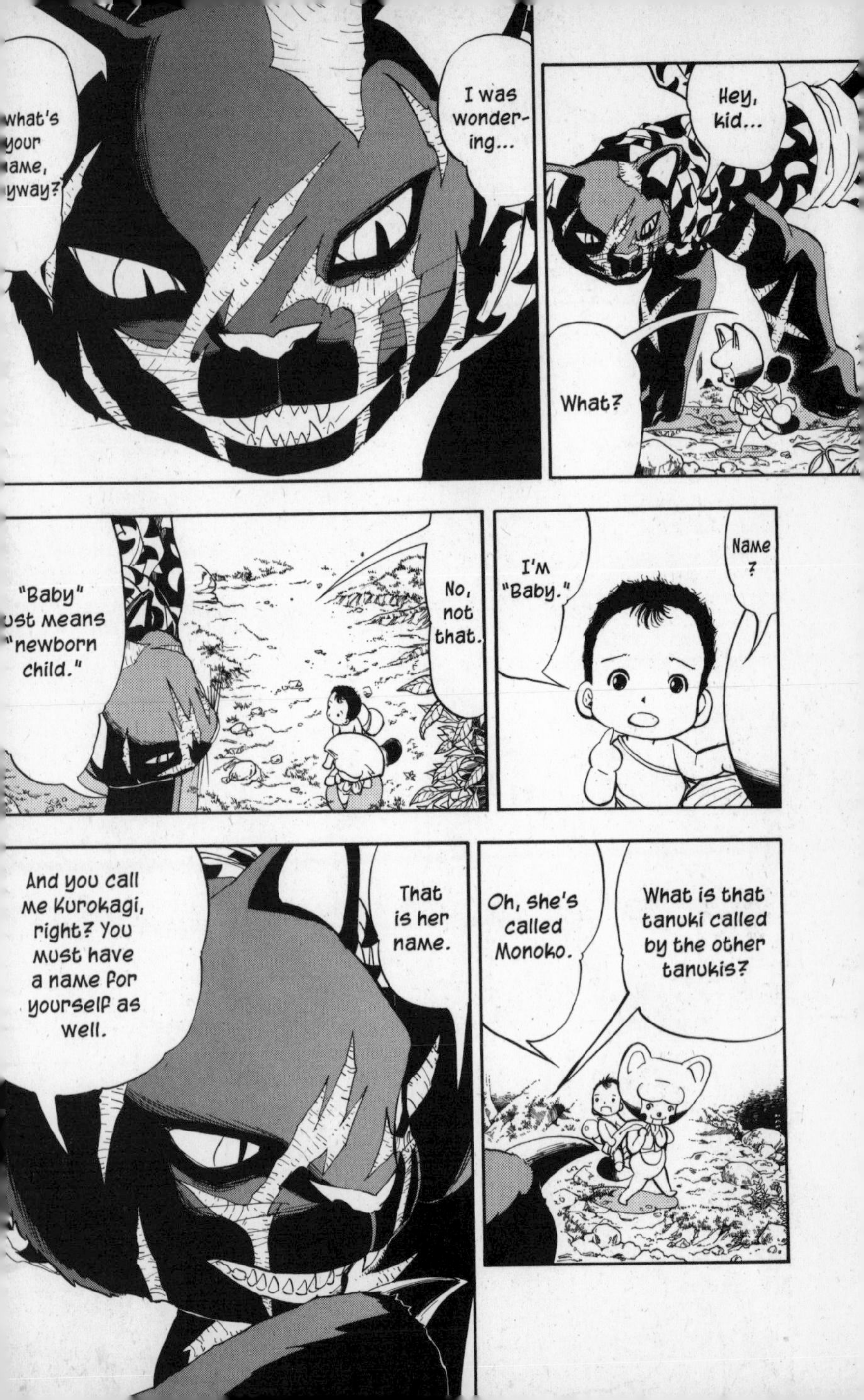
Hey, kid...
What?
I was wonder-ing...
what's your ame, yway?
Name?
I'm "Baby."
No, not that.
"Baby" ust means "newborn child."
What is that tanuki called by the other tanukis?
Oh, she's called Monoko.
That is her name.
And you call me Kurokagi, right? You must have a name for yourself as well.

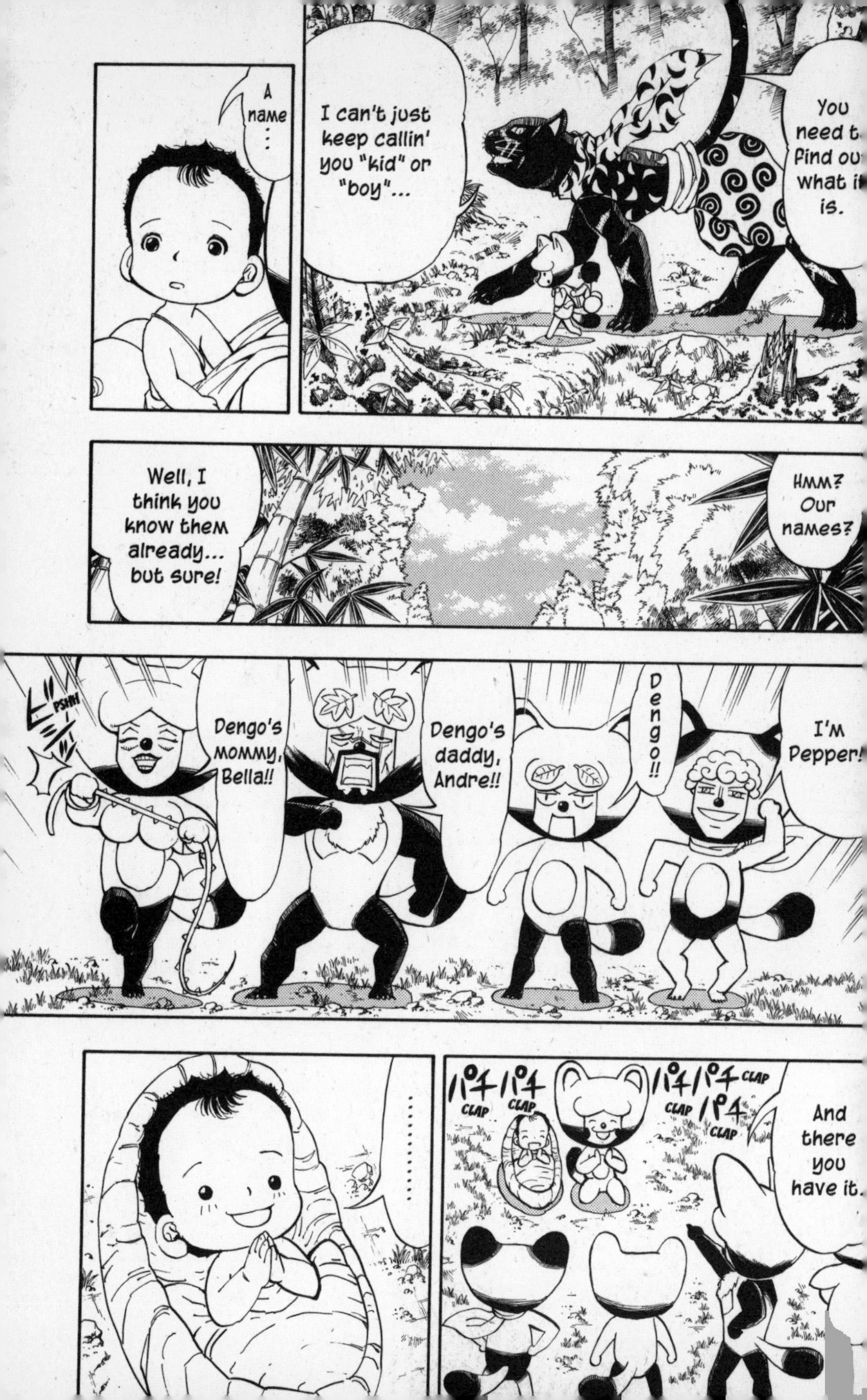
You need t find ou what i is.
I can't just keep callin' you "kid" or "boy"...
A name...
HMM? Our names?
Well, I think you know them already... but sure!
I'M Pepper!
Dengo!!
Dengo's daddy, Andre!!
PSHH
Dengo's MOMMY, Bella!!
And there you have it.
パチパチ CLAP CLAP パチ CLAP
パチパチ CLAP CLAP
......

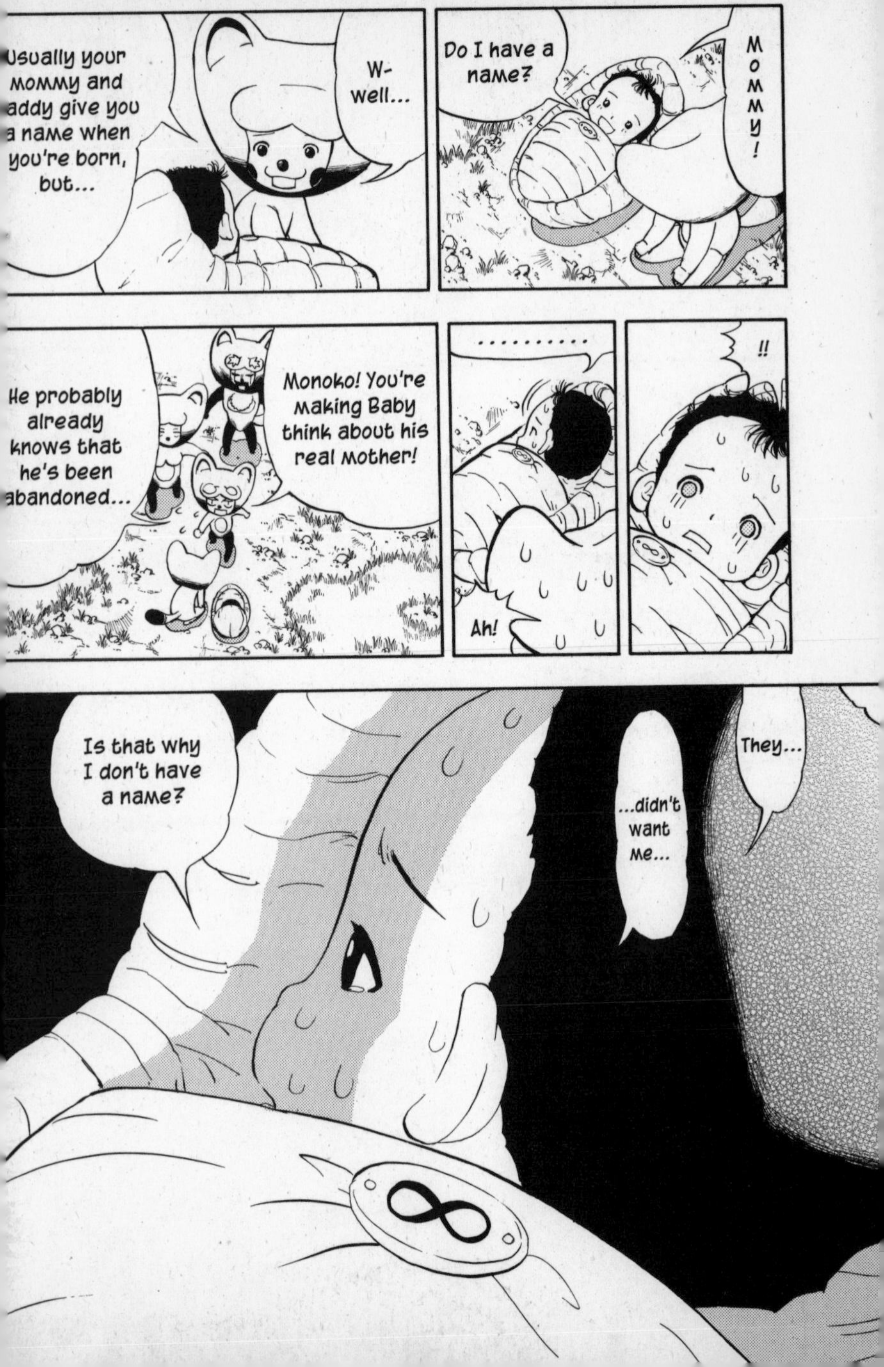

MOMMY!
Do I have a name?
W-well...
Usually your mommy and addy give you a name when you're born, but...
!!
....
Ah!
Monoko! You're making Baby think about his real mother!
He probably already knows that he's been abandoned...
They...
...didn't want me...
Is that why I don't have a name?

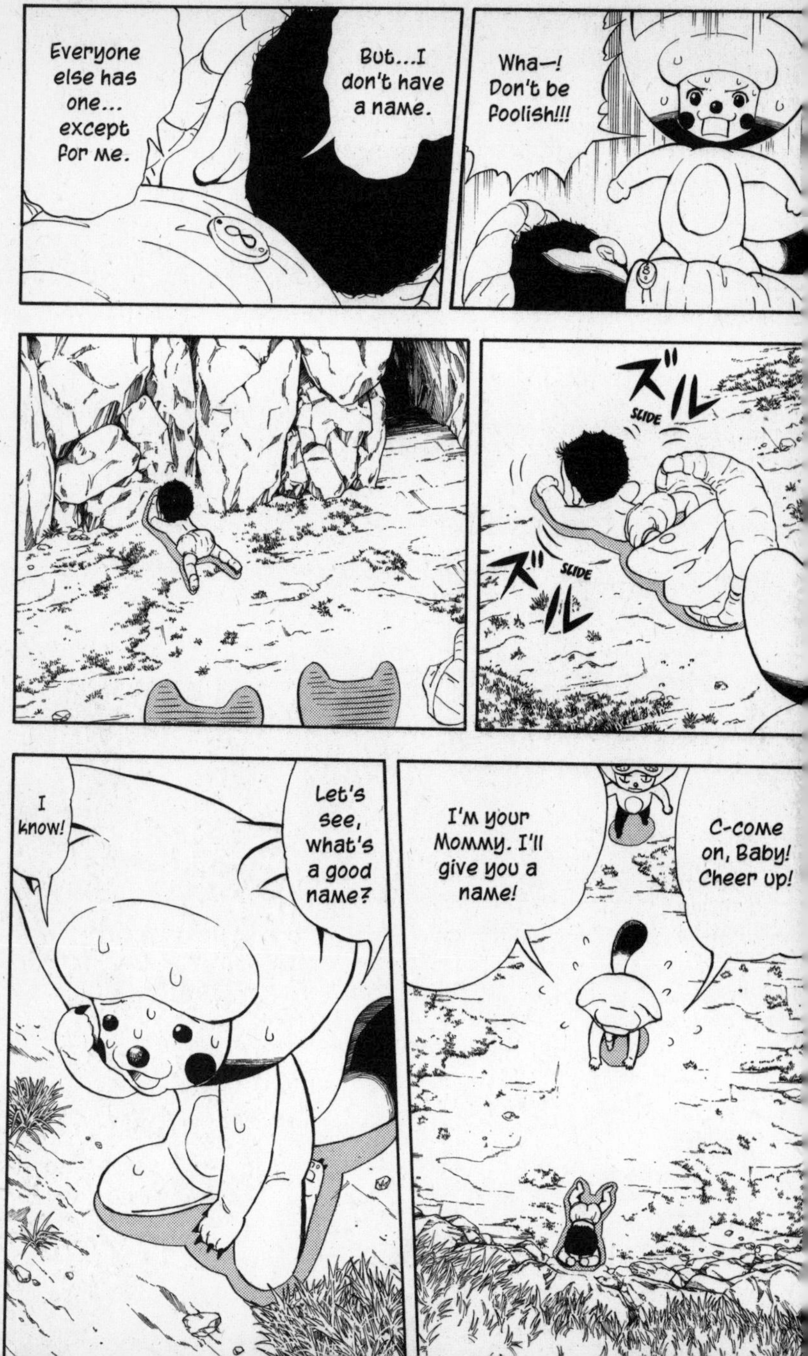
Wha—! Don't be foolish!!!
But...I don't have a name.
Everyone else has one... except for me.
ズル
SLIDE
ズル
SLIDE
C-come on, Baby! Cheer up!
I'm your Mommy. I'll give you a name!
Let's see, what's a good name?
I know!

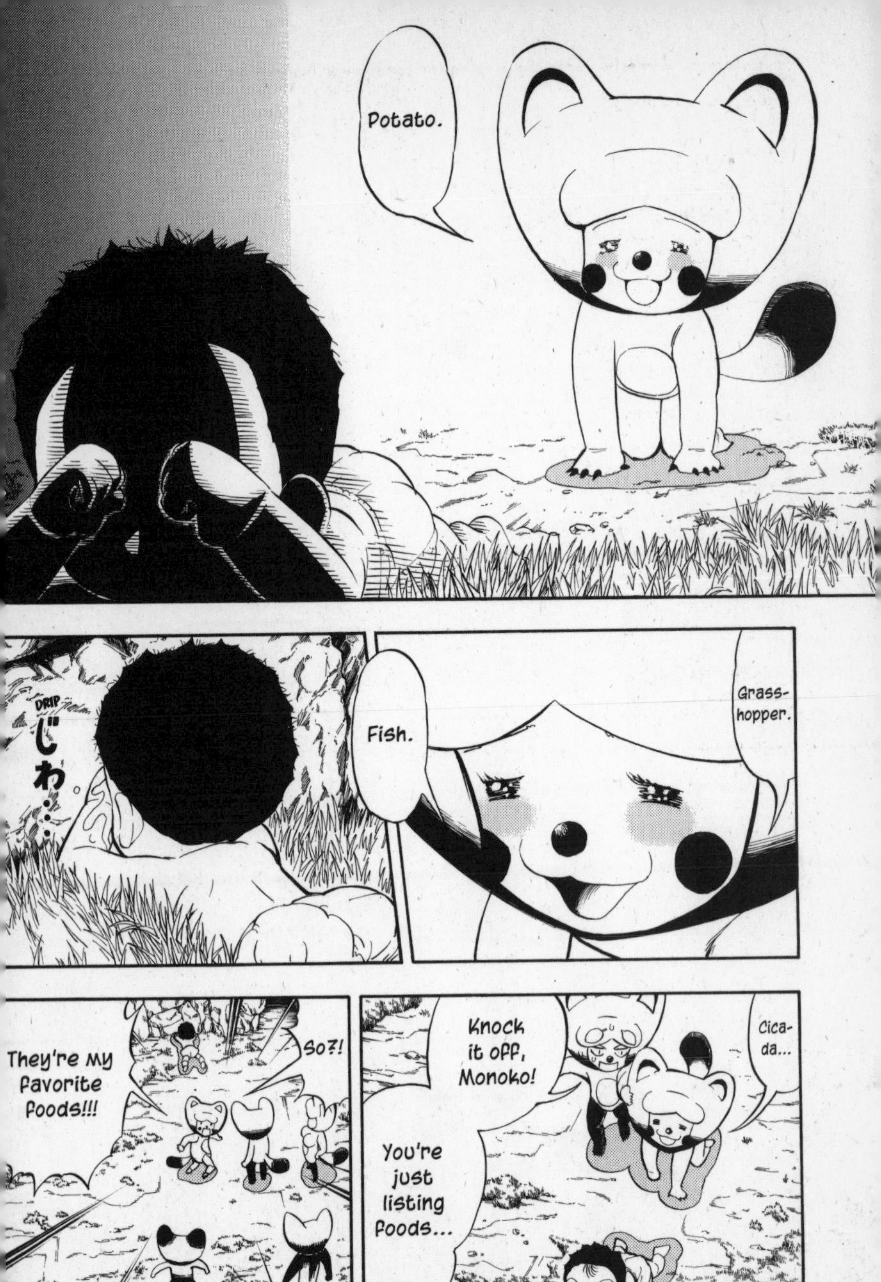

Potato.
Grass-hopper.
Fish.
DRIP
じわ…
Cica-da...
Knock it off, Monoko!
You're just listing foods...
So?!
They're my favorite foods!!!

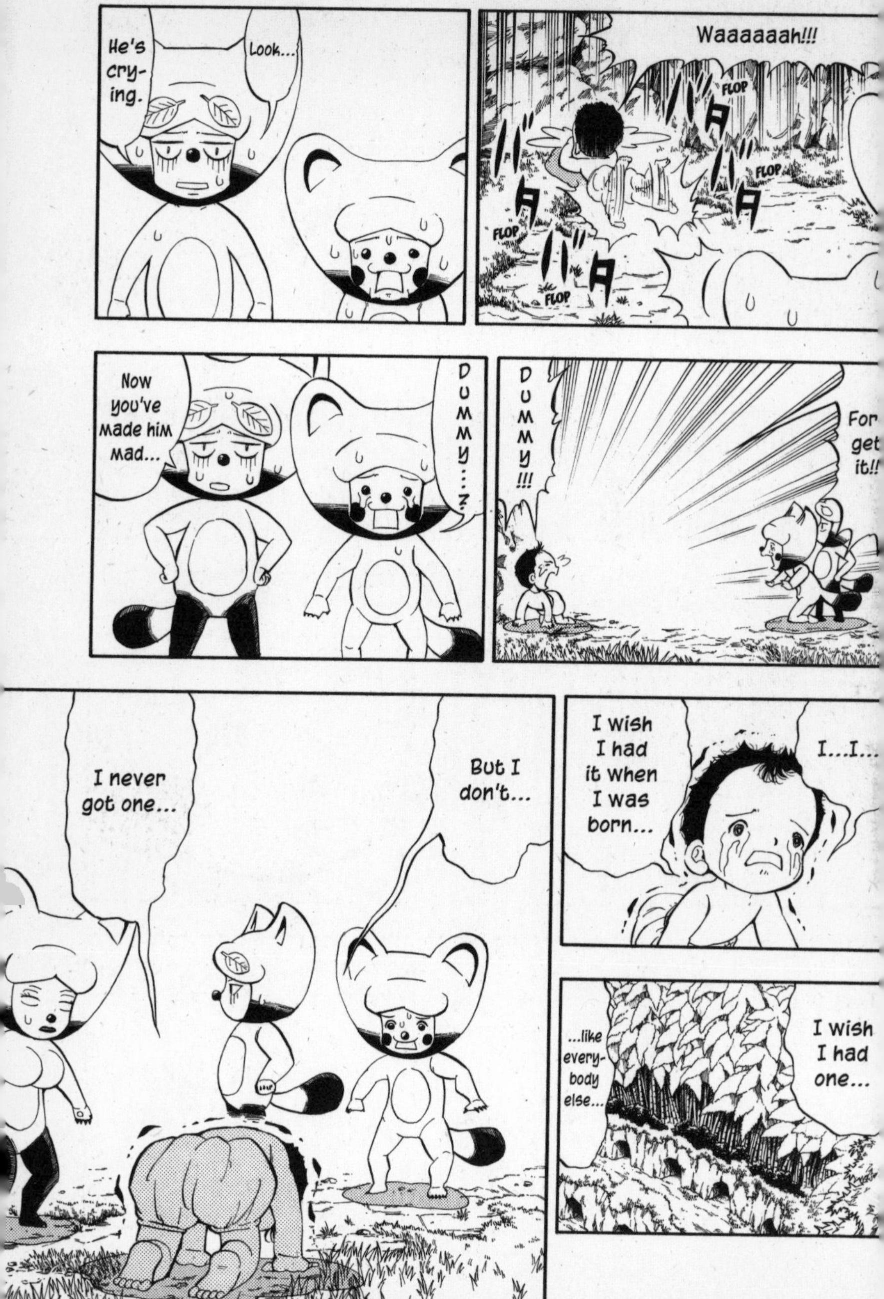
Waaaaaah!!!
FLOP
FLOP
FLOP
FLOP
Look...
He's crying.
DUMMY!!!
Forget it!!
DUMMY...?
Now you've made him mad...
I...I...
I wish I had it when I was born...
I wish I had one...
...like everybody else...
But I don't...
I never got one...

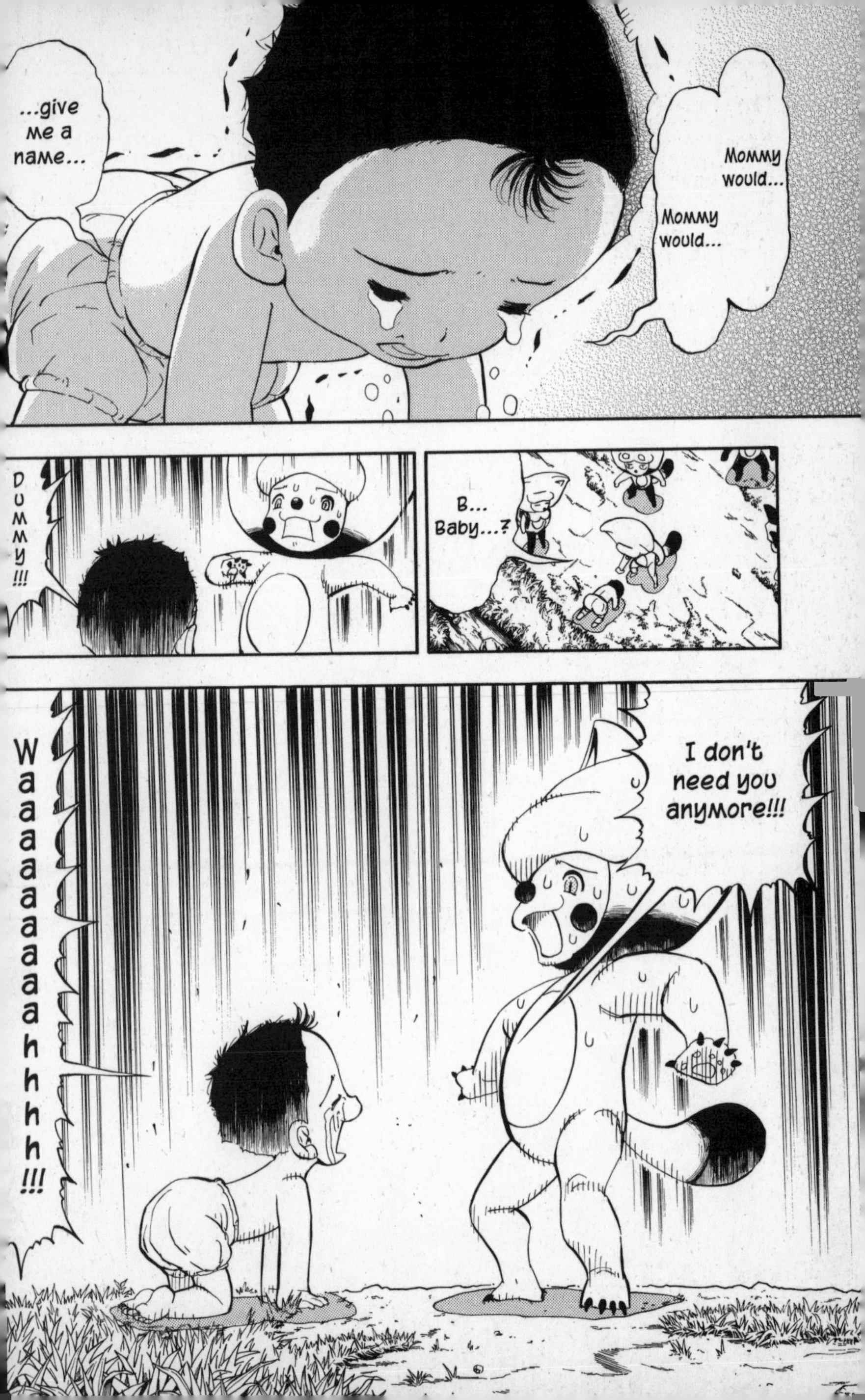
Mommy would...
Mommy would...
...give me a name...
B... Baby...?
DUMMY!!!
I don't need you anymore!!!
Waaaaaaaaaaahhhh!!!

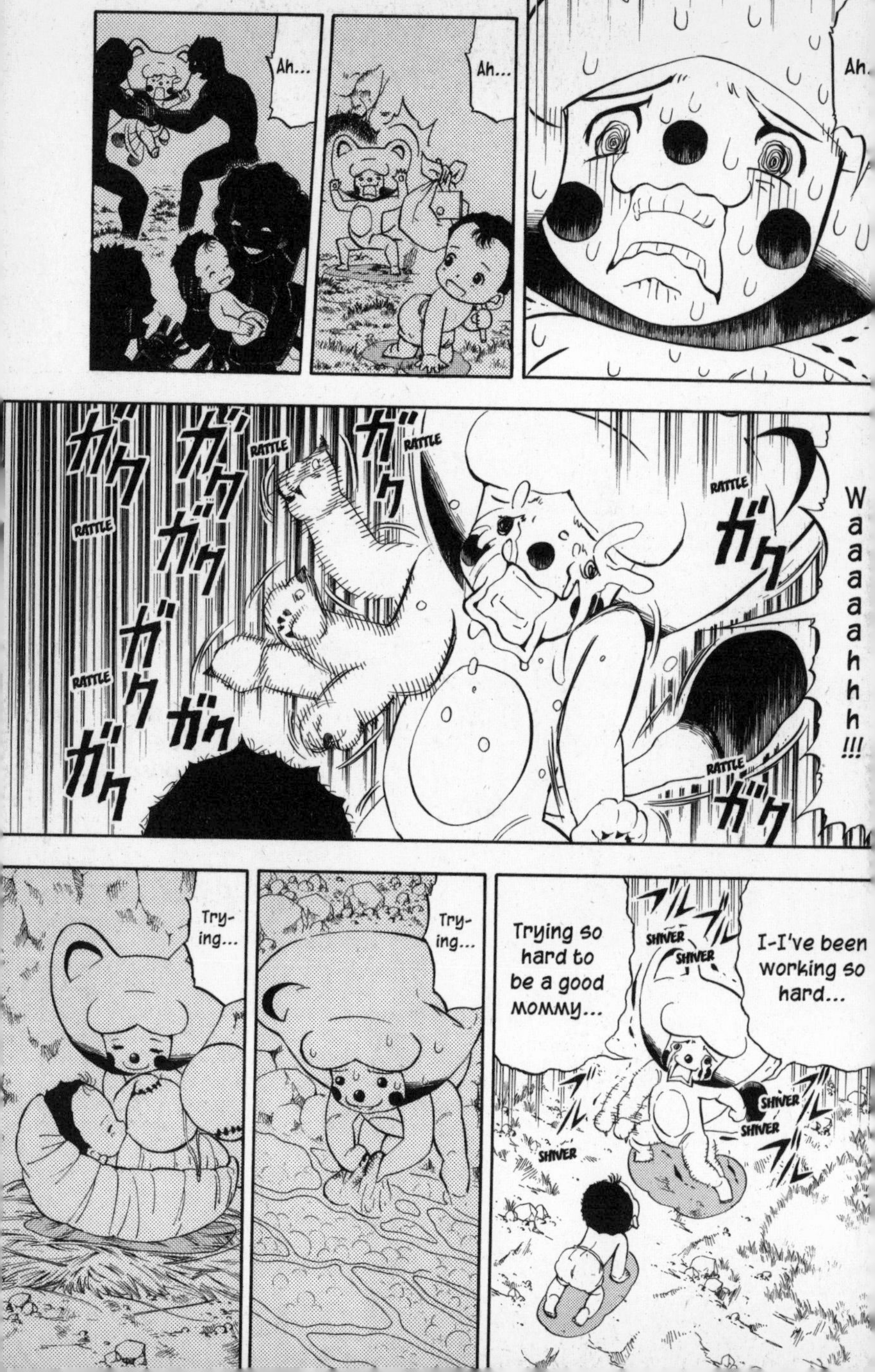

Ah.
Ah...
Ah...
Waaaaaahhh!!!
RATTLE
ガク
RATTLE
ガク
ガク
RATTLE
ガク
ガク
ガク
ガク
RATTLE
ガク
RATTLE
ガク
ガク
I-I've been working so hard...
Trying so hard to be a good mommy...
SHIVER
SHIVER
SHIVER
SHIVER
SHIVER
Try-ing...
Try-ing...

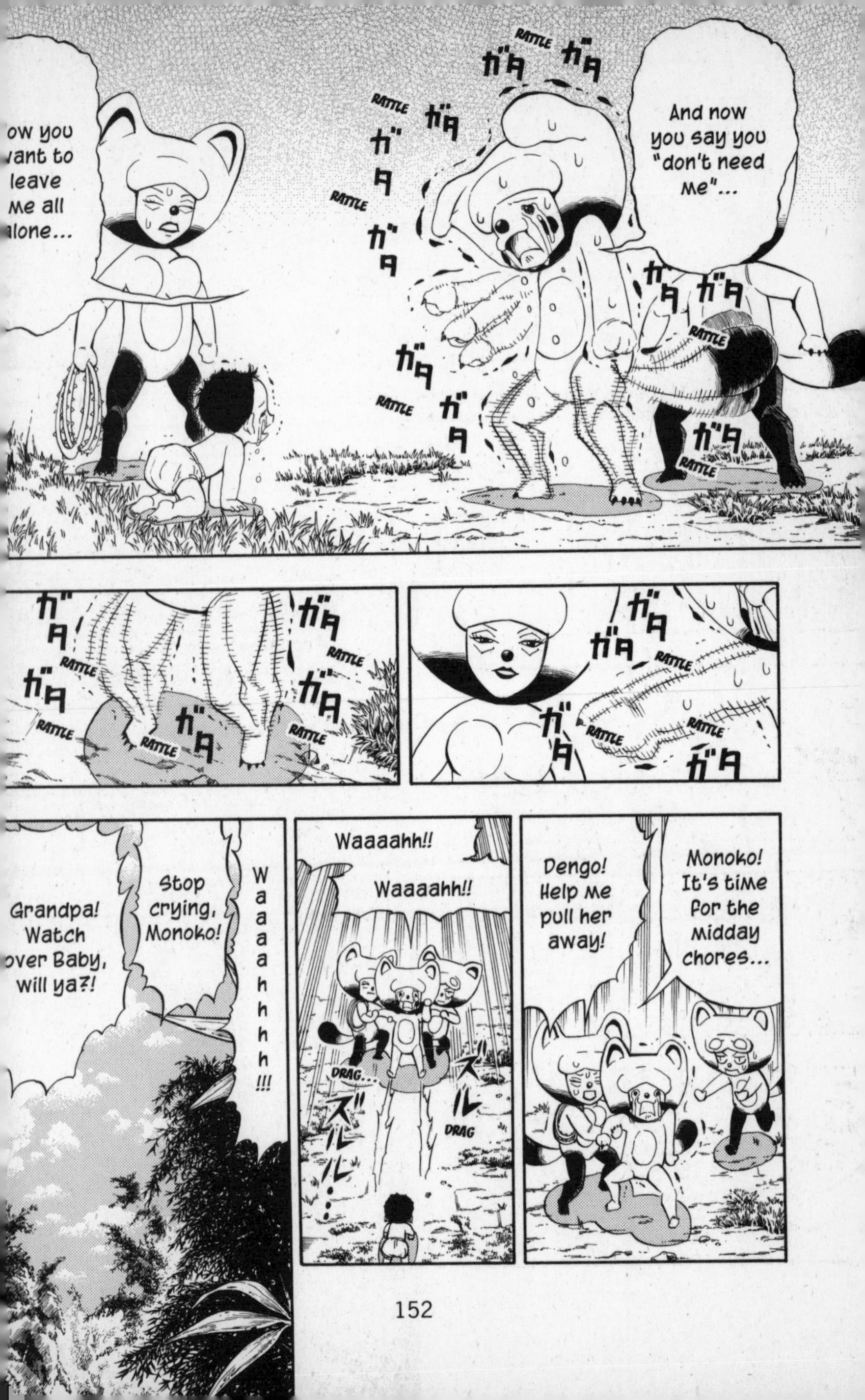

And now you say you "don't need me"...
ガタ
RATTLE
ガタ
RATTLE
ow you vant to leave me all alone...
ガタ
RATTLE
ガタ
RATTLE
ガタ
RATTLE
ガタ
RATTLE
Monoko! It's time for the midday chores...
Dengo! Help me pull her away!
Waaaahh!!
Waaaahh!!
DRAG...
ズル
DRAG
ズル
Waaaahhhhh!!!
Stop crying, Monoko!
Grandpa! Watch over Baby, will ya?!

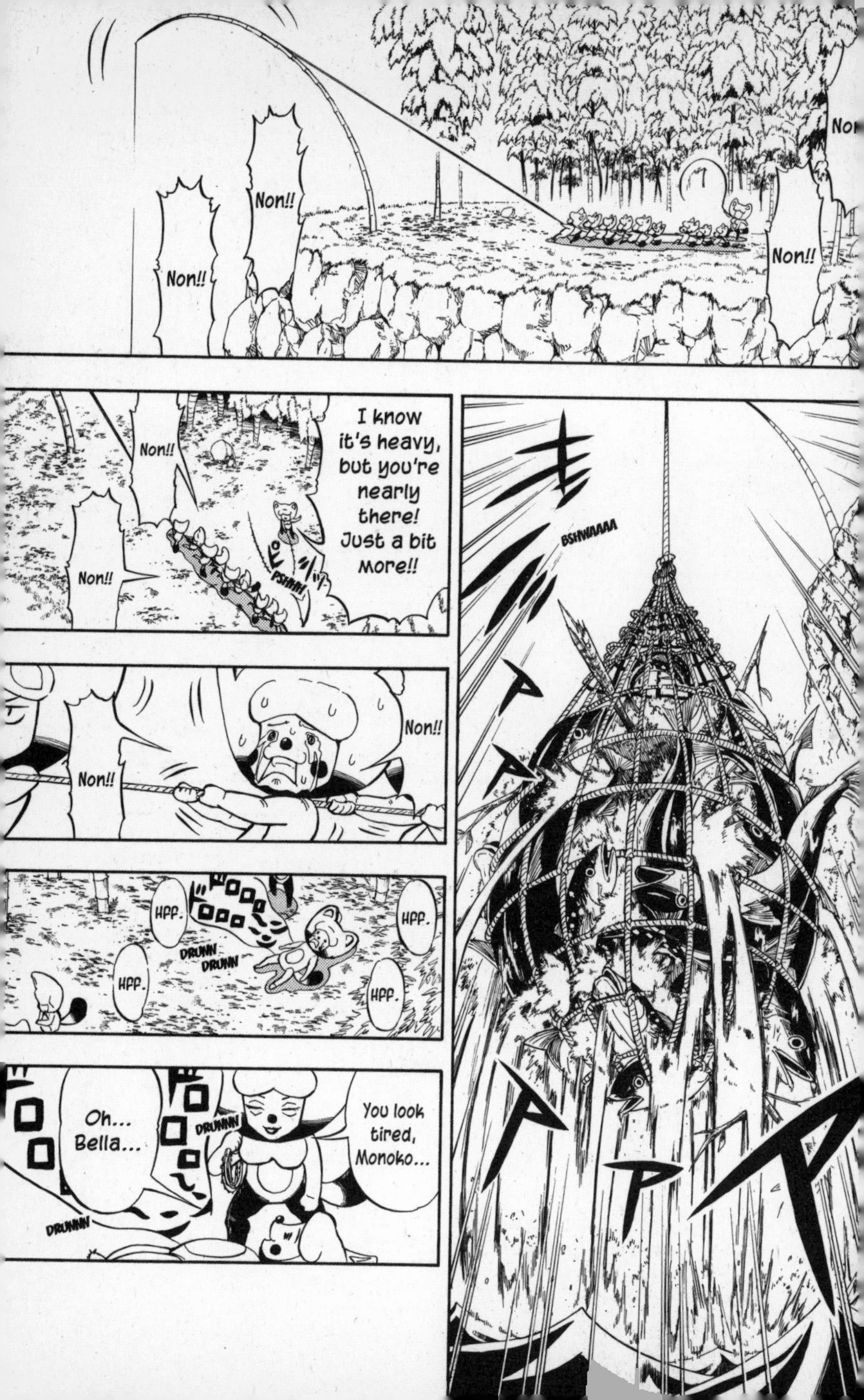
Non
Non!!
Non!!
Non!!
BSHWAAAA
I know it's heavy, but you're nearly there! Just a bit more!!
Non!!
PSHHH
Non!!
Non!!
Non!!
Hff.
Hff.
DRUNN DRUNN
Hff.
Hff.
You look tired, Monoko...
DRUNNN
Oh... Bella...
DRUNNN

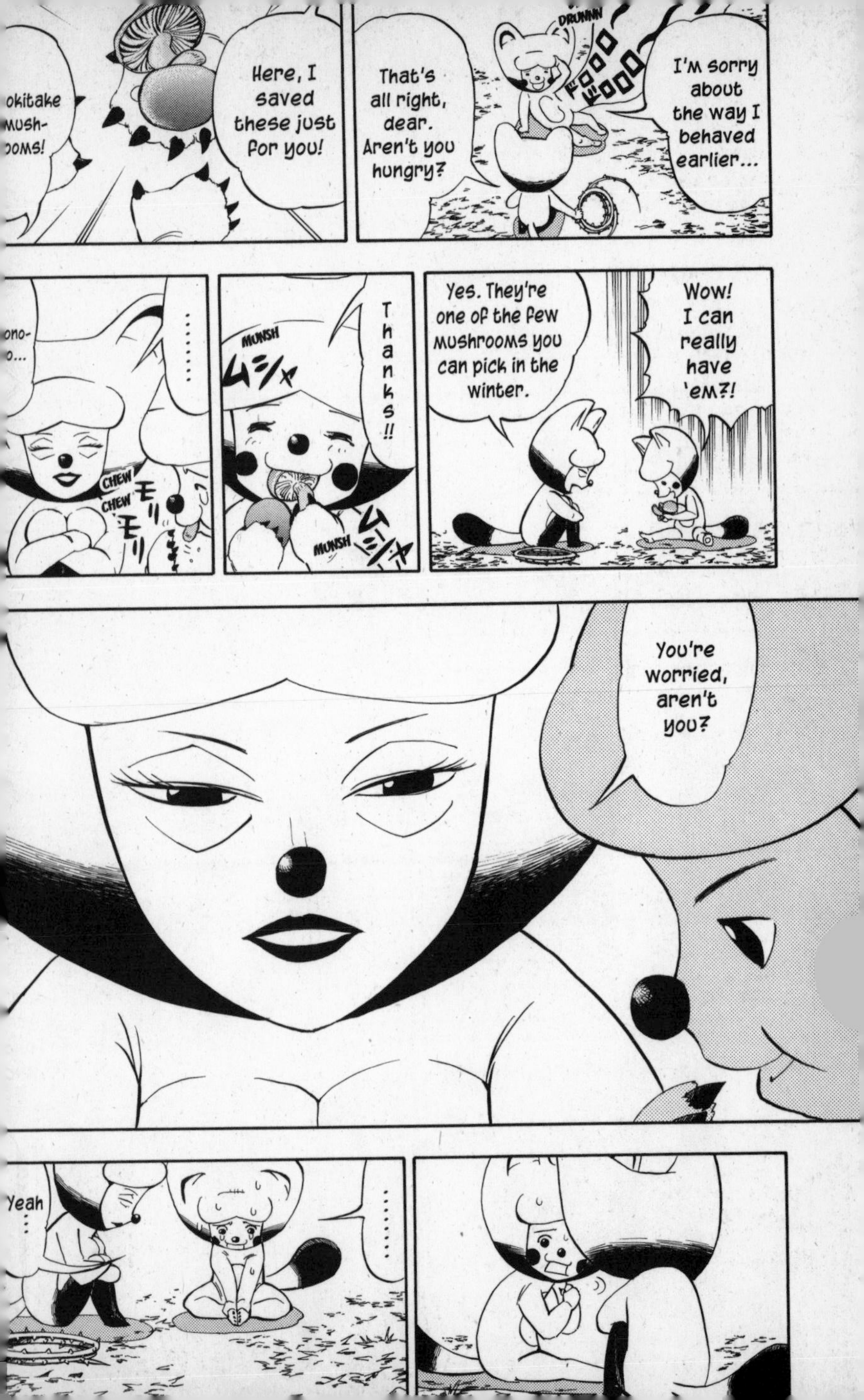
DRUNNN
FOOD FOOD
I'm sorry about the way I behaved earlier...
That's all right, dear. Aren't you hungry?
Here, I saved these just for you!
okitake mush- ooms!
Wow! I can really have 'em?!
Yes. They're one of the few mushrooms you can pick in the winter.
Thanks!!
MUNSH
MUNSH
......
ono- o...
CHEW
CHEW
You're worried, aren't you?
......
Yeah ...

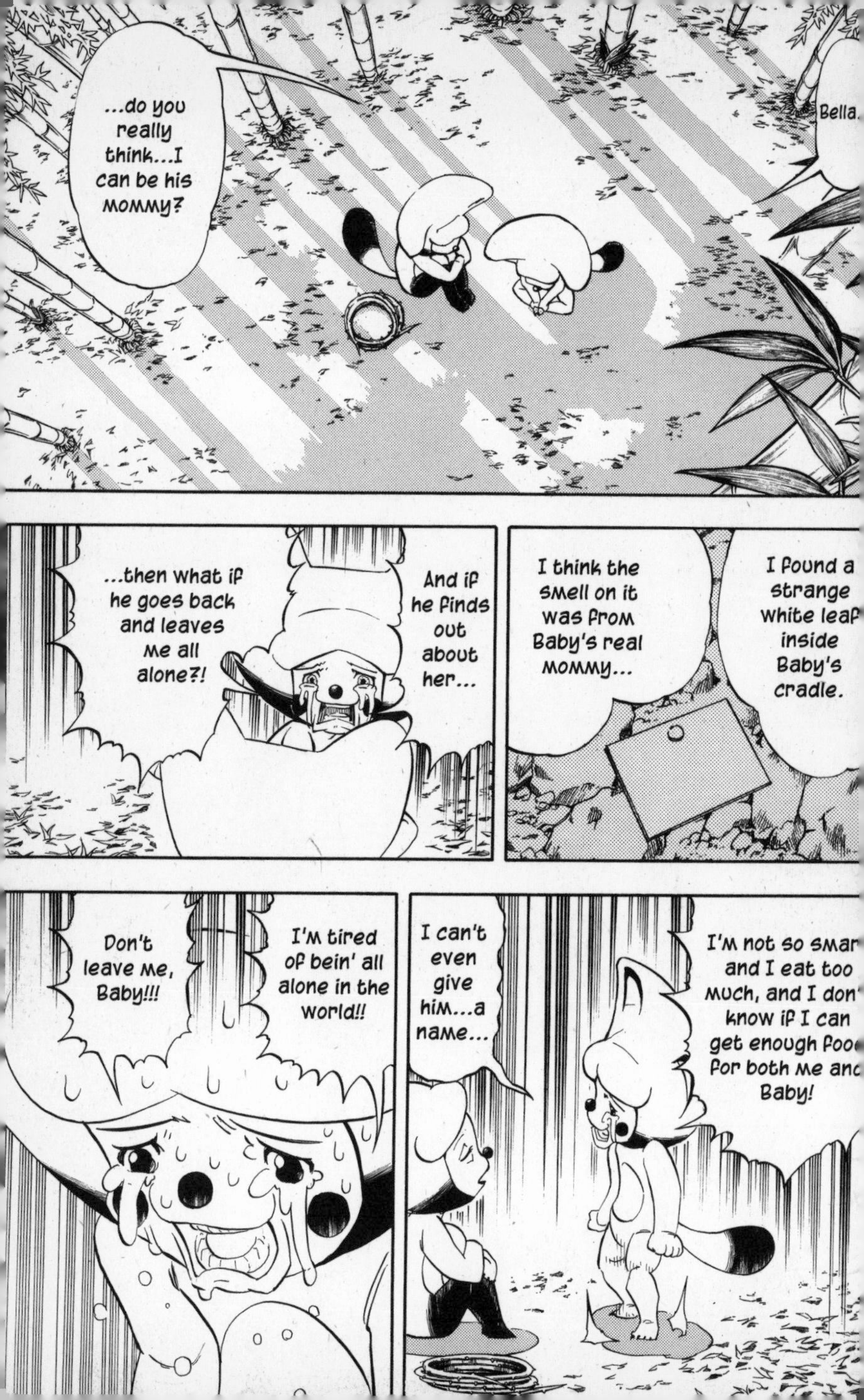
Bella.
...do you really think...I can be his mommy?
I found a strange white leaf inside Baby's cradle.
I think the smell on it was from Baby's real mommy...
And if he finds out about her...
...then what if he goes back and leaves me all alone?!
I'm not so smar
and I eat too much, and I don
know if I can get enough foo
for both me an
Baby!
I can't even give him...a name...
I'm tired of bein' all alone in the world!!
Don't leave me, Baby!!!

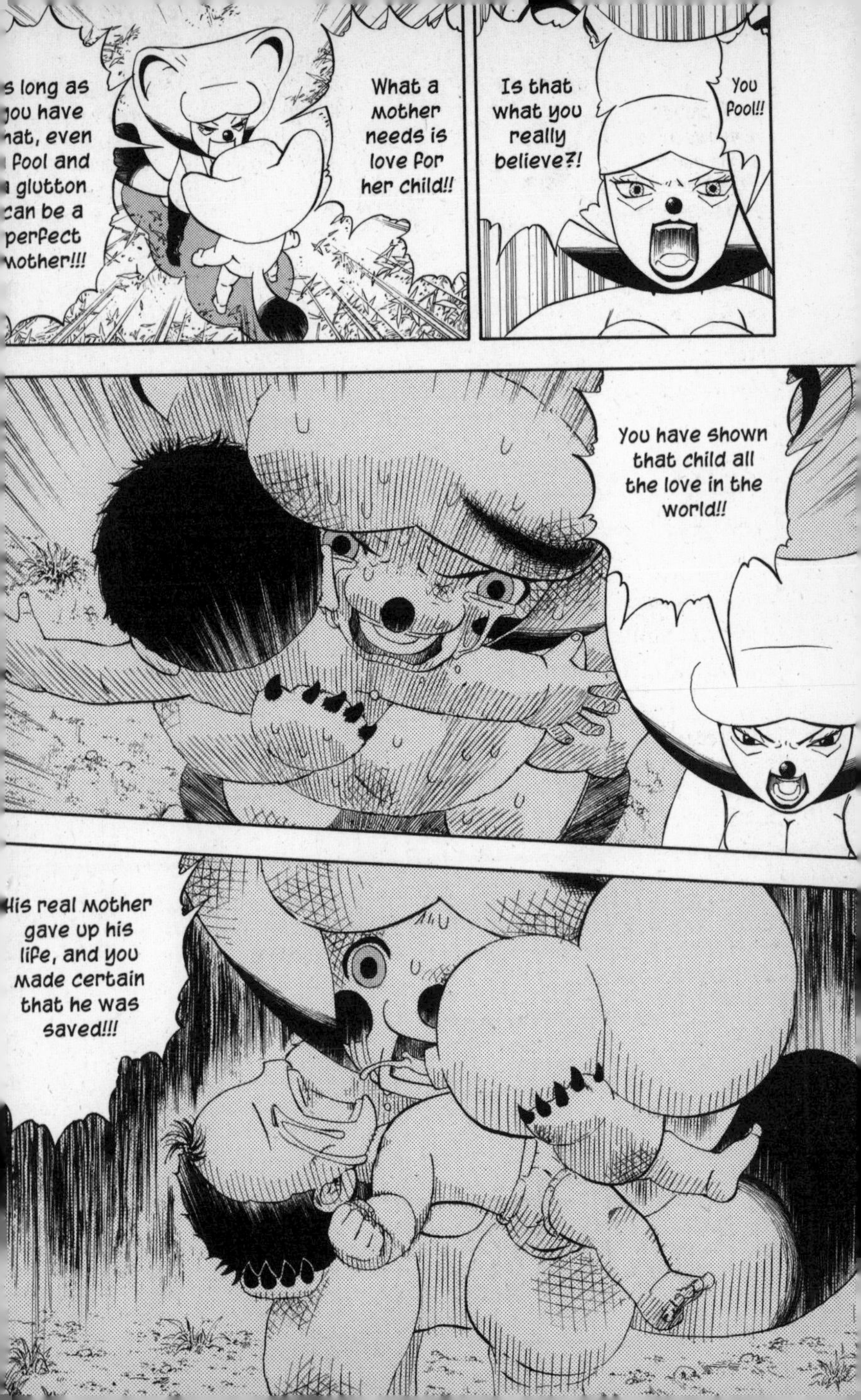
You fool!!
Is that what you really believe?!
What a mother needs is love for her child!!
s long as you have hat, even fool and a glutton can be a perfect mother!!!
You have shown that child all the love in the world!!
His real mother gave up his life, and you made certain that he was saved!!!

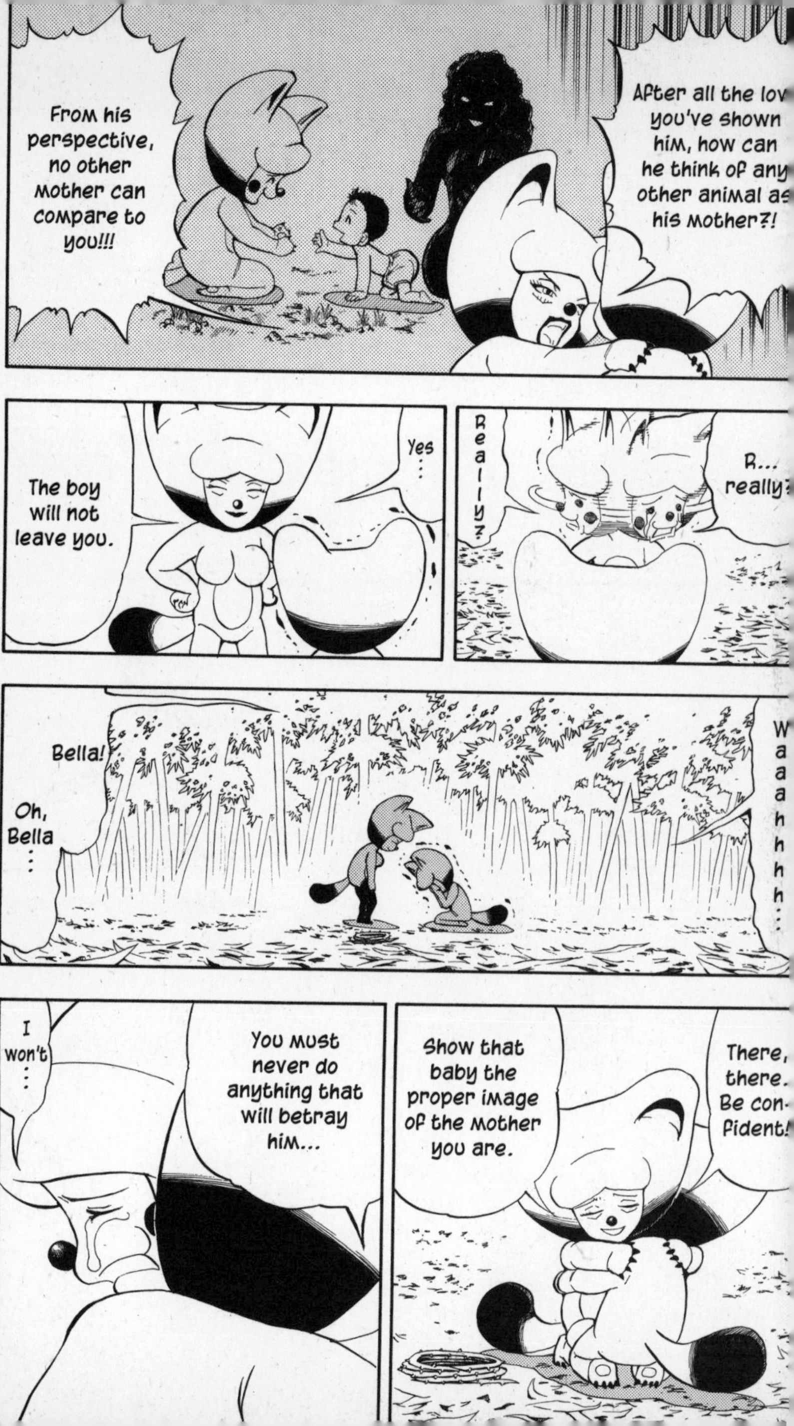
After all the lov you've shown him, how can he think of any other animal as his mother?!
From his perspective, no other mother can compare to you!!!
R... really?
Really?
Yes...
The boy will not leave you.
Waaahhhhh...
Bella!
Oh, Bella...
There, there. Be con-fident!
Show that baby the proper image of the mother you are.
You must never do anything that will betray him...
I won't...

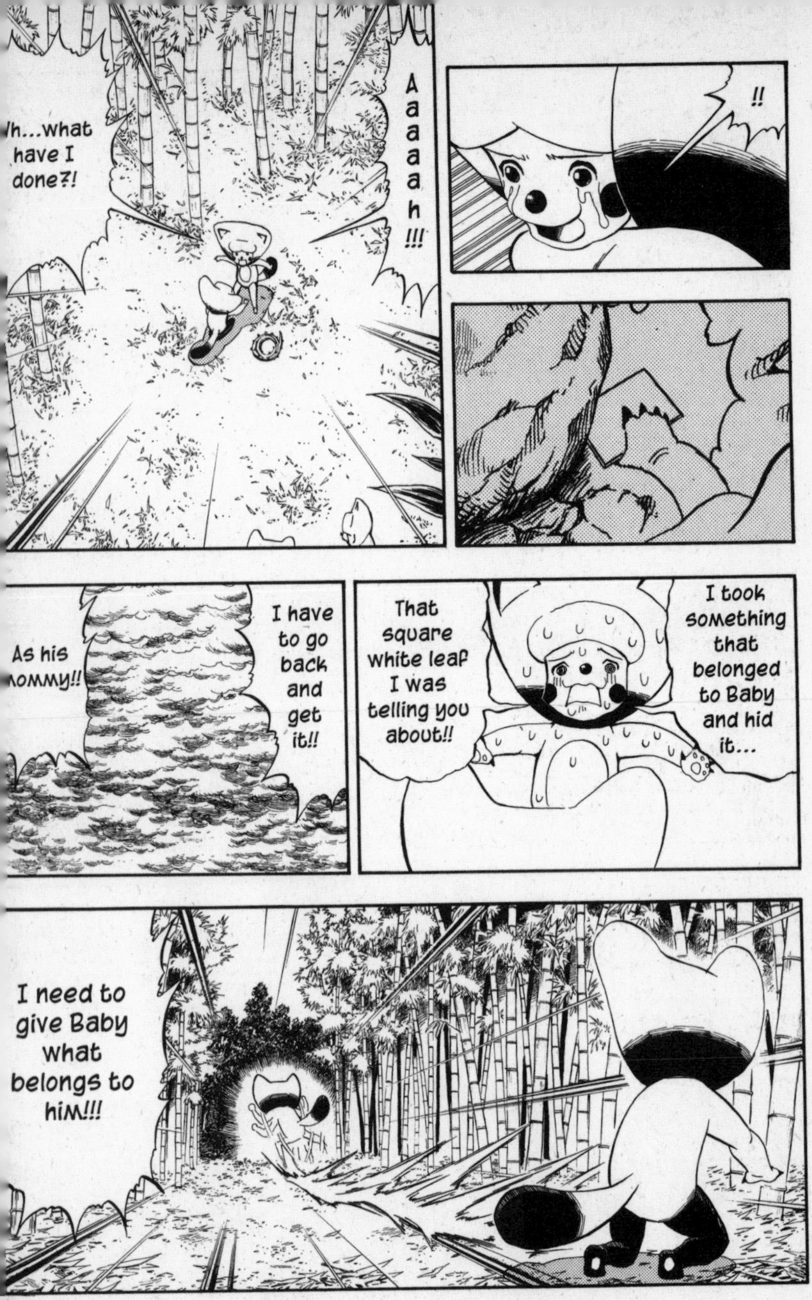
!!
Aaaaah!!!
h...what have I done?!
I took something that belonged to Baby and hid it...
That square white leaf I was telling you about!!
I have to go back and get it!!
As his ommy!!
I need to give Baby what belongs to him!!!

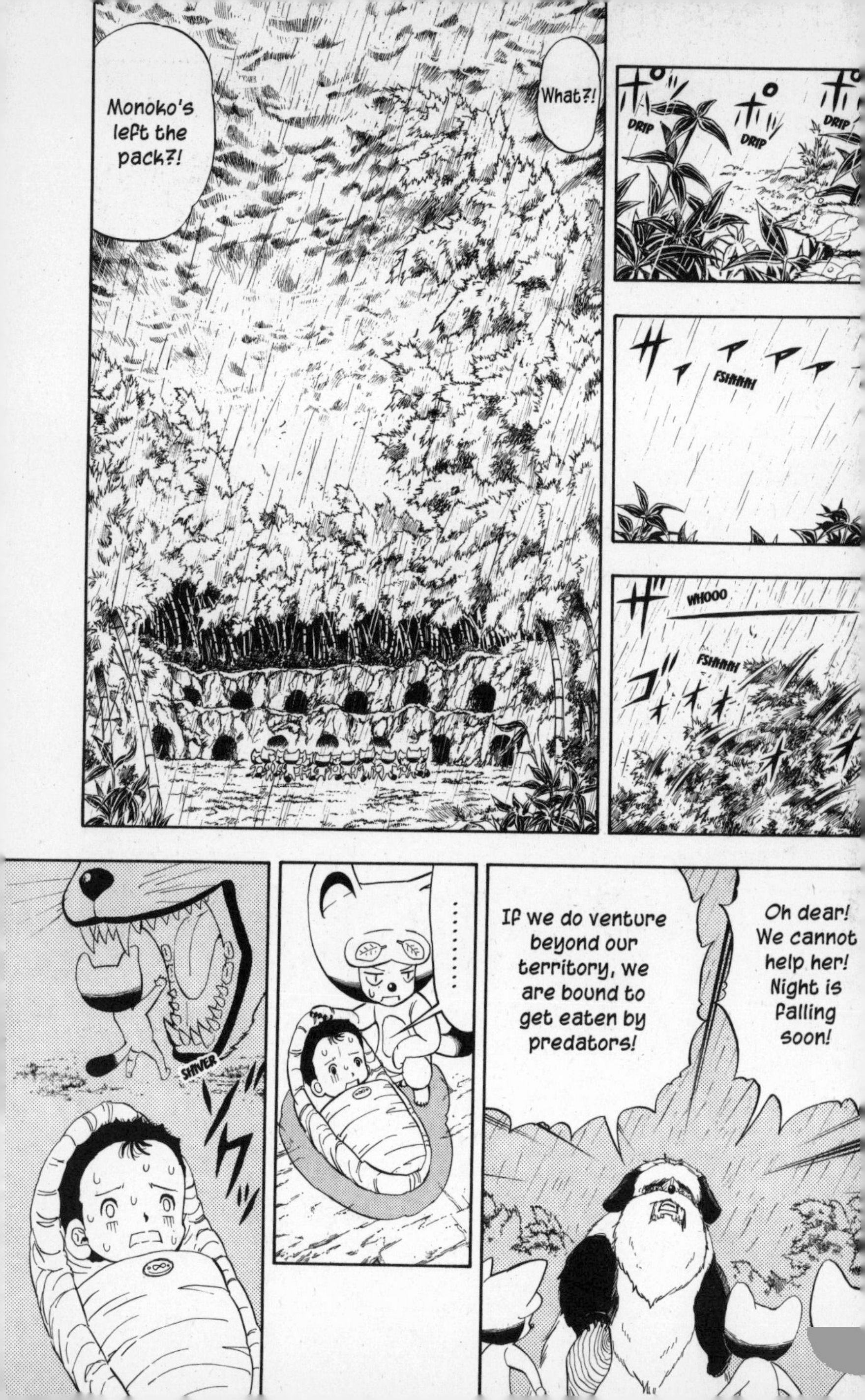
DRIP
DRIP
DRIP
FSHHHH
WHOOO
FSHHHH
What?!
Monoko's left the pack?!
Oh dear! We cannot help her! Night is falling soon!
If we do venture beyond our territory, we are bound to get eaten by predators!
......
SHIVER

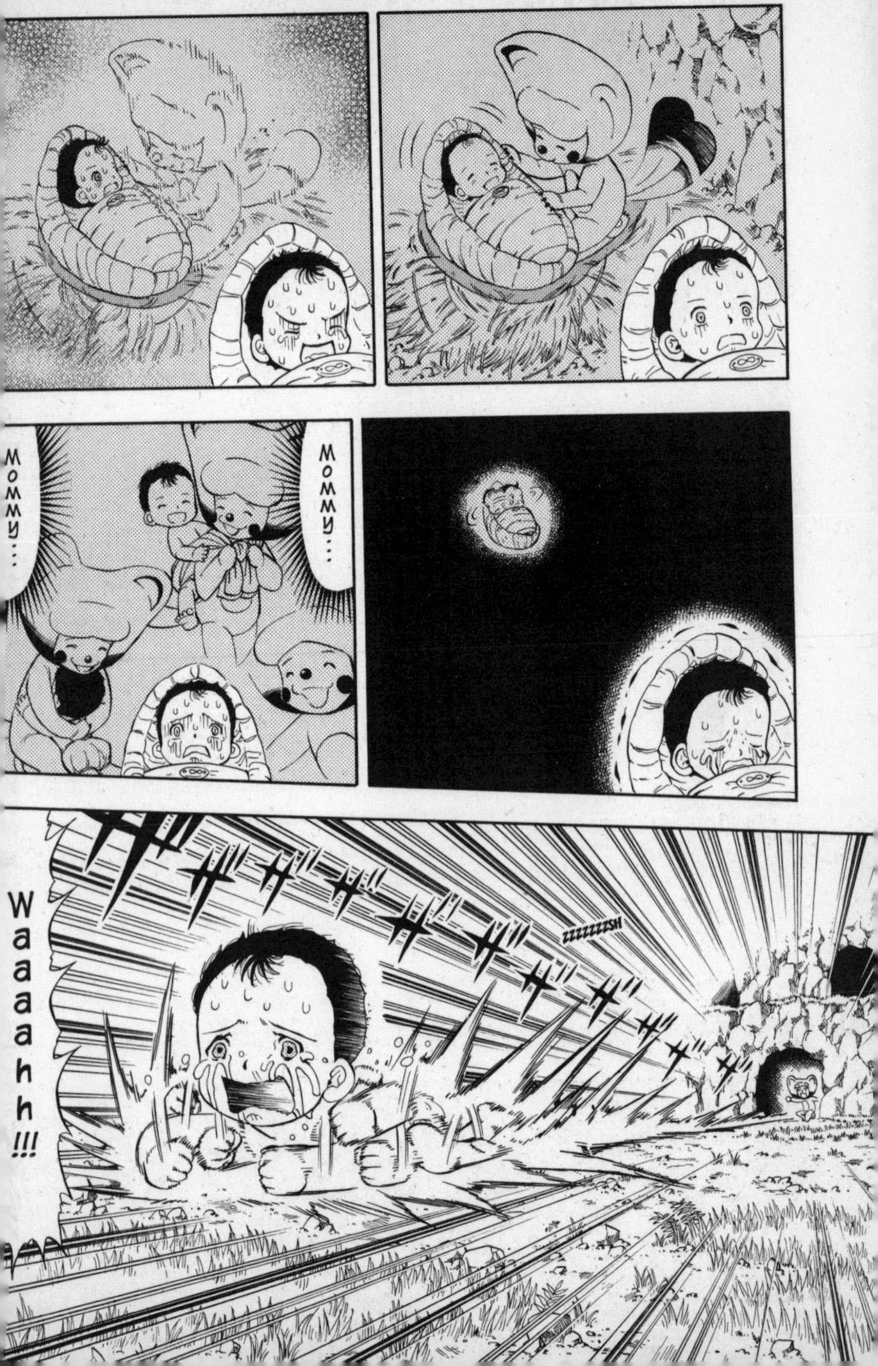
Mommy...
Mommy...
ZZZZZZZZSH
Waaaaahh!!!

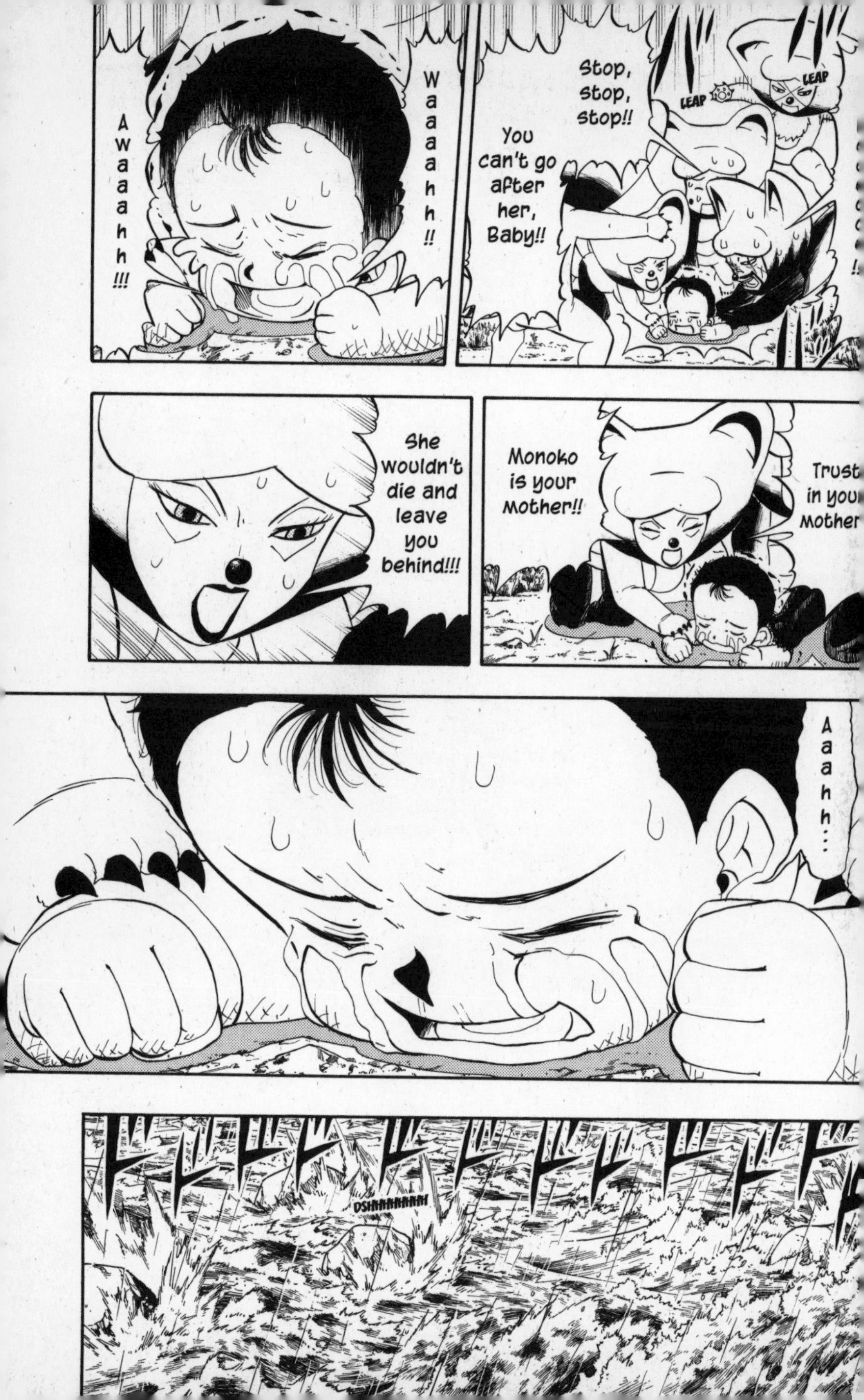

LEAP
LEAP
Stop, stop, stop!!
You can't go after her, Baby!!
Waaaaahh!!
Awaaaahh!!!
Trust in you Mother
Monoko is your Mother!!
She wouldn't die and leave you behind!!!
Aaahh...
DSHHHHHHHH

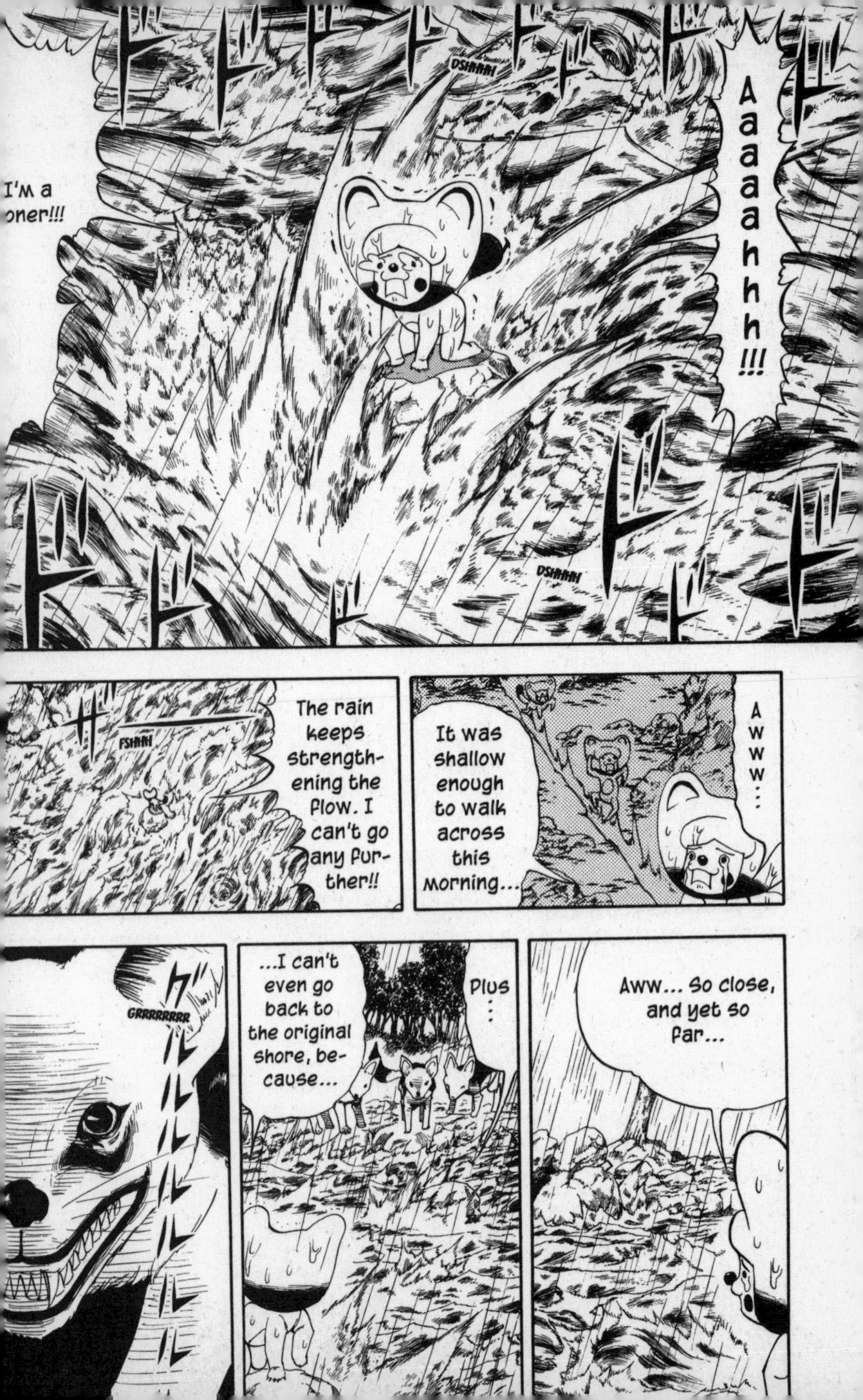
Aaaaahhh!!!
DSHHHH
I'M a
oner!!!
DSHHHH
Awww...
It was shallow enough to walk across this morning...
The rain keeps strength-ening the flow. I can't go any fur-ther!!
FSHHH
Aww... So close, and yet so far...
Plus...
...I can't even go back to the original shore, be-cause...
GRRRRRRRR

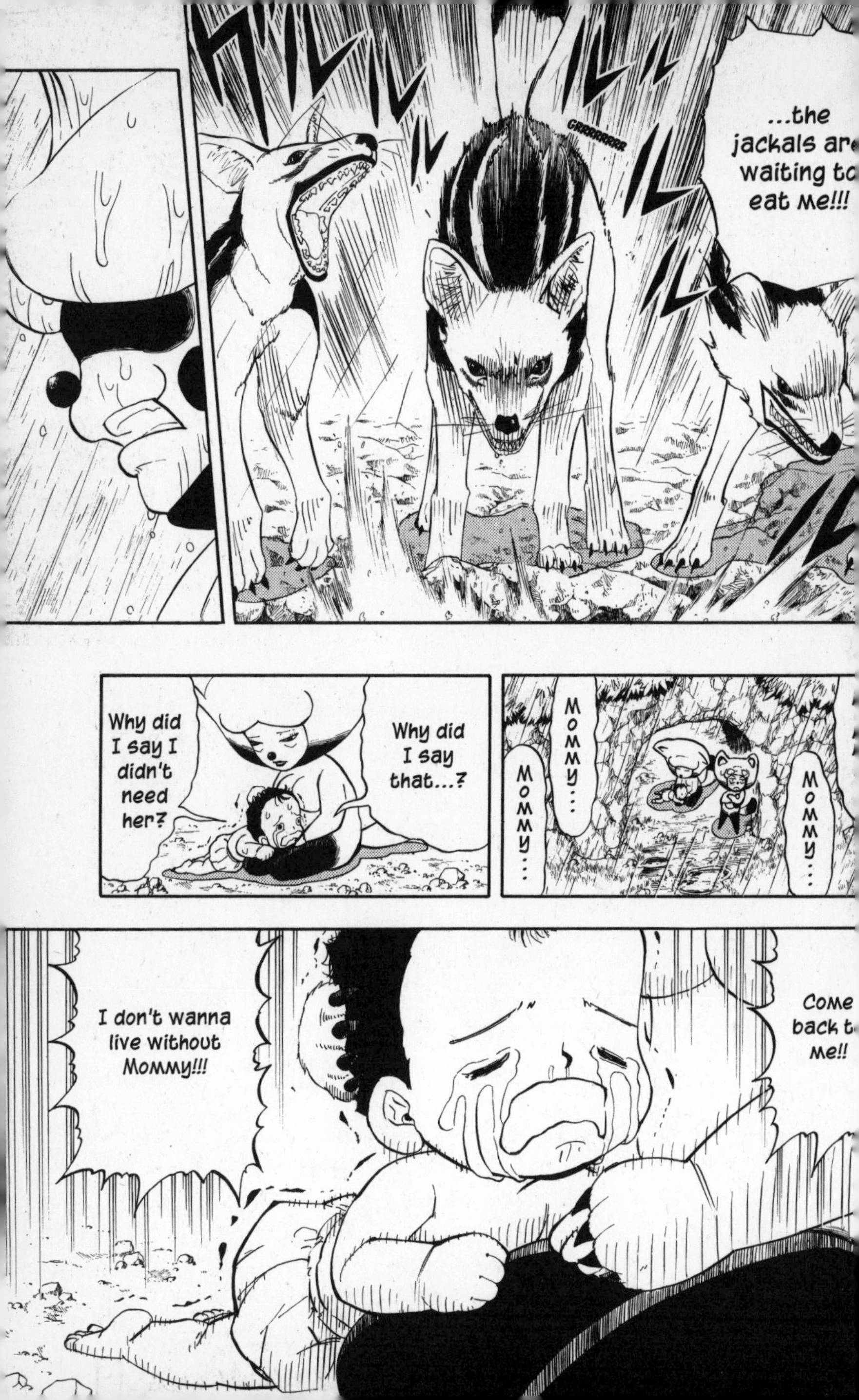
GRRRRRRRR
...the jackals are waiting to eat me!!!
Mommy...
Mommy...
Mommy...
Why did I say that...?
Why did I say I didn't need her?
Come back t me!!
I don't wanna live without Mommy!!!

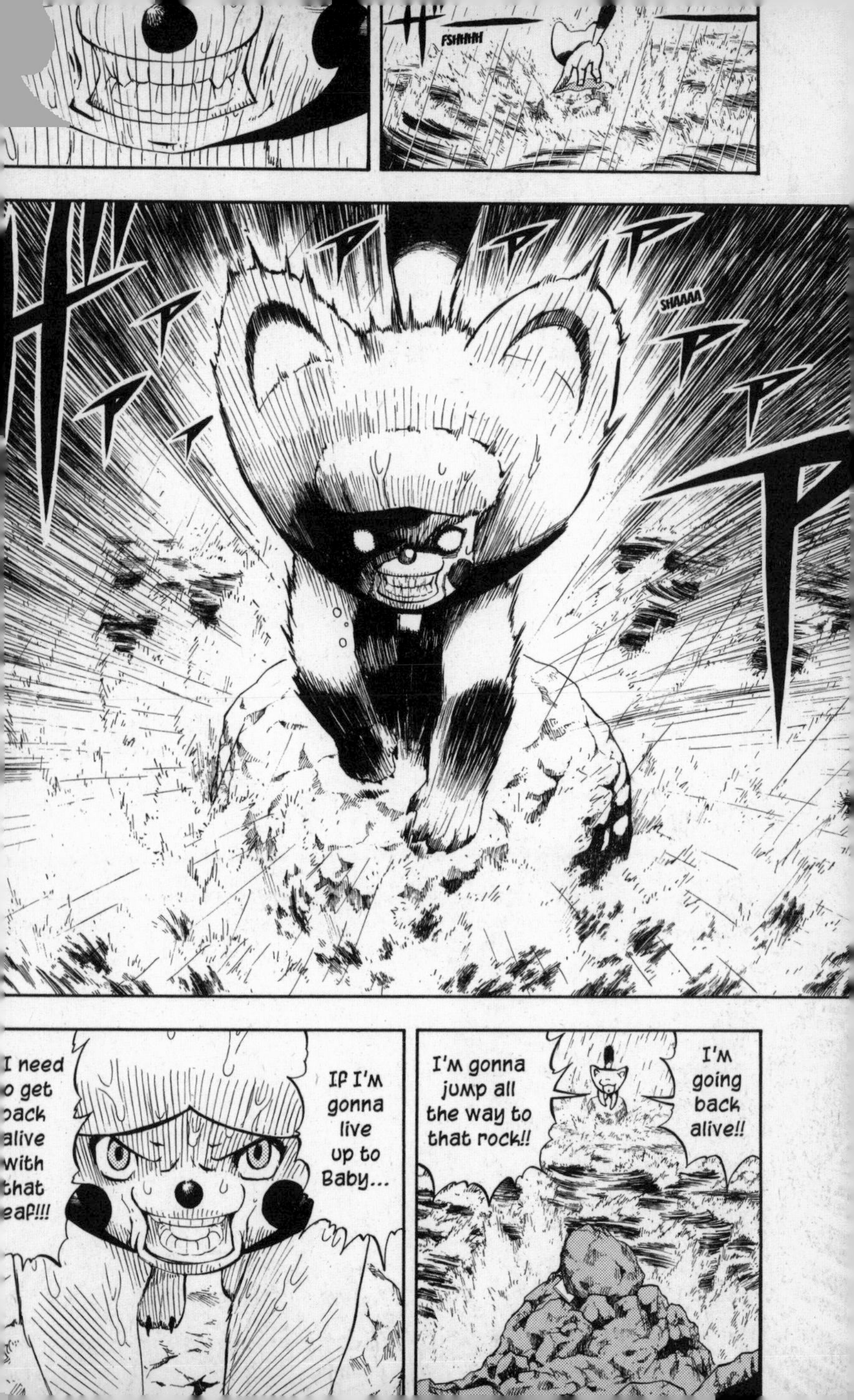
FSHHHH
SHAAAA
I'M going back alive!!
I'M gonna jump all the way to that rock!!
If I'M gonna live up to Baby...
I need o get back alive with that eaf!!!

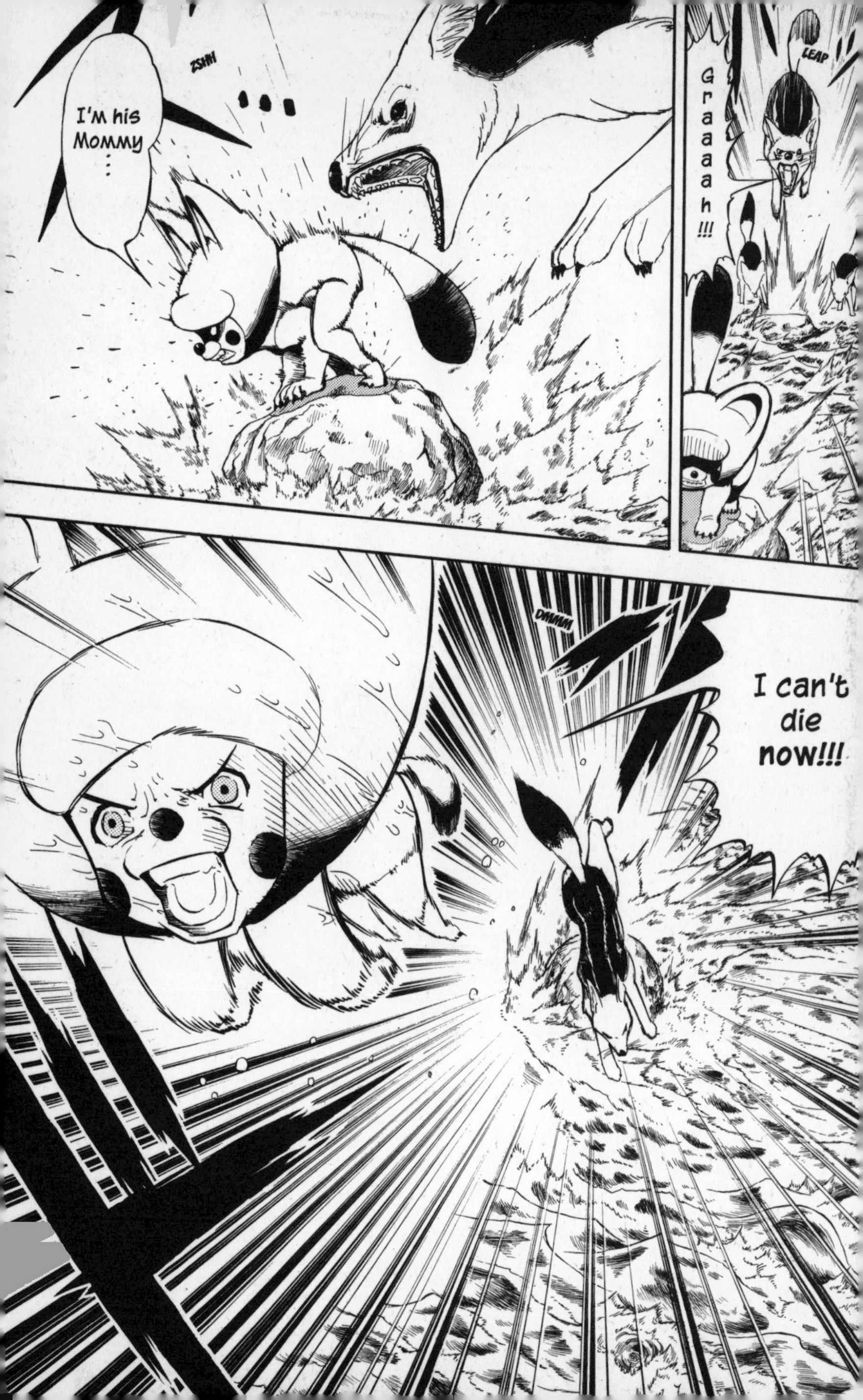
LEAP
Graaaah!!!
ZSHH
I'm his Mommy ...
DMMM
I can't die now!!!

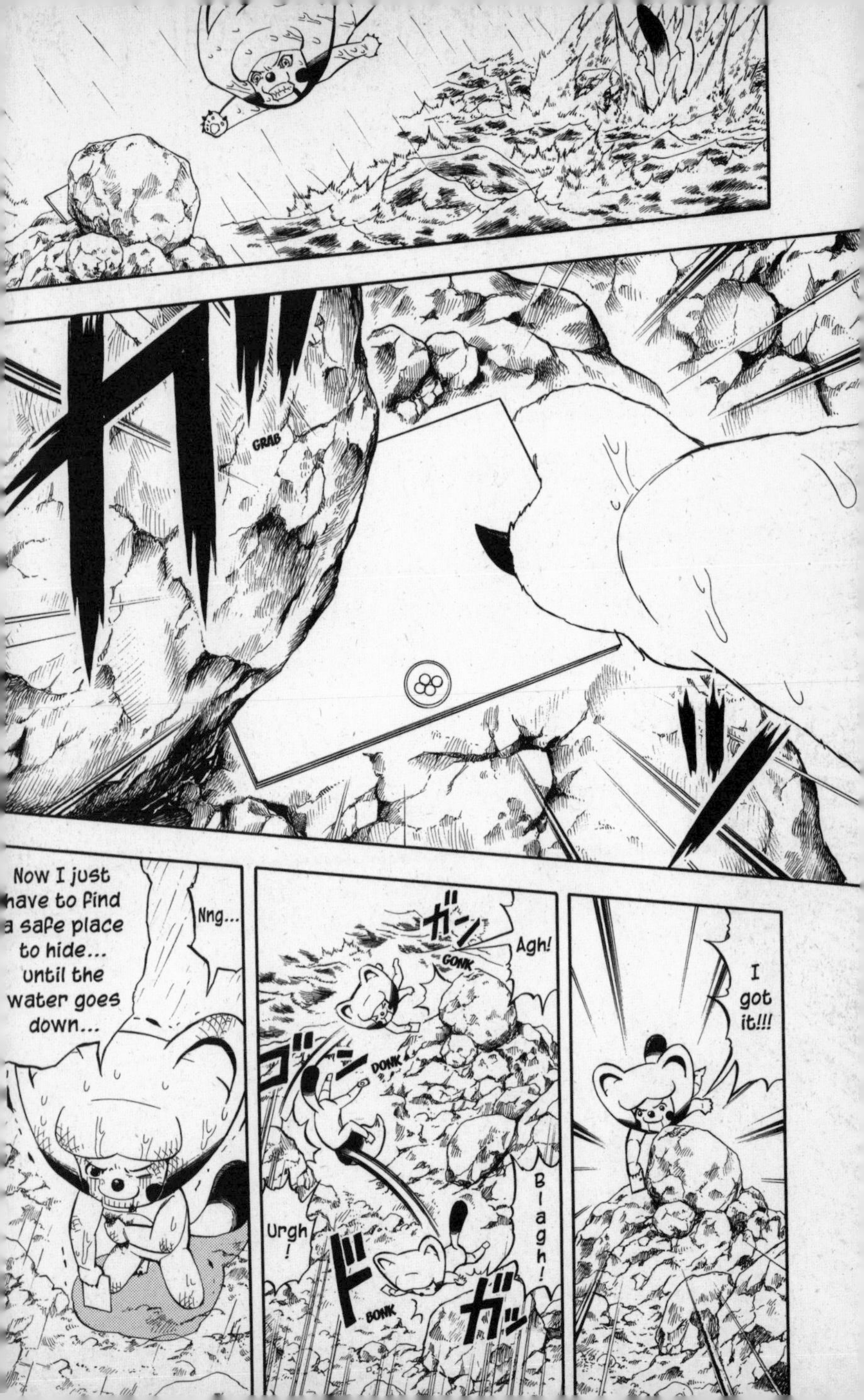
GRAB
I got it!!!
Agh!
GONK
DONK
Blagh!
Urgh!
BONK
Nng...
Now I just have to find a safe place to hide... until the water goes down...

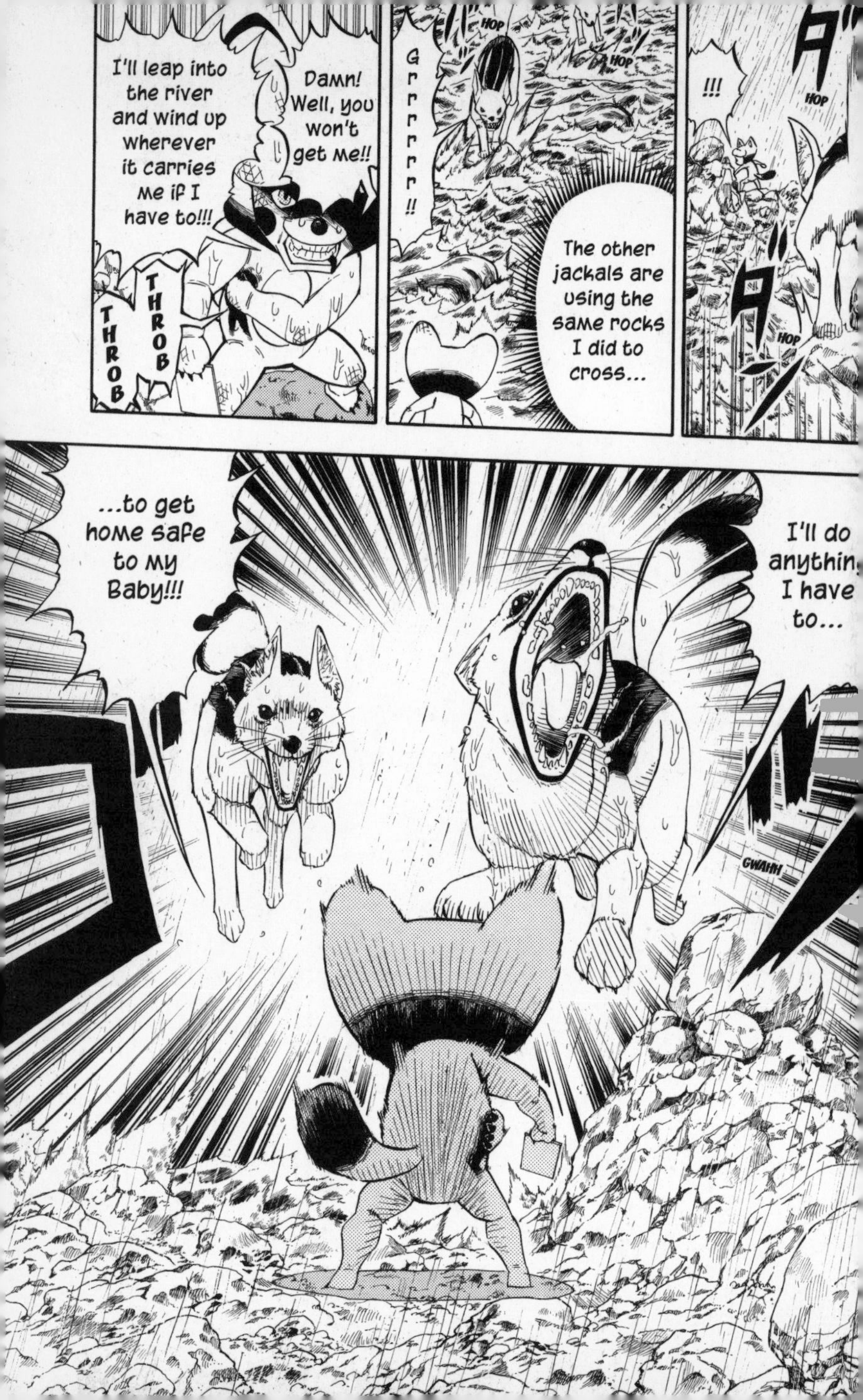
!!!
HOP
HOP
HOP
HOP
Grrrrrr!!
The other jackals are using the same rocks I did to cross...
Damn! Well, you won't get me!!
I'll leap into the river and wind up wherever it carries me if I have to!!!
THROB
THROB
I'll do anythin I have to...
GWAHH
...to get home safe to my Baby!!!

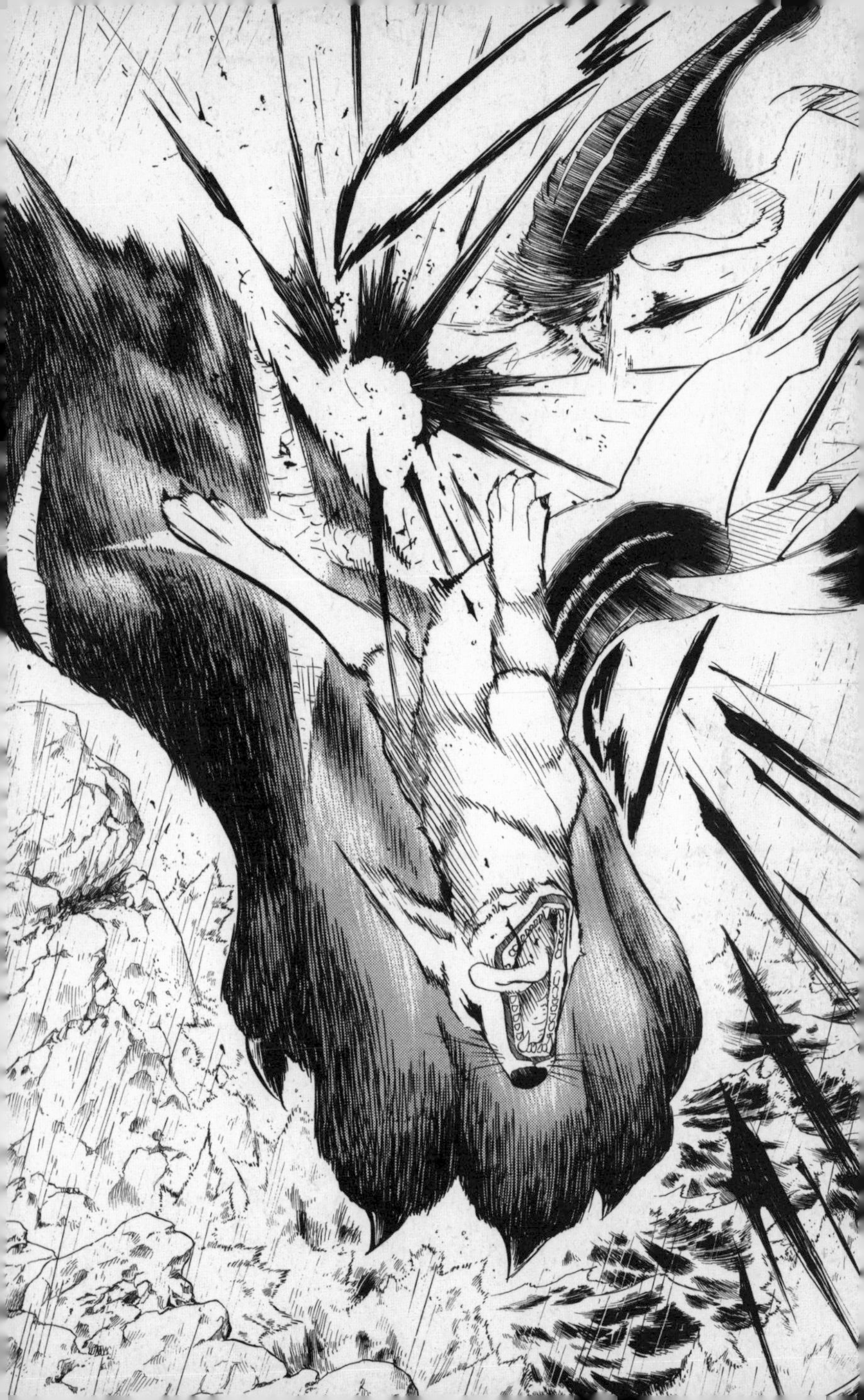

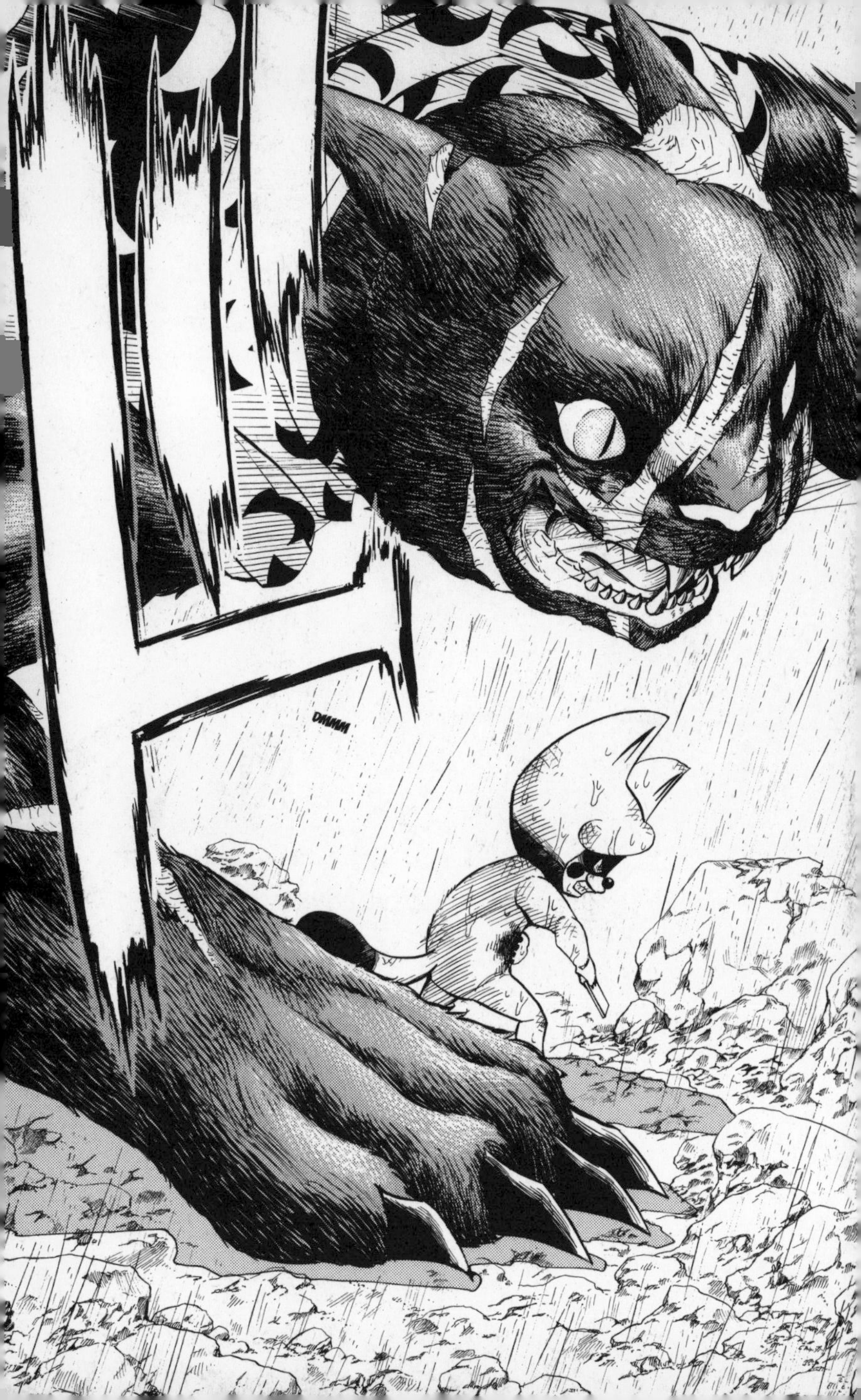
DMMM

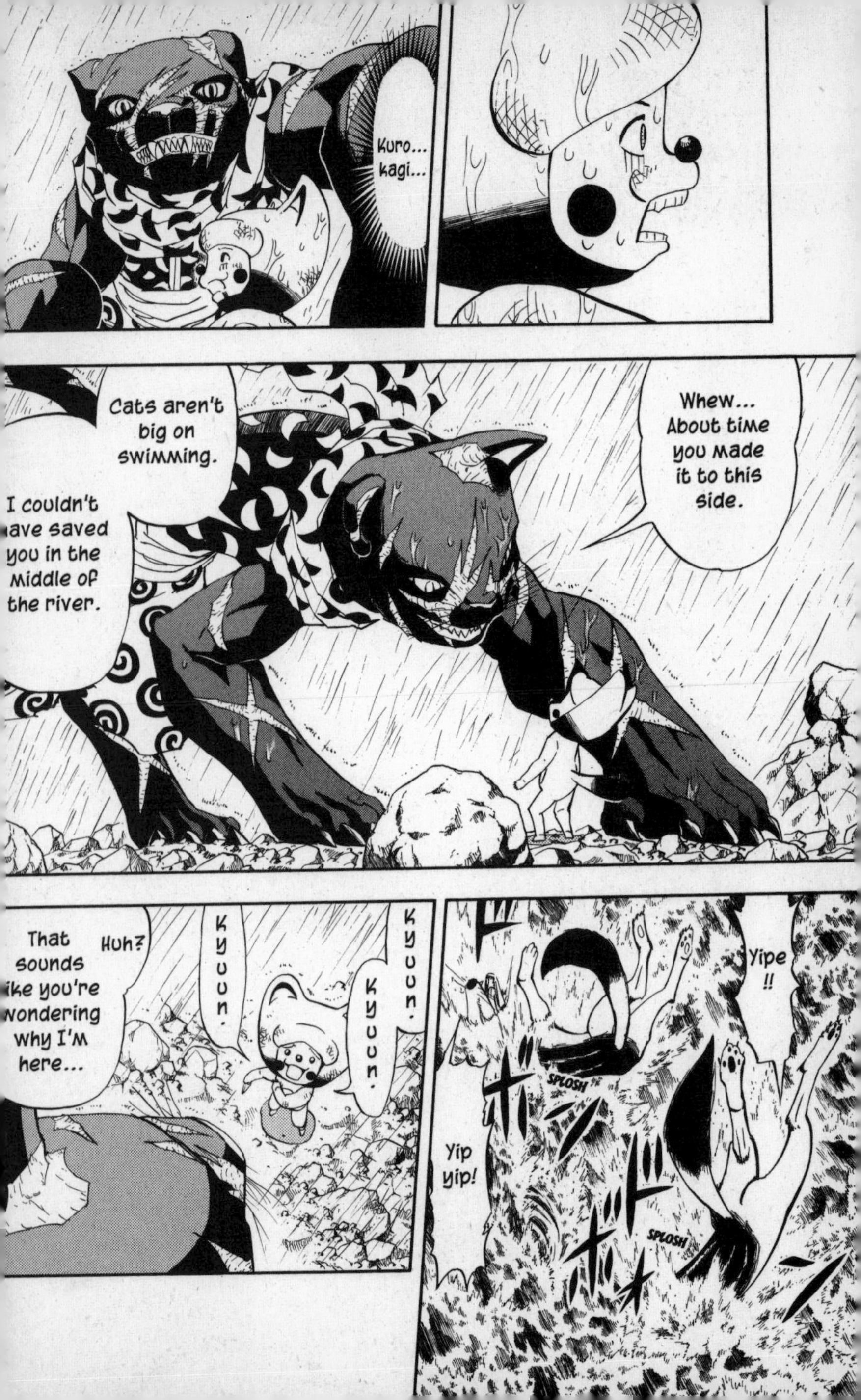
Kuro... kagi...
Whew... About time you made it to this side.
Cats aren't big on swimming.
I couldn't ave saved you in the middle of the river.
Yipe !!
SPLOSH
Yip yip!
SPLOSH
Kyuun.
Kyuun.
Kyuun.
Huh?
That sounds ike you're wondering why I'm here...

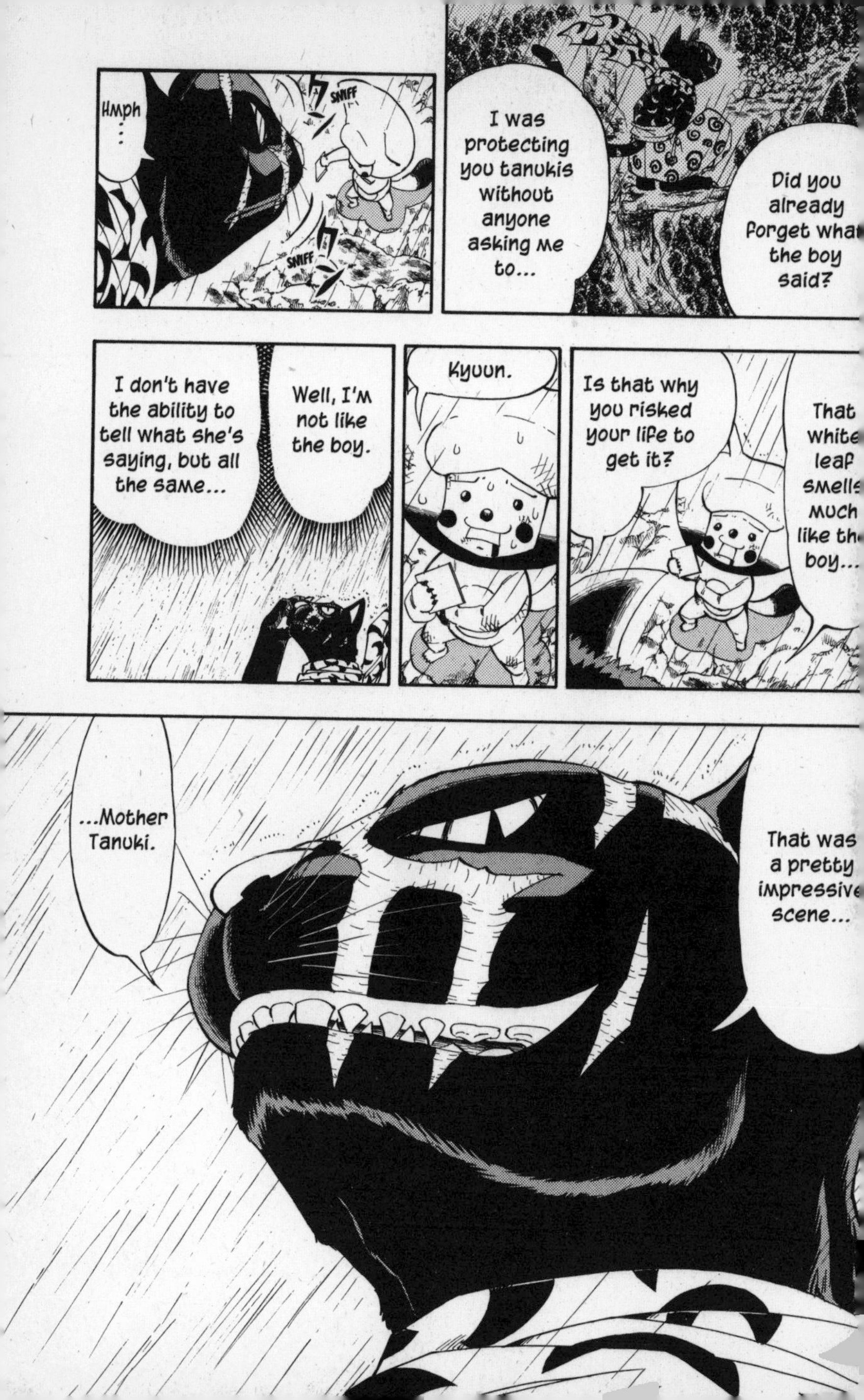
Did you already forget what the boy said?
I was protecting you tanukis without anyone asking me to...
SNIFF
SNIFF
Hmph...
That white leaf smells much like the boy...
Is that why you risked your life to get it?
Kyuun.
Well, I'm not like the boy.
I don't have the ability to tell what she's saying, but all the same...
That was a pretty impressive scene...
...Mother Tanuki.

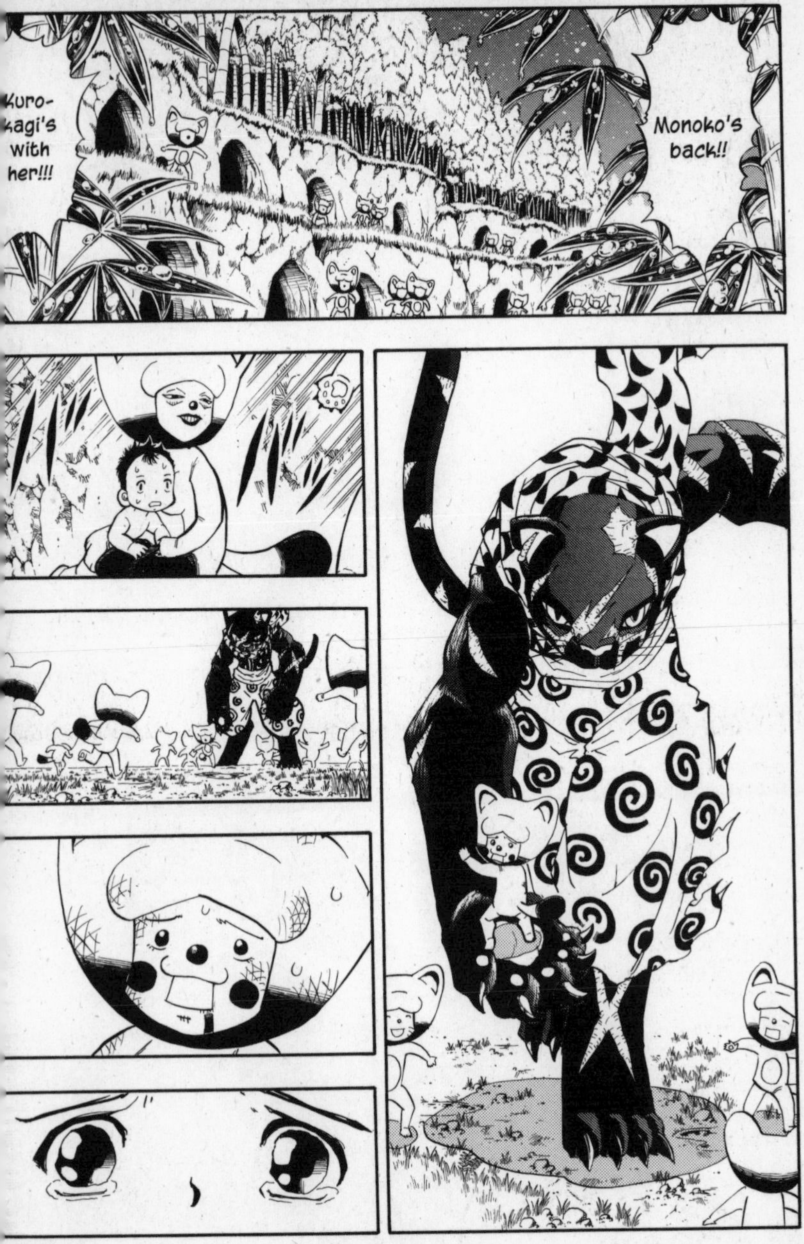
Monoko's back!!
Kuro-kagi's with her!!!

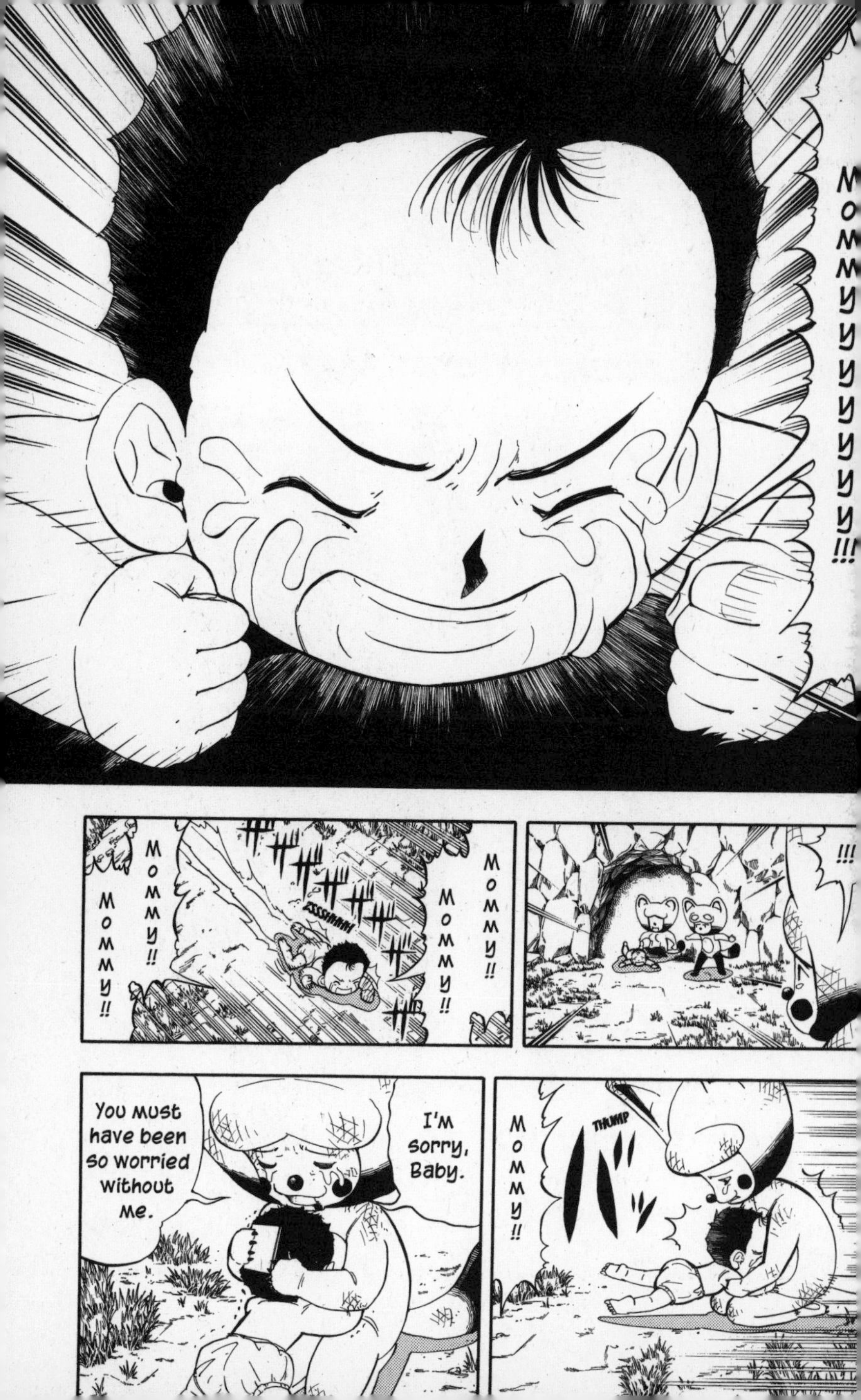

MOMMYYYYYYYY!!!
!!!
MOMMY!!
ZSSSHAAAH
MOMMY!!
MOMMY!!
MOMMY!!
THUMP
MOMMY!!
I'm sorry, Baby.
You must have been so worried without me.

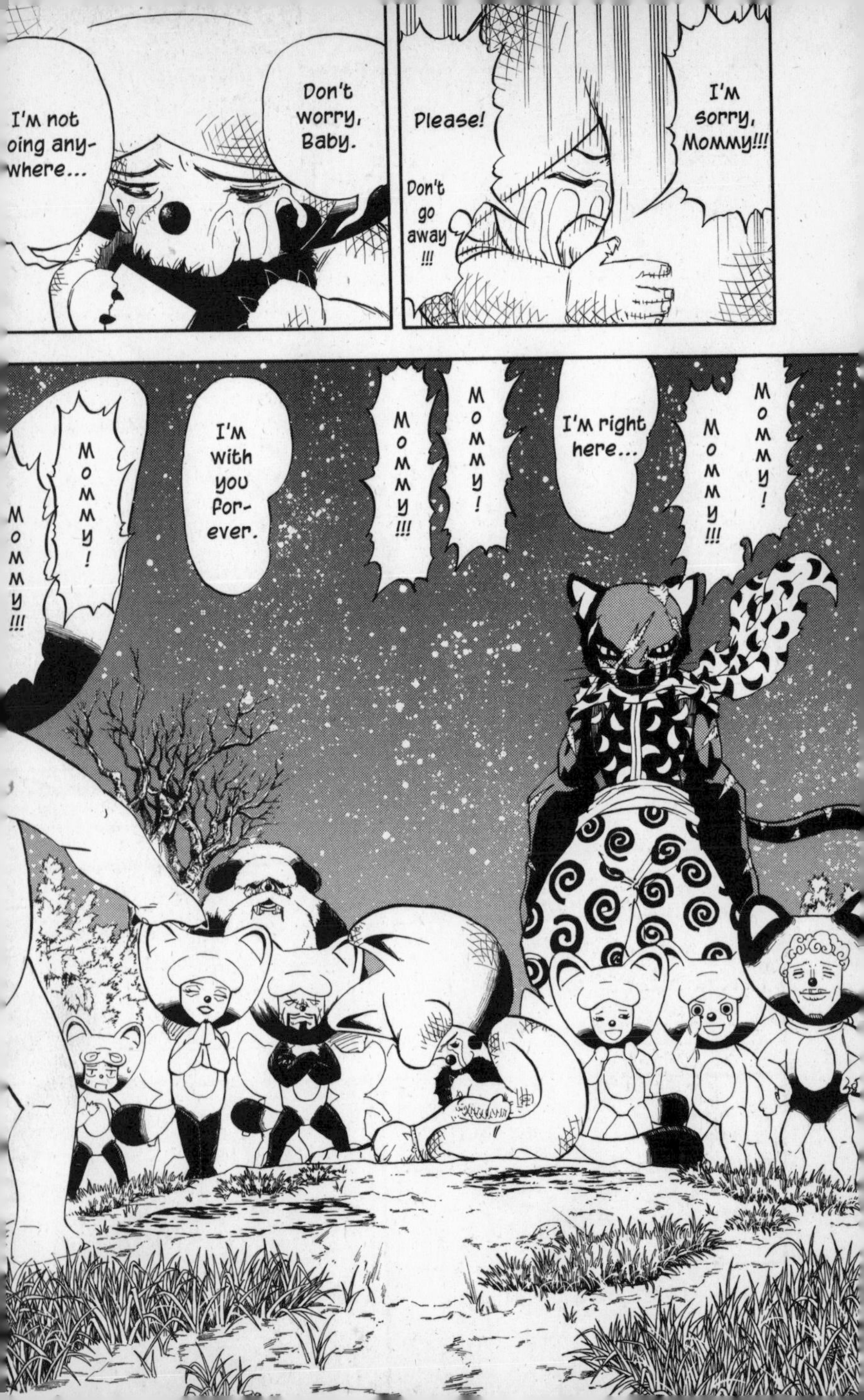
I'm sorry, Mommy!!!
Please!
Don't go away!!!
Don't worry, Baby.
I'm not oing any-where...
Mommy!
Mommy!!!
I'm right here...
Mommy!
Mommy!!!
I'm with you for-ever.
Mommy!
Mommy!!!

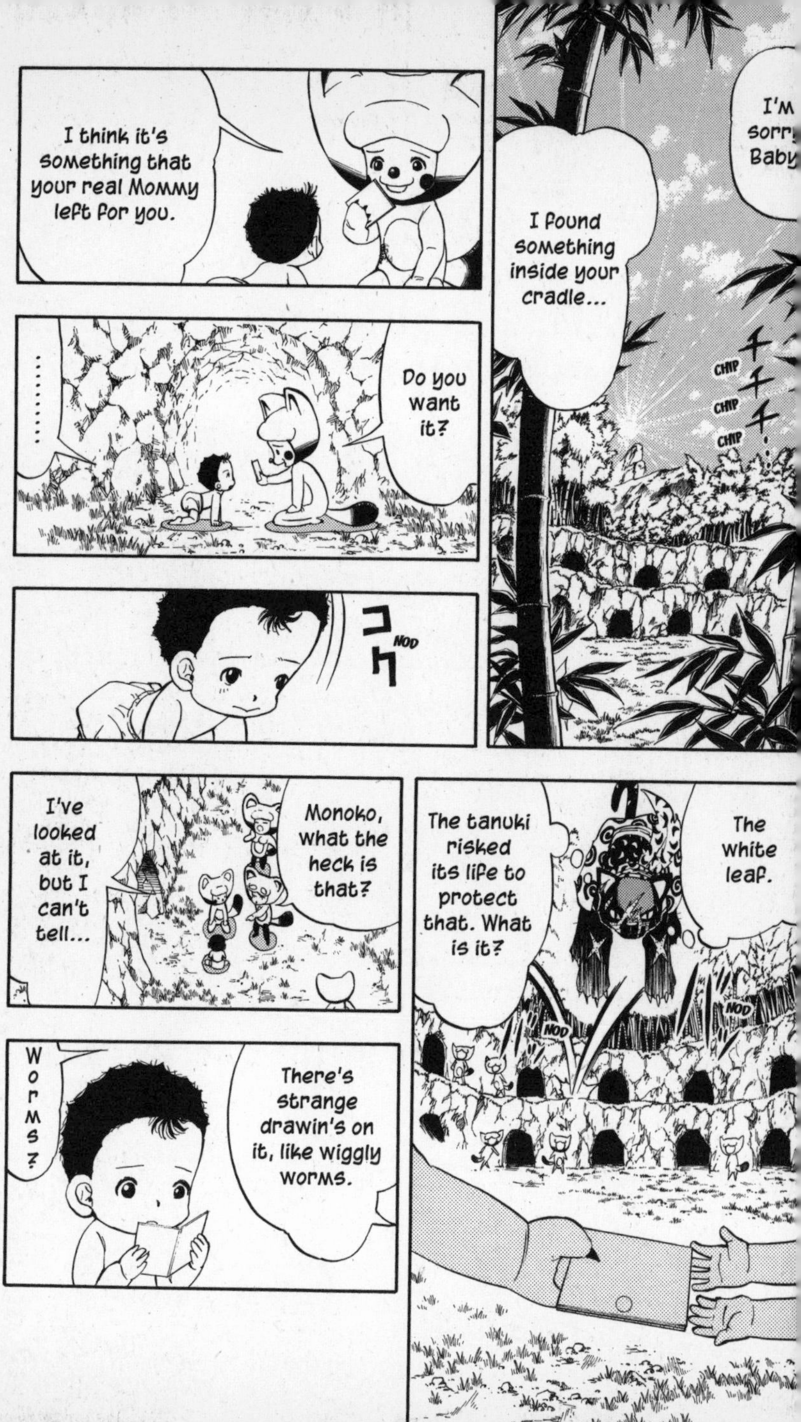
I'M sorr Baby
I found something inside your cradle...
CHIP
CHIP
CHIP
I think it's something that your real Mommy left for you.
Do you want it?
....
NOD
The white leaf.
The tanuki risked its life to protect that. What is it?
NOD
NOD
Monoko, what the heck is that?
I've looked at it, but I can't tell...
There's strange drawin's on it, like wiggly worms.
Worms?

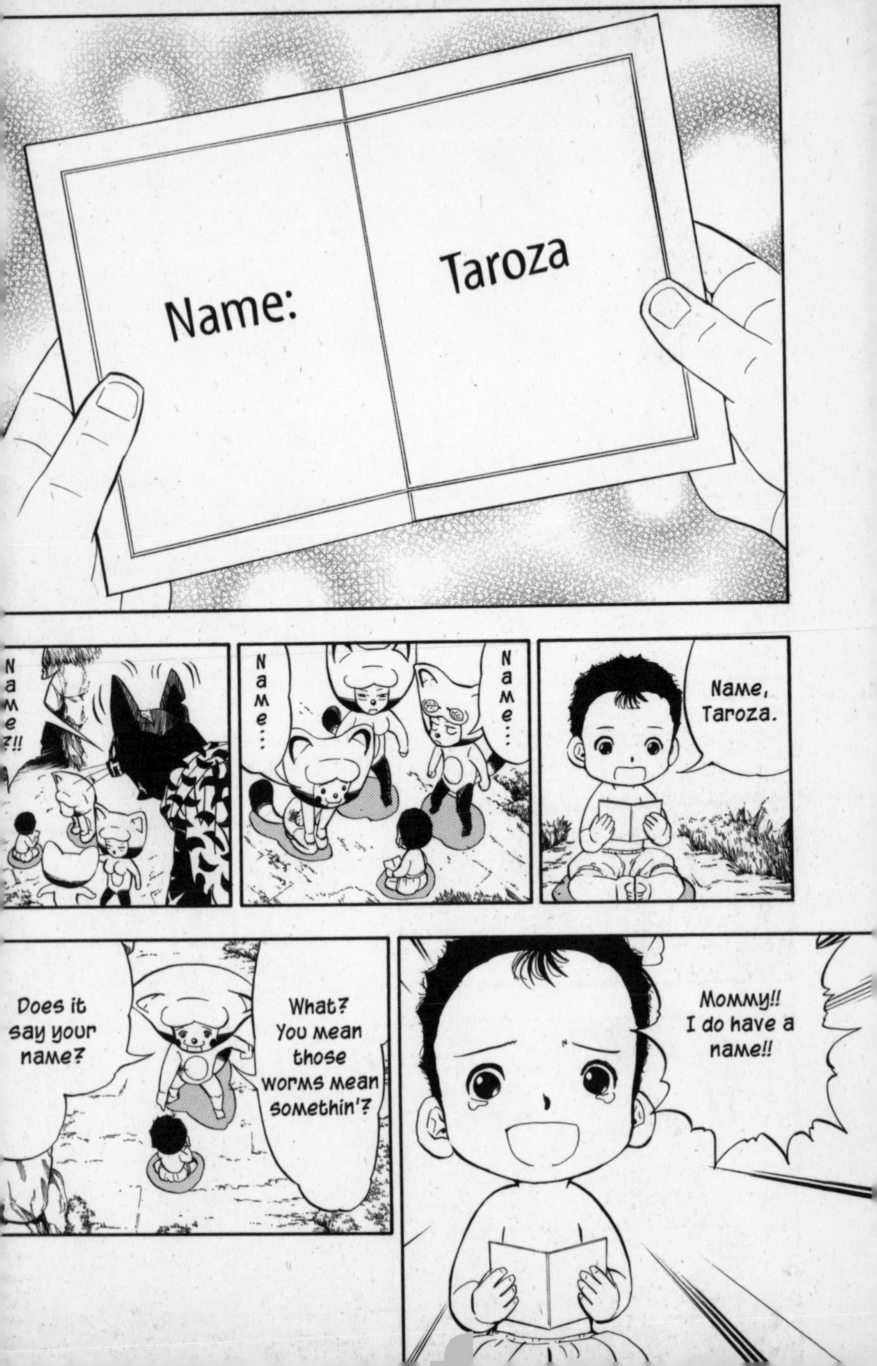
Name:
Taroza
Name, Taroza.
Name...
Name...
Name?!!
Mommy!! I do have a name!!
What? You mean those worms mean somethin'?
Does it say your name?

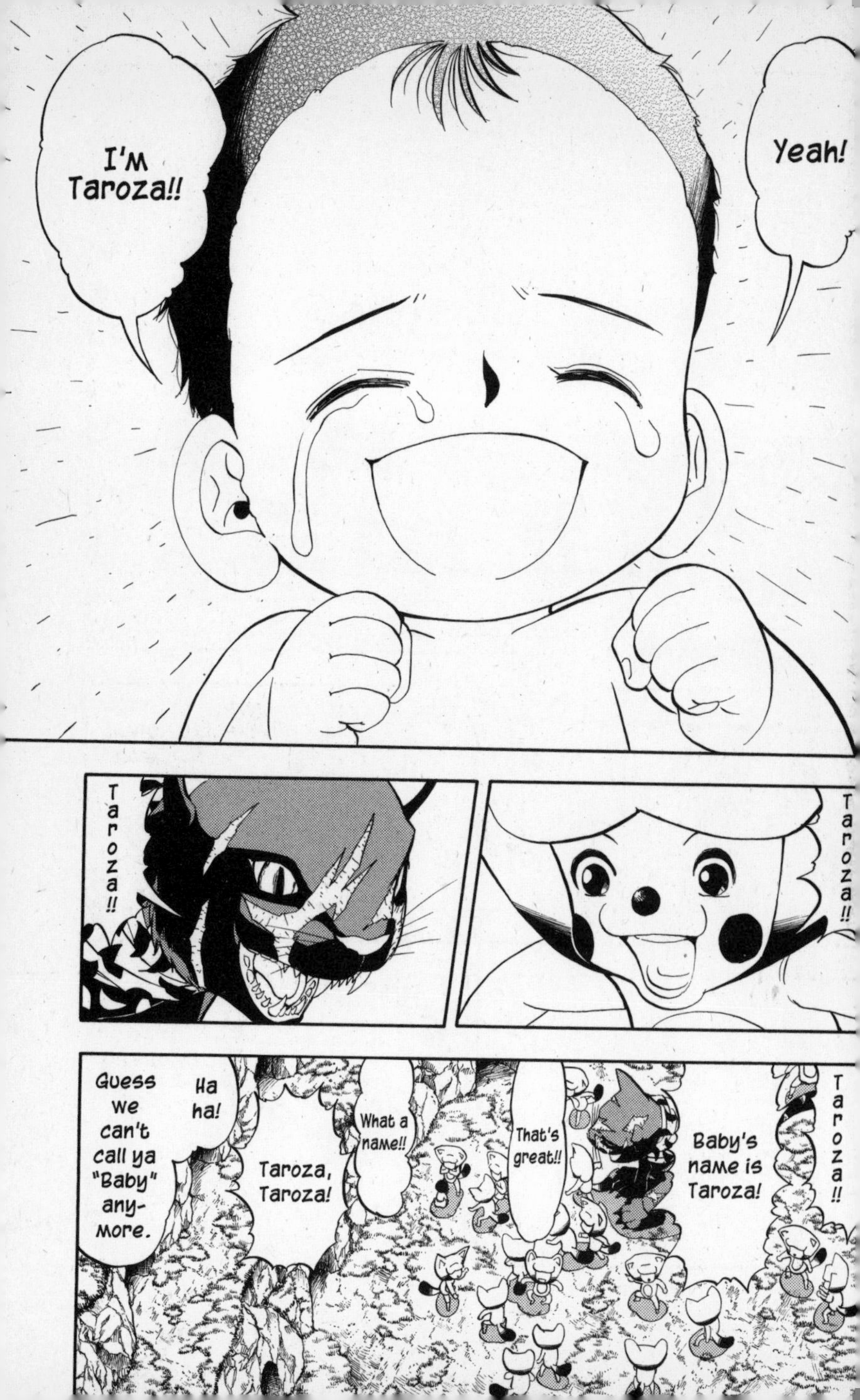
Yeah!
I'M Taroza!!
Taroza!!
Taroza!!
Taroza!!
Baby's name is Taroza!
That's great!!
What a name!!
Taroza, Taroza!
Ha ha!
Guess we can't call ya "Baby" any-more.

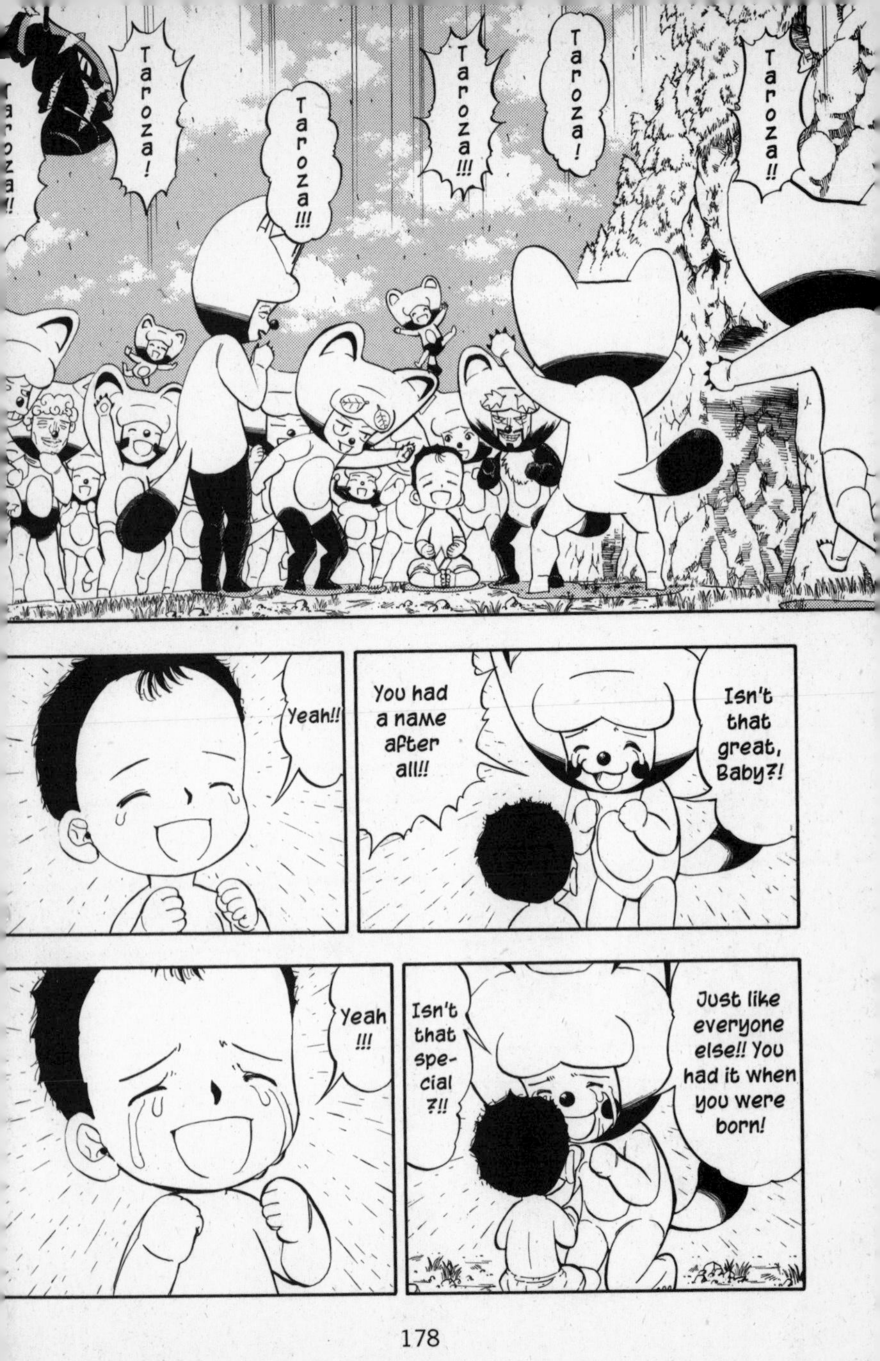
Taroza!!
Taroza!
Taroza!!!
Taroza!!!
Taroza!
Isn't that great, Baby?!
You had a name after all!!
Yeah!!
Just like everyone else!! You had it when you were born!
Isn't that spe-cial?!!
Yeah!!!

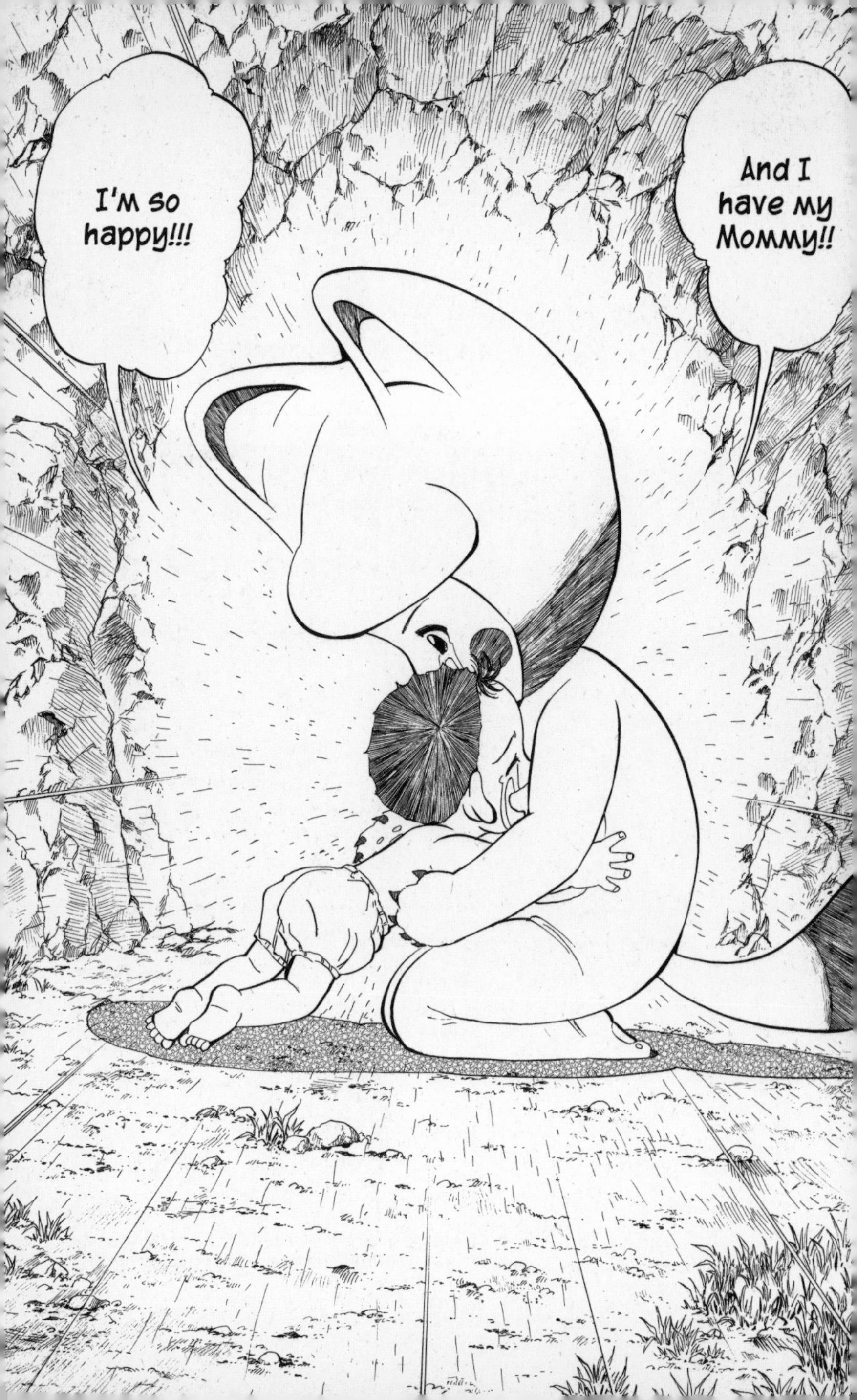
And I have my Mommy!!
I'm so happy!!!

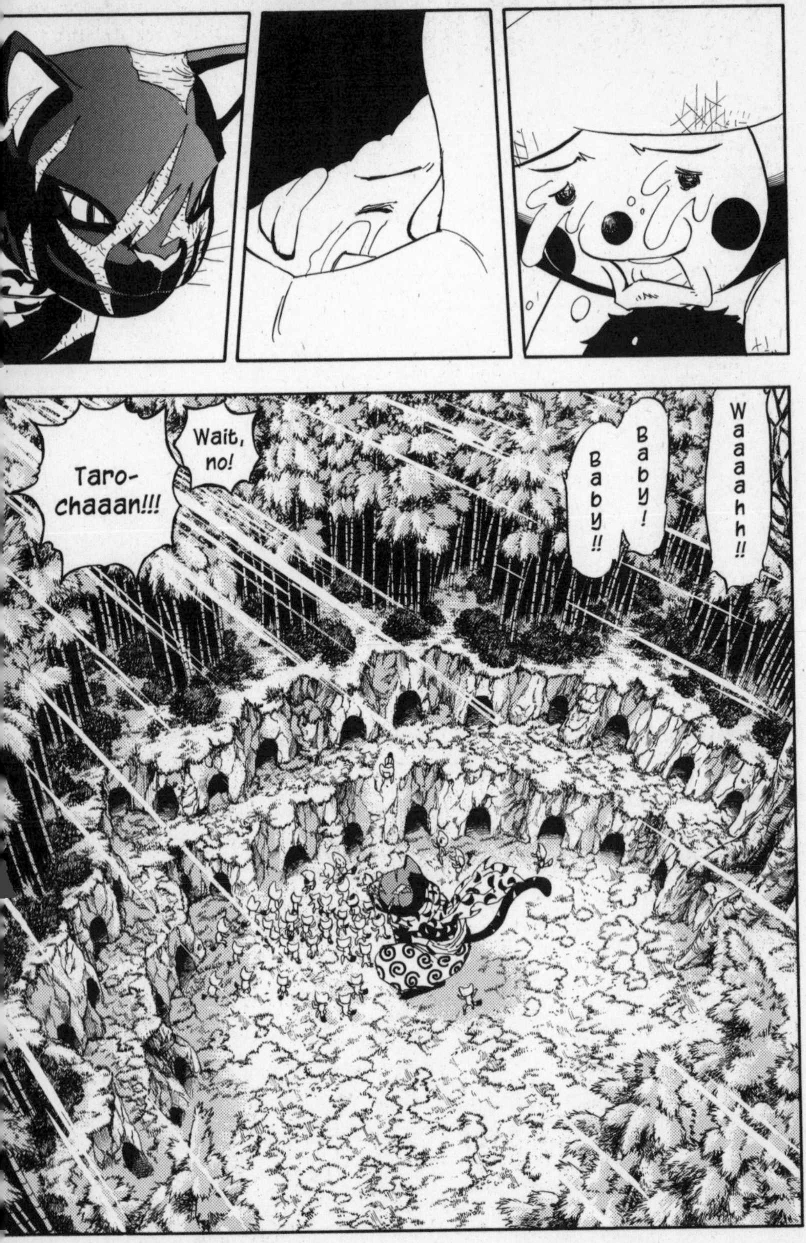
Waaaaahh!!
Baby!
Baby!!
Wait, no!
Taro-chaaan!!!

To be continued in Volume 2, Word 4

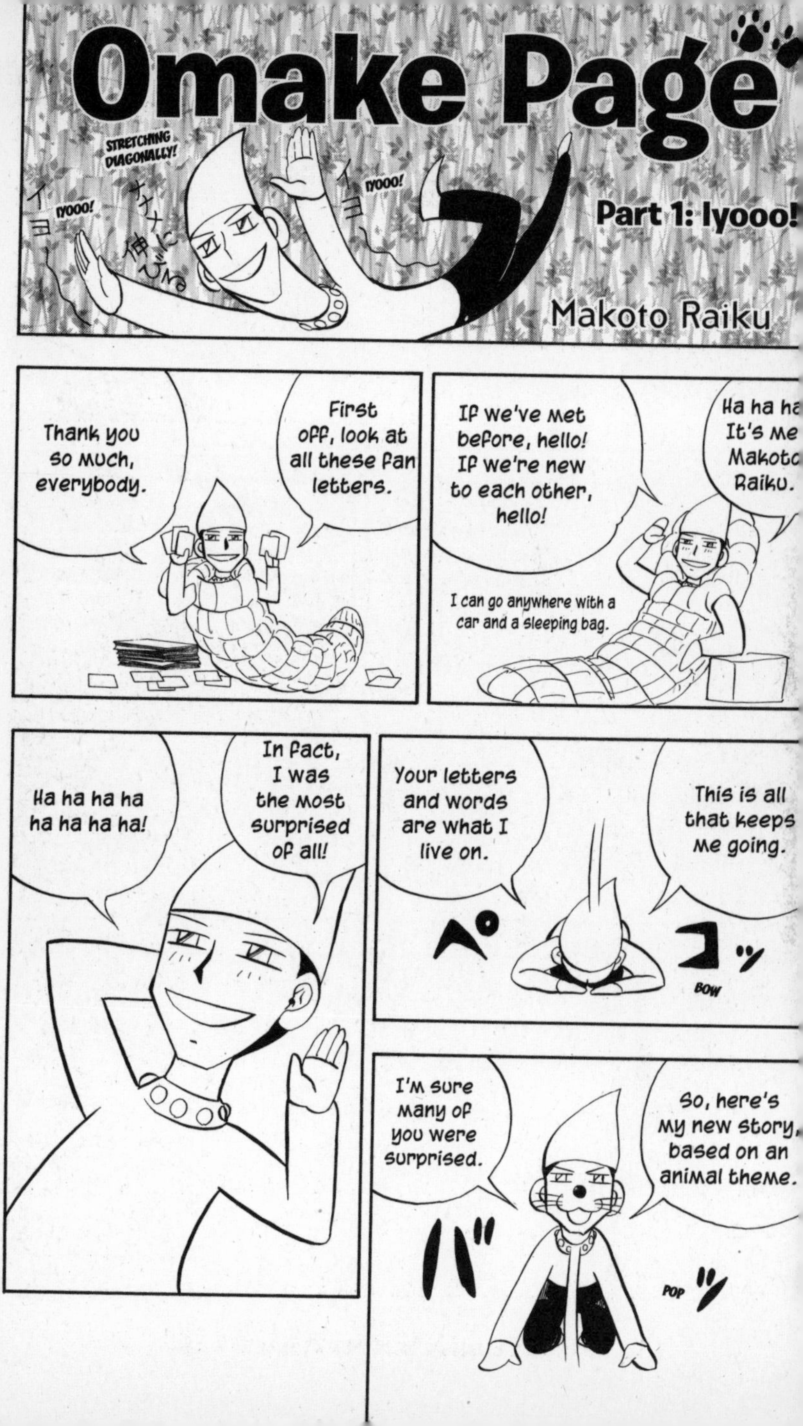
Omake Page
STRETCHING DIAGONALLY!
IYOOO!
IYOOO!
Part 1: Iyooo!
Makoto Raiku
Ha ha ha It's me Makoto Raiku.
If we've met before, hello! If we're new to each other, hello!
I can go anywhere with a car and a sleeping bag.
First off, look at all these fan letters.
Thank you so much, everybody.
This is all that keeps me going.
Your letters and words are what I live on.
BOW
So, here's my new story, based on an animal theme.
I'm sure many of you were surprised.
POP
In fact, I was the most surprised of all!
Ha ha ha ha ha ha ha ha!

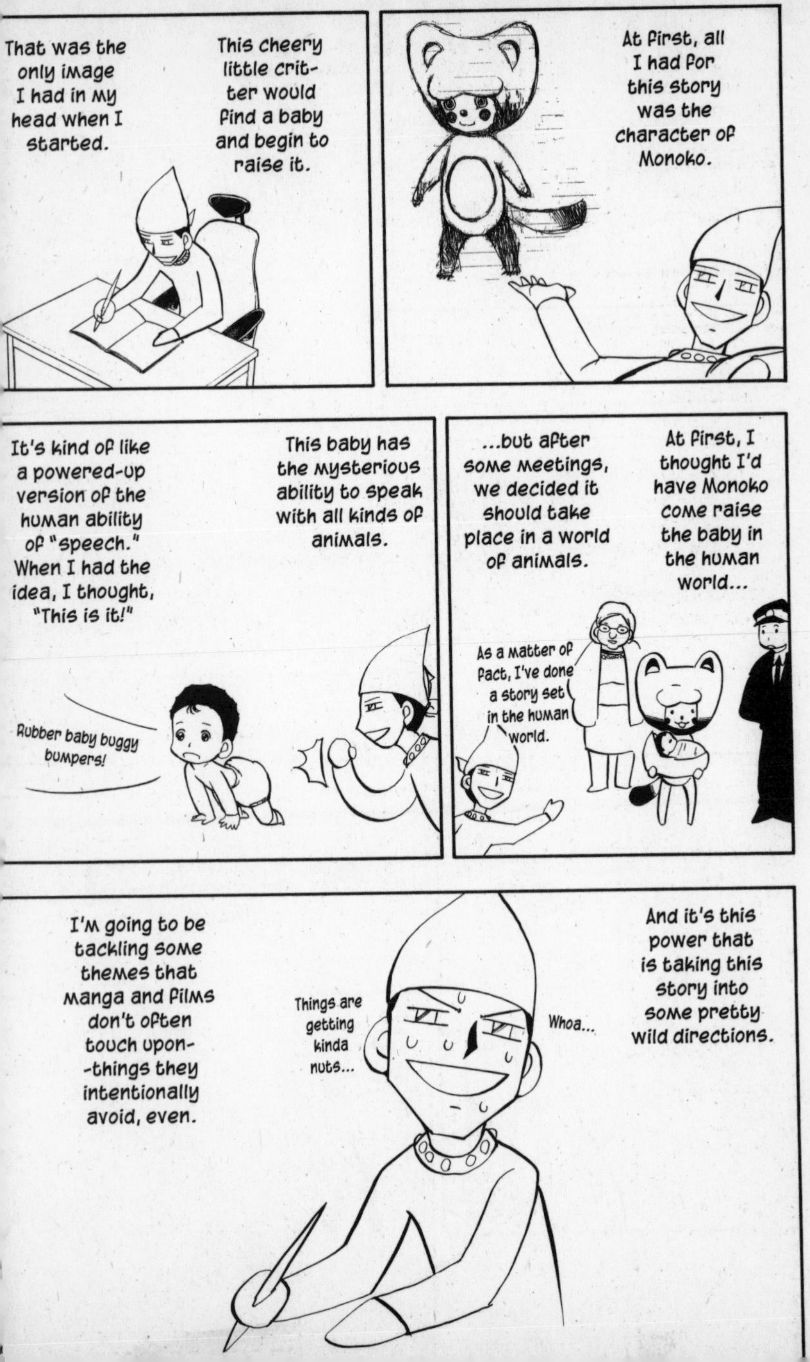
At first, all I had for this story was the character of Monoko.
This cheery little critter would find a baby and begin to raise it.
That was the only image I had in my head when I started.
At first, I thought I'd have Monoko come raise the baby in the human world...
...but after some meetings, we decided it should take place in a world of animals.
As a matter of fact, I've done a story set in the human world.
This baby has the mysterious ability to speak with all kinds of animals.
It's kind of like a powered-up version of the human ability of "speech." When I had the idea, I thought, "This is it!"
Rubber baby buggy bumpers!
And it's this power that is taking this story into some pretty wild directions.
Whoa...
Things are getting kinda nuts...
I'm going to be tackling some themes that manga and films don't often touch upon--things they intentionally avoid, even.

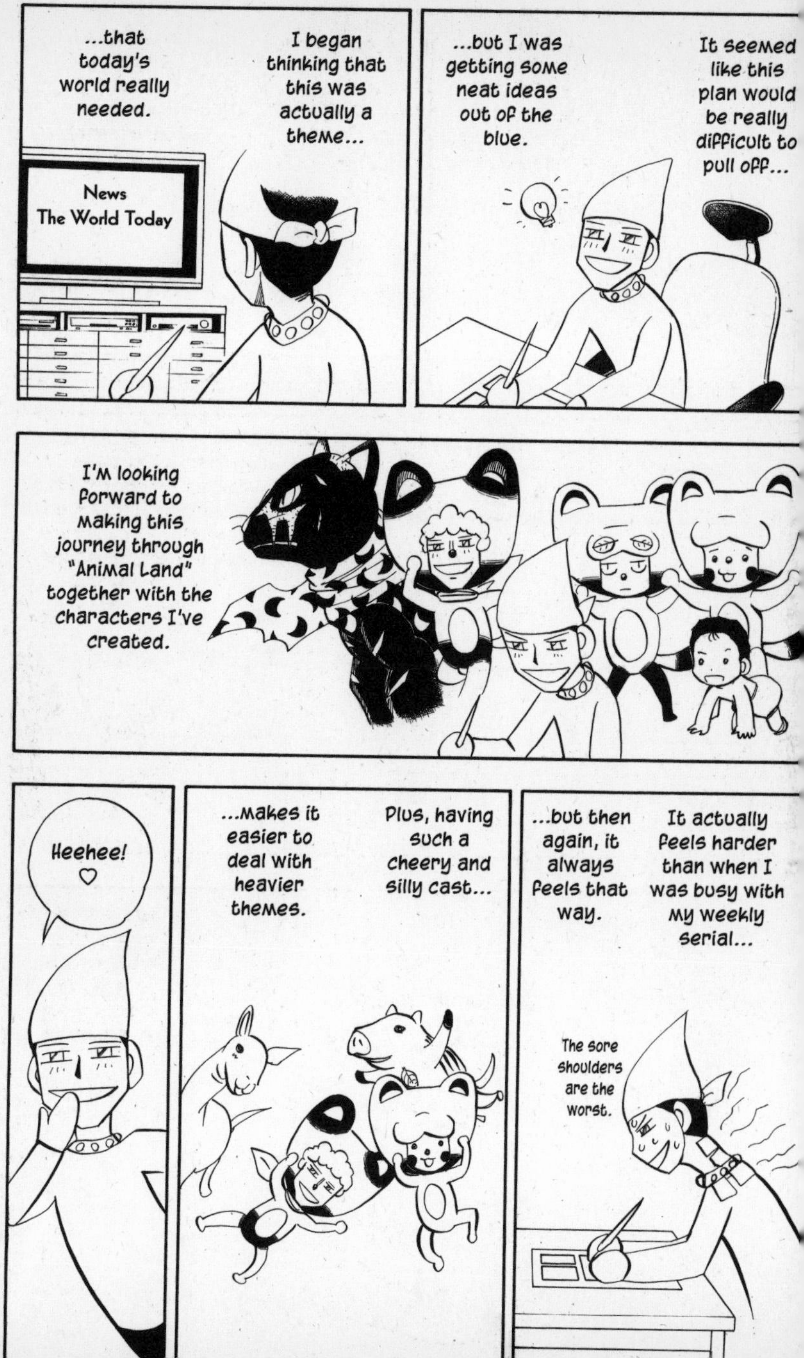
It seemed like this plan would be really difficult to pull off...
...but I was getting some neat ideas out of the blue.
I began thinking that this was actually a theme...
...that today's world really needed.
News
The World Today
I'm looking forward to making this journey through "Animal Land" together with the characters I've created.
It actually feels harder than when I was busy with my weekly serial...
...but then again, it always feels that way.
The sore shoulders are the worst.
Plus, having such a cheery and silly cast...
...makes it easier to deal with heavier themes.
Heehee! ♡

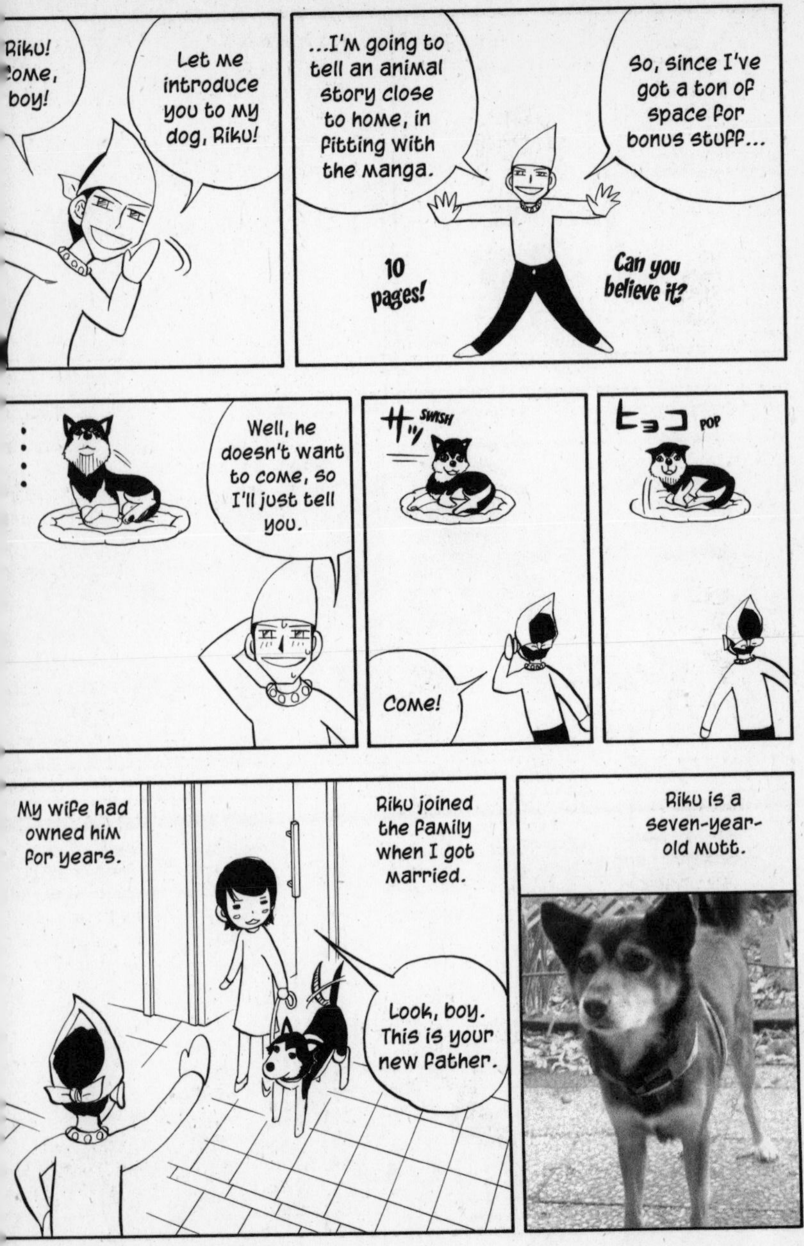
So, since I've got a ton of space for bonus stuff...
...I'm going to tell an animal story close to home, in fitting with the manga.
Can you believe it?
10 pages!
Let me introduce you to my dog, Riku!
Riku! Come, boy!
ヒョコ POP
サッ SWISH
Come!
Well, he doesn't want to come, so I'll just tell you.
....
Riku is a seven-year-old mutt.
Riku joined the family when I got married.
My wife had owned him for years.
Look, boy. This is your new father.

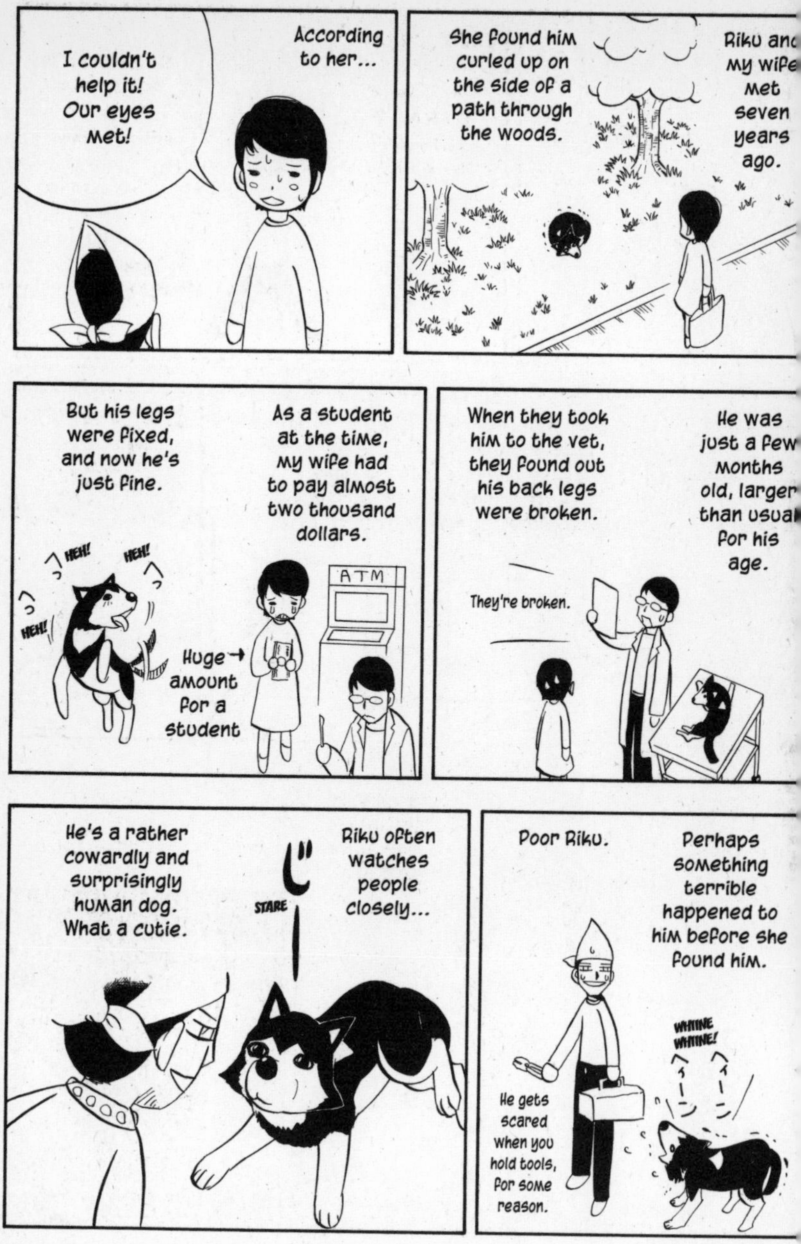
Riku and my wife met seven years ago.
She found him curled up on the side of a path through the woods.
According to her...
I couldn't help it! Our eyes met!
He was just a few months old, larger than usual for his age.
When they took him to the vet, they found out his back legs were broken.
They're broken.
As a student at the time, my wife had to pay almost two thousand dollars.
ATM
Huge amount for a student
But his legs were fixed, and now he's just fine.
HEH!
HEH!
HEH!
Perhaps something terrible happened to him before she found him.
Poor Riku.
He gets scared when you hold tools, for some reason.
WHIINE WHIINE!
Riku often watches people closely...
じー
STARE
He's a rather cowardly and surprisingly human dog. What a cutie.

howing the belly is a sign of submission. Lots of times, it just means they want it rubbed, though.

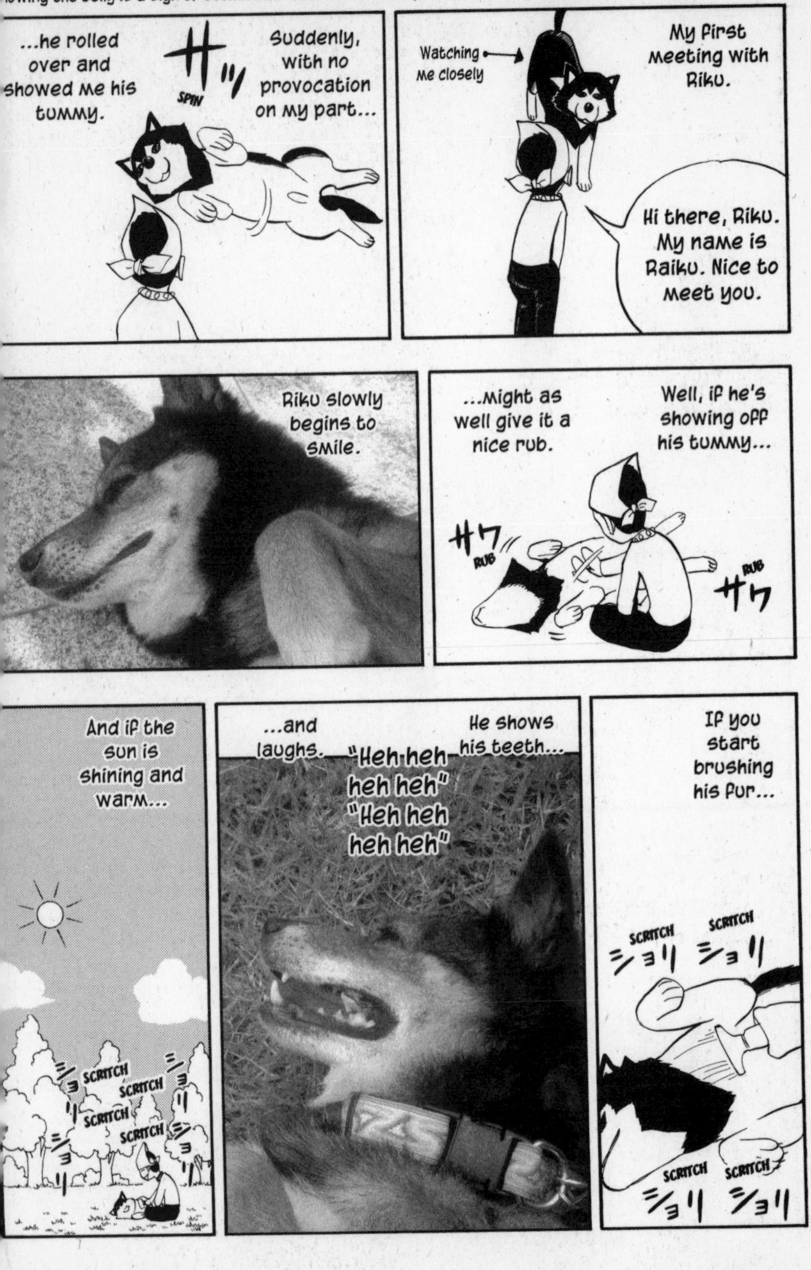

My first meeting with Riku.
Watching me closely
Hi there, Riku. My name is Raiku. Nice to meet you.
Suddenly, with no provocation on my part...
SPIN
...he rolled over and showed me his tummy.
Well, if he's showing off his tummy...
...might as well give it a nice rub.
RUB
RUB
Riku slowly begins to smile.
If you start brushing his fur...
SCRITCH
SCRITCH
SCRITCH
SCRITCH
He shows his teeth...
...and laughs.
"Heh heh heh heh"
"Heh heh heh heh"
And if the sun is shining and warm...
SCRITCH
SCRITCH
SCRITCH
SCRITCH

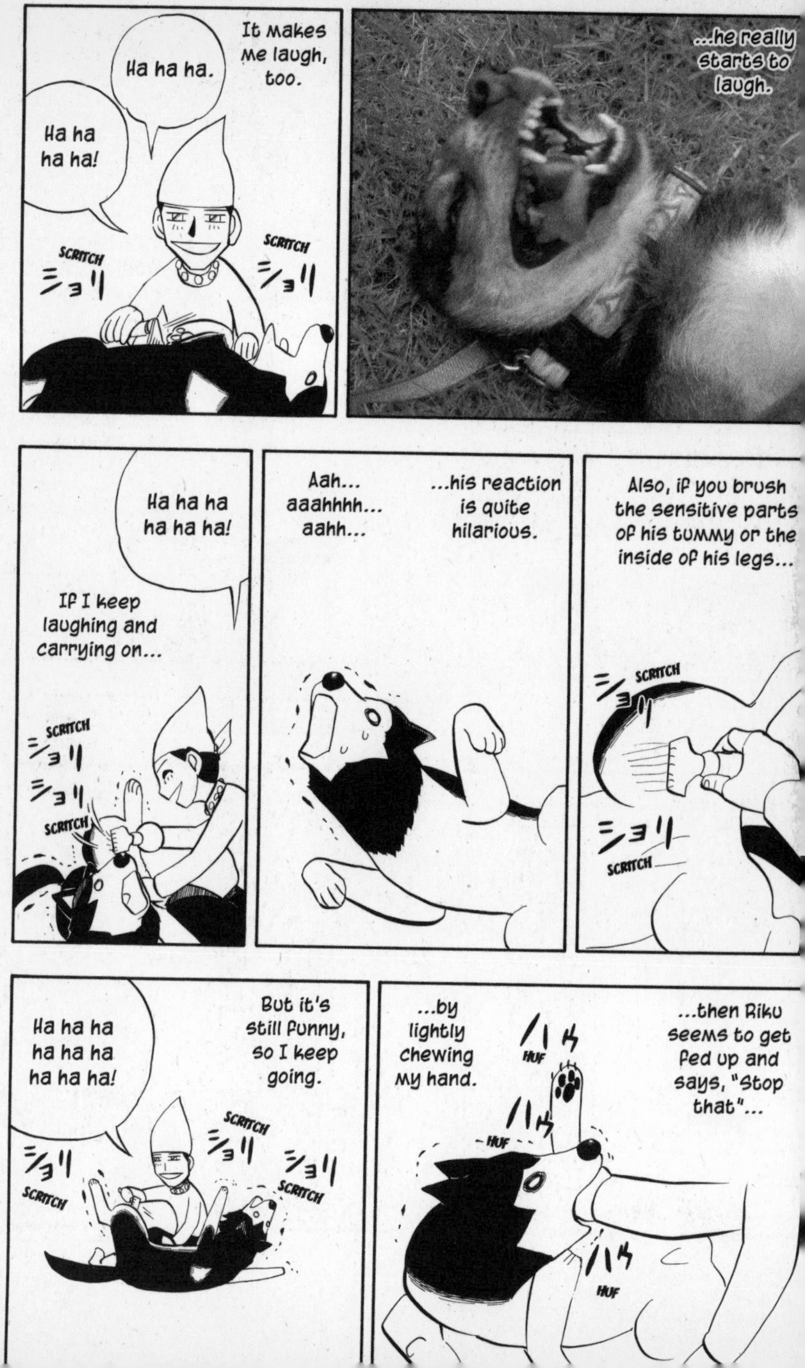
...he really starts to laugh.
It makes me laugh, too.
Ha ha ha.
Ha ha ha ha!
SCRITCH
ショリ
SCRITCH
ショリ
Also, if you brush the sensitive parts of his tummy or the inside of his legs...
SCRITCH
ショリ
ショリ
SCRITCH
...his reaction is quite hilarious.
Aah... aaahhhh... aahh...
Ha ha ha ha ha ha!
If I keep laughing and carrying on...
SCRITCH
ショリ
ショリ
SCRITCH
...then Riku seems to get fed up and says, "Stop that"...
...by lightly chewing my hand.
ハフ
HUF
ハフ
HUF
ハフ
HUF
But it's still funny, so I keep going.
Ha ha ha ha ha ha ha ha ha!
SCRITCH
ショリ
ショリ
SCRITCH
ショリ
SCRITCH

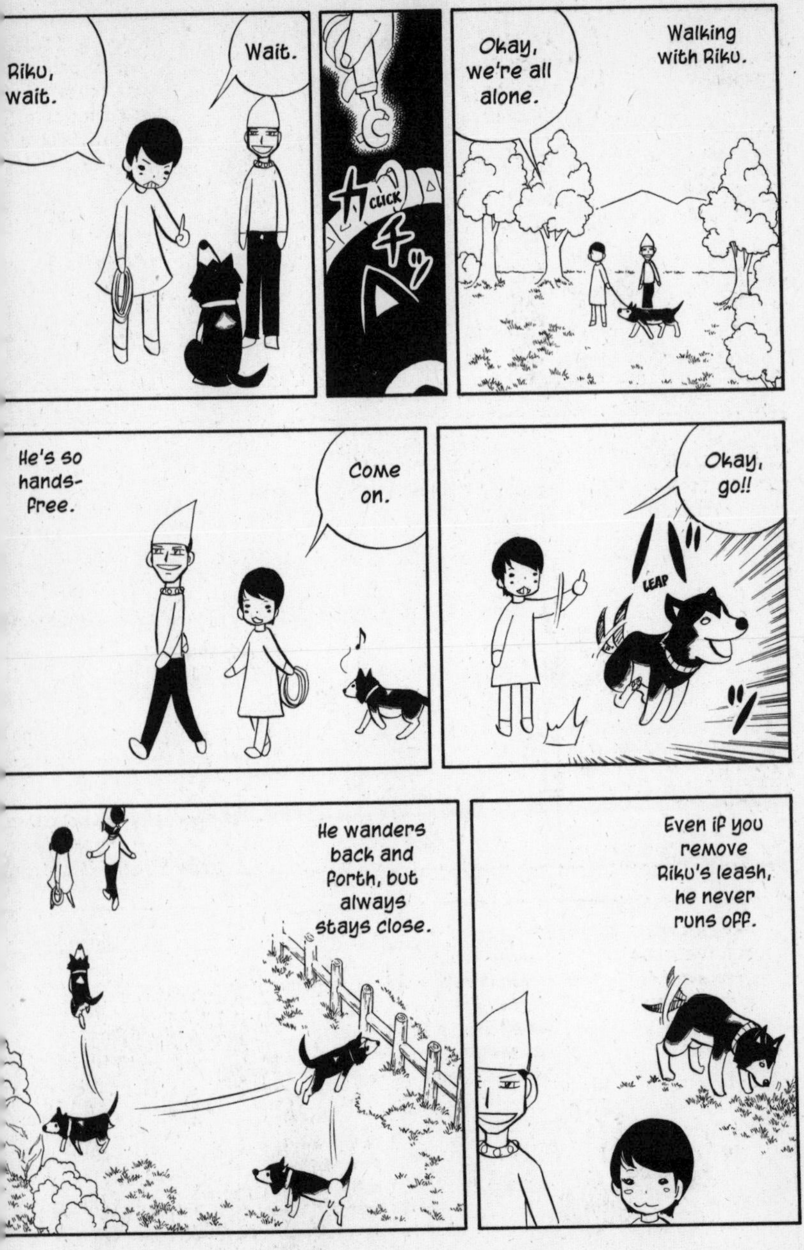
Walking with Riku.
Okay, we're all alone.
カチッ
CLICK
Wait.
Riku, wait.
Okay, go!!
LEAP
Come on.
He's so hands-free.
Even if you remove Riku's leash, he never runs off.
He wanders back and forth, but always stays close.

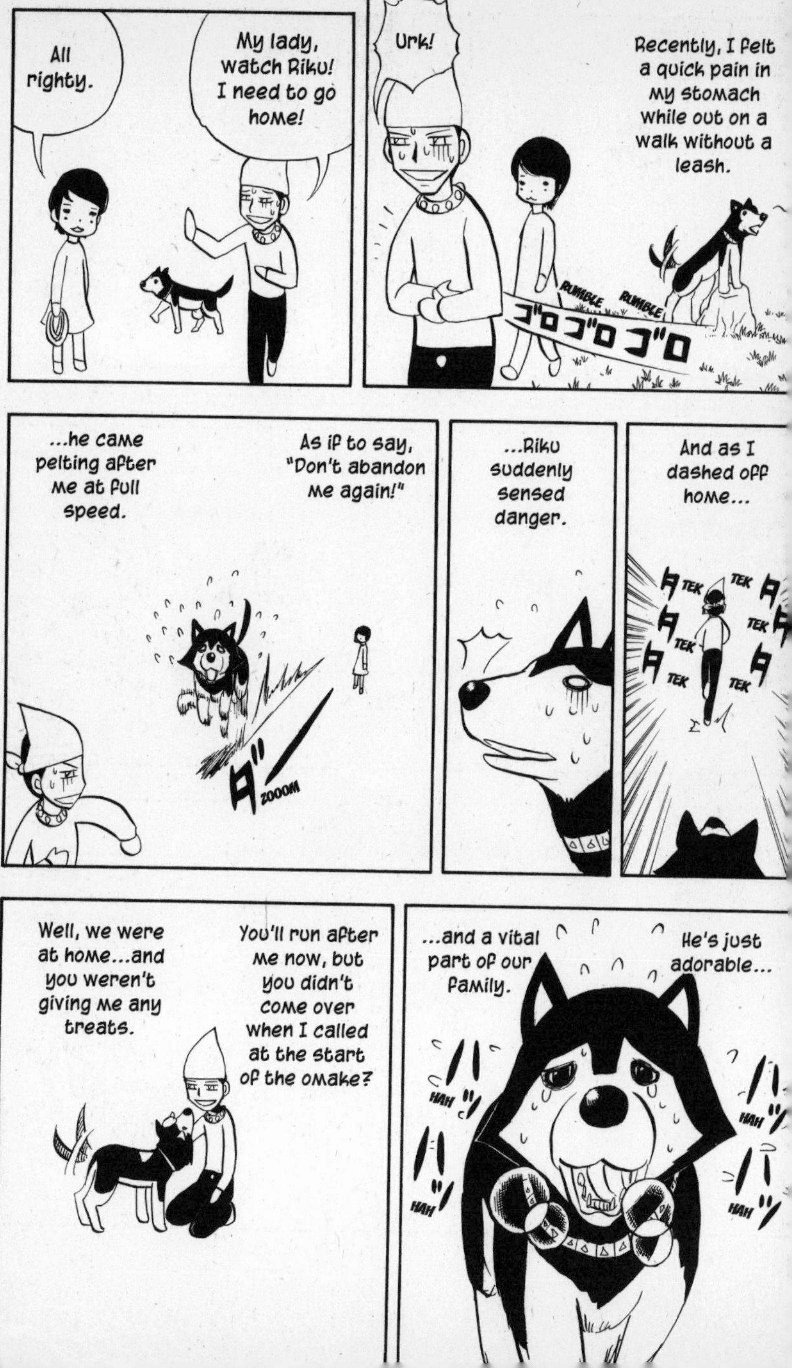
Recently, I felt a quick pain in my stomach while out on a walk without a leash.
Urk!
RUMBLE RUMBLE
ゴロゴロゴロ
My lady, watch Riku! I need to go home!
All righty.
And as I dashed off home...
TEK TEK TEK TEK TEK TEK
...Riku suddenly sensed danger.
As if to say, "Don't abandon me again!"
...he came pelting after me at full speed.
ZOOOM
He's just adorable...
...and a vital part of our family.
HAH HAH HAH HAH
You'll run after me now, but you didn't come over when I called at the start of the omake?
Well, we were at home...and you weren't giving me any treats.

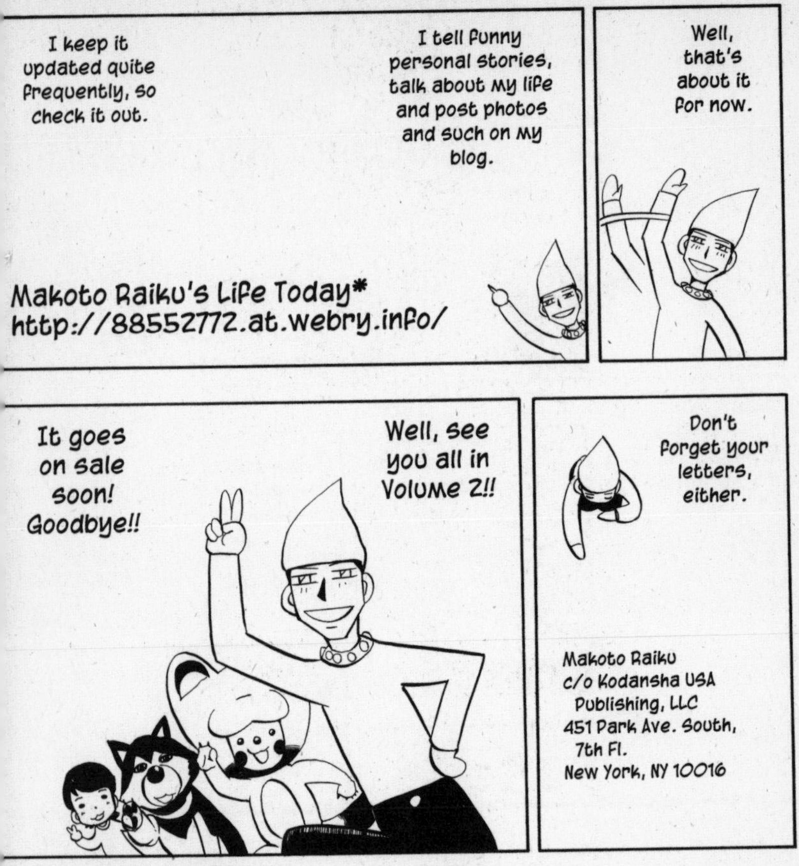
Well, that's about it for now.
I tell funny personal stories, talk about my life and post photos and such on my blog.
I keep it updated quite frequently, so check it out.
Makoto Raiku's Life Today*
http://88552772.at.webry.info/
Don't forget your letters, either.
Makoto Raiku
c/o Kodansha USA Publishing, LLC
451 Park Ave. South, 7th Fl.
New York, NY 10016
Well, see you all in Volume 2!!
It goes on sale soon! Goodbye!!

Please note the blog is in Japanese.

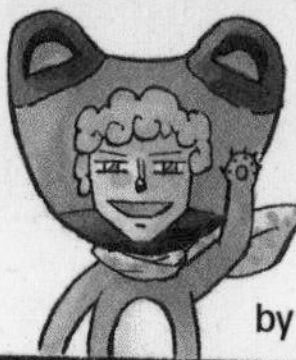

Pepper's Life

by Makoto Raiku

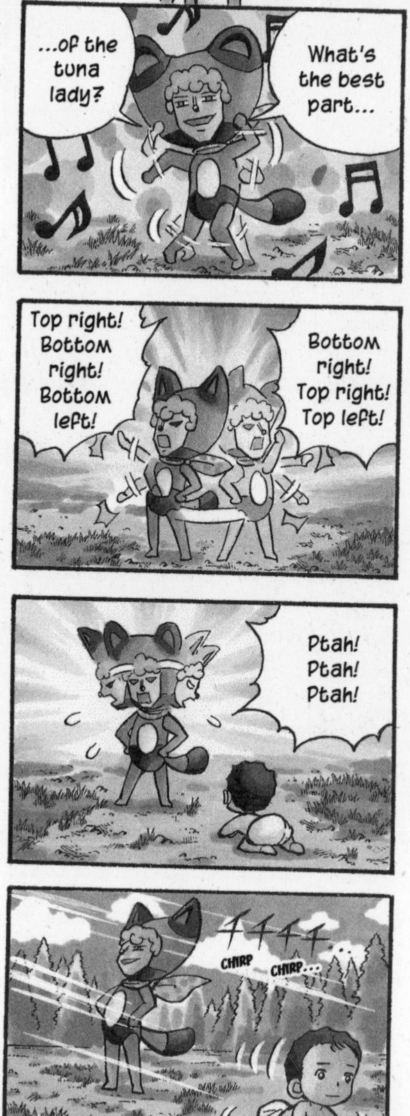
What's the best part...
...of the tuna lady?
Bottom right! Top right! Top left!
Top right! Bottom right! Bottom left!
Ptah! Ptah! Ptah!
CHIRP
CHIRP...

Translation Notes

Japanese is a tricky language for most Westerners, and translation is often more art than science. For your edification and reading pleasure, here are notes on some of the places where we could have gone in a different direction with our translation of the work, or where a Japanese cultural reference is used.

Tanuki, page 1

Tanuki is the Japanese name for what is otherwise known as the "raccoon dog" in English, a loose relative of dogs and foxes that is indigenous to east Asia. As one of the most recognizable wild species found in Japan, it plays a large part in Japanese folklore, where the tanuki is commonly considered a trickster or shapeshifter.

Preview of
Animal Land, volume 2

We're pleased to present you a preview from
Animal Land, volume 2. Please check our website
(www.kodanshacomics.com) to see when this volume
will be available in English. For now you'll have to
make do with Japanese!

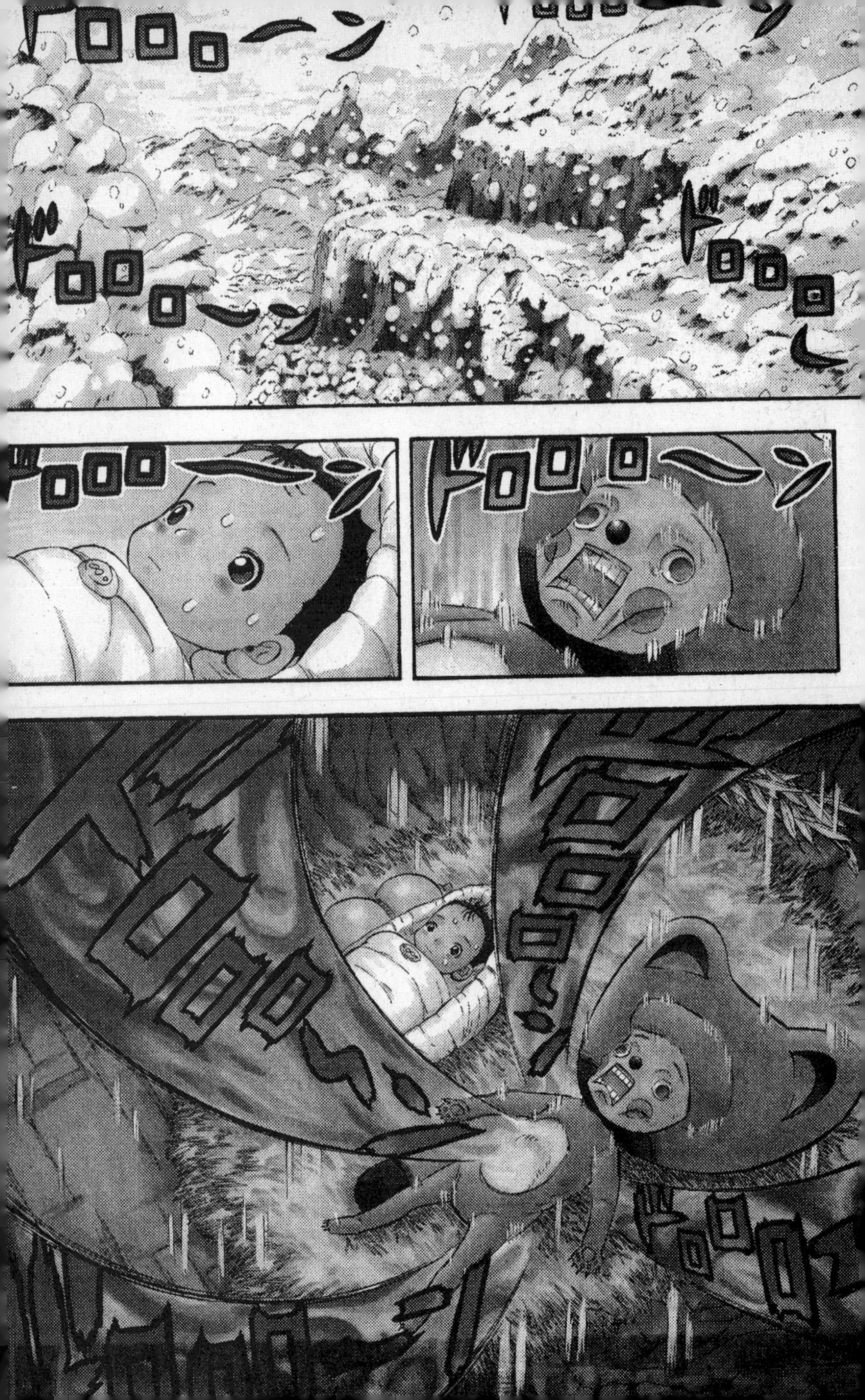
ドロロロ〜ン
ロロロ〜ン
ドロロロ〜ン
ドロロロ〜ン
ロロロ〜ン
ドロロロ〜
ドロロロ〜
ドロロロ

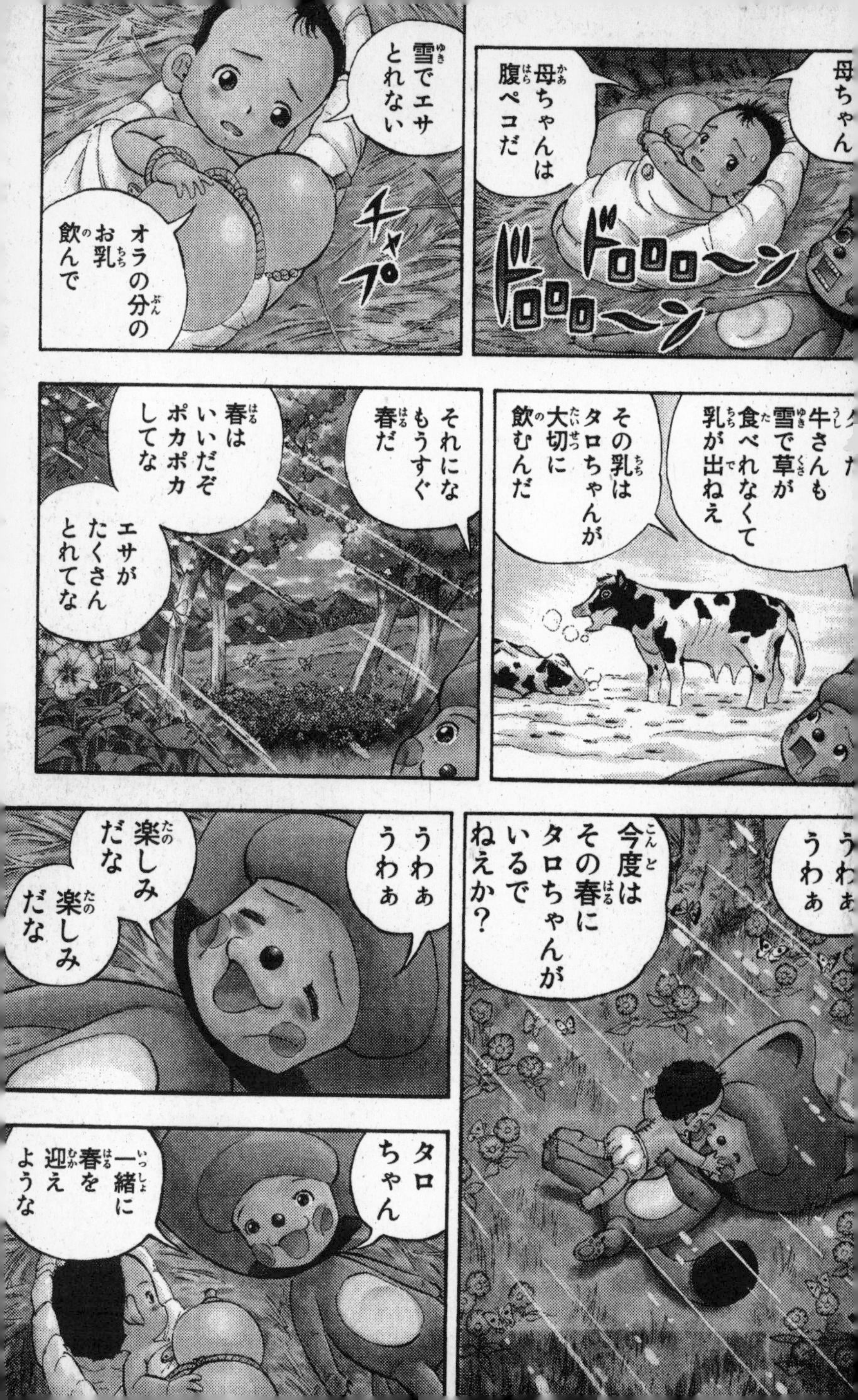
母ちゃん
母ちゃんは腹ペコだ
ドロロ〜ン
ドロロ〜ン
雪でエサとれない
チャプ
オラの分のお乳飲んで
牛さんも雪で草が食べれなくて乳が出ねえ
その乳はタロちゃんが大切に飲むんだ
それにもうすぐ春だ
春はいいだぞポカポカしてな
エサがたくさんとれてな
うわぁうわぁ
今度はその春にタロちゃんがいるでねえか?
うわぁうわぁ
楽しみだな
楽しみだな
タロちゃん
一緒に春を迎えような

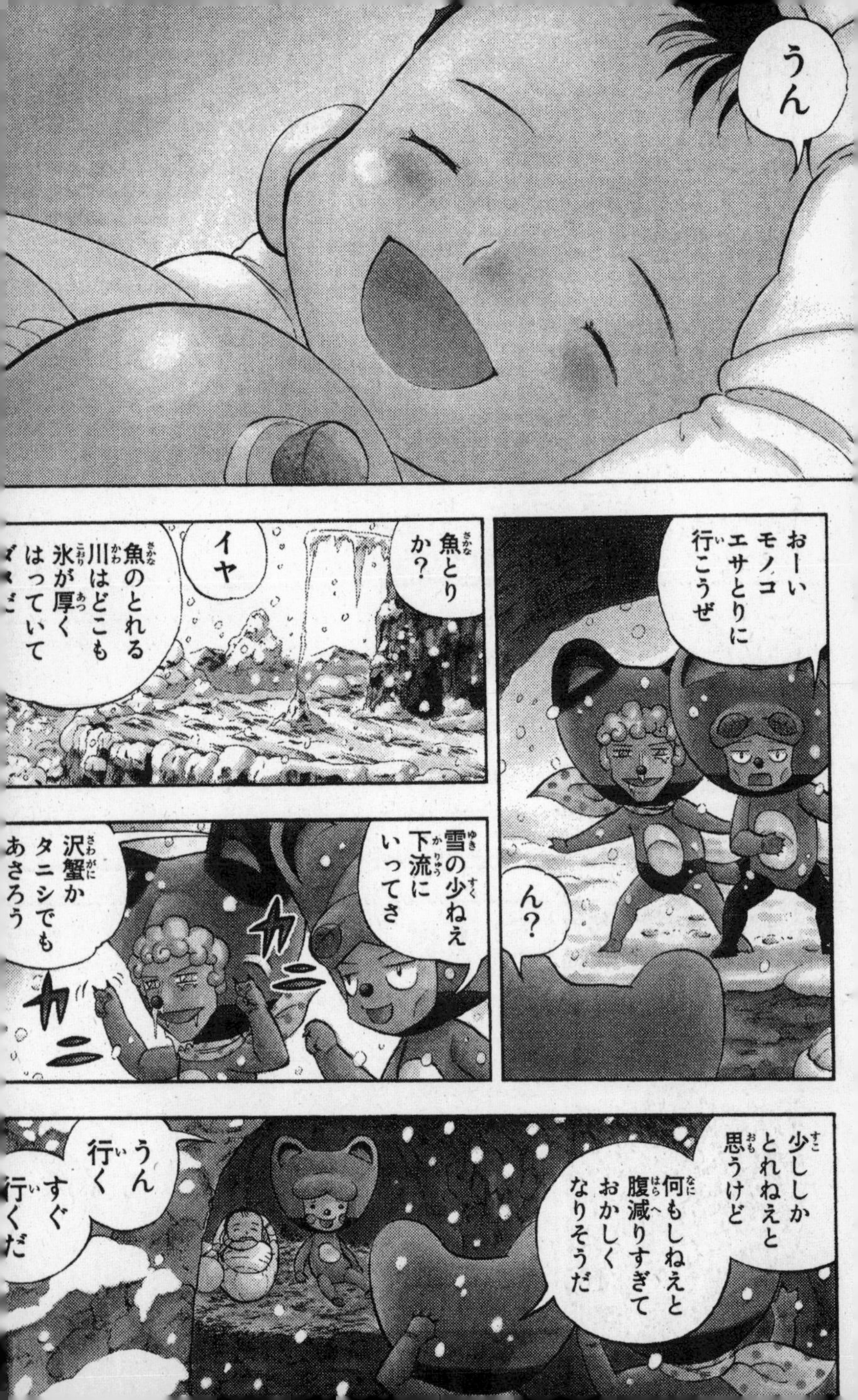
うん
おーい
モノコ
エサとりに
行こうぜ
ん？
魚とり
か？
イヤ
魚のとれる
川はどこも
氷が厚く
はっていて
雪の少ねえ
下流に
いってさ
沢蟹か
タニシでも
あさろう
少ししか
とれねえと
思うけど
何もしねえと
腹減りすぎて
おかしく
なりそうだ
うん
行く
すぐ
行くだ

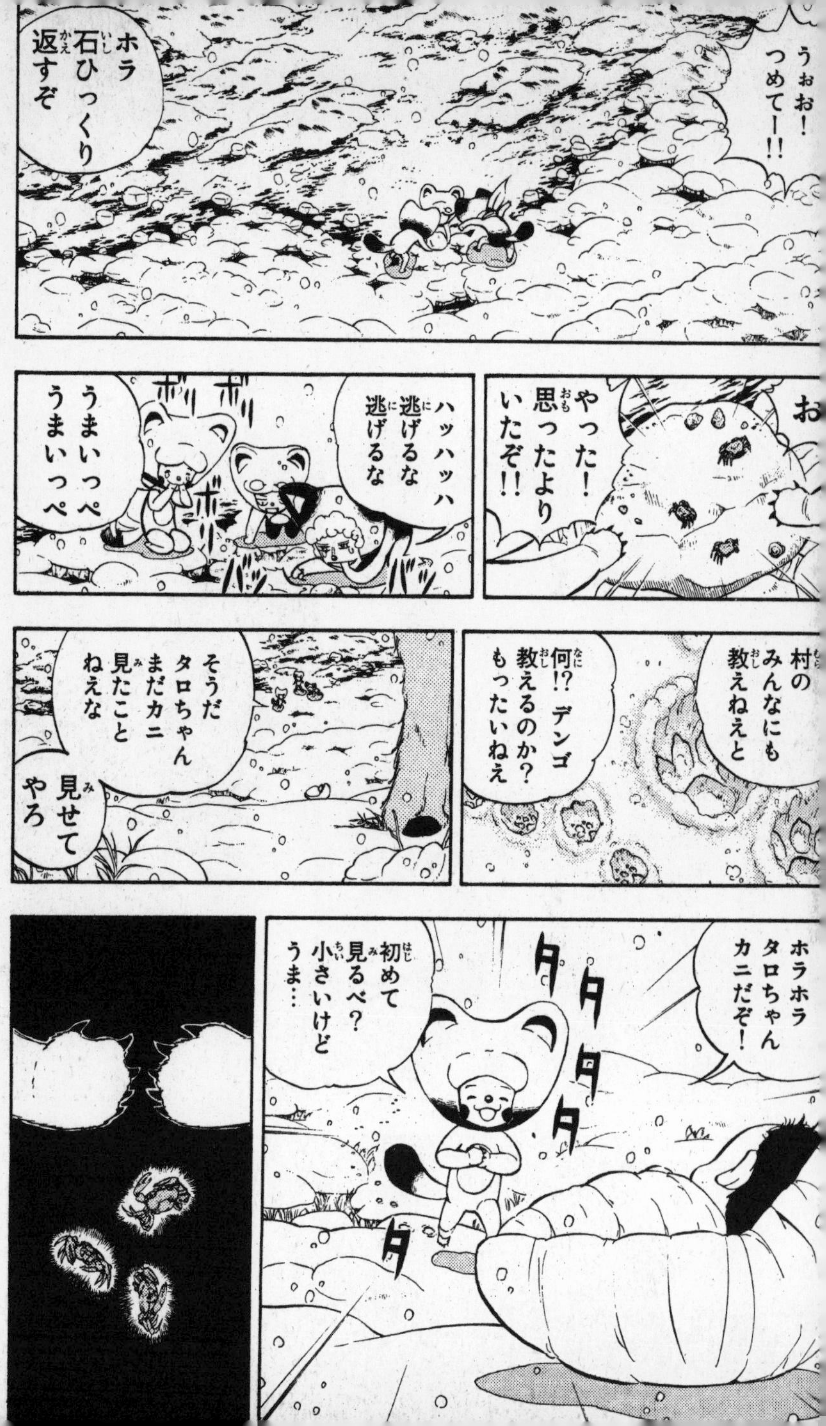
うぉお! つめてー!!
ホラ 石ひっくり返すぞ
お
やった! 思ったより いたぞ!!
ハッハッハ 逃げるな 逃げるな
ボリ ボリ ボリ
うまいっぺ うまいっぺ
村のみんなにも教えねえと
何!? デンゴ 教えるのか? もったいねえ
そうだ タロちゃん まだカニ 見たことねえな
見せてやろ
ホラホラ タロちゃん カニだぞ!
タタタタタ
初めて見るべ? 小さいけど うま…

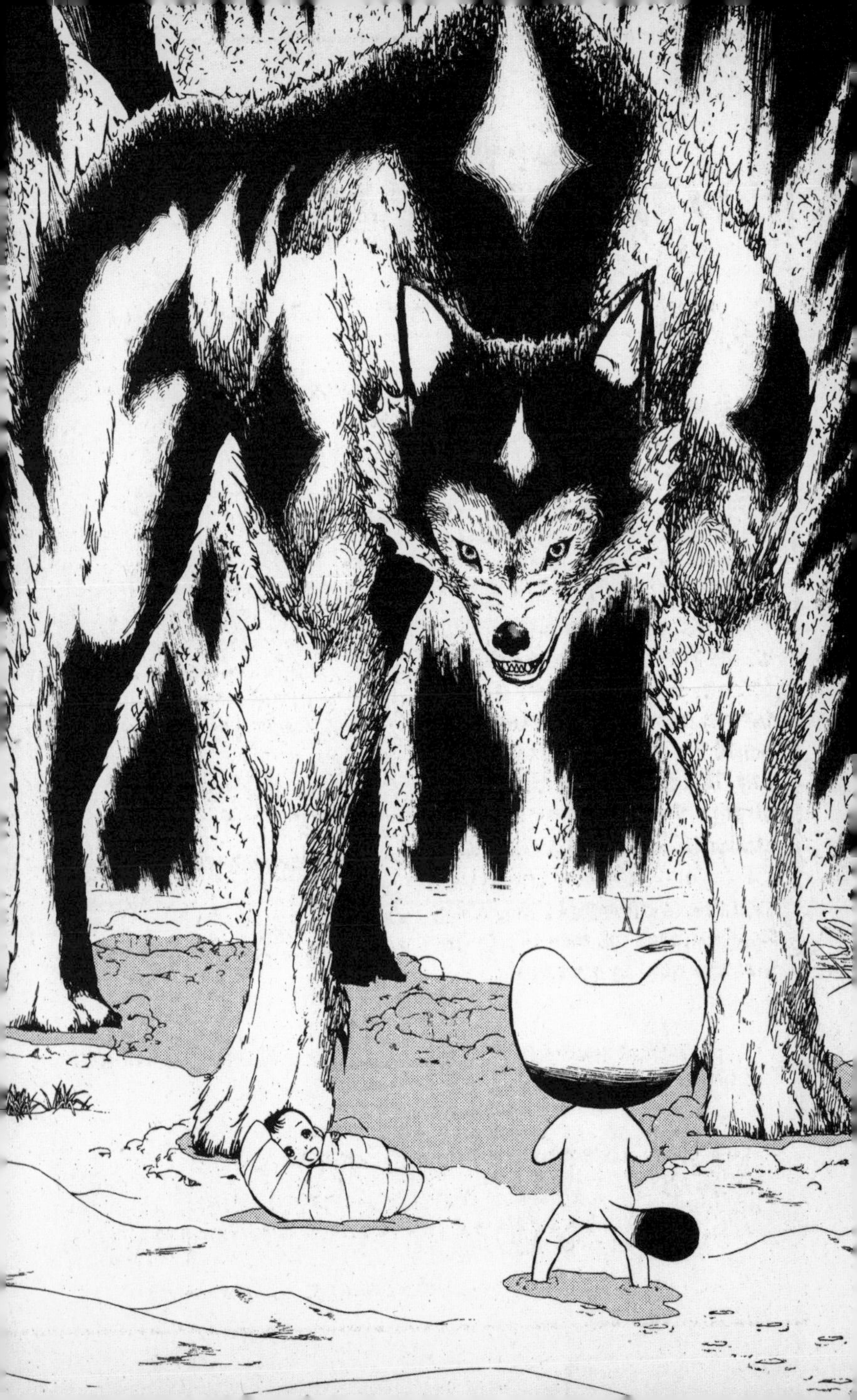

NEGIMA!
MAGISTER NEGI MAGI

BY KEN AKAMATSU

Negi Springfield is a ten-year-old wizard teaching English at an all-girls Japanese school. He dreams of becoming a master wizard like his legendary father, the Thousand Master. At first his biggest concern was concealing his magic powers, because if he's ever caught using them publicly, he thinks he'll be turned into an ermine! But in a world that gets stranger every day, it turns out that the strangest people of all are Negi's students! From a librarian with a magic book to a centuries-old vampire, from a robot to a ninja, Negi will risk his own life to protect the girls in his care!

Ages: 16+

Special extras in each volume! Read them all!

VISIT WWW.KODANSHACOMICS.COM TO:
- View release date calendars for upcoming volumes
- Find out the latest about new Kodansha Comics series

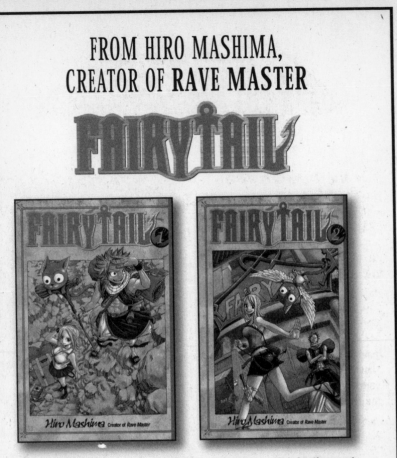

AIRGEAR

BY OH!GREAT

AIRGEAR
1
Oh!great

Itsuki Minami needs no introduction—everybody's heard of the "Babyface" of the Eastside. He's the strongest kid at Higashi Junior High School, easy on the eyes but dangerously tough when he needs to be. Plus, Itsuki lives with the mysterious and sexy Noyamano sisters. Life's never dull, but it becomes downright dangerous when Itsuki leads his school to victory over vindictive Westside punks with gangster connections. Now he stands to lose his school, his friends, and everything he cares about. But in his darkest hour, the Noyamano girls give him an amazing gift, one that just might help him save his school: a pair of Air Trecks. These high-tech skates are more than just supercool. They'll enable Itsuki to execute the wildest, most aggressive moves ever seen—and introduce him to a thrilling and terrifying new world.

Ages: 16+

Special extras in each volume! Read them all!

KC KODANSHA COMICS

VISIT WWW.KODANSHACOMICS.COM TO:

- View release date calendars for upcoming volumes
- Find out the latest about new Kodansha Comics series

TOMARE! [STOP!]

You are going the wrong way!

Manga is a completely different type of reading experience.

To start at the beginning, go to the end!

That's right! Authentic manga is read the traditional Japanese way—from right to left, exactly the opposite of how American books are read. It's easy to follow: Just go to the other end of the book, and read each page—and each panel—from right side to left side, starting at the top right. Now you're experiencing manga as it was meant to be.